Center or Margin

The Apple-Zimmerman Series in Early Modern Culture
Susquehanna University Press
Editors: Phyllis Rackin, University of Pennsylvania
Carole Levin, University of Nebraska

This interdisciplinary series will include books that examine a wide range of aesthetic works and moments in their original cultural milieu. This would include, for example, the works of Shakespeare and his contemporaries as the products of the burgeoning theatrical industry, designed for the entertainment of heterogeneous audiences who lived in a rapidly changing world where politics, religion, national identity, and gender roles were all subjects of contestation and redefinition. We solicit manuscripts from fields including, but not limited to, literature, history, philosophy, religion, and political science, in order to enable a truly multifaceted understanding of the early modern period.

Titles in This Series

On the Web at http://www.susqu.edu/su_press

Center or Margin

Revisions of the English Renaissance in Honor of Leeds Barroll

Edited By
Lena Cowen Orlin

Selinsgrove: Susquehanna University Press

Associated University Press
2010 Eastpark Boulevard
Cranbury, NJ 08512

The paper used in this publication meets the requirements of the American National Standard for Permanence of Paper for Printed Library Materials Z39.48-1984.

Library of Congress Cataloging-in-Publication Data

Center or Margin: revisions of the English Renaissance / edited by Lena Cowen Orlin
    p. cm – (The Apple-Zimmerman Series in early modern culture)
Includes bibliographical references and index.
ISBN 10: 1-57591-098-5 (alk. paper)
ISBN 13: 978-1-57591-098-7 (alk. paper)
    1. English literature–Early modern, 1500–1700–History and criticism. 2. Shakespeare, William, 1564–1616–Criticism and interpretation. 3. Renaissance England. 4. Literature and society–England–History–16th century. 5. Literature and society–England–History 17th century. 6. England–Civilization–16th century. 7. England–Civilization–17th century
I. Orlin, Lena Cowen. II. Barroll, Leeds (John Leeds), 1928– III. Series.
    PR423.C45 2006
    820.9'003–dc22   2005031325

Contents

Part III: The Human Figure on the Stage

(Title of Chapter Ten in Leeds Barroll's
Shakespearean Tragedy: Genre, Tradition, and Change in Antony and Cleopatra, 1984)

Part IV: Artificial Persons

(Title of Leeds Barroll's First Book, 1974)

Illustrations

Introduction

Lena Cowen Orlin

THE AUTHORS OF THIS VOLUME CAME TOGETHER out of shared admiration for Leeds Barroll. We have known him in many ways: as the founder of the Shakespeare Association of America, as the originating editor of the journals *Shakespeare Studies* and *Medieval and Renaissance Drama in England*, as the leader of advanced research seminars at the Folger Shakespeare Library, as invited plenary speaker at countless academic conferences, as the author of four influential books and many other publications, as a colleague at the University of Maryland Baltimore County, as a friend, as a mentor, as an inspiration. His influence has myriad aspects; this book represents just some of them.

The range of his scholarship is remarkable, encompassing critical theory and formalist literary criticism, intellectual history and cultural biography, archival research and textual editing. He is known particularly in the fields of Shakespeare studies and Renaissance theatrical history; Stuart court studies, court patronage, and the royal masque; early modern women's studies and women's writing; and the contact histories of Jacobean England and the East. In the wide reach of his work, the concerns that surface most repeatedly are metacritical and historiographic. These seem to have brought him to the frequent theme indicated by publication and presentation titles like "Privileged Biographies, Marginal Shakespeare," "Centering the Arts," and "England at the Margins." For his study of *Shakespearean Tragedy*, for example, Barroll deconstructs the tragic canon. Other critics have homogenized examples of the genre, reflexively and with the First Folio as a warrant, not always acknowledging their implicit mission to make the genre itself cohere. Barroll suggests instead that the first way to approach Shakespeare's tragedies is to study *a* tragedy. Then he chooses not *Hamlet, Othello, Macbeth,* or *King Lear*—the four works that A. C. Bradley brought so lastingly to the center—but instead *Antony and Cleopatra,* a play that has been marginalized ever since Bradley excluded it from his own influential register. The very decentering of characterologic focus in this play, and perhaps especially the resulting implications for the gendering of the genre, have traditionally cost it a prominent place in the Shakespearean canon.

Leeds Barroll has never been sentimental about the stature of the "great" tragic heroes. "Too often," he writes, we take Hamlet and Lear as "our defining moralists"; instead we should "insist on Lear as character, not Lear as spokesman." We should understand Lear's statements to speak to his dramatic characterization rather than to our personal philosophies. Barroll is equally unsparing about romantic notions of the inspired frenzy that poets purportedly require in order to produce their works of genius, arguing instead in *Politics, Plague, and Shakespeare's Theater* that Shakespeare wrote on demand and as the seasonal schedules and plague closings of open-air playhouses allowed. He is skeptical that Shakespeare was at the center of dramatic events like the Essex Rebellion and, in "A New History for Shakespeare and His Time," questions the ways we manufacture our accounts in order to advance longed-for biographies. Barroll holds no illusions that royal status confers upon a monarch the sort of cultural prescience that would have led James VI and I to bestow his personal favor on the playwright whom we most admire. And in *Anna of Denmark* he goes further to relocate the center of artistic patronage in seventeenth-century England, making the case that we have overlooked a more potent cultural catalyst than the king. Barroll is similarly tough-minded about the handful of privileged documents upon which we have based others of our most cherished contextualizing narratives, whether they proceed from the old historicism or the New. He has exhorted us to explore the archives more widely and more rigorously and, in the course of doing so himself, has also transformed many of our notions of the English Renaissance.

Even in his most radically revisionist scholarship, however, Leeds Barroll has demonstrated a large and generous spirit. He wrote in his first book, *Artificial Persons,* that just because Renaissance authors "did not think precisely in our terms is not necessarily to conclude that they did not think at all." This was an early indication of the scrupulous respect he has brought to bear upon all his professional activities: respect not only for the peoples of other places and other times but also for his fellow researchers, for ideas, for intellectual endeavor, and for the academic enterprise. For a scholar so centrally positioned in the Shakespeare world, it is especially remarkable that Barroll has unfailingly been willing to engage new fields even in their earliest and most marginal stages. These include the theory of representation (in *Artificial Persons*), feminist criticism (he published some of the first and most important feminist work in *Shakespeare Studies* before himself writing on *Antony and Cleopatra,* Aemilia Lanyer, and *Anna of Denmark*), new history (in the award-winning *Politics, Plague, and Shakespeare's Theater: The Stuart Years*), and global culture (he organized a groundbreaking conference on "The Impact of the Ottoman Empire on Early Modern

Europe"). It is with the last of these topics—and the most recent of Leeds Barroll's interests—that this volume opens. From there, we move back through the work of several decades, with the closing chapters of this collection in dialogue with his first book.

All these essays offer challenges to received wisdoms about the Renaissance, in what seems the most fitting tribute we could make to the scholar in whose name we have assembled. Those in the first section, "England at the Margins," investigate the island nation's precarious global status in the Renaissance and some of the ways in which the commercial theater worked to negotiate England's sense of its place in the world. The second section, "Researching the Renaissance," turns to the English domestic scene with a particular emphasis on gender relations, presentational modes, and cultural anxieties. The third section, "The Human Figure on the Stage," deals with Shakespeare's strategies for distinguishing characters in groups, and in particular with individual attributes of masculinity, charisma, and voice. The fourth section, "Artificial Persons," addresses the subjectivities and heightened realities of fictionalized and mediated experience. Most of the essays are rigorously historicizing, but those in the last group also recognize some of the continuities between our present and the early modern past.

ENGLAND AT THE MARGINS

(Title of a paper presented by Leeds Barroll at the 28th Annual Meeting of the Shakespeare Association of America, 2000)

In "Marginal England: The View from Aleppo," Peter Stallybrass shows how centrally the Mediterranean figured in the Elizabethan imagination, how marginal England was to global centers of empire, and how assiduously the Shakespearean theater labored nonetheless to depict this island nation as an imperial power. There were, for example, dramatizations of "inflated" accounts of English conquests, demonizations of the Turks, and the exaggeration of marginal events like the short-lived victory in Lepanto. The key to the literature of the period was the English view *of* Aleppo, an uneasy mix of "reluctant admiration" for its sophisticated material culture and fear of the further advances of Ottoman control. But, more surprisingly and more revisionistically, Stallybrass also portrays the view *from* Aleppo, where England was of surpassingly small interest. All Western Europe was backward with respect to the cosmopolitan culture and intellectual capital of the East, and England, still at this time the "hinterland" of Antwerp, was at an even further remove from international status. The Tudor merchant John Eldred was dismayed to discover that no one in Aleppo wanted to buy his inferior goods, and the Jacobean diplomat Sir

Thomas Roe was humiliated when his gift to the Mughal emperor Jahangir was returned as "too poor of value." England was "not at all respected," Roe observed. Until English adventurers succeeded in exploiting the precious metals, sugar, and tobacco of the New World, they had nothing of interest to the East. But, in the Shakespearean moment, did England fully comprehend how unimportant it was? Roe was in possession of an international knowledge that was marginalized by the more urgent local discourses that were represented on the Elizabethan stage in nationalistic themes and rhetorics. The commercial theater was so successful at mythologizing England's centrality for its immediate audiences that it has also misled those of us who encountered the period through the plays. We, too, have fallen subject to anglocentric ideas that, while culturally necessary for the development of national identity in the early modern period, should be less so in our historical interpretation. The world views of *Othello* and *Macbeth* did important cultural work in their own time, but Stallybrass shows that they do not get the Renaissance right.

In "Incising Venice: The Violence of Cultural Incorporation in *The Merchant of Venice*," Philippa Berry explores the Shakespearean meanings of a Renaissance city that centered itself through its potent marginality, making mercantile capital from a geographically liminal position between East and West, and in this establishing a unique claim on that Elizabethan imaginary which Stallybrass also addresses. Berry, too, observes the combination of fascination and aversion with which Elizabethans viewed the Mediterranean. In both Stallybrass's discussion of Othello's nature and Berry's analysis of *Merchant*'s setting, notions of hybridity feature strongly. The composite culture of Venice was built out of exotic commodities which passed through its markets, and Berry describes the effects of its internationalized trade as a layering of diverse inscriptions and ornamentations, the multiple incisings of the city's receptive surface. This idea of Venice, she goes on to argue, was also for Shakespeare a medium for exploring the complex processes of other cultural mediations and incorporations, including those of his own time which involved the negotiation of the recovered past. Thus, the surface of *The Merchant of Venice* is elaborated with echoes of the classical and biblical stories of Jason and the Golden Fleece, Medea and Aeson, Dido and Aeneas, Troilus and Cressida, Pyramus and Thisbe, Jacob and Laban, and Jacob and Isaac. Most of these involve instances of cutting, severing, separation, and dislocation, as do so many elements of the plot, themes, and imagery of the play: Shylock's bond, Launcelot Gobbo's name (a near-homophone of the surgical instrument for bleeding), Jessica's estrangement from her father. Because inscribing is related to incising and ornamenting to wounding, these associations provide ways for Berry to talk also about the violence that accompanies transactions in cultural difference, including the Renaissance binding together of its disparate heritages. In Berry's reading, *The Merchant of Venice* is a bricolage of references to the marking of surfaces: the inscribed knife of a "cutler," the "insculpted" angel of English coins, the flayed fleece of Colchis, the extruded gum of the manna tree, the etched ring of Nerissa. Each may seem trivial in its own right, but together they are central to the meanings of the play, to English ideas of Venice as a place imprinted by diverse societies, and also to the nature of the Renaissance as a time overwritten by archaic texts and knowledge.

In "Barbers, Infidels, and Renegades: *Antony and Cleopatra,*" Patricia Parker continues an emphasis on England's understanding of its relationship to the Mediterranean. Where Berry assembles a complex of interrelated details and decodes their cumulative significance, Parker begins with a single image from which meanings exfoliate. Her starting point is one of the most memorable passages of *Antony and Cleopatra,* as Enobarbus describes Antony's first view of Cleopatra in a barge that "burned on the water" of the Cydnus. The Roman general accepts the invitation of the Egyptian queen and, in a seemingly trivial particular, goes "barbered ten times o'er" to her feast. Like shaving, cutting, depilating, and curling, Parker proceeds to show, barbering was related in classical Rome to youth, effeminacy, transvestism, gelding, and eunuchry. In the second temporal register in which this play works, the early modern, barbering was also associated both with sexual license, inasmuch as harlots were known to lose their hair from syphilis, and with what Parker calls " 'infidel' inflections," because the "barbarous" Ottoman Turks reportedly shaved Christian captives as signs of enslavement. All these implications were alive in *Antony and Cleopatra,* a play based on Roman sources, written for a Renaissance audience, and overlaid with Jacobean notions of the East as a place populated by renegades, pirates, gypsies, and enchantresses. Tellingly, this last cluster of phobic fantasies enters the classical legend only in its early modern incarnation, in further evidence of the centrality of the Mediterranean to the Shakespearean imaginary. Because of the associations inspired by his name and known history, it is especially significant, Parker also suggests, that Enobarbus, or Red-Beard, delivers the central speech with its marginal detail of Antony's barbering. He is nominal kin to the Barbarossa who defeated the Roman Emperor at a new battle of Actium in 1538, in a signal triumph of the Ottoman power so much feared in England. His name also evokes the red beard of the stage Jew, and he was himself a renegade to Antony. If he seems in all these ways to be linked to the "barbarous East," in his final defection to Rome Enobarbus allied himself instead to the "civil West." Thus he constitutes a secret suspicion that undermined those binary oppositions which were otherwise so central not only to *Antony and Cleopatra* but also to England's sense of itself in the Renaissance.

Researching the Renaissance

(Title of graduate seminars led by Leeds Barroll at the Folger Shakespeare Library, 1991–1999)

In "Our Canon, Ourselves," Phyllis Rackin again sets in motion two time periods, the Shakespearean past and the academic present. Like Peter Stally-brass, she is concerned with ways in which our reading of Shakespeare's plays has distorted our understandings of his age, but she also goes one step further to argue that our misunderstandings of the Renaissance have misdirected our reading of the plays. Her subjects are the status of early modern women and the vicious circularities of misogyny. On the one hand, she says, we recognize that Shakespeare was historically situated, and we take his plays as compelling witnesses to contemporary hostility toward women—even though other Renaissance playwrights sometimes showed themselves more sympathetic to women than he. On the other hand, however, we believe that Shakespeare wrote "not for an age but for all time," and thus we assume his plays demonstrate that the inferior standing of women is transhistorically "true"—despite the transparent fallacies involved in naturalizing female subordination. To close the misogynist circle, she continues, our own biases—or, more specifically, the biases of a profession long dominated by male and masculinist scholars—have informed the way we read Shakespeare. We have chosen to derive what we think of as Shakespeare's view of women from the most antifeminine of his plays, and have done so in every genre. Not coincidentally, the more stridently patriarchal plays are also the more canonical: the *Henry IV* tetralogy, not that of *Henry VI*; *The Tempest,* not *The Winter's Tale*; *Hamlet,* not *Antony and Cleopatra*; and *The Taming of the Shrew,* not any of the later romantic comedies. As plays fully focused on women, sex, and gender, comedies make a particularly cogent case for Rackin's argument. *The Taming of the Shrew,* she points out, is flagrantly self-deconstructing, with an induction that reminds us both that it is only a play and also that the play is a farce. Moreover, *Shrew* was rebutted in its own time by John Fletcher's table-turning *The Tamer Tam'd.* And yet it has been a principal source on gender relations in the period. What if, Rackin asks, we were to put *The Merry Wives of Windsor* at the center of Shakespeare's canon, of our notion of his ideas on women, and of our sense of his time? This would be to rethink a fundamental paradigm for the Renaissance.

In "Artificial Couples: The Apprehensive Household in Dutch Pendants and *Othello,*" Harry Berger, Jr., moves the discussion of gender relations into one of its subsets, marital relations, and turns from what seems to be Shakespeare's experiment in city comedy with *The Merry Wives of Windsor* to his only gesture at another subgenre of the period, the domestic tragedy. Berger's discussion of *Othello* develops within the contexts of early modern ideology and Dutch portraiture. All three arenas (dogma, painting, and drama) purveyed powerful new fictionalizations of family life, and their strenuous representations of perfection engendered what Berger terms "performance anxiety." He describes how the new, nuclear form of family organization accompanied new forms of state organization and became a central "ideological apparatus" of the state. Marriage was an institutional mechanism for control and surveillance of the population. But the state's powers of containment have been exaggerated in historicist narratives, Berger asserts, and faultlines in domestic ideals—for example, an inherent tension between the notional reciprocities of conjugal love and explicit mandates for the patriarch's domestic supremacy—provided the occasion for fears of failure. Marital roles were publicly performed in the pairs and pendants of Dutch portraiture. These, too, had coercive functions, with their limited repertory of poses communicating information about rank, status, and, especially, gender. A principal instance of the genre's "political correctness," says Berger, was that husbands characteristically occupied the position on the left. Thus they assumed the roles of presenters, introducing their wives to the world and mediating between women and their environments. As in the political context, however, it was also the case in the painted context that there were irregularities. Wives seemed often to assert visual claims for equal performative rights; Berger makes much of unconformable elbows in pendant margins. Finally, the stageplay provided another platform for the performance of gender troubles. In his fantastic accusations that Othello has usurped his conjugal rights, Iago cynically parodies the "sexual and proprietary insecurity of husbands and fathers" in the patriarchal cultures of the Renaissance. However, he then suffers his own experience of marital anxiety. Because his plot against Othello relies upon Emilia's silence, especially about the lost handkerchief, Iago has given her a power that is perilous to him. Divided spousal authority in *Othello* embodies Berger's argument about the early modern family as a central site of danger and, in its prescriptive poses, a place of theater.

In "Spaces of Treason in Tudor England," I bring this section on domestic themes to a close by turning to household interiors. The established inventory of bedchambers, dining chambers, and service rooms in English homes was expanded in the sixteenth century with a new and unusual space, the long gallery. Galleries were built long and narrow in order to allow for walking indoors in inclement weather and, in their extravagant square-footage, were associated with status competitions in the Renaissance. They also had unintended meanings for the history of a personal privacy to which we have paid little attention. The sources of anxiety described in this chapter surrounded the difficulty of securing confidential conversations in the early modern house. As Harry Berger,

Jr., has demonstrated for gender relations, so this subject of concern was also dramatized on the Elizabethan stage, where plots were frequently advanced by eavesdroppings and overhearings. With no room for potential listeners to hide in the long gallery, however, the space came to be associated with uninhibited discourse. At one end of his long gallery, Thomas Wolsey staged his conferences for viewers at the other end, publicly performing his access to privacy. Elizabeth, Countess of Shrewsbury ("Bess of Hardwick") found herself frustrated by conversations she could not monitor in the vast length of her gallery at Hardwick Hall. The long gallery featured most dramatically, however, in records compiled during William Cecil's investigation into the so-called "Ridolfi Plot." When Thomas Howard, fourth Duke of Norfolk was found guilty of treason, he protested that much of the evidence against him was circumstantial. And indeed, one of the incriminating circumstances seems to have been the fact that a great many clandestine meetings took place in the conspirators' long galleries. This in itself served to indicate their dangerous intentions to be secretive. The "Ridolfi" depositions are thoroughly well known, having been transcribed out of the Salisbury papers as long ago as the mid-eighteenth century. They are put to new uses here, with the teasing out of a marginalized narrative, the spatial history of treason, and a recentering of the cultural unease that surrounded conversational privacy in the Renaissance.

THE HUMAN FIGURE ON THE STAGE

(Title of Chapter Ten in Leeds Barroll's Shakespearean Tragedy: Genre, Tradition, and Change in *Antony and Cleopatra, 1984)*

In "Stage Masculinities, National History, and the Making of London Theatrical Culture," Jean E. Howard carries forward the interests of earlier chapters in the social functions of Elizabethan drama and the performance of early modern gender roles. She seeks to recenter questions of masculinity that have lately been overshadowed by feminist concerns (and that are also addressed in this volume by Patricia Parker). Howard reminds us of how marginal the public theaters were in the 1590s, with their suburban locations, socially precarious actors, plague closings, and antitheatrical opponents. Nonetheless, the institution came to occupy a dominant position in popular culture, as witnessed in the reports of foreign visitors, the size of playhouse audiences, and the growth of dramatic repertoires. Some of this success, she argues, proceeded from an emergent cult of celebrity located in actors like Edward Alleyn, Will Kemp, and Richard Burbage, star players in a system that employed only men. Their public fame was created in large part by characterologic strategies developed in Shakespeare's early, experimental history plays. There, we see him learning how to adapt narrative chronicles to poetic drama, how to interweave multiple plots, and how, especially in a theatrical economy that relied upon doubling, to fix the identities of the human figures on the stage. Howard points out that while there were no more than five women characters in any of the plays of Shakespeare's first tetralogy, *Henry VI, Part 1* included thirty-two men; *Henry VI, Part 2,* fifty men; *Henry VI, Part 3,* forty-two men; and *Richard III,* thirty-seven men. To distinguish among these vast casts was to differentiate stage masculinities. Thus, the plays give us the effeminate Henry VI, disabled politically and domestically by his "feckless masculinity"; the heroic Talbot, a poignant symbol of lost military prowess; the performative Suffolk, modeled on the courtiers of aristocratic conduct books; the artisanal Jack Cade, fierce with class-based anger; and the Machiavellian Richard III, embued with a metatheatrical celebrity. In plays as focused on stagecraft as statecraft, Shakespeare learned to manage theatrical male bodies, discovering also how to capitalize on the particular qualities of the actors at his disposal and how to cultivate glamour as a commodity of the new entertainment industry. Shakespeare's dramaturgic successes were to help center the commercial theater in Renaissance society.

In "Charisma and Institution-Building in Shakespeare's Second Tetralogy," Raphael Falco takes us from the first tetralogy to the second and from individual personation to group relations. He describes the later history plays as dominated by conflicts between traditional and charismatic forms of authority, though his emphasis, like that of Jean Howard, is on finely calibrated distinction rather than polar opposition. Thus, he attends to the degrees of charisma which narrow the gaps between one kind of public authority and another. Max Weber, for example, identified three forms of charisma: personal (or pure), lineage (or inherited), and office (or institutional). Like Freud, Weber located many of his ideal types in literature, including Shakespeare's plays, and Falco shows how compatible Weber's categories are with the second Henriad. But he also demonstrates that the plays reinforce recent refinements to Weber's taxonomy. Henry IV, for example, can be seen to have made a personal charismatic claim on the English throne. Because institutionalization is necessary to his legitimization, however, Henry then confronts the challenge of "routinizing" his charisma and converting his group of rebels to courtly supporters. This process eventually results in Henry VI's secure possession of a lineage authority. Between the two, Henry V not only demonstrates both pure and institutional charisma but also displays his awareness of his own "dual existence." Falco revises our understanding of Hal's early delinquency in describing it as a means by which the character enacts his personal charisma and organizes his followers; his authority resides not only in the fact that he is "human," as is traditionally argued, but also in his participation in such communal charismatic experiences as those of the tavern scenes and the disguised-monarch scene. Creating disorder that only he can manage and then routinizing his charisma in the institutions of marriage, succession, and rule, Hal disproves Weber's notion that pure charisma is always socially disruptive. He is politically effective in exploiting the wonder that accompanies transition from one charismatic status to another. Finally, Falco's essay engages the place of theory in Shakespearean studies. With other authors in this volume, principally Bruce R. Smith and Catherine Belsey, he recenters an influential theoretical paradigm by historicizing it. Shakespeare may not have known the word "charisma," Falco says, but he would have understood its nature, "because the concept was so much a part of sixteenth-century religious idealism."

In "Mona Lisa Takes a Mountain Hike, Hamlet Goes for an Ocean Dip," Bruce R. Smith undertakes to decenter the most central of Shakespeare's tragic heroes by reconstructing the sea of sound he inhabited as a figure on the Jacobean stage. Hamlet has seemed as dominant in his play as the first-person narrator of a nineteenth-century novel; he was a model patient for the Freudian psychoanalysis of the twentieth century; and he would appear to constitute a perfect instance of Derridean logocentrism for the twenty-first century. But Smith demonstrates that this last can be true only if, as Derrida assumes, there is such a thing as a universal, undifferentiated circumstance for sound and if, further, speakers hear their speech in biologically transhistorical ways. Smith suggests that the apparent simultaneity of thought and speech exhibited by the character Hamlet is an effect—just as is the compositional device that centers the Mona Lisa in her pictorial space by framing her bosom with river channels and aligning a distant horizon with her eyes. The Hamlet-effect is technical, too, but in a specific, historically conditioned way. For example, the character's "physical frame" was the newly constructed Globe. There, Hamlet emerged into vocal centrality out of first-scene sounds dispersed around the platform; throughout the play, he had always to struggle against "acoustic oblivion" amid stage noises, other actors' voices, and the claps and shouts of those in the pit and the galleries. Within his "dramaturgical frame," meanwhile, the character came to "consciousness" in third person, as described by Horatio, was then referenced in second person, by Claudius, and finally achieved his first-person presence in soliloquy. The subsequent reversal of this process is sharply underscored in the Folio version of the text, where omission of the "How all occasions do inform against me" soliloquy consigns Hamlet to dialogue alone for the last third of the action. Finally, Smith asserts that Hamlet must also be placed inside the "physiological frame" that conditioned Renaissance understandings of how sound related to speech and speech to identity; this is an aspect of what he calls "historical phenomenology." Attempting to "hear green" and to reintegrate the Cartesian separation of spoken message and speaking messenger, Smith argues that even that aural sense which seems most immutable must be historicized. To do so is to discover that Shakespeare's most famous tragic hero occupies "a position of logomarginality."

Artificial Persons

(Title of Leeds Barroll's first book, 1974)

In "Psychoanalysis and Early Modern Culture: Lacan with Augustine and Montaigne," Catherine Belsey challenges two conflicting notions which are so familiar in Renaissance studies that each has acquired a powerfully suasive status. First, many critics have objected that it is anachronistic to bring psychoanalysis to bear on early modern texts; instead, they privilege the claims of historicism in interpretation. Second, defenders of psychoanalytic criticism have often argued that while Freudian understandings of unconscious desire awaited a vocabulary in the nineteenth century, they nonetheless informed the subjectivities of the sixteenth century; fundamentally, this is to appeal to apprehensions of universal and transhistorical "truths" about human nature. Contesting both positions, Belsey also confutes their perceived polarity. Psychoanalysis and historicism can be reconciled, she suggests, in an awareness that there were early modern authors who commented on psychological processes in terms that are recognizable to us from the work of Freud. Joseph Hall, for example, wrote that dreams could reveal the content of the human heart, and Montaigne acknowledged motivations not immediately accessible to consciousness, including those of the male's "unruly member." But the case for the historical standing of psychoanalysis is not only a matter of discovering that some of its central themes were anticipated by Renaissance authors. Belsey also traces direct lines of influence. In Augustine, the story of the Fall is represented as the refusal of man to obey the divine will, even as the condition of fallen man is represented in the refusal of sexual organs to obey human will. If this seems in sympathy with Lacan's theories of the phallus, then it is also worth noting that Lacan stated directly that Augustine "foreshadowed psychoanalysis." Lyotard was even more explicit in acknowledging debts to Augustine. Connections can also be made between Augustine's nonreferential theory of language and Saussure, and between postmodern notions of how people think and Montaigne's associative, digressive essays; Lacan knew Montaigne, too. Finally, says Belsey, psychoanalysis goes less to explanatory significance in texts than to methodological insight about ways of approaching them, and these are insights that would seem to have descended through time. In this fashion she makes a forceful case for recentering psychoanalysis in discussions of the "artificial persons" of the Renaissance.

In "Abdiel Centers Freedom," Susanne Woods returns to the subject of the uses to which fictional characters are put by their authors. Like Patricia Parker (and in contrast to Bruce R. Smith), she focuses on the importance of a minor figure. In fact, she terms Abdiel, in Milton's *Paradise Lost,* a marginal character. The angel features in just three hundred lines of the poem and is, in addition, distanced from the reader by narrative layerings. We are aware of Milton depicting Raphael, and then of Raphael describing to Adam a rebellion within a rebellion, Abdiel's refusal to join Satan. Milton's rhetorical strategy with this "small narrative" dramatizes the process of getting to its center, which is the meaning contained in the story and the moral that Adam is expected to realize. The fact that the tale comes at the structural center of the poem adds formal weight to an incident that demonstrates the individual power of choice and an exercise of personal freedom. One significance of the tale of Abdiel, then, is what it shows about Milton's craftsmanship. Another is interpretive, because it foregrounds the theme of liberty which, Woods says, was emphasized in nearly all of the poet's works; he was the first major author to feature it so consistently. The Abdiel episode also informs the central issue of *Paradise Lost,* the question of whether the Fall was a fortunate one. It was not, Woods argues, even despite God's plan for redemption. Abdiel embodies the choice Adam declines to make, and so reminds us of the lost possibility of an alternative human history. Finally, the tale of Abdiel also has important historical meanings. The idea of freedom circulated in seventeenth-century English-speaking culture in axes of power distinct from the Crown (among members of the noble, gentle, and mercantile classes), in documents like the Petition of Right, in the execution of Charles I for oppressing public freedoms, and in the arguments of John Locke and Thomas Jefferson. Abdiel illustrates Milton's conviction that God's creatures have free will and also shows what he means by this: they have been endowed with the strength to make right decisions. The poem invites readers to judge between Abdiel and Adam, and in so choosing to enact their own liberty in the moment of textual encounter.

In "Artificial Intensity: The Optical Technologies of Personal Reality Enhancement," Barbara Stafford contributes an essay reflecting upon a recent (2001) exhibition at the Getty Museum of Art. "Devices of Wonder: From the World in a Box to Images on a Screen" assembled displays and demonstrations of optical technologies from the sixteenth through the twenty-first centuries. As Stafford indicates, there was a strong concern among the exhibition organizers that early mirrors, microscopic and telescopic lenses, magic lanterns, camera obscuras, and perspective boxes should not be seen merely as outdated implements. This would have been to relegate them to the status of "imperfect stages" in a developmental narrative about technology, one that finally achieves a temporary consummation in the films, virtual experiences, computer simulations, and artificial intelligence of the present day. Instead, however, Stafford emphasizes continuities of desire across five hundred years of human invention, recognizing that these "eye-machines" document an extended history of fascination with enhanced realities. There was never a time free of optical technology, she argues, since the eye itself is a tool that extends our perception beyond the boundaries of our own body. And even in prehistoric cave-shelters there was undoubtedly shadow play against the walls. But she also emphasizes the significance of the optical innovations of the Renaissance. These demonstrate that ever since the sixteenth century, identity has been constituted in an "instrumentalization of the biological self." Thus she remarks "the surprising age, depth, and complexity of the mediated world"; reality, she asserts, "has long had a competitor." Each device or mechanism possesses an individual history that is specific to its original context, but together these objects represent an ongoing investment in encounters with the hyperreal. In Stafford's description of the synthetic universes created by perspective boxes, and especially in the context of this volume, it is also possible to make connections between the effects of these optical devices and those of the Shakespearean theater, which intensified human experience through its contrived plots and artificial persons. Stafford could speak as cogently for Renaissance drama when she describes optical technologies not as substitutes for reality but instead as extensions of it.

Stafford also talks about wonder cabinets, with which, like most collections of essays, this volume shares certain affinities. It seeks to provide no more comprehensive or complete a view of the Renaissance than do such apparently random gatherings of marvelous objects. Of course, the principle of selection is more immediately apparent here, in that each of the chapters speaks to the scholarship of Leeds Barroll. Stafford, for example, makes an explicit homage to work that he has conducted across the traditional disciplines, especially those of literature and history. Other shared interests are acknowledged more and less directly, with Catherine Belsey writing on ways of making sense of the figures who populate Shakespeare's stage; Raphael Falco, on the playwright's group strategies with his artificial persons; Jean Howard, on the role of theater in early modern culture; Patricia Parker, on the tragedy of *Antony and Cleopatra;* Bruce Smith, on the decentering of a tragic hero; Phyllis Rackin, on the place of women in Renaissance society; Philippa Berry, on the idea of Venice in Elizabethan England; Peter Stallybrass, on the marginality of England in the Renaissance world; Susanne Woods, on the polymorphism of the early modern state; Harry Berger, Jr., on the privileging of regiocentrism and theatrocentrism in traditional narratives; and I, on new histories from familiar documents.

Finally, though, wonder cabinets work to develop order from disparity, and in their assemblings and groupings and foregroundings they beguile us into recognizing what Stafford calls a "network of correspondences" among alien curiosities. These connections might never have been apparent had the objects not been dislodged from their native environments and displayed as near neighbors. In just this way, the essays assembled here share themes and sympathies that become evident through proximity and juxtaposition. These have to do with how the academy centers some issues, what it marginalizes, and why these practices have consequence for our historical understanding. Together, the authors aim to take their individual acts of tribute forward into a collaborative revision of some aspects of the Renaissance.

Center or Margin

Part I
England at the Margins

(Title of a Paper Presented by Leeds Barroll at the 28th Annual
Meeting of the Shakespeare Association of America, 2000)

Marginal England:
The View from Aleppo

Peter Stallybrass

And say besides; that in *Aleppo* once,
Where a *Malignant,* and a *Turband Turke,*
Beate a *Venetian,* and traduc'd the State;
I tooke bi'th'throate the circumcised dog,
And smote him thus. *He stabs himselfe.*
                                    —*Othello*

SO *OTHELLO* MOVES TO ITS CONCLUSION.[1] But before his suicide, Othello, formerly general of the Venetian forces, has securely occupied Cyprus. The Ottoman forces have been beaten back by storms at sea. The only Ottoman remaining is the turbaned Turk who beat a Venetian in Aleppo. In his final speech, Othello, both turbaned Turk and upholder of the Venetian state, undoes his own hybrid nature. The Venetian Othello turns against the "Turkish" Othello and kills him. With Othello's death, the last Turk is erased. Venetian hegemony is reasserted, a hegemony achieved by the exorcism of Turk and Venetian Moor alike. But Venetian rule is not static. It is imagined as expanding ever further east, from Venice to Cyprus, from Cyprus to Aleppo. "*The* State" is the Venetian state as if Aleppo was still Cyprus or even Venice itself. The turbaned Turk appears paradoxically as an aggressive interloper even within the boundaries of the Ottoman Empire.[2] Yet it is nevertheless in Aleppo that the final scene of malignancy is imagined.

Curiously, Aleppo reappears in *Macbeth.* Drawing upon the Scottish witch trials of the 1590s, Shakespeare represents the First Witch as sailing in a sieve to revenge herself upon the husband of a woman who has offended her. The husband is a sailor, master of a ship called the *Tiger,* and he has gone to Aleppo (1.3.7).[3] But now, Aleppo is no longer a place of malignancy. If anything, it is a merchant city where one might hope to evade the malignancy whose place of normal residence is Scotland. But even fleeing to the Eastern Mediterranean cannot protect the ship's master from the malignancy that pursues him from the west.

Where is the place of danger? Where is the place of safety? What counts as "home"? Freud found the *unheimlich* (the strange, the foreign, the uncanny) rooted in the very concept of the *heimlich,* the homely.[4] But unhomeliness was drastically enacted in Renaissance Europe with the massacres and expulsions of Catholics by Protestants, of Protestants by Catholics, with the continuing and extended persecution of Jews, with the expulsion of the Moors from Granada and the enslavement of Africans on a wholly new scale. While England had already expelled the Jews in the thirteenth century, Granada followed suit in 1492. It was to the Ottoman Empire that many exiled Muslims and Jews migrated. Mehmed II had conquered Constantinople in 1453, taking over "a collection of villages" and transforming them into the most cosmopolitan capital in the world, a capital composed of "Muslim merchants and skilled craftsmen, Greeks, Armenians, and Jews from Caffa in the Crimea, and Muslims and Jews from the Granadian diaspora."[5] This cosmopolitan capital was also an imperial center which, like the imperial centers of Europe, had its own violent hierarchies. But Constantinople was religiously and culturally diverse in ways that were unimaginable in Christian Europe.

Aleppo was equally diverse. The shock that Renaissance English travelers registered in Aleppo was the shock of the *toleration* of such diversity. In 1600, John Cartwright traveled to Aleppo and his account, published in 1601, echoes the accounts of previous travelers. Aleppo, he wrote, "is now become the third capital of the Turkish Empire. And well it may be so accounted, since it is the greatest place of traffic for a dry town in all those parts; for hither resort Jews, Tartarians, Persians, Armenians, Egyptians, Indians, and many sorts of Christians, all enjoying freedom of conscience, and bringing hither all kinds of rich merchandise: the trade and traffic of the which place, because it is so well known to most of our nation, I omit to write of."[6] For Cartwright, Aleppo is both familiar and unfamiliar. Familiar as a trading city whose goods were known both through earlier accounts and through the commodities that it exported and that were readily available in London shops. Unfamiliar, because it offered a "freedom of conscience" that had only the remotest echo in England in the "strangers'" churches—the churches of the Huguenots and other Protestant exiles.[7]

To those exiled from Western Europe by violence, the "malignant" Turks of Aleppo and Constantinople were hospitable in ways that could only be dreamed of in Granada or Paris. Indeed, it's hard to imagine Othello's Aleppo within the same frame of reference as Cartwright's Aleppo. If English merchants did have some cause for fear in Aleppo, it was primarily the Europeans (the Portuguese, the French, the Venetians) whom they feared. John Eldred arrived in Aleppo in 1583 in a ship that, like the master's ship in *Macbeth,* was called the *Tiger.*[8] He was later imprisoned but only because he was accused by Portuguese and Venetian merchants of being a spy. And Eldred specifically contrasts the fate of English merchants to that of other European merchants. "There is," he wrote, "no nation that they seek for to trouble except ours."[9] The English encountered trouble not only because they were mercantile interlopers but also because Francis Drake's piracy was objectionable to the Portuguese and the Ottomans alike.

But the view of Aleppo as a cosmopolitan center of trade has to be set against the wider fear of Ottoman hegemony. Nowhere is that fear *raised* and *erased* more fully than in *Othello*. In the play, the imperial power of the Ottomans is simply dissolved. Cyprus remains Venetian; even Aleppo is exorcised of the "malignant" Turk. In 1571, the year after the Ottomans had captured Cyprus (and been welcomed as rescuing Cyprus from the persecutions of Venetian Catholics), the so-called Holy League of Christian powers defeated the Ottoman fleets at the Battle of Lepanto. Throughout Europe, the victory of the Holy League was celebrated as a victory for Christendom. As Fiona Kisby has shown, special prayers were printed in London to celebrate Lepanto and several parish churches still own the pamphlets that they bought on the occasion.[10] The Mediterranean figured centrally in the English imaginary.

The celebration of Lepanto, however, occluded the most obvious fact. Far from Lepanto being a deathblow to the Ottoman Empire, it was no more than a prelude to the expansion of Ottoman hegemony in the Mediterranean. In 1572 Selim II completely rebuilt his navy, and in 1573 he regained Cyprus from the Venetians and increased the annual tribute that they had to pay for commercial privileges.[11] The Ottomans went on to capture Tunis in 1574 and Fez in 1576, thus insuring their control of most of North Africa as well as of much of the Western Mediterranean. They also extended their frontiers into Hungary toward Vienna. *Othello,* in other words, exactly reverses the shifting boundaries of the late sixteenth century. Historically, the Ottoman Empire had recaptured Cyprus long before the play was written.[12] It is, no doubt, the remarkable *successes* of the Ottomans, both military and commercial, that partially account for the proliferation of phobic representations of the malignant Turk.

But we should not take such representations as exhaustive, or necessarily typical, of European and Ottoman interactions.[13] It is not even clear that an antithesis between "Europe" and the Ottoman Empire is sustainable. When Cesare Vecellio published his book on the costumes of "all the world" in Venice in 1590, he dedicated the first book to Europe ("L'Europa"), beginning with ancient Rome and ending with contemporary Turkey. For Vecellio, Turkey was *part* of Europe. This was not, I think, an appropriative gesture but rather a realistic acknowledgment of the proximity of the Ottoman Empire to Venice and of its central role in the shaping of the Mediterranean world. While denouncing Turkish treatment of

Christian slaves, Vecellio remains above all impressed by the grace and magnificence of Ottoman material culture. Even when praising Venetian textiles, Vecellio repeatedly turns to Ottoman textiles for relevant comparisons. Vecellio's detailed and largely admiring account of Turkey is in stark contrast to his brief and sometimes bizarre account of England. England, indeed, scarcely registers for Vecellio, and he never mentions its significance in terms of trading and clothmaking. He does, however, assert that the English are passionately fond of red-haired people, and that when they meet a foreigner with red hair they say, "what a pity he's not English." England, in other words, appears as Ultima Thule to Vecellio.[14] The future, as he imagines it, will be shaped by the Ottomans, not by the distant and marginal English. Vecellio's view was shared by many of the English traders who went to Aleppo. John Eldred noted in 1583 that, "whereas we had thought to have sold in this place great store of our commodities, we cannot sell." And he later complains, "we have offered to give our Commodities *at price,* but no man will deal with us."[15]

Eldred was only registering an acute version of what Portuguese, Venetian, and French merchants had already discovered: that the Ottoman, Persian, and Indian empires were largely unimpressed by the material culture of Western Europe. As Michel Morineau puts it, "while the wealth of the East fascinated the Westerners, the reverse was certainly not true."[16] Western Europe highly valued the silks, dyes, jewels, and spices of the East, but it had little to offer in exchange. Hence, the crucial exploitation of the Americas. It was bullion (above all silver) from the Americas that allowed the Western European powers to enter into negotiations for a wide range of Asian goods that it otherwise had no means to purchase. As John Newberry noted in Baghdad in 1583, "without money there is here at this instant small good to be done."[17] Newberry was not registering the obvious but rather the overthrow of his and his compatriots' notion of the basis of trade: the export and sale of English and reexported commodities on the outgoing voyage; the import and reexport of Ottoman, Persian, Indian, and Chinese commodities on the return voyage. But the tin and textiles that the English traders offered could not begin to buy the silks, pepper, cloves, cinnamon, indigo, musk, pearls, and feathers that they desired. Only in the seventeenth century would English traders be able to export American goods to the East, so that, by 1621, "drinking" tobacco was said to be widespread in Girisk and Quandahar. And later, coffee and even indigo from the West Indies would make inroads along the trade routes of the Levant, competing with the existing Asian markets.[18]

If the Asian empires desired the bullion that Western Europe brought from the Americas, it should still be stressed that in 1600 *intra*-Asian trade was far more important than Asian-European trade.[19] However rapidly it expanded in the seventeenth century, the English East India Company was established only in 1600 and it met with fierce resistance from the Portuguese and Dutch.[20] While the Ottoman Empire, and above all Aleppo, was dependent upon its situation on the great trading routes from the East, it was not only a reexporter to the West, charging, like Persia, its own tariffs along the way. It was also the final destination for a wide range of Indian commodities, above all cotton fabrics and mixtures. Imports from India according to Ottoman customs regulations included eleven different kinds of muslin, five sorts of cotton/silk mixture, four sorts of satin, eleven sorts of ikat fabric, and chintz in five colors. Indigo was exported from Agra in northwest India in large quantities and was crucial for the development of Ottoman textile production in the seventeenth century.[21]

The Ottoman Empire was the Westernmost outpost of the intra-Asian trade that dominated the global economy in 1600. If Europe used American silver to get a foothold in that economy, it remained of secondary importance in it. And despite its previous history of European conquests, England in 1600 was marginal even within Europe. It is possible to view England at this juncture as only beginning to emerge from its status as the hinterland of Antwerp.[22] While England was an important producer of wool and unfinished cloth, it remained incapable of producing the sophisticated dyeing and finishing processes that were established in the Low Countries, Italy, Persia, India, and China. The Cockayne project in 1614 legislated that only *finished* cloth could be exported from England. The project was a catastrophic failure and had to be rapidly revoked. If the Low Countries successfully imposed an embargo on the importing of any English cloth, no one wanted to buy finished cloth of such poor quality anyway.[23] Despite the relative power of England as a state-formation, economically it remained a small island on the margin of Western Europe. In the seventeenth century, England's position in the global economy was transformed through the triangular trade in slaves, sugar, and tobacco between England, Africa, and the Americas. Western-facing ports like Liverpool in England and Glasgow in Scotland would eventually take on new significance because of their geographical position facing across the Atlantic. But in 1600, Liverpool and Glasgow faced Ireland and a vast expanse of water that was only beginning to be charted and turned to violent profit.[24]

As English ambassadors discovered when they traveled to the East, it was difficult to maintain the imperial pretensions of Elizabethan and Jacobean propaganda when the gifts they had to offer were often seen as worthless and useless commodities. If English writers sometimes scorned Eastern textiles as the materializations of oriental luxury and lechery, English merchants aspired to produce just such textiles themselves. Even the monarchy was involved in the attempt to develop on native soil textile skills that remained elusive. Charles I commissioned the painter Nicholas Wilford to search out the "excellencies" of Persian textiles. Wilford was particularly requested to "take notice" of the manufacture of "Cloth of Gould Silke with its colours and dies."[25] But the search for the mysteries of Persian and Indian textile production largely failed. In the 1680s, there were riots in England against the importing of Indian cloths which, being both cheaper and of better quality than English cloths, threatened the collapse of English textile production. In fact, Indian clothworkers were using a mordant unknown in Europe that gave their dyes a durability that Europeans could not match.[26]

Along the trade routes that ended in the Eastern Mediterranean came not only goods but also languages and tales of other worlds.[27] In *Macbeth*, the demonic may already inhabit Scotland, but it is reimagined through the languages of the East. Contemplating the murder of Duncan, Macbeth says:

> If it were done when 'tis done, then 'twer well,
> It were done quickly: If th'Assassination
> Could tramell vp the Consequence . . .
> . . . .
> Wee'ld iumpe the life to come. (1.7.1–6)

The *Oxford English Dictionary* cites this passage as the first use of "assassination" in English. The word "assassin," literally a "hashish-eater," is first recorded in Richard Knolles's *History of the Turks* in 1603, where the "Assassines" are defined as "a company of most desperat and dangerous men among the Mahometans."[28] In Speed's *History of Great Britain,* eight years later, the word was sufficiently unfamiliar to retain its Italian form. Speed writes of "that bloudy Sect of Sarazens, called *Assassini,* who, without feare of torments, vndertake . . . the murther of any eminent Prince, impugning their irreligion."[29] Italians, remaining the main European distributors of eastern languages as well as goods, had adopted the word decades before marginal England. But, perhaps surprisingly, in a play on the public stages of professional companies, the *Assassini* had already been Englished—or, at least, Scottished.

Yet Macbeth's "Assassination" still conjures up an almost unimaginable deed. So unimaginable that he can only name the act as "it." "If *it* were done, . . . then 'twer well, / *It* were done quickly." Agent and action are alike erased. To then name the deed as an "Assassination" was surely to imagine it as above all alien and unfamiliar. In *Macbeth,* though, the alien and unfamiliar do not inhabit an elsewhere, whether Aleppo or India. The *unheimlich* already resides within the "home." The bloody sects "over there" are already, or perhaps have always been, the bloody sects "over here." In fact, one striking feature of the "Britishing" of the assassin is how rapidly the word came to name the other within. In 1611, when the word was still so foreign that Speed wrote it in Italian, a French pamphlet was translated into English attacking the Jesuits for their "abhominable assassinancie."[30]

If "eastern malignancy" named the unnameable that was already present within Europe, one of the crucial aspirations of Protestant scholars could best be fulfilled not in Elizabethan and Jacobean England but in the land of the "infidels." From the late sixteenth century, radical Protestants made the journey to Istanbul to learn Hebrew from the large Jewish community there and even to debate openly with Jews in synagogues. At the same time, the reformers collected Jewish manuscripts, which now constitute a significant part of the Bodleian Library's collection in Oxford.[31] Aleppo was also a center of scholarship. It was in Aleppo that Edward Pococke "studied Arabic, Hebrew, Syrian, and Ethiopic." On his return, Pococke published "the first book to be printed in Arabic type in England (1636)."[32] And in Catholic countries, merchants brought back from the Levant not only commercial goods but also unique religious imports: "the veil of St. Anne" (in fact, an Islamic veil); a vase from the marriage at Cana (a fourteenth-century Spanish Islamic vase that the Ottomans had taken from Cyprus in 1571). In the Marienkirche in Gdansk, a dalmatic (one of the Catholic priest's vestments) was composed of five silk textiles including one with parrots and the Arabic inscription "the sultan, the wise," probably from Khorasan in what is now northeast Iran, as well as a fourteenth-century textile from Mamluk Egypt. It is likely that these last two textiles ended up in Gdansk by traveling from Egypt to Venice, from Venice to Charles IV in Prague, and from Charles IV to the Teutonic Knights who ruled Gdansk.[33]

India, Persia, and the Ottoman Empire materialized Europeans. That is, they provided much of the *matter* (fibers, textiles, dyes) that shaped European bodies. In 1600, the opposite was not true, not because Western Europe was not familiar to the Ottomans but because it was marginal to the Indian Ocean, which remained dominant in the global network of trade.[34] And if mainland Europe was marginal, England was yet more so. England discovered its distance from India, and its marginality to the centers of global power, when Sir Thomas Roe was sent as the first English ambassador to the Mughal Empire in 1615. As Sir William Foster noted from the perspective of early twentieth-century British imperialism: "There is nothing more striking to a present-day reader than the indifference towards Europeans displayed by the Emperor and his ministers. Jahangir's memoirs, while daily chronicling the arrival of missions from Persia and other neighbouring countries, and minutely detailing many trivial details, make no direct allusion to the English ambassador . . . To the sovereign of Hindustan there were only two other monarchs who could even pretend to equality with himself—the Persian Shah, and the still more distant ruler of Constantinople and its dependencies."[35] The humiliation of the English ambassador was the greater because Jahangir had an extensive knowledge of and interest in European culture and found at least some aspects of it worth collecting. For instance, a surviving automaton of Diana on a stag made by Joachim Fries is almost identical to an automaton depicted in a Mughal miniature in 1618, held by the Mughal Ambassador to Persia.[36]

The Mughal court's sophisticated interest in European culture preceded Jahangir. His father, Akbar, left twenty-four thousand books at his death: "Each part of the library is subdivided according to the value of the books and the estimations of the sciences are held of which the book treats. Prose books, poetical works, Hindi, Persian, Greek, Kashmirian, Arabic, are all equally placed . . . Experienced people bring them daily and read them before his Majesty, who hears every book from beginning to end."[37] All the books, we are told, were catalogued and numbered. Akbar also prided himself on his artistic connoisseurship. Emulating his father, Jahangir acquired a substantial knowledge of Italian painting and Netherlandish engraving from Jesuit missionaries. And although neither Akbar nor Jahangir acquired a printing press, Mughal artists were trained to copy in minute detail the cross-hatchings of European engravings.[38] Akbar also incorporated aspects of Christian iconography into his imperial cult, and a crucified Christ appears in the Mughal marginalia to a Persian love poem.[39] If Persian and Chinese art had a greater influence on Mughal painting,[40] European Renaissance motifs (including cupids) appear to striking effect. But while European art had an increasingly important influence on Mughal painting, it in no sense posed a technical mystery. When Sir Thomas Roe presented Jahangir with "a smale limned picture of a woeman" by Isaac Oliver, the Emperor claimed that he could "call four paynters, my cheefe woorke men," who would make a copy so exact "that yow shall not knowe your owne." When presented with the copies, Roe could only "discerne which was which" with the greatest difficulty, much to Jahangir's amusement.[41]

If Roe's embassy left no trace in Jahangir's memoirs, it is indirectly alluded to in a miniature by Bichitr, now called *Jahangir Preferring a Sufi Shaikh to Kings,* painted ca. 1615–18.[42] Bichitr incorporated James I, Roe's master, in the bottom left hand corner, with a figure who may be Bichitr himself standing in front of James, holding up a miniature. The depiction of James closely follows John de Critz's portrait of him, down to the details of hat, jacket, and hose.[43] But we can plausibly infer that there were other versions of the de Critz portrait, since Bichitr shows James wearing a ruff, not a falling collar. The couplet at the bottom of the miniature can be translated as "Although to all appearances kings stand before him, He looks inwardly towards the dervishes [for guidance]." Jahangir is thus represented as turning away from the worldliness of James and of the

Ottoman sultan above him to the Sufi Shaikh Hassain. James is incorporated but only so as to be marginalized. At the same time, English artistic technique is placed quite literally at the margins, whereas the motifs of Italian art are complexly integrated into the whole composition. Jahangir sits on top of an hour glass through which the sands of time are running. But two Italianate angels write upon the hourglass: "O Shah, may the span of your life be a thousand years." Above Jahangir, either side of the rising sun that acts as an enormous halo for his head, two naked European *putti* bestride the air. The *putto* on the left holds a bow in his left hand, but with his right hand he raises a broken arrow. The *putto* on the right holds his head in his hands in shame or mourning. With extraordinary sophistication, Bichitr redeploys European motifs in the service of the Mughal imperial cult. The cupids of European love conventions are humbled before Jahangir's supposed sanctity, which is itself upheld as a millennial rule by two clothed angels.

Sir Thomas Roe was profoundly impressed by the Mughal court artists: "In that arte of limninge," he wrote, "[Jahangir's] paynters woorke miracles."[44] But if Roe was impressed, he failed to impress himself: "For presents, I have none, or so meane that they are woorse then none; so that I have resolved to give none." But before giving "none," Roe had already had the humiliating experience of having one of his gifts returned "as too poore of valewe."[45] The humiliation was the greater because the Portuguese were able to offer "rich presents" and "many rarietyes."[46] And English trading goods fared no better than English gifts. Roe complained that the Indians "seeme to buy our comodityes for almes. . . . For our trade, or any thing wee bring, [it is] not att all respected."[47] From the Mughal empire, even more than from Aleppo, England appeared not just distant but marginal. What, after all, did it have to offer?

Given the global centrality that "Great Britain" achieved in the eighteenth century, it is hard now to imagine just how marginal England was to the global economy of c. 1600. Even the greatest European powers were overshadowed by the expansion of the Ottoman Empire and the dominance of the trade networks in the Indian Ocean. As Philip Curtin notes, "The 'European Age' in world history had not yet dawned [in the sixteenth and early seventeenth centuries]. The Indian economy was still more productive than that of Europe. Even the per capita productivity of seventeenth-century India or China was probably greater than that of Europe. . . . Europe's clear technological lead was still limited to select fields like maritime transportation, where the design of sailing ships advanced enormously through the sixteenth and seventeenth centuries. Otherwise, Europe imported Asian manufactures, not the reverse."[48] Om Prakash further observes that Asian producers were "in a position of advantage over their European counterparts in the production of a variety of manufactured goods" throughout the seventeenth century. "The only major item Europe was in a position to provide to Asia was precious metals."[49] The exploitation of the mineral resources of the Americas can, indeed, be seen as a necessary precondition for the expansion of European trade with Asia. Without precious metals, Europe had little to exchange that Asia wanted. If the exploitation of the Americas gave England (and later Britain) a privileged position on the westernmost margins of Europe, it was relations with the East that dominated both the economy and the diplomacy of Europe in 1600. While Venice, Portugal, and Holland were all struggling to maintain old and develop new markets in Asia, England in 1600 was not yet in a position to compete. Against the inflated accounts of English conquests upon the London stage, we should recall that Sir Thomas Roe's visit to the Mughal court left no trace in Jahangir's extensive diplomatic records of visiting ambassadors. England was too marginal to count.

NOTES

1. This paper was brought into existence by Leeds Barroll, who asked me to write about a topic I had not thought about till then for a panel he chaired for the Shakespeare Association of America in Montreal in 2000. The quotation is from William Shakespeare, *The Tragedy of Othello* (London: Thomas Walkley, 1622), 99 (5. 2. 353–7). I am also deeply indebted to Ania Loomba for sharing her work with me, and in particular her "Signs Not Taken for Wonders—the View from Agra" (unpublished ms.). See also her "Shakespeare and Cultural Difference," in *Alternative Shakespeares 2,* ed. Terence Hawkes (London: Routledge, 1996), 164–91.

2. On the geography of the play, see Virginia Mason Vaughan, *Othello: A Contextual History* (Cambridge: Cambridge University Press, 1994), 13–50, and John Gillies, *Shakespeare and the Geography of Difference* (Cambridge: Cambridge University Press, 1994). The extensive commentary on the "turban'd Turk" includes Dennis Bartholomeusz, "Shakespeare Imagines the Orient," in *Shakespeare and Cultural Traditions: the selected proceedings of the International Shakespeare Association World Congress, Tokyo, 1991,* ed. Tetsuo Kishi, Roger Pringle and Stanley Wells (Newark: University of Delaware Press, 1994) and Daniel Vitkus, "Turning Turk in *Othello,*" *Shakespeare Quarterly* 48 (1997), 159–61. See also Richard Levin, "*Othello*'s American Indian," *Shakespeare Newsletter* 50: 2, no. 245 (Summer 2000), pp. 35–6.

3. *Macbeth* in *The Norton Facsimile: The First Folio of Shakespeare,* ed. Charlton Hinman (New York: Norton, 1968), TLN 105 (1. 3. 7). Curiously, William Davenant changed Shakespeare's "Her Husband's to *Aleppo* gone" to "Her Husband's to the *Baltick* gone." See Christopher Spencer, *Davenant's "Macbeth" from the Yale Manuscript* (New Haven, CT: Yale University Press, 1961), 1.3.7. I am at a loss to explain this change.

4. See Sigmund Freud, "The Uncanny," in *The Standard Edition of the Complete Psychological Works of Sigmund Freud,* ed. James Strachey (London: Hogarth Press, 1955), 17, 218–52, especially 220–26.

5. Metin Kunt, "State and Sultan up to the Age of Süleyman: Frontier Principality to World Empire," in *Süleyman the Magnificent and His Age: The Ottoman Empire in the Early Modern World* ed. Metin Kunt and Christine Woodhead (London: Longman, 1995), 19–21 and Stanford J. Shaw, *History of the Ottoman Empire,* vol. 1, "Empire of the Gazis: The Rise and Decline of the Ottoman Empire, 1280–1808" (Cambridge: Cambridge University Press, 1976), 55–60.

6. John Cartwright, *The Preacher's Travels* (London: Walter Burre, 1611), as quoted in Kenneth Parker, ed. *Early Modern Tales of Orient* (London: Routledge, 1999), 107. See also P. R. Harris, "The Letter Book of William Clark, Merchant at Aleppo, 1598–1602" (PhD dissertation, University of London, M.D.) and S. A. Skilliter, *William Harborne and the Trade with Turkey, 1578–1582: A Documentary Study of the First Anglo-Ottoman Relations* (Oxford: Oxford University Press, 1977). For later developments, see Bruce Masters, *The Origins of Western Economic Dominance in the Middle East: Mercantilism and the Islamic Economy in Aleppo, 1600–1750* (New York: New York University Press, 1988) and Ralph Davis, *Aleppo and Devonshire Square: English Traders in the Levant in the Eighteenth Century* (London: Macmillan, 1967).

7. See Patrick Collinson, "The Elizabethan Puritans and the Foreign Reformed Churches in London," *Proceedings of the Huguenot Society of London,* 20:525–55. Repr. in *Godly People: Essays in English Protestantism and Puritanism* (London: Hambledon Press, 1983), 245–72.

8. Richard Hakluyt, *The Principal Navigations, Voyages, Traffiques & Discoveries of the English Nation* (London: J. M. Dent, 1937), 3:323.

9. Ibid.

10. Fiona Kisby, "Books in London Parish Churches, c. 1350–1603," lecture, the History of Material Texts seminar, University of Pennsylvania, March 27, 2000.

11. Shaw, *History of the Ottoman Empire,* 1: 177–79. See also Vaughan, *Othello,* 23–8; Kunt, "State and Sultan," 3–38; and Ann Williams, "Mediterranean Conflict," in Kunt and Woodhead, *Süleyman the Magnificent,* 39–54.

12. Shaw, *History of the Ottoman Empire,* 1:179–81.

13. On the complexities of this interaction in Britain, see Nabil Matar, *Islam in Britain, 1558–1685* (Cambridge: Cambridge University Press, 1995), particularly 1–49.

14. Cesare Vecellio, *Degli habiti antichi, et moderni di diverse parti del mondo* (Venice, 1590), 364, 366, 373, 205. I am indebted to Ann Rosalind Jones and Margaret Rosenthal for this reference.

15. Hakluyt, *Principal Navigations,* 3: 268, 270.

16. Michel Morineau, "Eastern and Western Merchants from the Sixteenth to the Eighteenth Centuries," in *Merchants, Companies, and Trade: Europe and Asia in the Early Modern Era,* ed. Sushil Chaudhury and Michel Morineau (Cambridge: Cambridge University Press, 1999) 116–44, particularly 130. For an account of an earlier period, see Janet L. Abu-Lughod, *Before European Hegemony: The World System A.D. 1250–1350* (Oxford: Oxford University Press, 1989).

17. Hakluyt, *Principal Navigations,* 3:274.

18. Niels Steensgaard, "The Route through Quandahar: The Significance of the Overland Trade from India to the West in the Seventeenth Centuries," in Chaudhury and Morineau, *Merchants, Companies, and Trade,* 55–73, particularly 61 and 67, and Halil Inalcik, *An Economic and Social History of the Ottoman Empire,* vol. 1, 1300–1600 (Cambridge: Cambridge University Press, 1994), 1:358–59.

19. For the centrality of intra-Asian trade, see Gilles Veinstein, "Commercial Relations Between India and the Ottoman Empire (Late Fifteenth to Late Eighteenth Centuries" in *Merchants, Companies, and Trade,* 95–115 (see note 16), and Halil Inalcik, *An Economic and Social History,* 315–63.

20. Om Prakash, *The New Cambridge History of India*, vol. 2, part 5, "European Commercial Enterprise in Pre-Colonial India" (Cambridge: Cambridge University Press, 1999), 72–85.

21. Veinstein, "Commercial Relations Between India and the Ottoman Empire," pp. 95–115.

22. Writing about the development of London in the sixteenth century, Derek Keene still emphasizes its dependency upon Antwerp and the Low Countries. See his "Material London in Time and Space," in *Material London, ca. 1600,* ed. Lena Cowen Orlin (Philadelphia: University of Pennsylvania Press, 2000), 55–74. On the importance of Antwerp in the sixteenth century and the beginnings of its decline, see Jan van der Stock, *Antwerp: story of a metropolis,* ed. (Gent: Smoeck-Duceju and Zoon, 1993), H. Van der Wee, *The Growth of the Antwerp Market and the European Economy* (The Hague: Nijnoff, 1963), and G. D. Ramsay, *The Queen's Merchants and the Revolt of the Netherlands: The End of the Antwerp Mart* (Manchester, UK: Manchester University Press, 1986). The long history of England's "low tech" exports and "high tech" imports is suggested by Vanessa Harding, "Cross-Channel Trade and Cultural Conflicts: London and the Low Countries in the Later Fourteenth Century," in *England and the Low Countries in the Middle Ages,* ed. Caroline Barron (Stroud, Gloucestershire: Sutton, 1995), 153–68. In 1384, for instance, Clays Johansen imported to England earthenware dishes, bakestones, Holland linen cloth, and beer, while his only export was cloth. In the same year, Robert Stavele made three trips, importing linen cloth, metalware, flax, garlic, and tallow, but exporting only butter and cheese (and possibly cloth), while Laurence Chesse used his large ship to import "66 barrels of pitch, woad, iron, and other goods, 20 thousandweight of woad, madder, flax, and copper, nearly 2,000 lb. of baterie (beaten metal wares), several thousand Baltic furs, several thousand ells of linen cloth from Westphalia, Flanders, Hainault, and Zeeland, and a small quantity of Italian silk textiles. Chesse's recorded export cargo was less than 50 quarters of grain, 25 cloths, and 900 boards of wainscot, but perhaps he carried wool as well" (158–59). As Harding further notes, "there was clearly a high demand for a wide range of imports, which drove trade to the extent that some ships could find no export cargoes in London and apparently left without one" (163).

23. Conrad Russell, *The Crisis of Parliaments: English History 1509–1660* (Oxford: Oxford University Press, 1971), 283–84.

24. On England's early role in the slave trade, see, for example, Hilary Becles, "The 'Hub of Empire': The Caribbean and Britain in the Seventeenth Century," and P. E. H. Hair and Robin Law, "The English in Western Africa to 1700," in *The Origins of Empire* ed. Nicholas Canny (Oxford: Oxford University Press, 1998), 218–40 and 241–63.

25. R. W. Ferrier, "Charles I and the Antiquities of Persia: The Mission of Nicholas Wilford," *Iran* 8 (1970): 51–56, particularly 51.

26. Michel Morineau, "The Indian Challenge: Seventeenth to Eighteenth Centuries," in *Merchants, Companies, and Trade* (see note 16), 243–74, particularly 257. For later developments, see Dietmar Rothermund, "The Changing Pattern of British Trade in Indian Textiles," in ibid., 276–86.

27. For an overview of Shakespeare's linguistic "imports," see Jeffrey McQuain and Stanley Malles, *Coined by Shakespeare: Words and Meanings First Used by the Bard* (Springfield, MA.: Merriam-Webster, 1998). See also Marjorie B. Garber, *Academic Instincts* (Princeton, NJ: Princeton University Press, 2001), 104, 124–38, 168.

28. Richard Knolles, *The Generall Historie of the Turks* (London: Adam Islip, 1638), 120.

29. John Speed, *The History of Great Britaine* (London: John Sudbury and George Humble, 1611), 9.10.5.

30. Anon., *Anti-Coton, or a Refutation of Cottons Letter declaratorie: touching the killing of kings,* translated by G. H. (London: Richard Boyle, 1611), 48. It is significant that this is an

Englishing of a French pamphlet, so, as in Speed, the word arrives through an explicitly double (and in fact multiple) migration. It is also notable that the Jesuits' "assassinancie" is, like Macbeth's, specifically "the killing of kings."

31. I draw here upon the brilliant unpublished work of Josef Hacker of the Hebrew University, Jerusalem, presented during the year on "Christian Hebraists, Jews, and the Study of Judaism in Early Modern Europe," the Center for Advanced Judaic Studies, University of Pennsylvania, 1999–2000.

32. Parker, *Early Modern Tales of Orient*, 3–4.

33. Jay A. Levenson, ed., *Circa 1492: Art in the Age of Exploration* (New Haven, CT: Yale University Press, 1991), 133.

34. See the quote below from Philip D. Curtin, *Cross-Cultural Trade in World History* (Cambridge: Cambridge University Press, 1984), 149. See also Prakash, *New Cambridge History of India*, vol. 2, part 5, 1–7.

35. Sir William Foster, ed., *The Embassy of Sir Thomas Roe to India, 1615–1619* (London: Oxford University Press, 1924), xliii.

36. Ebba Koch, *Dara-Shikoh Shooting Nilgais: Hunt and Landscape in Mughal Painting* (Washington, DC: Smithsonian Institution, 1998), Occasional Papers, 1:12–14: "In the famous Freer Gallery painting of the imaginary meeting of Jahangir and Shah Abbas of Persia, the Mughal Ambassador to the Persian court, Khan-i Alam, holds in one hand a precious hunting falcon, and in the other a clockwork with the gilt group of Diana, the Roman goddess of the hunt, seated upon a stag. Such Diana groups were produced in Augsburg, Germany, around 1600. . . . The object testifies to Jahangir's taste as a collector of the latest European art and to his passion for the hunt." (The latter was a passion that he shared with James VI of Scotland and I of England.)

37. Milo Cleveland Beach, *The Imperial Image: Paintings for the Mughal Court* (Washington, DC: Smithsonian Institution, 1981), 9–10.

38. Gauvin Alexander Bailey, *The Jesuits and the Grand Mogul: Renaissance Art at the Imperial Court of India, 1580–1630* (Washington, DC: Smithsonian Institution, 1998), Occasional Papers, 2:18–33.

39. Ibid., 33–34.

40. Amina Okada, *Indian Miniatures of the Mughal Court*, trans. Deke Dusinberre (New York: Harry N. Abrams, 1992), 62–95 and Milo Cleveland Beach, *Early Mughal Painting* (Cambridge, MA: Harvard University Press, 1987), pp. 33–36.

41. Foster, *Embassy of Sir Thomas Roe*, xxxix. See also 189–90 for a conflicting account. For an excellent modern account of English painting at the Mughal court, see Ania Loomba, "Signs Not Taken for Wonders."

42. See Beach, *Imperial Image*, 29–37 and 168–69, and *Early Mughal Painting*, 168–69. See also Okada, *Indian Miniatures*, 45–47.

43. Beach, *Imperial Image*, 30.

44. Foster, *Embassy of Sir Thomas Roe*, xxxix.

45. Ibid., xxxiii.

46. Ibid., xxxvii.

47. Ibid., xxxviii.

48. Philip D. Curtin, *Cross-Cultural Trade in World History* (Cambridge: Cambridge University Press, 1984), 149.

49. Prakash, *New Cambridge History of India*, vol. 2, part 5, 84–85.

Incising Venice: The Violence of Cultural Incorporation in *The Merchant of Venice*

Philippa Berry

THIS ESSAY READS SHAKESPEARE'S VENICE AS A geographical and cultural site which, in its marking by significant rifts and fissures, can offer us new insights into the fragmented and fragmenting character of Renaissance or early modern culture. Rejecting what is sometimes implied to be the cultural and epistemic homogeneity of this moment, I want to configure it instead as a layered or palimpsest-like surface, upon which the remnants of other cultures and systems of knowledge exercised an uncanny potency, as they left subtle yet significant incisions or marks upon the parchment-like skin of the dominant culture.[1]

The first mythological image invoked in the play, that of "two-headed Janus," hints that the concerns of the *The Merchant of Venice,* like those of Renaissance culture in general, may be curiously bifocal. For of course it was the excavation, revaluation, and partial cultural incorporation of archaic knowledge systems—in the first instance, by Renaissance humanists—which paradoxically helped to inspire the forward momentum of the early modern era. Hence while the Renaissance or early modern era was energetically future-oriented in its anticipation of a new age, it was haunted at the same time by a multiplicity of half-acknowledged fathers: in other words, by a diversity of putative cultural "origins."

My contention is that Shakespeare uses the geographically and culturally liminal location of Venice to explore the contradictions inherent in this complex process of cultural mediation and incorporation, in a play which foregrounds the contemporary fascination with, yet simultaneous abjection of, those parts or remnants of other cultures with which Renaissance or early modern culture was so lavishly ornamented. Writing of the early modern delight in inscribing epigrammatic utterances or "posies" upon a variety of material surfaces, Juliet Fleming has observed that "The posy is the written form that calls attention to the fact that writing is 'set' on something."[2] Yet at the same time, the Renaissance or early modern text was itself characteristically embellished or inlaid with numerous citations and echoes from ancient texts. And the cultural remnants that are exchanged in this comedy are not only the exotic commodities acquired from other cultures, many of them non-European, in which merchants such as Antonio would have traded; they also include the textual fragment, as the play's subtle use of textual citation parallels but also obliquely comments upon that compelling bricolage of bits and pieces of diverse texts which was characteristic of early modern textuality. Indeed, both texts and textual inscriptions are accorded an objective material status on several occasions, as the play uses a number of highly charged dramatic contexts to stress the affinity of a new textual mobility—a cultural exchange of both texts and textual fragments—with a heightened faculty of visual perception which may be read as analogous to the emergence of increasingly subtle practices of reading.

Through this emblematic staging of texts or fragments of text, we appear to be invited to register a distinct anxiety about the inherent strangeness of surfaces or appearances that is a general theme of the play, in its repeated juxtaposition of the aesthetically beautiful surface with others—like the "streaked and pied" or "particoloured" lambs which form the basis of the biblical Jacob's growing flock, evoked by Shylock in 1.3—that appear disfigured or monstrous, and consequently seem to reflect upon the disturbing liminality or porosity of the skin or surface of European Renaissance culture. In her brilliantly nuanced exposition of that "intellectual distress" for which the tattoo "stands as figure," Juliet Fleming has suggested that within the new Euclidean space of early modern art "the two-dimensional skin functions as a material remainder that haunts the 'objective' spatial depth within which the Cartesian subject is driven to locate itself."[3] And in its specifically aesthetic preoccupation with surfaces, the Renaissance repeatedly fractures its putative cultural integrity, through a persistently troubled awareness of the simultaneously alien yet compellingly seductive appeal of diverse forms of ornamentation.

So Bassanio comments of the gold and silver caskets which threaten to mislead any culturally naive suitor for Portia's hand: "Ornament is but the guilèd shore / To a most dangerous sea, the beauteous scarf / Veiling an Indian beauty" (3.2.97–99). And of course the narrow escape of a tragic fate by the merchant Antonio affords a vivid figure for the anxieties which were seemingly being evoked by the dangerous trade in cultural difference, reminding us that the exotic or archaic object, commodity, or text may carry a hidden cost in terms of cultural disturbance. For while the Renaissance incorporation of alien cultural remnants might have appeared to serve a merely ornamental function, it was also producing subtle yet significant epistemic effects—changes in knowledge—within the dominant culture.

Superficially, of course, *The Merchant* sets up an apparently unequivocal polarization between Jewish and Christian models of cultural and economic

activity, in the form of usury versus mercantilism, illegitimate versus legitimate forms of trading, and Jewish revenge versus Christian "mercy." Its
conclusion implies that this binarism can be resolved by the act of social
and cultural violence, masquerading as "mercy," which is Shylock's
coerced conversion to Christianity; this cutting off or deracination of the
Jew from his own community is the symbolic Christianized substitute for
his intended revenge in the physical cutting off of Antonio's flesh
required by Shylock's bond. However, the prominence given to citations
from both the Old Testament and Greek myth in this play would have
alerted any attentive spectator to its striking memorial preoccupation
with archaic cultural origins—and even more specifically, with elements
from these archaic cultures that were curiously associated with separation, severance, or cutting off. Of course the Old Testament was a vener-
ated Christian text; however, through its dramatic citation by Shylock in
this play, it is effectively made strange—temporarily de-Christianized—as
it is culturally relocated as the original possession of the Jewish people. In
the contest over its meanings in 1.3 and 4.1, along with its final citation
by Lorenzo, the play dramatizes a continuing cultural struggle for interpretative possession of this text, while subtly reminding us of its pre-
Christian origins.

A key series of citations occurs in acts 1 and 5, and may therefore be
said to frame the play. In each case, it is interesting to note that an allusion to the Old Testament is balanced by or juxtaposed with a reference to classical literature and myth. Most significantly, the extended
metaphor of Portia as the Golden Fleece, introduced by Bassanio in
1.1, is followed a scene later by Shylock's retelling of the curious biblical episode of Jacob and Laban's sheep, in a justification of his taking
of "interest." The introduction of magical sheep (or rams) in each narrative fragment can be variously explained, but seems on one level to
remind us that the production of "interest" is an activity that is not necessarily restricted to Jews, but might have had some obscure analogue
in the world of pagan antiquity.

But in act 5, the "interest" that can be generated via acts of cultural as well
as sexual miscegenation is subtly incorporated into the Christian community
of Belmont, in a process that is initiated by the installation within Portia's
house of the mixed-race couple of Lorenzo and Jessica.[4] As the act begins
the lovers appear obliquely to allude to the obstacles that impede this work
of miscegenation, in their evocation of a series of unhappy lovers from different races who were familiar from classical myth and literature:

> *Lorenzo.*   The moon shines bright. In such a night as this,
>   When the sweet wind did gently kiss the trees
>   And they did make no noise—in such a night

> Troilus, methinks, mounted the Trojan walls,
> And sighed his soul toward the Grecian tents
> Where Cressid lay that night.

Jessica.   In such a night
> Did Thisbe fearfully o'ertrip the dew
> And saw the lion's shadow ere himself,
> And ran dismayed away.

Lorenzo.   In such a night
> Stood Dido with a willow in her hand
> Upon the wild sea banks, and waft her love
> To come again to Carthage.

Jessica.   In such a night
> Medea gatherèd the enchanted herbs
> That did renew old Aeson.

Lorenzo.   In such a night
> Did Jessica steal from the wealthy Jew,
> And with an unthrift love did run from Venice,
> As far as Belmont.

Jessica.   In such a night
> Did young Lorenzo swear he loved her well,
> Stealing her soul with many vows of faith,
> And ne'er a true one.

Lorenzo.   In such a night
> Did pretty Jessica, like a little shrew
> Slander her love, and he forgave it her.
>   (5.1.1–22)

However, the classical sequence ends with a dissonant and Ovidian coupling, that of daughter and father figure: these are Medea and Aeson, the father of her lover Jason. Medea has significantly been omitted from Bassanio's opening appropriation of the narrative of the Golden Fleece in order to legitimate and idealize his courtship of Portia. But in this near-climactic context, we can plausibly read Medea as representative of the cultural remnant's uncanny, even magical potency. At the end of this closing act, however, we turn back to the Old Testament, in what seems to be a final and pivotal moment of cultural appropriation by the Christian community of the play. This occurs in Lorenzo's brief but highly charged allusion to God's distribution of manna to the Israelites during their long exodus.

Since all of these citations focus upon a quasi-magical object, figure or event, they suggest that the cultural fragment carries a powerful surplus of alterity, by virtue of its frequent association with alien concepts of the supernatural, the uncanny, or the divine. The potentially troubling effect of this cultural alterity or difference seems to be most explicitly troped in this play in terms of a mysterious process of cultural incision: that is, as leaving a figurative wound in the surface of the dominant culture which aimed merely to assimilate and recuperate, with relative ease, the bits and pieces of other cultures.

The Merchant makes several allusions to both cutting off and cutting into—whether as wounding, lancing, or incising—as an activity that is implicitly associated with a cultural or perceptual difference—most directly, with Shylock and Morocco, who are emblematically equipped with knife and scimitar respectively. But there is also the mysterious and seemingly despised figure of the "cutler" whose inscribed knife is evoked by Gratiano near the end of act 5. *The Merchant* also comically personifies this strange preoccupation with cutting in the figure of the Clown, Launcelot Gobbo, whose name, as Patricia Parker has recently pointed out, is homophonically associated with a surgical instrument used for bleeding, the lancet or lancelet.[5] At the same time, while this is a play whose action hinges precisely on the protection of a Christian skin from a Jewish knife, it also accords a striking emblematic status and potency to individuals who are figuratively severed or cut off from a site of origin: not only are Shylock and Jessica both severed, for different reasons, from their cultural and religious origins, but in her comparison both to the Golden Fleece and to the Colchian Medea the fatherless Portia is also troped as one who is cut off from an originating source; even the clown Launcelot Gobbo has a dislocated relationship to his father, as is evidenced in their muddled meeting in 2.2, which echoes the biblical narrative of Jacob and Isaac's mistaken blessing. But alongside this focus on the individual who is deracinated or cut away, the play also alludes to several aesthetic surfaces that bear the diverse marks of cultural incision, in an implication that this imagery of a cultural cutting into may constitute or define a new level of meaning—providing not just a curious perspective from which to think about the inherent strangeness of ornamentation or beauty, but also a more nuanced understanding of the troubling question of cultural difference.

St. Paul had alluded in his Epistle to the Romans to the breaking or cutting off of the Jews from God, along with the possibility that they would finally "be graffed in" to God's grace:

For if the casting away of them, be the reconciling of the world [in enabling the substitution in God's favour and consequent salvation of the Gentiles], what shall the receiving of them be, but life from the dead? For if the first fruites be holy, the whole lumpe also is holy: And if the roote be holy, the branches also. And if some of the branches be broken off, and thou being a wilde Olive tree, wast graft in among them, and made partaker of the roote and fatnesse of the Olive tree. . . . Thou wilt say then, The branches are broken off, that I might be graft in. Well; because of unbeleefe they were broken off, and thou stoodest steadfast in faith. Be not high minded, but feare. For seeing that God spared not the naturall branches, take heed lest it come to passe, that he spare not thee. Behold therefore the kindenesse and rigorousnesse of God: on them which fell, rigorousnesse; but towards thee, kindenesse, if thou continue in kindenesse: or els thou also shalt be hewen off. And they [alluding to the Jews], if they bide not still in unbeliefe, shall be graffed in: for God is of power to graffe them in againe.[6]

This Christian perspective upon cutting off and grafting is a valuable intertext for the Christians' enforced conversion of Shylock, but it does not fully elucidate the play's evident interest in the ambivalent effect of the alien concept or cultural fragment upon the "skin" of that culture which appropriates it. The strangeness of this effect may rather be clarified by reference to a concept borrowed from the very detailed and extensive theoretical work undertaken by Gilles Deleuze (later shared with Felix Guattari) on the phenomenology of the concept.

In his attempt to develop a new relationship between thoughts and things, Deleuze shifts the interpretative emphasis from the idea itself to the "incorporeal" effect that he defines as being produced by the interaction between what he calls bodies or entities.[7] My understanding of this formulation is that Deleuze's "bodies" may be individually or socially constituted, and can therefore be equated with the body of a given culture or social group: "Incorporeal entities do not exist, but persist, subsist, or inhere in relations between bodies; they materialize *at the surface of bodies* without being themselves corporeal or substantial materials. . . .Corporeal bodies are things, while incorporeal entities are effects; corporeal bodies are objects, incorporeal entities are events" (my emphasis).[8] The incorporeal effect is not a go-between as such, but might rather be understood in terms of the effect that is produced by acts of cultural mediation. It is a "singularity," Deleuze emphasizes, in that it has no origin, and must consequently be interpreted separately from the situation and time in which it occurs. For this reason, the incorporeal effect has a ghostly or "phantasmic" property, and Deleuze stresses "the extreme mobility of the phantasm and its capacity for 'passage.' It [the phantasm] is a little like the Epicurean envelopes and emanations which travel in the atmosphere with agility."[9] At the same time, a figurative connection between the incorporeal effect and the attribute "of being cut" is explicitly introduced by Deleuze, as he traces his elaboration of this concept back to Stoic thought.[10]

In Sonnet 15, Shakespeare briefly tropes his writing as a cutting and grafting activity, telling the young man that "As he [Time] takes from you, I engraft you new" (1.14). And as it hints at the potent, even quasi-magical, influence that can be effected by the cultural remnant, as an incorporeal entity or event that operates precisely on the surface, *The Merchant* appears simultaneously to be articulating a conception of writing as a highly visual form of cultural marking or wounding, performed upon a skin-like surface by an alien hand. When Lorenzo receives a note from the Jew Jessica, he converts the racial difference and erotic agency of his mistress into an undifferentiated white surface that implicitly invites cultural (re)inscription, as he declares, "I know the hand. In faith, 'tis a fair hand, / And whiter than the paper it writ on / Is the fair hand that writ" (2.4.12–14). When Bassanio receives the news of Antonio's losses, and hence of Antonio's obligation to redeem Shylock's bond with his own flesh, he subsumes Antonio's authorship of the letter into the agency of the Jew, whose murderous intentions have converted words into "gaping wounds": "O sweet Portia, / Here are a few of the unpleasant'st words / That ever blotted paper. . . . Here is a letter, lady, / The paper as the body of my friend, / And every word in it a gaping wound / Issuing life-blood" (3.2.249–65).

More generally, the play implicitly mirrors and comments upon the peculiar signifying effects of the many incised and highly textured surfaces of Renaissance culture, as it configures the ambiguous, highly charged activity of cultural incision as a cutting away that is also an inscription. The number of verbs used in the play to evoke the cognate activities of inscribing, marking, tearing, or inserting is notable. These include: inscroll, incise, inlay, insculp, stamp, [en]grave, infold, insert, cut in, infuse, seal, rend, and tear, along with pill (for peel) and enthrone. The dark-skinned and culturally abjected Morocco, who swears "by this scimitar" (2.1.24), appeals to Portia: "Bring me the fairest creature northward born, / Where Phoebus' fire scarce thaws the icicles, / And *let us make incision for your love* / To prove whose blood is reddest, his or mine" (2.1.4–7; my emphasis).

But Morocco's failure to pass the test of the caskets reveals the unsettling difference that is at work in the activity of cultural incision/inscription, for "the saying [en]graved in gold" upon the golden casket conceals only a skull, in whose eye socket a mocking text has been inserted or "inscrolled." In part, the death's head serves as an emblem of time, and hence it may be read as a reminder that, within this new work of cultural incision, a strangely hybrid, double-eyed (a Janus-like) model of cultural temporality is also implicit. The incorporation, within *The Merchant,* of particular textual fragments or textual remains may question the plausibility of ever leaving archaic or abjected cultural origins completely behind.

But it also suggests that the relics of a different culture, once *cut off* from their originating context, and "inserted" or "inscrolled" in an alien cultural surface, can acquire new *interest*—an exaggerated significance whose "incising" effect is "incorporeal" in that it verges on the uncanny, phantasmic, or spectral—precisely because of the loss of an original cultural context or frame. Indeed, Morocco reminds us that the very coins which are the implied objective of both Christian and Jewish forms of trading are figuratively marked by the incorporeal effects of cultural inscription, here troped as a dual process of "stamping" and "insculping." "They have in England," he observes, "A coin that bears the figure of an angel / Stamped in gold; but that's insculped upon" (2.7.55–57).

This figurative detail certainly suggests that in the play's explicit meditation upon the ethics of commercial trading, the mystery of economic profit is seen as closely allied to the effect produced by those other forms of "trading" or "going-between"—artistic and epistemological as well as bodily and sexual—which produced the rich and strange "hybridity" of Renaissance or early modern culture. In *The Location of Culture,* Homi Bhabha defines hybridity as follows: "Hybridity is a problematic of colonial representation and individuation that reverses the effects of the colonialist disavowal, so that other 'denied' knowledges enter upon the dominant discourse and estrange the basis of its authority—its rules of recognition."[11] In *The Merchant,* as later in *Othello,* Venice is a macrocosmic version of this ambiguous process of cultural miscegenation: a place where the complicated articulations of racial and cultural difference through storytelling are both censored and licensed, and where the racial and cultural outsider whose freight of cultural wisdom is both admired and contested is either explicitly or implicitly circumcised.[12] In Shakespeare's Venice, these fragmentary narratives of different races and cultures—of the Jew, the Moor, and also, more indirectly, the Greek, the barbarian, and the Egyptian—are not only accorded a brief dramatic attention, but are also used to shape the wider figurative patterning, inscribing, or inlaying of each play. In *Othello,* the unsettling effects produced in Venetian society by the deracinated figure of the Moor are paralleled, of course, by the overwrought surface of his handkerchief. The handkerchief functions as a palimpsestic emblem of that pervasive ornamentation of cultural surfaces with foreign cultural details that was characteristic of Renaissance culture, as I have noted, but which is configured here not as European but as Egyptian in provenance; by implication, it is this heavy weight of indecipherable meaning or cultural "work" that tragically overdetermines the lives of the play's two protagonists.

When the "incorporeal effect" of the cultural fragment is localized in the disturbingly mobile handkerchief, it becomes an emblem of a surface mutability within nature as well as in signs that is interpreted by the jealous

Othello as specifically feminine. And in *The Merchant*'s thick mesh of biblical and classical allusion, it is the barbarian witch Medea, whose implied
affinity with Portia has been noted by several critics, who most obviously
emblematizes the conversion of the ambivalent process of cultural excision
and incision into an obscure activity of renewal through cultural difference.
The allusion in act 5 to her gathering of "the enchanted herbs that did renew
old Aeson" is to her magical restoration of vigor to Jason's father by cutting
into his flesh and anointing it with her magical balm: according to Ovid,
"Medea unsheathed her knife and cut the old man's throat; then, letting the
old blood run out, she filled his veins with her brew."[13]

Bassanio's description of Portia to Antonio in 1.1 positions her, like
Medea, as a problematic kind of cultural as well as social remnant: an
unfathered daughter "richly left" in the strangely indeterminate location of
Belmont. But although this speech makes no reference to Medea, it associates Portia with motifs of wounding and cutting through two other classical affiliations:

> In Belmont is a lady richly left,
> And she is fair, and, fairer than that word,
> Of wondrous virtues. Sometimes from her eyes
> I did receive fair speechless messages.
> Her name is Portia, nothing undervalued
> To Cato's daughter, Brutus' Portia;
> Nor is the wide world ignorant of her worth,
> For the four winds blow in from every coast
> Renownèd suitors, and her sunny locks
> Hang on her temples like a golden fleece,
> Which makes her seat of Belmont Colchis' strand,
> And many Jasons come in quest of her.
> (1.1.161–72)

The Roman Portia was renowned for wounding herself in the thigh in order
to prove her worthiness to share the secret of her husband Brutus and his fellow conspirators, while the Golden Fleece was the hide, pelt, or skin of a magical golden ram, sent by Zeus to carry a brother and sister to safety in Colchis
by swimming or flying from Greece. On arriving at Colchis, according to the
account in the *Argonautica* of Apollonius of Rhodes, the ram instructed the
brother, Phrixus (whose sister Helle had fallen and drowned in the renamed
Hellespont) to sacrifice it, after which its flayed fleece was hung in a sacred
grove until it was finally recovered—or stolen—and returned to Greece by
Jason and Medea. Portia is therefore troped at the very beginning of the play
as the remainder of an obscure system of values in which "wondrous virtues"
are associated with individuals, objects, and surfaces that are emblematically
incised or cut away; she will later tell Bassanio, "I stand for sacrifice."

But whereas the word "virtue" is repeatedly used by Shakespeare, throughout his work, in quasi-Paracelsan terms, to denote the mysterious powers concealed *within* particular natural objects, an understanding of Portia's "wondrous virtues," as Bassanio himself will learn, seems to require instead a heightened attention to the ambiguous potency of surfaces: to the metal casket, to Antonio's skin exposed to Shylock's knife, to mercy as the falling of rain upon the ground, to the superficial yet significant adornments of flesh which are the misplaced wedding rings, and finally, to the letters of good fortune which she delivers at the end of the play, troped by Lorenzo as manna.

For as I mentioned earlier, one of this play's most suggestive fragmentary allusions to the Old Testament occurs at its very end, when the multiple blessings that Portia and Nerissa miraculously bestow upon the Venetian Christians—significantly, in the form of letters—is troped by Lorenzo as the dispensation of manna. The reference is to God's miraculous nocturnal feeding of the Israelites during their forty years in the wilderness which is described in Exodus. Lorenzo exclaims: "Fair ladies, you drop manna in the way of starvèd people" (5.1.293–94). This almost magical distribution by Portia of supplementary good fortune, following the release of Antonio, affords a symbolic parallel to Shylock's taking of "interest."

The evanescent wafers of manna which are described in the Old Testament can hardly be regarded as substantial things; as mobile signs of God's blessing which are all surface and no depth, and which consequently have a distinctly phantasmic or uncanny character, they can plausibly be described as "incorporeal entities": "And when the dew was gone, beholde upon the ground in the wildernes there lay a smal rounde thing, as smal as the hoare frost on the ground. And when the children of Israel sawe it, they said every one to his neighbour, it is Manna, for they wist not what it was. And Moses said unto them, This is the bread which the Lord hath given you to eate."[14] Yet the Renaissance herbalist or botanist identified manna with a particular substance. This was a gum produced by making incisions in the bark of the Manna Ash, a tree native to southern Italy. In this botanical context, manna would have been understood as extruding through a skin-like rind or bark, which was marked by a figurative wound. The prominence of this trope so near to the end of the play consequently directs our attention to the peculiar potency of a highly fluid, yet almost insubstantial surplus: a surplus of meaning that constitutes a seeming enigma—an incorporeal effect—not just within the seemingly opposed domains of nature and spirit, but also within the cultural milieu of the play. From a botanical perspective, manna could be extracted from the fissured surfaces of trees. From a biblical perspective, it was a paradoxically material—if fleeting—manifestation of the divine blessings afforded by God to the Children of Israel.

According to Genesis, God's blessing of Abraham conferred a physical and material fruitfulness upon both him and his descendants that was crucially dependent upon a cutting off of masculine "flesh" (that is, upon the ritual act of circumcision).[15] By implication, the blessing is what is exchanged for the sacrificed membrane of skin. Portia's invalidation of Shylock's bond will precisely hinge, of course, on a question of cutting, in what several critics have seen as a covert allusion to the issue of circumcision. At the bodily level, Portia's ability to intervene in the Shylock-Antonio conflict seems partly attributable to the fact that both she and Nerissa are already "gelt" or castrated, with no genital "pens" to "mar" in a literal cutting off (5.1.143, 236). The self-description of Antonio in the trial scene as a "tainted wether of the flock"—a castrated ram—positions another image of an excessive or complete cutting off at the very center of the play. But while Antonio is symbolically disabled by this imagery of cutting away, Portia's parallel identification with the Golden Fleece of Greek myth is with the quasi-magical, supplementary value, not of a body rendered sacred by excision, but rather of a skin-like remnant—a nonhuman "thing" that has itself been cut off, skinned, or separated, to be left as a highly textured surface: this surface is also, by implication, the site of a wound. Yet the Fleece's mysterious conjunction of severance with a distinctive surplus of value or meaning is also signalled by its peculiar conjunction of goldenness with hairiness.

In Genesis, it was the simulation of hairiness, by covering the skin of his forearms with the hides of goats, that had enabled Jacob to trick his blind father Isaac into awarding the divine blessing conferred on Abraham upon his youngest, not his eldest son. Hence, whereas both the casket test and Shylock's coffers found a cultural integrity or substantiality that is identified with the father on an implied opposition between protected exteriors and inner value, the equation of Portia with the Golden Fleece directs our attention quite explicitly to a very different kind of cultural power, one that is inherent in the ambivalence of decorated or textured surfaces. This is a power that had seemingly been deployed by the patriarch Jacob, who is also the archetypal trickster figure of the Old Testament, as evidenced in the story of Laban's sheep. In the Gospel of St. John, Christ contrasts the food that he represents to the "bread" of manna that was dispensed to "our fathers" (6:31). Yet it seems that at the very point when Jessica and Shylock have voluntarily and involuntarily been assimilated into Christian society, the Belmont community figuratively reverses the process, in a symbolic exchange of cultural places that substitutes for the Christian blessing of the Eucharist the very different, because economic as well as spiritual, blessing that was conferred by God upon the descendants of Abraham. In its complicated work of cultural incision, therefore, the play also appears to be creating a network of figurative substitutions in which the father as cultural origin is both unmasked—as a trickster figure whose "law" is effectively a chimera—but also displaced or replaced by the figure of the equally duplicitous daughter, who is severed or cut off from her own origins in a rather different sense than was the deracinated patriarch and his exiled descendants.

The play's last act weaves together several different figures of the incorporeal effects that are allied to acts of cultural incision. For in between the quasi-sacrificial renewal of the father Aeson (which we are surely invited to read as a metamorphosis) by Medea's pouring of her brew into a seemingly deadly wound, and Portia's emblematic distribution of the letters (like another set of divine commandments), imaged as a gumlike manna that drops as it were from a cultural wound as well as from a heavenly aperture, are two further figurative incisions in the dramatic narrative. These are, firstly, Lorenzo's rapt contemplation of "the floor of heaven," which he sees as "thick inlaid with patens of bright gold"—in other words, with stars. The stars are troped here as alien bodies in the floor of heaven, for they are configured as highly material, like golden disks inlaid in a costly pavement. But since patens were the dishes used to serve the Eucharist, the implication also appears to be that this fissuring or inlaying of the floor of heaven with an alien substance is necessary, if heavenly qualities are to be transmitted to man.

Yet in vivid contrast to this otherworldly image, the incising inscription that is finally foregrounded in *The Merchant*'s last act appears to be negligible, even banal. This is the trite motto or "posy" inscribed on Nerissa's ring, which Gratiano dismissively describes as "For all the world like cutler's poetry / Upon a knife—'Love me, and leave me not'" (5.1.149–50). In this curious figurative substitution of knife for ring, we are reminded once again of the shadow of violence—like the lion's shadow which "afeared" the Ovidian Thisbe—that necessarily attends the binding together of disparate elements within a particular society—whether in the context of marriage, or via the process of cultural incorporation. For all their seeming contrast—since the figurative movement here appears to be from the sublime to the banal—both tropes focus upon a subtle affinity discovered between highly material surfaces (the patens or dishes of gold, the ring itself) and concepts of immateriality (the heavenly spheres and their soul-piercing music, and the death-do-us-part oath of the marriage ceremony), precisely through the work of inlaying or inscription.

I have tried to read the inscribing incisions of *The Merchant of Venice* as the peculiar interest—the strangely productive yet "incorporeal" effects—of the violence that informed the enormous cultural complexity within which the play is embedded. The play appears to articulate a subtle comment on the cultural conventions that shaped the Renaissance, by showing how deracinated ideas and images from archaic cultures function as semiotic go-betweens: marking the intersection of old with new cultures, and consequently producing "incorporeal" effects that cannot be reduced to either cultural context. Through its allusions to the Old Testament, the play appears to interpret the disturbing figure of the "assimilated" Jew and his cultural tradition as a residue or remnant whose significance may now be entirely questionable, precisely because it goes or is passed between different cultural locations, but which acquires a new, quasi-magical potency precisely by virtue of its complete deracination or cutting off from a cultural origin. What is finally accomplished through Portia's agency in the play is a subtle process of cultural *revaluation* which departs from the models of both usury and mercantilism, as our attention is directed instead to those "wondrous virtues"—the surplus of cultural value, we might say—that inhere in the most "paltry" or unvalued things: in objects like Nerissa's ring, which seem to have a highly disjointed or undervalued relationship to the cultural context in which they are incorporated. At one level, we can plausibly read Portia as the personification, within the play, of the recently revaluated idea of cultural "wonder"—here given a specifically classical inflection—that informs so much of Renaissance or early modern culture. Yet she can also be seen as redirecting that wonder, as in the test of the caskets, to the curious properties of incised or inscribed surfaces.

NOTES

1. My interest in the prominence of the cultural surface in *The Merchant of Venice* has been invaluably clarified by Juliet Fleming's *Graffiti and the Writing Arts in Early Modern England* (London: Reaktion, 2001).

2. Ibid., 43.

3. Ibid., 86.

4. In "From Imagination to Miscegenation: Race and Romance in Shakespeare's *The Merchant of Venice*," *Renaissance Drama*, n.s. 29 (2000): 137–64, Elizabeth A. Spiller argues that miscegenation in this comedy also involves a mixing of generic kinds, in a dramatization of the reciprocal relationship between new understandings of race and new types of romance.

5. Patricia Parker, "Barbers and Barbary: Early Modern Cultural Semantics," in *Renaissance Drama* n.s. 33 (2004). Parker cites Thomas Thomas's *Dictionarium Linguae Latinae et Anglicane* (1587) on "*Scalper.* . . . Any kinde of instrument or yron toole, to make incision, to scrape, cut, or grave with a graving yron, a lancelot, scissers," and Gabriel Harvey, who observes in his *New Letter* (1593), 12: "Pierces Supererogation . . . is less beholding to the penknife: Nashes S. Fame hath somewhat more of the launcelet."

6. Romans 11:15–23, from *The Bishops' Bible* (London, 1602).

7. The concept is most extensively discussed in *The Logic of Sense* (1969), trans. Mark Lester with Charles Stivale, ed. Constantin Boundas (London: Athlone, 1990), 4–11.

8. This helpful explication of Deleuze's formulation is by Paul A. Harris, in his unpublished paper "Nothing: A User's Guide."

9. Ibid., 217.

10. Ibid., 5.

11. Homi Bhabha, *The Location of Culture* (London: Routledge, 1994), 114.

12. In *Shakespeare and the Jews* (New York: Columbia University Press, 1996), James Shapiro describes late sixteenth-century Christian attitudes to circumcision. Shapiro notes the prominence of ideas and tropes related to circumcision within *The Merchant.*

13. Ovid, *Metamorphoses,* 7: 285–87.

14. Exodus 16:14–15, from *The Bishops' Bible.*

15. Genesis 15:1; 17:1–14.

Barbers, Infidels, and Renegades:
Antony and Cleopatra

Patricia Parker

> Our courteous Antony . . .
> Being barber'd ten times o'er . . .
> —*Antony and Cleopatra*

One of the most memorable of Shakespearean speeches describes Antony's first meeting with Cleopatra on the Cydnus, in Cilicia in Asia Minor or early modern Turkey. In a speech famous for its "Asiatic" excess as well as the more detached perspective of its speaker Enobarbus, Roman Antony is described as "barber'd ten times o'er":

> The barge she sat in, like a burnished throne,
> Burned on the water; the poop was beaten gold;
> Purple the sails, and so perfumed that
> The winds were love-sick with them. . . .
> . . . .
> Upon her landing, Antony sent to her;
> Invited her to supper. She replied
> It should be better he became her guest,
> Which she entreated. Our courteous Antony,
> Whom ne'er the word of "No" woman heard speak,
> Being barber'd ten times o'er, goes to the feast . . . (2.2.196–238)[1]

"Barber'd" here is an apparently minor or marginal detail in this famous speech, often forgotten in commentaries on this memorable passage. Its resonances, however, are central to the multiple implications of barbering it manages to suggest, across both Roman and early modern registers.

"Barber'd" here is an extraordinary compound term, compressing into a single word so much of what Egypt and the East are assumed to represent. As coiffed and groomed, it anticipates the reprise of this first meeting on the Cydnus in Cleopatra's elaborate preparations to meet her "curled Antony" (5.2.30) in death, lines whose "curled" summons one of the principal Roman indices of Eastern effeminacy and decadence. As evocation of Roman Antony's enchantment by a "barbarian" queen, it recalls the Battle of Actium that provided the historical climax of this first encounter, where (in Virgil's Augustan rendering) Antony's Egyptian forces include barbarian races and "barbaric" wealth. As a term suggestive of eunuchry and castration, it evokes the Barbary or *Barbaria* associated in the period with cutting and shaving of all kinds, including in contemporary narratives preoccupied with renegades and the "infidel" Turk.

Enobarbus's "barber'd" Antony is also part of the emphasis on beards as indices of masculinity, both within and beyond this play. The scene of the set speech itself begins with Enobarbus's pointed reference to the shaving of Antony's own "beard," in the exchange with Lepidus in Rome, before the meeting between Antony and Octavius Caesar, the figure who would rule as the Emperor Augustus after Antony's Actium defeat:

> I shall entreat him
> To answer like himself. If Caesar move him,
> Let Antony look over Caesar's head
> And speak as loud as Mars. By Jupiter,
> Were I the wearer of Antonio's beard,
> I would not shav't today!
>
> (2.2.4–8)

Here, the invocation of Mars and the traditionally bearded "Jupiter" identified with an older Roman *virilitas* is combined with the early modern "Antonio" by which Roman Antony in this play is alternately known, counterpart to the anachronistic identification of Virgil and Plutarch's Egyptian queen with a more contemporary "gypsy."

What I want to explore, in beginning from these marginal lines, is not only their centrality in relation to such outward signs but their importance in relation to both of this play's historical registers, ancient Roman and early modern at once.

barbers who pluck out the hair of these effeminate creatures. . . .
—Clement of Alexandria

barberous barbers. . . . alongst these shores of Barbaria
—Dekker, *The Gull's Hornbook*

The Roman significance of barbering and of beards was familiar from texts well known to early modern writers. As classicist Maud W. Gleason observes, "hairiness in general" in these texts is one of the visual signs that "announce from afar, 'I am a man' "; and "chief of these signs is the beard."[2] Since the seductive attractiveness of the "boy" was "conventionally held to fade with the arrival of body hair and the beard," shaving, cutting, or depilating—multiple Roman forms of barbering—were associated with attempts to return to the smoothness of the catamite or Ganymede. Ovid in *The Art of Love* counsels men against depilatories as well as curling. The elder Seneca condemns curling, depilation, and shaving, contrasting such practices with the virility of Cato and an older Rome. Seneca the Younger condemns "those who pluck out, or thin out, their beards," declaring of such "effeminate" practices: "How incensed they become if the barber gets careless, as if he were trimming a real man!" *Glaber* ("hairless") was the term used to describe "young men, usually slaves, who were considered sexually attractive because of their smoothness, whether natural or artificially attained." Pliny writes that "dealers in slave-boys, in order to keep their merchandise as marketable as possible, used blood from the testicles of castrated lambs to delay the growth of the beard." Plautus features the depilated player and transvestite male dancer or *saltator,* the well-known Latin word for "leaper" or "dancer" echoed in the condemnation of "wanton" dancing in Stubbes's *Anatomy of Abuses* and other early modern texts, a possible resonance within the "Salt Cleopatra" of Shakespeare's play, as both female seductress and transvestite "boy."[3]

Roman texts associate effeminate barbering with the East in particular. Juvenal's Second Satire aligns the supposed pathic sexuality of the depilated *cinaedus* with the *gallus* or Eastern eunuch. Martial contrasts his own vaunted manliness to an easterner with curled hair and shaven legs. Part of the tradition surrounding Julius Caesar—which may give a homoerotic inflection to the emphasis on "cuts" in Shakespeare's *Julius Caesar*—was his depilation and overconcern for the grooming of his hair, together with the pathic role he is said to have taken (in the ambiguous transition between boy and man) in the East of Asia Minor, under Nicomedes a foreign king, transforming this famous Roman *vir* (in Suetonius's famous phrase) into "Queen of Bithynia." Antony himself—trained in the "Asiatic" style that was associated with eunuchs and the effeminacy of Alexandria and the East, contrasted with more virile "Attic" style and "hirsute philosophy"—was derided not only as a "*catamitus*" but as a male *sponsa* or "bride" to Curio in Cicero's *Philippics,* the satirical attack that famously led to the latter's death.[4]

In the Roman texts on barbering and beards best known to early modern writers, the "natural" and the "constructed" (as Gleason observes) dizzyingly interact, complicating the opposition of bearded and smooth not only by the practices of such Roman leaders, in a period in which most Romans were shaven (in contrast to the older bearded ideal), but by the way in which the beard functioned as a notoriously deceptive index. Juvenal's Second Satire—directed against effeminate or *mollis* men—opens with those "who ape the Curii" of ancient Rome but "live like Bacchanals," observing that "Men's faces are not to be trusted." Martial's epigrams are filled with examples of hidden or secret *cinaedi* or pathics, concealing their identity under the appearance of "an ascetic bearded philosopher."[5]

Both this Roman tradition and its contradictions were transmitted to early modern Europe and England by other texts that underscored the multiple inferences of barbering, cutting, and shaving. Athenaeus's *Deipnosophists* includes beards and the origins of shaving in a passage on the love of boys, which begins with hypocritical Stoics who have smooth-shaven "favourites" and ends with the connection between "shaven chins and posteriors." Dio Chrysostom (in a discourse directed to the inhabitants of Tarsus in Cilicia) traces a degeneration that begins with trimming or cutting the beard and ends with the production of "epicenes," a combination reflected in the "Barber" named "Cutbeard" in Jonson's *Epicoene*. Clement of Alexandria associates shaving with "unnatural acts," complaining of those who ("although they are men") go to barbers to get "their whole bodies made smooth" and of the "barbers who pluck the hair of these effeminate creatures," removing the "beard" that is "the badge of a man" and "shows him unmistakably to be a man," castrating or cutting the visible sign of manhood itself.[6]

Shakespeare's "Roman" play and the lines on the "barbering" of Antony reflect the influence of this Roman tradition, transmitted both by classical texts and by later writers such as Clement of Alexandria, frequently cited in English antitheatrical treatises. What needs to be added is the "infidel" inflection this classical and Roman representation of alleged Eastern practices was given in early modern texts, where barbering of various kinds was increasingly associated with Barbary and the Ottoman Turk, or the new Islamic rulers of both Egypt and the East. For the description of Antony as "barber'd" by Cleopatra *not* to have such contemporary overtones would be difficult—given the growing interest in the Turk on the English stage and the publishing of accounts that associated "Barbarie" or the North African coast and the "barbarous Turk" with multiple forms of barbering. By the time of the play (1606–7), Egypt and Alexandria themselves had already been subsumed into the expanding Ottoman Empire for almost a century; and the shaving of Joseph in Egypt (part of the biblical narrative of Egyptian captivity) had its counterpart in illustrations that depicted the Pharaoh of the Exodus as a turbaned Islamic ruler.

As Nabil Matar, Jean Howard, Daniel Vitkus, and others have reminded us, dramatizations of the Turk and the Barbary coast had already become prominent on the English stage. The beardless eunuch associated with Egypt and the East in Roman writing was a staple of early modern accounts of the smooth or gelded eunuchs of Ottoman courts. What was claimed as the Turkish custom of castrating prisoners (as well as the circumcising of rene-gades, frequently conflated with castration) was detailed in popular dramatic and other accounts of the "great Turke." Mason's *The Turk* (1607–8) features not only Mulleasses, the Turk of its title, but a slave who was "a free borne Christians sonne in Cyprus, / When Famagusta by the Turke was sackt," who when captured was made "an Eunuch, / Disabled of those masculine functions, / Due from our sex." "Muly" (like Mulleasses)—the name identi-fied with Barbary and the Turk through Peele's Muly Hamet and contempo-rary travel writings—was itself associated with gelding or cutting, conflated with the "mule" that was a sign both of the hybrid mingling of kinds and of barbering in this other sense. Middleton's *Spanish Gipsy* makes the connec-tion explicit ("A beast? is't a mule? send him to Muly Crag-a-whee in Bar-bary," 4.1.22–23).

The anachronistic combination of Roman texts with early modern rep-resentations of the Turk was commonplace in English writing. George Sandys's account of his travels, for example, applies Juvenal's Sixth Satire on the gelded eunuch ("so smooth, / so beardless to kiss . . . What the sur-geon chops will hurt nobody's trade but the barber's") to the eunuch of the "Turkes," describing the boys "the *Turkes* do buy" and "castrate, mak-ing all smooth," in a passage that cites the lines of Juvenal on the *despera-tio barbae,* or "chins that of beards despaire."[7] The insertion of Roman excerpts into contemporary accounts of Barbary and the Turk had its counterpart in the anachronistic incorporation of Ottoman references into plays set in ancient Rome. Marlowe's *Dido Queen of Carthage,* though focused on Dido and Roman Aeneas, resonates with reminders of the Barbary coast. "Moores" suggest both ancient and contemporary reso-nances in Jonson's *Sejanus* (1603), while plays such as Dekker's *Satiromas-tix* included anachronistic reference to the Turk in a Roman plot.

The identification of "barbering" with "Barbary" (as well as a "bar-barous" nicking or cutting) is a striking feature of other contemporary English texts. In the First Part of Heywood's *Fair Maid of the West*—usu-ally dated between 1597 and 1604, though it may be later—the apprentice (Clem) who accompanies Bess to "rich Barbary" (5.1.82) appears there as a cultural transvestite, dressed in the clothing of a "fantastic Moor."[8] Enamored of the wealth of the Barbary coast (one of the motives for turn-ing Turk in the period), this English apprentice, who mishears "geld" for Barbary "gold," initially praises the "barbers" of Barbary ("for your coun-try's sake, which is called Barbary, I will love all barbers and barberies the better," 5.1.125–29). But after he is invited to "taste the rasor" (5.2.103), in order to be raised to favored status as a "eunuch," he protests this "Moorish preferment" that would "rob a man of his best jewels," calling the "barber" of Fez not "Davy" but "shavy" and resisting what he calls the Barbary barbers' "cutting honor" (5.2.126–31).

Dekker's *Gull's Hornbook* (1609), which features an entire chapter devoted to "Long Hair," similarly rails against "base barberous barbers" in a passage on the importance of "laweful heirs" (or hairs) and a text whose later references to an "abominable shaving" combine ingles or catamites with the theft that Dekker elsewhere identifies with renegade English pirates. Expressing disgust for the contemporary "polling and shaving world," Dekker compares it to the barbering to which Christian captives are subjected by the "Mahommedan cruelty" of the "Turks," who "no sooner lay hold on a Christian, but the first mark they set upon him, to make him know he's a slave, is to shave off all his hair close to the skull." The association of "base barberous barbers" with the barbarous "Turk" is retroactively underscored by the opening sentence of the next chapter, which professes to be "weary with sailing up and down alongst these shores of Barbaria."

The association of barbering, shaving, and cutting with Barbary and the Turk was at the same time part of accounts of English and European renegades and captives on the Barbary coast and in Alexandria itself. Captivity narratives reported the forcible shaving of Christian captives, as well as their "barbering" in other senses, including circumcising, gelding, and sodomizing or pathic subjection. Hakluyt includes a voyage to Tripolis in "Barbarie" in 1583, in "a ship called the Jesus," in which Englishmen were not only taken captive but "forceably and most violently shaven, head and beard" (5:301). The "plagues and punishments" visited on "Barberie" (5:308)—in the redemptive ending given to this narrative—recall the plagues on Egypt prior to the Exodus deliverance. But the texts devoted to this major international incident in the pages of Hakluyt include not only captives, but a willing renegade and a figure who has become a "eunuch" in Barbary, who is challenged by Elizabeth's "Ambassador with the Grand Signor" in Constantinople to be like "Joseph" in "Egypt," keeping his "true christian mind & English heart" free from Turkish "vices," notwithstanding that "your body be subject to Turkish thraldom."

Alexandria—already under Ottoman control from the early sixteenth century—provides the locus of other captivity narratives that conflated the biblical Egypt with the "captivitie of the Turkes," including another account in which Christian captives are forcibly barbered or shaved. In the version printed in the 1589 edition of Hakluyt, entitled "The woorthy enterprise of John Foxe an Englishman in delivering 266. Christians out of the captivitie of the Turkes at Alexandria, the 3. of Januarie 1577"

(5:153–64), Englishmen in a ship bound from Portsmouth to Seville in 1563 are "beset round with eight gallies of the Turkes" (5:152). Despite "manfully" resisting (an emphasis on "manhood" the account repeatedly stresses), they are "caried prisoners unto an Haven nere Alexandria" (5:156). Hakluyt's narrative focuses on John Foxe, who was "somewhat skilfull in the craft of a Barbour" (5:156), and on a barbering in reverse, in which this English "Barbour" with "an olde rustie sword blade" (5:158), rescues his fellow captives from "thraldome and bondage" (5:163). When the story is re-told by Anthony Munday, in an account that includes a renegade reluctant to leave Alexandria, explicit attention is called to the barbering of the captives by the Turk. As sign of their subjection as "slaves" to this "barbarous . . . tyrant" (before escape from "so barbarous a thraldome"), the "first villany and indignitie that was done to them" was "the shauing off of all of the hayre both of heade and beard."[9]

Barbering in the sense of cutting or shaving (already associated with Barbary pirates or being shaven by thieves) came simultaneously with multiple sexual overtones in the period, combined with Barbary, "infidels," and Turks. "Barbarie pidgeon" was a well-worn synonym for harlot in early modern English, as was turning "Turk," contemporary slang not only for the cutting of eunuchry or circumcision but for the sexual "turning" evoked in Antony's description of Cleopatra as "a triple-turn'd whore," a turning that suggests both turning Turk and turning whore.[10] The association of harlots with barbering derived from the loss of hair from syphilis— routinely described as a "foreign" disease. Robert Greene's *Disputation* (1592) features a "French Barbar," whose spelling combines barbering by a foreigner with a sexualized Barbary ("hee was strangely washt alate by a French Barbar, and had all the haire of his face miraculously shaued off"). Weever's *Faunus* (1600), translating Persius's Roman satires, pictures the removal of "the beard" from "Philosophers" by "Some shamelesse whore," while Rowlands's *Knaue of Harts* (1612) has jacks complain that because they "haue no beards," they are assumed to be panders "whose naked Chinnes are shauen with the Poxe." Joseph Swetnam, in the *Araignment of Lewd, idle, froward, and unconstant women* (1615), compares a lascivious woman to "a Barbers chaire, that so soone as one knaue is out another is in." "Barbers" in the sexual sense thus caused what the "Barber" was supposed to cure. Florio (1598), defining *Barbiera* as both "shee-barber" and "common harlot," cites under "*Andar in barberia,* to go and be cured or laide of the pocks," one of the contemporary functions of the barber surgeon. A bawd in Marston's *Dutch Courtesan* is described as being the "supportress of barber-surgeons" (1.2). Antony Nixon's *Black Yeare* (1606) warns those "conversant with *Venus*" that "the very haires shal be banished from their heads, and poore Barbers be made beggers for want of work."

The name "Shavem" is given to a harlot in Massinger's *City Madam* (1632), while Davies of Hereford exploits the commonplace conflation of "hairs" and "heirs" (or "heires apparant") in warning of the "dry-shauing" to be given by a "Kate."

The barber's pole and barber's balls (evoked in Jonson's "half-witted Barbarism! which no Barber's art, or his balls, will ever expunge or take out") were repeatedly associated with the phallic member and the "balls" that could be barbered or gelded. But barbering (and barbaring)—like Barbary itself—was also inseparable from overtones of pathic subjection, as well as eunuchry or gelding: in English texts where "sodomy" was described as "barbarously diverting Nature," by "metamorphosing humane shape into bestiall forme," in the account (in 1594) of a youth of "rare beauty" captured by pirates and "barbarously handled," or in narratives of enslavement by the Turk that included the threat of sodomizing among "barbarous" practices, like the account in Hakluyt of English captives in "Barbarie" which moves from their forcible shaving to the Islamic ruler who desired them. The sodometry already associated with piracy was also ascribed to renegades who "turned Turk" in Barbary, such as the notorious English pirate Ward. His "Sodomie" is decried in contemporary texts, including Daborne's *A Christian Turn'd Turk* (1612), where the cutting or circumcising that is part of his converting or turning Turk in Tunis on the Barbary coast is represented as his being pathically "handled" by "Mahomet" himself.[11]

> Thou art a Roman, be not barbarous . . .
> —*Titus Andronicus*

Both the Roman and "infidel" associations of barbering are reflected in the "smooth-fac'd catamites" and smooth or beardless chins of early modern writing. In Rabelais, the Asiatic "Bacchus, the god of bibbers, tipplers, and drunkards," is described as "most commonly painted beardless and clad in a woman's habit, as a person altogether effeminate, or like a libbed eunuch." The beardless "Ganymede" and the association of beardlessness with effeminacy are already familiar parts of the Shakespeare corpus: from Francis Flute's "Let me not play a woman, I have a beard coming" and the "green corn" that "hath rotted ere his youth attain'd a beard" (2.1.95) in *A Midsummer Night's Dream* to the "beardless vain comparative" (3.2.67) and shaven "chin" of the messenger ridiculed by Hotspur for his "holiday and lady terms" in *Henry IV, Part 1* (1.3.33–46); from the "smooth-faced gentleman, tickling commodity" (2.1.573) and "beardless boy" called a "cockred-silken wanton" in *King John* (5.1.69) to "the beards of Hercules and frowning Mars" in *The Merchant of Venice* (3.2.85). *As You Like It* and *Much Ado* depend on the external "note" or sign of the beard as the ostensible marker of difference between men and boys, as between men and women. *Bearding* in the sense of braving or challenging appears as a comparative index of virility in *Henry VI, Part 1* (4.1.12: "No man so potent breathes upon the ground, / But I will beard him") and *Coriolanus* ("If e'er again I meet him beard to beard, / He's mine, or I am his," 1.10.11–12). In the famous anachronism of *Henry V*—which assumes an Ottoman conquest that had not yet occurred—Henry's hope for a son who will "go to Constantinople and take the Turk by the beard" (5.2.222) applies this familiar topos to the contest with the Turk, famously bearded as well as associated with barbering renegades, captives, and boys.

The association of the Turk with eunuchry and other forms of barbering likewise appears repeatedly in Shakespeare. In *All's Well That Ends Well* (2.3.94)—which includes a "barber's chair that fits all buttocks" (2.2.17)—youths of "little beard" are said to be fit to send "to the Turk to make eunuchs of" (2.3.87–88). In *Twelfth Night,* Viola's plan to become a "eunuch" in Illyria (1.2.56–63) suggests not just the castrato evoked by the name of "Caesario" (from *caesus,* "cut") but the eunuchry identified with the Turk, whose dominions included Illyria, an "infidel" reference underscored when Malvolio is called a "renegado," after the famous "C-U-T" of the letter scene and his fantastic change of clothes.[12] Even the reference in the early texts of *Hamlet* to something in need of cutting ("It shall to th' Barbars [Q2 barbers] with your beard") may be part of the multiple topical allusions in the play to contemporary as well as ancient empires, to turning Turk, and to the Diet of Worms, which was concerned not only with the Lutheran schism but with the Ottoman threat.[13]

In addition to the associations of the beard with the manliness of the full-grown male, and of eunuchry and cutting with the Turk, the Shakespeare corpus directly conflates barbering with the barbarous, both before and after Enobarbus's description of the barbering of Antony. "Barbary" in the Folio text of *The Two Noble Kinsmen* appears as "Barbery" in the Quarto, in the Morris dance scene which calls attention to the "coast of Barbary" (3.5.60), to cutting (3.5.61), and to the Morisko or "Moor" (3.5.118). In *Titus Andronicus* (1593–4), the "barbarous Moor" appears as a "barberous" Moor in the Quarto version, which similarly renders Lucius's "O barbarous" as "O barberous," in response to the Moor's narrative of Lavinia's barbaric cutting or trimming. Although the play is set in Rome, the "barbarous" (or "barberous") Moor responsible for so much of its barbering suggests a more contemporary Mediterranean geography, the Barbary of the so called "infidel" as well as "coal-black" Moor, a more contemporary frame of reference suggested by the Moor's sending of his racially mixed son to *"Muliteus* my Countriman," emended by Steevens to the familiar Islamic "Muly."[14]

> On th'other part with all *Barbaria* force of diuerse armes
> Anthonius drags his traine of nacions thick. . . .
> —*Aeneid,* trans. Thomas Phaer (1573)

> Upon a tawny front . . .
> —*Antony and Cleopatra*

An "infidel" overlay on the Roman plot of *Antony and Cleopatra* would not be unexpected in relation to a pair whose well-known Virgilian counterparts, the potential renegade Aeneas and Dido the other African Queen, were already part of an anachronistic early modern overlay with Barbary and the Turk. Jerry Brotton, glossing "This Tunis, sir, was Carthage" in relation to the Mediterranean geographies of *The Tempest,* notes the conflation of ancient Roman imperial struggles with more contemporary references in "Thomas Phaer's highly influential translation of the *Aeneid*" (1573), where Iarbas, Dido's African suitor, is compared to "the Turkes."[15] In Roman writing, Cleopatra is repeatedly represented as "barbarous." In Virgil's Battle of Actium description, the Egyptian queen's "barbaric wealth" (*ope barbarica*), is the counterpart of the earlier description of the "gold on which Dido's Carthage is founded" (*Aeneid* 1.357–60).[16] The "barbaric" wealth of both African queens was updated in the "gold of Barbary" familiar from Peele's *Battle of Alcazar* and the enticement of the barbered renegade of Heywood's *Fair Maid.*

Phaer's influential rendering of Virgil's imperial epic translates it into unmistakable early modern accents, both in its description of Aeneas in Carthage and in its version of the confrontation at Actium.[17] Editors and critics of *Antony and Cleopatra* cite the parallel between Antony's subjection to Cleopatra and Virgil's Aeneas dressed in the clothing of Dido in Carthage. Phaer's culturally translated *Aeneid* pictures Aeneas in Carthage in terms that unmistakably evoke the Tunis that replaced it: "shining read in roabe of *Moorishe* purple, mantle wise, / Hae stood, and from his shoulders down it hing *Morisco* gise." Here, Aeneas captivated by Dido and become what he soon after calls Dido herself—"a Moore among the Moores" (4.377)—is expressly described in terms that align him with the Moriscos and renegades of the early modern Barbary coast.

In Virgil's description of the Battle of Actium, which provides one of Shakespeare's principal sources, Antony and his "Egyptian wife" are ranged with the "powers of the East." But *Orientis* in Virgil's famous description of Cleopatra's "barbaric wealth" had already—by the time of Shakespeare's play—long been part of the title by which European monarchs addressed the Turkish sultan, as Emperor of the East. In Phaer's version of the clash of West and East at Actium, Virgil's *ops barbarica* and the "nacions" of Africa and the East ranged on the side of Antony and Cleopatra his "*Gyptian* wife," are compounded within what he calls "all *Barbaria*": "On th'other part with all *Barbaria* force of diuerse armes / Anthonius drags his traine of nacions thick." When Phaer's translation renders their ignominious retreat, the territories associated with Antony and this "*Gyptian*" Cleopatra sound in both historical registers at once ("All *AEgypt* than, all *Inde* downe couched lowe, / All nations wilde of South *Arabia* . . . / All *Asia* scattring fled, all *Sabey* kingdoms turnd their backs").

The Battle of Actium itself had already been transplanted to this new early modern context, in the confrontation between the Ottoman power and the new "Roman" Emperor Charles V and his European successors. The Battle of Lepanto (in 1571)—led by Charles's bastard son Don Juan of Austria—was celebrated as another Actium, though its victory over the new forces of the "barbarous" East was shortlived.[18] Even more strikingly, in 1538, the forces of this new Roman emperor engaged the Turkish fleets at Prevesa or the site of Actium itself, in a celebrated battle in which history was reversed, yielding as victor not the "Roman" West (which was hopelessly divided) but the new sea power of the Ottoman Turk, which as a result of this victory at this new Actium became virtual master of the seas, and made the Barbary ports and Alexandria itself attractive magnets for renegades who flocked to North Africa from all over Europe. This new Battle of Actium was described at length in Knolles's *Generall Historie of the Turke* (1603), already acknowledged as an influential source for *Othello* in the following year.

Well before *Antony and Cleopatra,* literary and other accounts had already conflated the confrontation between Octavius and Antony with engagements on two fronts—the New World and the territories of Asia, Africa, and the Turk. The "barbarian hordes" of the East in Virgil's Actium description found their early modern counterparts in the Saracen army of Tasso's *Jerusalem Delivered,* whose English translation by Fairfax in 1600 may be echoed in Enobarbus's speech on Antony and Cleopatra's first meeting. Cleopatra, the Egyptian enchantress of Roman descriptions, had already been given an "infidel" inflection in the well-known epic-romances of Ariosto, Tasso, and Spenser, whose Acrasia evokes in her very name the mingling or mixture condemned as part of the adulterous Roman-Egyptian union of this famous pair. In Tasso, the infidel enchantress Armida—whose role is to impede the Christian crusade to regain Jerusalem by captivating its forces, as Antony was captivated—is described (like Cleopatra) as a "barbarian queen" ("la barbara reina").

Enobarbus's speech on Cleopatra and the "barber'd" Antony summons reminders of the more contemporary overlay the *Aeneid* had already been given. Editors of the play have remarked that its "burned" and "burnished" ("The barge she sat in, like a burnished throne, / Burned on the water") recall not only the flames of Virgil's Actium but also Tasso's palace of Armida, whose gates are inscribed with the Actium story of Antony and Cleopatra's "barbaric" forces, imitated by Spenser and others in the 1590s even before its English translation by Fairfax in 1600.[19] The passage in Fairfax (after evoking Hercules effeminated by Omphale) describes the Battle of Actium carved into the door of the palace of Armida, the infidel enchantress whose impeding of an earlier Christian crusade to regain Jerusalem reverberated with reminders of the crusading ambitions of the new "Roman" Emperor Charles V and other European rulers.

Cleopatra was thus already assimilated to the "infidel" East, as well as identified with Alexandria, controlled by the Turkish Sultan together with its neighboring Barbary coast. *Antony and Cleopatra* goes out of its way to recall this identification of the "gypsy" Cleopatra with the "spells" of such enchantresses—in Antony's "I must from this enchanting Queen break off" (1.2.132) and allusions to her as a "witch" as well as a "Fairy" Queen (4.8.12–18), whose "spell" and "charm" (4.12.2–13) hold Antony captive in Egypt. The triumph of "will" over "reason" that Enobarbus blames for Antony's Actium retreat (3.13.4–5) is an inversion familiar from contemporary accounts of captivating "infidel" enchantresses, both before 1606–7 and in "Turk" plays that retroactively situate Shakespeare's Cleopatra in relation to the problem of renegades and turning Turk. In Massinger's *Renegado,* the potential infidel enchantress Donusa, niece to the Ottoman Emperor or Great Turk himself, recalls the Cleopatra of the Shakespeare play in which Antony dies a renegado, in a play that rewrites both its plot and that of Daborne's *A Christian Turned Turk* (1612), by its conversions or re-turnings in the opposite direction. The "triple-turn'd whore" of Antony's description is assimilated to the sense of turning as both sexual and religious in the period, just as the designation of Shakespeare's Cleopatra as a "gypsy" aligns her with these early modern counterparts— an association that Jonson makes explicit in *The Gypsies Metamorphosed,* where "Queen *Cleopatra,* / The Gypsies grand-matra" is remembered in the "Turk gypsy" of its compound description.[20]

Enobarbus's description of Antony as "barber'd" by Cleopatra thus invokes the keyword not only of Virgilian and Roman writing but also of accounts of English and European renegades in Barbary and the "witchcraft" and "spells" of "infidel" enchantresses. Even the most familiar speeches and scenes of the play sound in these double registers. The play's own opening lines, which are put into the mouth of "Philo" (an invented character whose name, like that of Eros, suggests the different loves with which Antony and Cleopatra are identified), describe the "dotage" of Antony in terms that not only cast him as the most famous renegade of Roman history but underscore his own turning, toward a more contemporary gypsy:

> *Philo.*   Nay, but this dotage of our general's
>   O'erflows the measure. Those his goodly eyes,
>   That o'er the files and musters of the war
>   Have glow'd like plated Mars, now bend, now turn
>   The office and devotion of their view
>   Upon a tawny front; his captain's heart,
>   Which in the scuffles of great fights hath burst
>   The buckles on his breast, reneges all temper,
>   And is become the bellows and the fan
>   To cool a gipsy's lust. . . .
>   (1.1.1–10)

"Bend" and "turn" sound in these opening lines the familiar terms in the period for turning renegade or Turk, here associated with a "bending" and "turning" upon a "tawny front." "Tawny front" itself combines in a single phrase both the territorial and the personal—the "tawny" forehead of the "gypsy" Cleopatra whom Shakespeare makes "tawny" and "black" rather than Greek and (through the double meaning of "front" as "forehead" and military "front") the Eastern or Egyptian territory to which Antony has "turned." "Reneages" in the Folio text of these opening lines is usually glossed in the sense of "renounces" or "denies." But from the earliest editions (compounding the *renego* appropriate to a "Roman" play), it has also been identified with Old French *reneyes* and Spanish *renegar,* the root of "renegado" or renegade, familiar in its shifting orthography in the period from descriptions like Nicholas de Nicholay's of Algiers on the Barbary coast, as composed "for the most part of Christians reneid."[21]

Perhaps because of Egypt's identification with the "Orient" or East and because Antony and Cleopatra had already been aligned with the "infidel" Turk and the Virgilian counterparts of Aeneas and Dido in Tunis, the history of editorial commentary on the play has itself been inflected in this direction. Hanmer's reading of "reneages" as a variant of Spanish *renegado* identifies the figure the Folio renders as "Anthonio" with the Italian, English, and other European renegades who were flocking to Alexandria, Algiers, and other Barbary ports. In the eighteenth century, the Folio's puzzling "Arme-gaunt Steede" was read as a textual corruption for

"Termagant," the alleged Turk or Saracen deity. Even "ribaudred nag" was read as "renegade" by at least one former editor, while the "Terrene" of Antony's "Terrene Moone" has been glossed as a reminder of the Mediterranean or "Terrene Sea" of Marlowe's *Tamburlaine, Part 2,* from the lines in which Tamburlaine speaks of Christian captives and "the cruel pirates of Argiers."[22] Even the reference to three kings in *Antony and Cleopatra*—usually assumed to be one of the adumbrations in the play of the Christian revelation to come under the *pax Romana* of Augustus—may recall the Battle of Alcazar on that same Barbary coast, familiarly known as the battle of Three Kings.[23]

In the context of this framework, the opening emphasis on turning to a "tawny front" and the anachronistic renaming of this Roman-Egyptian pair as "Anthonio" and his "Gypsy," even the set speech that includes Enobarbus's description of Antony as "barber'd ten times o'er" has been thought to have contemporary overtones. In her study of Shakespearean pirates, Lois Potter observes that the "pursed" of Enobarbus's lines on Cleopatra (who, "when she first met Mark Antony, pursed up his heart upon the River of Cydnus," 2.2.186–87) casts the gypsy queen herself as a pirate, in a play whose maritime marauders inevitably recall their early modern equivalents.[24] "Anthonio" as the name given to Shakespeare's Roman Antony allies him not only with the merchant of *The Merchant of Venice* but with the Antonio who is called a "salt-water thief" in *Twelfth Night.*

In Phaer's culturally translated *Aeneid,* Aeneas in the "Moorishe purple" of Dido Queen of Carthage is not only effeminized but dressed as a contemporary "Morisko," as we have seen.[25] In *Antony and Cleopatra,* another change of clothing is described by another North African queen:

> I drunk him to his bed;
> Then put my tires and mantles on him, whilst
> I wore his sword Philippan . . .
> (2.5.21–23)

This famous cross-dressing scene in *Antony and Cleopatra* is usually treated in relation to the play's inversions of gender or the exchange of male and female sexual roles. But it is also a dramatic scene of cultural transvestism, in which "tires" simultaneously evokes both "attire" and the Turkish and Eastern "tires" familiar in early modern writing. "Tires" in the sense of headdresses appear not only in Dekker's *Honest Whore, Part 2* ("The soldier has his morion, women ha' tires, / Beasts have their head-pieces, and men ha' theirs") but earlier in the Shakespeare canon itself, in the lines of *Merry Wives* that contrast exotic foreign tires (including "any tire of Venetian admittance," 3.3) with plainer English head coverings. Minsheu's *Guide unto the Tongues* (1617) observes that "The word *Attire* in English commeth from the Latine word *Tiara,* which is an ornament of the heads of the Persian Kings, Priests, and Women," a headdress which his Spanish *Dictionarie* describes as "a round rolle of linnen which Princes, Priests, &c. did weare in Persia, such as the Turkes weare at this day." Florio (1598) has for "Tiara, a turbant, or round wreath of linen for the head such as the Turks vse to weare." Cotgrave (1611) defines "Tiare" as "A round and wreathed Ornament for the head (somewhat resembling the Turkish Turbant) worne, in old time, by the Princes, Priests, and women of Persia." "Tire" in this early modern sense appears both long before and after the date of *Antony and Cleopatra.* Hall's *Chronicle* (1548) has "ladyes" with "marueylous ryche & straunge tiers on their heades." The Geneva Bible (1560) describes "round tyres" or "tyres of the head" as part of the dress of Babylonian harlots. The Great Bible (1539) portrays Jezebel (another foreign queen) as having "starched her face, and tired her head." Joseph Hall's *Paradoxes* (1653) asks "What Towers doe the Turkish Tires weare upon their womens heads?"[26]

The sense of Antony as barbared as well as "barber'd" or emasculated by Cleopatra is thus strengthened by the dressing of Antony in Cleopatra's "tires and mantles" (2.5.22), making this scene of cross dressing the counterpart not only of the classical emblem of Hercules' effeminization by the Amazon Omphale but also of the dressing of Aeneas as a "Morisko" in Phaer's description of the cultural transvestite at the court of another African queen. In a play whose Egypt summons simultaneously the ancient Egypt of the Ptolemies and Plutarch's *Life of Antony,* the biblical locus of captivity recalled in the description of Cleopatra as the "serpent of old Nile" (1.5.552), and the contemporary Alexandria familiar from accounts of renegades and captives, even the territories named in Antony's notorious "donations" of territory to his gypsy queen contribute to the layering of ancient and early modern within the play. The description by Octavius Caesar in act 3—of Cleopatra and Antony "publicly enthroned" in "chairs of gold"—recounts Antony's giving to Cleopatra (in the passage from Plutarch) "the stablishment of Egypt," and "absolute" authority over "lower Syria, Cyprus, Lydia" (3.6.4–11), territories associated with the "barbarous" East in the Roman time of the plot and with the dominions of the Turk at the time of the play itself. The play's still-unexplained neologisms "candy" and "discandy" (3.3.162–67; 4.12.20) may also summon the "Candy" or Crete familiar from contemporary accounts of the "infidel" East, as well as the melting or excess associated with Cleopatra's Egypt.

The play in which Antony or "Anthonio" is both "barber'd" on the Cydnus and turned infidel in his clothing is at the same time part of a contemporary context in which a so-called "Asiatic" rhetoric (familiar from Roman writing and the description of Antony's own training in Plutarch) had similarly been given an early modern inflection. Charles Sedley's *Antony and Cleopatra* (1677) would later present Antony as "a mere soft Purple Asian Prince," a description that combines the "purple" of assumed Asiatic decadence with the "purple" passages of "Asiatic" rhetoric condemned by Quintilian and others. What the most recent Arden editor of *Antony and Cleopatra* calls Shakespeare's Antony's "Asiatic" style, is termed a "rodomontade" by one eighteenth-century editor, a term that identifies the "Asiatic" rhetoric of speeches such as Antony's "Let Rome in Tyber melt" with the Saracen opposed to the representative of Rome in Ariosto's rewriting of the *Aeneid.* In the period of the play itself, excessive rhetoric or speaking "large" was identified with the Turk. Dekker's *Satiromastix* (1.2.379), for example, has Tucca say to Horace (or Jonson): "thy title's longer a reading than the style a the Big Turkes."[27]

The barbering or unmanning associated with Barbary—in the conflation of "Muly" as the familiar name of Islamic rulers with the gelded "mule" (reflected in Middleton's "mule" and "Muly Crag-a-whee in Barbary")—may itself be iterated in *Antony and Cleopatra,* in a passage that simultaneously describes Antony's forces at Actium as "unmann'd." "Muly"—the name shared by Peele's "Muly Hamet" (the "barbarous Moore" of Peele's *Battle of Alcazar*), as well as the Mulleasses of Mason's *The Turk* and the Mullisheg of Heywood's *Fair Maid*—may already be evoked in *Titus Andronicus* when Aaron (its "barberous" or "barbarous Moor") sends his racially mixed son to "*Muliteus* my Countriman," the name emended by Steevens to the Islamic "Muly."[28] In the years before *Antony and Cleopatra,* the association of mules with Turks is evoked in the allusion in *All's Well* (1602–3) to "Bajazeth's mule" (4.1.42), in a scene where Parolles contemplates the shaving of his own "beard" (4.1.49) and the play where "boys" of "little beard" are thought fit to be sent to the "Turk" to "make eunuchs of" (1.3.62, 88). *All's Well* itself not only invokes a "barber's chair" (2.2.17) but famously goes out of its way to make reference to the shrine in northwestern Spain identified with St. James, the Sant'Iago whose association with driving the Moors out of Spain provided the name for the nemesis of the Moor in *Othello.*

"Mules" in *Antony and Cleopatra* are explicitly evoked in the scene in which Enobarbus warns Antony that his ships are not "well-manned":

> *Enobarbus.*   Your ships are not well mann'd,
>   Your mariners are [muleters], reapers, people
>   Ingross'd by swift impress. . . .
>
>   (3.7.34–36)

Enobarbus's warning here to Egyptianized Antony, of the weakness of his forces, is drawn from the passage of Plutarch's *Life of Antony* which stresses the relation of Antony's fatal decision to engage Octavius by "sea" to his being "subject to a woman's will," in the sentence that goes on to record that his captains "prest by force all sorts of men out of Greece that they could take up in the field, as travellers, muleteers, reapers, harvest men, and yong boys, and yet could they not sufficiently furnish his galleys." The juxtaposition of "not well mann'd" with "muleters" changes the order of Plutarch's description, aligning the latter with the poorly "manned" that elsewhere in the play is suggestive of eunuchry or gelding. It is to this implication of the "barber'd" Antony that I now turn.

I'll spurn thine eyes
Like balls before me! I'll unhair thy head!
—*Antony and Cleopatra*

Read against the different historical moments its striking anachronisms align, not only Enobarbus's set speech but other familiar speeches in the play resonate in these multiple registers. *Antony and Cleopatra* repeatedly foregrounds beards, barbering, shaving and cutting, as the currency both of its internal or civil division (marked by the older Antony's contemptuous references to the "boy" Caesar) and of reversals within the familiar binary opposition between Egypt and Rome, starting from Cleopatra's own contemptuous reference to the "scarce-bearded Caesar" (1.1.22).

Both beards and hair as the traditional indices of generative virility—together with the sense of diverted patrimony that sounds in Antony's accusation against Cleopatra for preventing the "getting of a lawful race"—become associated with barbering, through the Folio text's sustained conflation of "heires" and "haires." Even Cleopatra's attack on the messenger come from Rome to announce that Antony is married to Octavia—"I'll spurn thine eyes / Like balls before me! I'll unhair thy head!" (2.5.63–64)—underscores (in ways abetted by the familiar bawdy senses of these terms) the un-heiring as well as unhairing or barbering associated with the Egypt in which Antony himself is symbolically castrated or gelded. Shamed, at the Battle of Actium, by a "coward's" flight with the woman he later calls by the generic name of "Egypt," this Roman renegade laments "I followed that I blush to look upon. / My very hairs do mutiny, for the white / Reprove the brown for rashness, and they them / For fear and doting" (3.11.12–15), lines that conflate the cultural semantics of barbering and "hair" with the racialized metaphorics of a mingled "white" and "brown," lawful and unlawful "heirs."

The imputation not only of unhairing (or unheiring) but of "cutting" in its multiple senses, compounded in the description of Antony as "barber'd ten times o'er," connects *Antony and Cleopatra* with other Shakespearean combinations of barbering and cuts. Enobarbus's speech on Antony's "barbering" by Cleopatra in act 2 prompts Agrippa's response "She made great Caesar lay his sword to bed. / He ploughed her, and she cropped." "Cropped" here may seem at first simply to complete the implication of generative or agricultural fertility in "ploughed." But—in its other sense of cropping or cutting—it simultaneously presents this famous moment, of the laying of a "sword" to "bed," as the unmanning of another Roman leader. "Caesarion"—issue of this earlier Roman encounter with Egypt's barbarous queen—shares with Julius "Caesar" the root of "cutting" itself, the *caedo/caeso* stressed in Varro, in Camden's *Remains,* and in Shakespeare's own *Julius Caesar,* by cuts that include "the most unkindest cut of all." In Suetonius's *Life of Octavius Caesar* and Samuel Daniel's *Cleopatra* (1594)—both important influences on *Antony and Cleopatra*—the name of "Caesarion" is alternately spelled "Cesario," the name Viola chooses in *Twelfth Night* (1601–2), when she announces her intention to become a "eunuch" in Illyria, in a play where the "C-U-T" of the letter read by Malvolio repeats the figure of castration or nicking invoked by the otherwise unrealized "eunuch" at its beginning, in the lines whose "mute" simultaneously evokes Illyria's Turkish connections.[29]

The familiar gender reversals of *Antony and Cleopatra* have been repeatedly rehearsed. But what has been less closely examined, both in general and in relation to the lines on the barbering of Antony with which we began, is the extraordinary emphasis on cutting that pervades this play. In the scene in which Antony announces Fulvia's death to Enobarbus, the latter offers consolation in the following terms: "Why, sir, give the gods a thankful sacrifice. When it pleaseth their deities to take the wife of a man from him, it shows to man the tailors of the earth; comforting therein, that when old robes are worn out, there are members to make new. If there were no more women but Fulvia, then had you indeed a cut, and a case to be lamented"(1.2.168–76). The sexual figure of the "cut" (and "case") as well as "members" is continued in the lines that follow, which turn on the sexual (and territorial) senses of broaching or breaching as well as of occupation or abode: "*Antony.* The business she hath broached in the state / Cannot endure my absence. / *Enobarbus.* And the business you have broached here cannot be without you, especially that of Cleopatra's, which wholly depends on your abode" (1.2.178–82). "Tailors of the earth"—a phrase that may appear to be only about attire or clothing—simultaneously sounds in its familiar early modern and Shakespearean resonance of "tailleur" or "cutter" as well as of a potentially castrated "tail."

The cutting of the phallic "member" is underscored in the emphasis on eunuchry throughout, beginning with the eunuchs in the Egyptian train of Antony and Cleopatra in the opening scene. The Cleopatra who (as both female monarch and boy player) says to Antony "I would I had thy inches!" (1.3.41) famously engages her own eunuch Mardian later in this opening act:

> *Cleopatra.*   Thou, eunuch, Mardian!
>
> *Mardian.*   What's your highness' pleasure?
>
> *Cleopatra.*   Not now to hear thee sing. I take no pleasure
>   In aught an eunuch has. 'Tis well for thee
>   That, being unseminared, thy freer thoughts
>   May not fly forth of Egypt. Hast thou affections?
>
> *Mardian.*   Yes, gracious madam.
>
> *Cleopatra.*   Indeed?
>
> *Mardian.*   Not in deed, madam, for I can do nothing
>   But what indeed is honest to be done.
>   Yet have I fierce affections, and think
>   What Venus did with Mars. . . .
>   (1.5.8–19)

Like the Caesario of *Twelfth Night* who seeks to become a "eunuch" or *castrato* in Illyria, the "unseminared" Egyptian eunuch here associated with an emasculating lack provides a figure for the sense of barbering or gelding identified with Egypt and the East in the familiar binaries of both Roman and early modern writing.

The sense of cutting or coming "too short," as well as of "balls" evoked in contemporary reminders of the castration associated with the "barber" (as in Jonson's equivocal reference to an incising "barbarism" and a punning "barber's balls" or the phallic overtones of the barber's pole) returns in Cleopatra's exchange with Charmian in act 2:

> *Cleopatra.*   Let's to billiards. Come, Charmian.
>
> *Charmian.*   My arm is sore. Best play with Mardian.
>
> *Cleopatra.*   As well a woman with an eunuch played
>   As with a woman. Come, you'll play with me, sir?
>
> *Mardian.*   As well as I can, madam.

> *Cleopatra.*   And when good will is showed, thou't come too short,
> The actor may plead pardon . . .
> (2.5.3–9)

"Come too short" here—in the context of a "will" that is repeatedly sex-ualized in Shakespeare—suggests not only the familiar assumption of the eunuch's deficiency or lack but its extension to Antony "barber'd" in Egypt.

Reminders of cutting or clipping (another of the overdetermined senses of barbering) are foregrounded throughout this play, even in descriptions that could employ other terms. Octavia reminds Antony of the "division" with her brother Octavius ("Wars 'twixt you twain would be / As if the world should cleave, and that slain men / Should solder up the rift," 3.4.30–32), in lines whose cleaving evokes the cutting or severing of Roman unity. The cutting of the cable proposed by the pirate Menas in the scene on the galley of Sextus Pompeius, pirate-son of Pompey the Great, metonymically juxtaposes cutting this cable with another kind of cutting ("cut the cable, / And when we are put off, fall to their throats," 2.7.72–73). In the charged phallic language of *Antony and Cleopatra,* "cut" is suggestively juxtaposed with "slackness," in reports of the Egyptianized Antony's war with Octavius, in the exchange in which Enobarbus warns Antony that "your mariners are [muleters]" (3.7.35). Antony's "Is it not strange, Canidius, / That from Tarentum and Brundusium / He [Octavius Caesar] could so quickly cut the Ionian sea / And take in Toryne?" (3.7.20–23) is followed by Cleopatra's "Celerity is never more admired / Than by the negligent" (3.7.24–25) and his "A good rebuke, / Which might have well becom'd the best of men, / To taunt at slackness" (3.7.25–28). "Cut" here (in "cut the Ionian sea") corresponds to the description in North's translation of Plutarch, of Octavius's quick passage. But the choice of "cut" and "slackness" draws the geopolitical contrast between the two in bodily as well as nautical terms.

Cutting—with the implication of castrating—is part not only of the eunuchry associated with Egypt and Barbary but also of the decapitation familiar from Shakespeare's Roman sources—including the severed head of Pompey presented to Julius Caesar in Egypt, recalled by Shakespeare in *Cymbeline.* Decapitation or cutting off a head is foregrounded in the allusion to the death of "Marcus Crassus" in act 3 (3.1.2), as well as in ear-lier echoes of this well-known story. The sense of decapitation similarly surrounds the lines in which the defeated Antony says "To the boy Cae-sar send this grizzled head, / And he will fill thy wishes to the brim / With principalities" (3.13.18–20), lines whose ambiguity is underscored by Cleopatra's immediately following question: "That head, my lord?" (3.13.20). Cleopatra's promise to have a "Herod's head" (3.3.4) summons

not only one of the play's reminders of the Christian dispensation that followed the triumph of Octavius at Actium, but also the severed head of
John the Baptist, adding the Levantine Salome or Herodias to the barbering of Antony by this Egyptian queen.

Antony is himself described as "plucked" (3.12.3), in the post-Actium
scene in which his schoolmaster-ambassador arrives to parley with the
triumphant Octavius ("Caesar, 'tis his schoolmaster; / An argument that
he is plucked, when hither / He sends so poor a pinion of his wing,"
3.12.3–5). The language of cutting, nicking, or emasculating continues in
the scene that immediately follows in Egypt, when Enobarbus responds to
the defeated Cleopatra's "Is Antony or we in fault for this?" (3.13.3):

> Antony only, that he would make his will
> Lord of his reason. What though you fled
> From that great face of war, whose several ranges
> Frighted each other? Why should he follow?
> The itch of his affection should not then
> Have nick'd his captainship, at such a point,
> When half to half the world oppos'd. . . .
>
> (3.13.4–9)

"Nick'd" here implies that Antony's "captainship" is conceived as "the
blade of a sword, which Cleopatra has damaged and made useless,"[30] in
lines that go out of their way to invoke the phallic idiom of "such a point."
OED cites this passage for the sense of "nick" as "To cut into or through"
as well as "cut short." That Antony is "nick'd" at such a "point" by "the
itch of his affection" simultaneously recalls the syphilis identified with the
unheiring strumpet—the Barbiera Florio reminds his readers could be both
a "shee-barber" and "common harlot"—here attached to the "gypsy"
denounced as a "triple-turn'd whore" by Antony himself. "Make his will /
Lord of his reason" summons not only gender inversion in general but
familiar contemporary accounts of enthrallment to "infidel" enchantresses,
including those already identified with this Egyptian queen.

Editors have frequently related Enobarbus's description of Antony's
"nick'd" captainship to the description of the Roman triumvirate and its
civil war as a "three-nook'd world" (4.6.6), a "nook'd" whose homo-
phonic-semantic link with the indented or "nick'd" had already been
exploited in the description of England as a "nook-shotten isle" in Henry
V. In the English context of civil war, nicking as indenting in the root
sense of incising or cutting is exploited in Henry IV, Part 1, in the scene
of "indentures tripartite" (3.1.79) dividing territory among the three
rebel leaders that calls attention to territorial broaching not only as a
"deep indent" (3.1.103) but as "Gelding the opposed continent" (108), in

a play of infidels within (2.3.29) that itself opens with the "knife" of "civil butchery" (1.1.13) and includes an extended exchange on a "gelding" named "Cut" (1.3.5–98). In the context of the Roman triumvirate, Antony's "nick'd" captainship at Actium is the fulfillment of this later play's opening lines on the "triple pillar of the world transform'd / Into a strumpet's fool" (1.1.11–12), which transfer to this phallic Roman "pillar" the figure of the nicked or gelded "fool" familiar from *The Comedy of Errors* (5.1.175). The nicking of Antony's captainship, in the lines that follow Enobarbus's description of the overmastering of his "reason" by his "will," at the same time recalls the nicking or cutting identified with the contemporary threat from the Turk and the North African coast. The Variorum glosses Caesar's "three nook'd world" by reference to Europe, Asia, and Africa as the "three Angles" of the Globe, and the three races emanating from Japheth, Shem, and Ham, a division capable of Roman and early modern reference at once. *Nick* was itself a keyword of contemporary dramatic plots of barbering in Barbary—from the "Nick" Bottom of *A Midsummer Night's Dream,* who remarks that he must to the "barbers" in the scene of his own enthrallment to an exoticized Fairy Queen, to the juxtaposition of "nick" and "Turk" in *The Knight of Malta,* to the transformation of "Nicke the Barbor" into a threatening "Barberoso" in *The Knight of the Burning Pestle.*[31]

But Why Enobarbus?

Both the lines on Antony as "barber'd" by Cleopatra and those on the shaving of "Antonio's beard" in Rome are, finally, put into the mouth of Enobarbus, whose own name and its link with beards or "barbes" the play goes out of its way to underscore, in its shortened form of "Enobarbe" (2.7.144). Even to call him "Enobarbus" (or "Red-beard") rather than "Domitius" (as Antony's lieutenant was also known) calls attention to the "barbe" or "beard" on which so much stress is laid, in Roman as well as early modern culture, as well as to the red beard he may have worn on stage. The association of Enobarbus or "Enobarbe" with shaving, barbering, and beards within the play is entirely Shakespearean, since this figure does not appear in earlier English or continental theatrical representations of this story.[32]

The influential brief note by Dawson in 1987—whose answer to the question "But Why Enobarbus?" has become a standard reference for editors and critics of this play—argued that Shakespeare's "Enobarbe" would have worn on stage the red beard associated with Jews and the defector

Judas, thus announcing from his first appearance the betrayal of Antony that would be his "place in the story."[33] I want, however, to suggest a historically more inclusive answer to this famous question, in relation to Barbary and infidels of all kinds, as well as the Roman significance of this Shakespearean figure. Critics and editors of *Antony and Cleopatra* have tended to depend primarily on Plutarch's *Life of Mark Antony* for details about Enobarbus, sometimes even assuming that Shakespeare constructed this memorable dramatic character out of two different historical figures briefly cited in this particular source.[34] But in fact there were numerous other accounts well known to Shakespeare and his contemporaries, which not only detailed the pivotal role and family history of this "Red-beard" or "Aheno-barbus" but repeatedly drew attention to beards, barbering, and shaving in ways that made clear his "place" in the "story" and called into question the binary opposition of civil West to barbarous East that *Antony and Cleopatra* famously both evokes and undoes.

Antony's Enobarbus (or "Domitius Enobarbus," to use both names by which he is called in the play) appears several times in Plutarch's *Life of Antony*—as the lieutenant of Antony who participates in the Parthian campaign, argues against Cleopatra's participation in the war, and finally deserts Antony in Egypt for Rome, though he repents his defection and dies soon after. Plutarch's striking ending then describes the ultimate Roman story in which Antony's Enobarbus was a pivotal figure: the marriage of his son to the daughter of Antony and Octavia and the combination of the families of Antony, Enobarbus, and Octavius or Augustus that produced the ultimate "Domitius Enobarbus," the emperor whose adopted name was Nero. The larger "story" of Enobarbus, which Plutarch goes out of his way to underscore, is thus one in which Actium itself was ultimately reversed by the imperial "Enobarbus" (product of Antony's "lawful race") who brought Alexandrian revels—and the theatricality condemned in both ancient and early modern antitheatrical treatises—into Rome itself. [35]

Enobarbus—and the history of the "Ahenobarbi" in which he is a pivotal figure—is also part of a larger Roman as well as early modern "story" of barbering and beards. Suetonius's *Life of Nero,* which Shakespeare had already recalled in the Claudius and matricidal "Nero" of *Hamlet,* begins with the entire history of the Ahenobarbus line, from the Red-beard origin of the name to the culminating Domitius Enobarbus renamed Nero when he was adopted as Claudius's stepson and heir. In the Latin text used by Shakespeare and others before Holland's English translation in 1606, "Ahenobarbi" appears as "Ahenobarborum," with other case endings that underscore the associations of barbering and "barbarian" that Enobarbus's famous speech exploits.[36]

Suetonius describes each generation of Ahenobarbi in turn, starting with Enobarbus's grandfather, Cnaeus Domitius Ahenobarbus, of whom it was said that "It was no mervaile he had a brasen beard whose face was made of Iron, and heart of lead."[37] This Enobarbus is described elsewhere as a defender of the *virilitas* of ancient Rome, opposing the introduction of Eastern practices, including the rhetoric associated with the "shaven" or smooth. His son (father of Antony's Enobarbus) is likewise aligned with the older republican Rome of Cato and opposition to the rise of Caesar. When Suetonius comes to the Enobarbus who was Antony's lieutenant ("worthy without question, to be preferred before all others of his name and linage"), he stresses not only his alternation between warring sides in Rome's civil wars before his final desertion of Antony for Octavius but (along with Tacitus and other sources known to Shakespeare) his command of a fleet and his crucial involvement in battles by sea.

Like Plutarch, Suetonius then fills in the history between Antony's Domitius Enobarbus and Nero as the culminating "Domitius AEnobarbus," starting with the son of Antony's lieutenant who, having married into the imperial line of Augustus, "produced upon the stage to acte a comicall and wanton Enterlude," anticipating the outrageous "theatricals" of Nero himself. That this subsequent history of Antony's Enobarbus was known well before the date of *Antony and Cleopatra* is underscored not only by its appearance in Suetonius and Tacitus (the latter the source of the more skeptical view of Augustus in Shakespeare's play) but also by the reference to this theatrical Enobarbus in the "villanous out-of-tune fiddler AENOBARBVS" of Jonson's *Poetaster* in 1601, a "fiddler" (in both musical and sexual senses) who proleptically evokes the Nero who fiddled while Rome burned. Suetonius then describes the Enobarbus of Tiberius's reign who was "father to Nero" himself, a riotous reveller, drinker, and lascivious adulterer, fitting progenitor (with the sexually transgressive Agrippina) to the climactic "Domitius Ahenobarbus" of the entire line.[38]

This larger place in the "story" of Shakespeare's Enobarbus calls repeated attention to the Roman significance of barbering, shaving, and beards. When Suetonius describes the Enobarbus whose name was changed to Nero, he records that his "Paedagogues" were a transvestite dancer (*saltator*) and a barber.[39] The link in sound between barber and Enobarbus does not work in Latin (where "barber" is *tonsor*, source of slurs against tonsured priests as "shavelings" in Protestant English polemics). But it does resonate with the "barbus" of "AEnobarbus" in Holland's 1606 translation, which recounts the slur of Nero's stepbrother Brittanicus, who continues to call Nero, after his adoption, by the name "AEnobarbus," an origin that haunted the adopted emperor throughout his history. This same section records not only Nero's castrating or gelding of "Sporus" as his male bride but this emperor's "prostituting" his "owne body" to "bee abused" in turn, being "by Doriphorus his freed-man . . . wedded like as Sporus unto him" (Holland, *Suetonius,* 2:123).

The description of the "gelding" of Sporus goes out of its way to call attention to Nero's "AEnobarbus" lineage—remarking of his castration of this
boy "whose Genitories he cut out" (assaying thereby to "transforme him
into the nature of a woman") that it was joked that "it might have beene
wel and happie with the World, if his father Domitius had wedded such a
wife," preventing the begetting of the heir who would become the imperial Enobarbus, or Nero.

Suetonius repeatedly connects barbering of different kinds with this
imperial Enobarbus, who "cut off the first beard that he had (*barbam pri-
mam*) and laid it in a golden box and consecrat[ed] it in the Capitol." His
narrative of Nero's matricide (Holland, *Suetonius,* 2:130) is followed by yet
another barbering, which relates the cutting of his first beard to the death
of the aunt (Domitia) in whose household he was tutored by a "dauncer"
and "Barber": when, after "handling the tender downe of his beard new
budding forth," she remarks "Might I but live to take up this soft haire
when it fals, I would be willing to dye," he responds by promising to
"streight wayes . . . cut it of(f)." The association of this ultimate "Domitius
AEnobarbus" with shaving, beards, and hair continues in different forms,
as the insult levelled at him by Britannicus's "Ahenobarbus" (ch. 7) is
repeated in taunts by his Roman subjects. Suetonius proceeds from "this
name appropriate to his house and family, wherewith he was thus in con-
tumelious manner twitted" to call equivocal attention to the long "hair" of
a "Gallus," the term that could mean both "Gaul" (origin of the red-
bearded Ahenobarbi) and "castrate," as in the eunuch "Galli" associated
with the castrated Attis. The Nero whose real name was "AEnobarbus" is
taunted with this double-meaning "Gallus" (ch. 43), when Romans object-
ing to his bringing Eastern entertainers from Alexandria, place a "curl" on
his statue in Rome, with a Greek inscription alluding to the long hair worn
by this new "Ahenobarbus" on his trip to the East. Suetonius's description
(ch. 12) of Nero's presiding over Eastern entertainments from his *cubicu-
lum* or "his owne Bed-chamber" (Holland)—the same Latin term used for
the "Bedchamber" of England's King James—provides an account of the
pyrrhic "daunces" of "ephebes" or young Greek males, who simply for
dancing were accorded Roman citizenship by an emperor who fre-
quented "Actours and players." At these games, Nero takes the prize for
rhetoric and lays the "harp" presented to him for his lyre playing at "the
Statue of Augustus" (*Suetonius,* 2:108)—implicating the line of Octavius in
this Easternizing of Rome's imperial seat.

Beards and hair continue to be foregrounded in Suetonius's description
of this imperial Roman "AEnobarbus," including in the chapters on his
bringing of Alexandrian revels into Rome itself, which picture him in his
"wastfull riotousnesse" wearing what Holland glosses (out of Dio Cassius)

as a "peruke and cap of counterfeit hair" (Holland, *Suetonius,* 2:272), immediately before the famous description of his "unnaturall abusing of boyes freeborne" (2:122) and his cutting of the "Genitories" of the boy Sporus, in the passage where taunting reference is once again made of his "Ahenobarbus" origins. When Tacitus records the "Juvenalia" in cele- bration of this first shaving of Nero's beard (*Annals* 14.15), he accompa- nies it with a passage on the obscene gestures or "postures" this imperial Enobarbus encouraged Roman actors to assume, described as "never meant for the male sex" (*ad gestus modosque haud virilis*). The passage—along with the hetero- and homoerotic *modi* or postures of Ovid and Martial—is famously recalled in Aretino and Giulio Romano, early modernizers of the "modi" or "I modi" that were the Italian coun- terpart of this Roman "*modus.*" In relation to the final English transla- tion of this "story" in Shakespeare's own simultaneously Roman and early modern play, we might see the extension of such postures in the lines of *Antony and Cleopatra* on the boying on the English stage of the greatness of Antony's Egyptian queen, by "some squeaking Cleopatra" in "the posture of a whore," in a play whose "Salt Cleopatra" may evoke not only the "salt" of female sexuality or a "gypsy's lust" but also the figure of the *saltator, salter,* or transvestite dancer familiar from Plautus and other Roman writers and from the condemnation of such spectacles in contemporary antitheatrical literature.[40]

The subsequent history of Antony's Enobarbus—familiar from Plutarch's *Life* as from Suetonius and Tacitus, already well-known Shakespearean sources—thus stresses the "story" of an imperial history in which the binaries opposing Rome (or its later emulators) to Egypt or a more contemporary "Turk Gypsy" are brought into "Rome" itself, including the theatricality that Shakespeare's Octavius emulates as well as ostensibly condemns.[41] In relation to barbering and beards, and the topos of decline from the *virilitas* of an old "bearded" Rome evoked in Enobarbus's "By Jupiter, / Were I the wearer of Antonio's beard, / I would not shave it today," Antony's Enobarbus occupies a pivotal posi- tion within a larger history that charts the breakdown of this very binary opposition—from the stern consul Enobarbus identified with resisting the importing of rhetoric and other Eastern practices into Rome to the ultimate Enobarbus or Nero, who brought Alexandrian revels into Rome's own imperial center. Shakespeare's Enobarbus thus has a piv- otal "place" in the "story" of Rome as well as the Ahenobarbus line and of the Roman history of barbering and beards, between the past of a bearded older Rome (signalled by the *barbus* of his own name) and the barbaring of Rome by the ultimate imperial "Domitius Enobarbus," heir not of a "barbarous" Egyptian but of the intermarriage or mingling of the "lawful race" of Antony, Enobarbus, and Octavius or Augustus himself.

Barbaroxa, a famous pyrate among the Moores which had a red beard . . .
—Minsheu (1599)

a eunuch of Solymans court, sent by him as Barbarussa his companion. . . .
—Knolles, *Generall Historie of the Turke* (1603)

The Enobarbus or "Enobarbe" of Shakespeare's play who delivers the lines on the danger of shaving "Antonio's beard" in Rome has both a name and a history that resonate with the supposedly natural Roman index of virility, even as his simultaneous reference to the "wearer" of that beard calls attention to the prosthetic stage beard that complicated the very categories of natural and constructed.[42] In the network of Latin and translated sources whose metamorphoric *Ahenobarbi* and *Ahenobarborum* resonate not only with *barbus* or beard but with the *barbarus* or barbaric, the fact that it is likewise Enobarbus who speaks the lines on Antony as "barber'd" on the Cydnus, in Cilicia or early modern Turkey, may connect this Roman defector and renegade Red-beard, finally, with two historical registers at once: not just the Roman history in which he is first a renegade with Antony and then defects back to Rome but also the more proximate history of renegades and defectors, and the Barbary and Egypt that were so central to early modern representations of barbering and beards. Suetonius, Tacitus, and others, like Plutarch, emphasize that Antony's Enobarbus was an experienced sea commander during the civil wars, who "commanded a fleet in the Adriatic against the triumvirs" before joining the side of Antony, the reason why he is the one who counsels Antony on his weakness by "sea." In relation to the Enobarbus of *Antony and Cleopatra,* who engages in the major exchange with the pirates of Sextus Pompeius and begs Antony not to give in to Cleopatra's desire to fight with Octavius by sea, where the Egyptian forces are not well "manned," it is important, then, to record that Enobarbus is not only a "master leaver" or deserter (after his sojourn with Antony, in Egypt, as a fellow renegade) but master of a "fleet" at sea.[43]

In his *Remains Concerning Britain* (1605), William Camden explicitly connects Roman "Aenobarbus" with his early modern counterpart "Barbarossa," as "red-beards" from both ancient and early modern worlds, commenting on what he calls "*Aenobarbus* of the Latines, or *Barbarossa* of the Italians," as simply different versions of the same name.[44] In relation

to the preoccupation of *Antony and Cleopatra* not only with piracy and battles by "land" and "sea" but also with barbering, barbaring, and beards,
and the description of the "barber'd" Antony that Shakespeare chooses to
put into the mouth of Enobarbus in Rome, it would not be inappropriate
to end with the most famous Red-beard defector of early modern memory. The story of this Red-beard renegade was detailed at length, only a
few years before, in Knolles's *Generall Historie of the Turke* (1603), already
an acknowledged influence on *Othello* (1604). From his origins in a renegade family, he spread the power of the new Emperor of the East from
Alexandria and Egypt across the entire North African coast, literally creating the Barbary ports associated with the taking of captives and with renegades who flocked from all over Europe, including to Tunis and Algiers,
the Barbary ports that would figure so prominently in the Mediterranean
geographies of *The Tempest.*

This renegade Barbarossa—whose name was rendered in one English
account as *Barbarus*—was none other than the naval commander who led the
forces of the East at the new Battle of Actium fought at Prevesa in 1538,
establishing Ottoman mastery and reversing the story of the ancient battle by
defeating the forces of the new Roman Emperor Charles V. Knolles's *Historie* recounts at length this reversal of East and West at this early modern
"ACTIVM" (687)—describing the Antony-like retreat of Andrea Doria,
leader of the Western forces, as done "in such hast" that "it seemed rather a
shamefull flight than an orderly retreat" (689–90). Knolles goes on to record
the scorn of the triumphant renegade "Barbarussa" at this western commander's loss of "honour" in so "shamefull a flight." And he then proceeds to
recount the story of a "sonne" taken captive with his father at this new
Actium battle, a "yong gentleman. . . . beautifull with all the good gifts of
nature, who afterwards presented to *Solyman,* turned Turke; and growing in
credit in *Solymans* chamber, after three yeares miserable imprisonment,
obtained his poore fathers libertie, and sent him well rewarded home againe
into SPAINE" (689), a Joseph-in-Egypt story in which the Egyptianized son
gains redemption for his family but does not himself return home.[45]

By the time of *Antony and Cleopatra,* this renegade Barbarossa or Red-
beard was an established part of the network linking barbering, Barbary,
and beards—appearing in Minsheu's 1599 dictionary as "Barbaroxa, a
famous pyrate among the Moores which had a red beard," as the Red-
beard "Barbaroja" in the Captive's Tale of *Don Quixote* (published in
1605, and circulating in English by 1607) recalling the red beard or *barba
roja* of the earlier "barber" named Nicolas or Nick, as "Barbarussa" in
Knolles's Turkish *Historie,* which remarks of the Battle of Lepanto in 1571
that it was only a temporary shaving of the Sultan's beard, and as the
assumed name of "Nicke the Barbor" in Beaumont's *Knight of the Burning*

Pestle, a "Barbarossa"/"Barberoso" who keeps captives in his cave.[46] In a play in which Roman Antony is called alternately "Antonio" (the name of the Merchant of Venice and in *Twelfth Night* of an alleged pirate or "saltwater thief") and in which (as Leeds Barroll has demonstrated) the exchange between Enobarbus and the pirates casts empire itself as a form of piracy,[47] it is not at all impossible that (as in Camden only a few years before) the Red-beard Enobarbus who so pointedly evokes this network of barbering may have recalled not only Judas or the stage beard of the Jew but the most memorable Red-beard from what *The Jew of Malta* calls the other "circumcised nation"—the Barbarossa who reversed not only Actium but the very direction of Enobarbus's defection and was a renegade who, like Antony, chose never to return.

NOTES

1. All quotations from Shakespeare are taken from *The Riverside Shakepeare,* ed. G. Blakemore Evans et al. (Boston: Houghton Mifflin, 1974).

2. Maud W. Gleason, *Making Men: Sophists and Self-Presentation in Ancient Rome* (Princeton, NJ: Princeton University Press, 1995), 68–69. For recent studies of the importance of the beard in early modern writing, see Will Fisher, "The Renaissance Beard: Masculinity in Early Modern England and Europe," *Renaissance Quarterly* 54, no. 1 (Spring 2001): 155–187, and Elliott Horowitz, "The New World and the Changing Face of Europe," *The Sixteenth Century Journal* 28, no. 4 (Winter 1997): 1181–1201.

3. See Gleason, *Making Men,* 113; on Pliny and the *glaber,* Craig A. Williams, *Roman Homosexuality* (Oxford: Oxford University Press, 1999), 26, 73; Plautus, *Men.* 513–14; *Asin.* 402; Bruce R. Smith, *Homosexual Desire in Shakespeare's England* (Chicago: University of Chicago Press, 1991), 169.

4. See Arthur L. Little, Jr., *Shakespeare Jungle Fever* (Stanford: Stanford University Press, 2000)(for the *Philippics* charge); Amy Richlin, "Not Before Homosexuality: The Materiality of the *Cinaedus* and the Roman Law against Love between Men," *Journal of the History of Sexuality* 3, no. 4 (1993): 523–73; Gleason, *Making Men,* 72–73; William J. Dominik, ed., *Roman Eloquence* (New York: Routledge, 1993), e.g. 41–46, 84–87, 91–107.

5. Gleason, *Making Men,* 73.

6. See Discourse 33 (to Tarsus) para. 62–64 (pp. 331–33 of vol. 3 of the Loeb *Dio Chrysostom,* trans. J. W. Cohoon and H. Lamar Crosby, 5 vols. (Cambridge, MA: Harvard University Press, 1940; reprinted in 1951); Clement of Alexandria, *Paidagogus,* book 3, chapter 3, trans. Simon P. Wood, *Clement of Alexandria: Christ the Educator* (New York: Fathers of the Church, 1954), 212–14, with the rest of chapters 3 and 4 (e.g. p. 221) on eunuchs and youths; chap. 11 (esp. pp. 246–48, 256, 258, on beards, hair, and barbers).

7. Cited from George Sandys, *A Relation of a Journey Begun An: Dom: 1610: Foure bookes* (London, 1615), 70.

8. On *Fair Maid,* see Jean E. Howard, "An English Lass Amid the Moors: Gender, Race, Sexuality, and National Identity in Heywood's *The Fair Maid of the West,*" in *Women, "Race," and Writing in the Early Modern Period,* ed. Margo Hendricks and Patrick Parker (London: Routledge, 1994), 101–17; Barbara Fuchs, *Mimesis and Empire: The New World, Islam, and European Identities* (Cambridge: Cambridge University Press, 2001), 129–34; and Jonathan Burton, "English Anxiety and the Muslim Power of Conversion: Five Perspectives

on 'Turning Turk' in Early Modern Texts," *Journal for Early Modern Cultural Studies*, 2, no. 1 (Spring/Summer 2002): 35–67, esp. 53–59.

9. See *The Admirable Deliverance of 266. Christians by Iohn Reynard Englishman from the captiuitie of the Turkes, who had been Gally slaues many yeares in Alexandria* (London, 1608), attributed to Anthony Munday, which describes the shaving of the captives' heads and beards on sig. B2r. Vitkus in *Piracy, Slavery, and Redemption: Barbary Captivity Narratives from Early Modern England*, ed. Daniel J. Vitkus (New York: Columbia University Press, 2000), 55–70, mentions (57) this different account, though it prints only the version from the 1589 edition of Hakluyt's *Principal Navigations.*

10. See Daniel J. Vitkus, "Turning Turk in *Othello:* The Conversion and Damnation of the Moor," *Shakespeare Quarterly* 48, no. 2 (1997): 145–76, esp. 154, 157–58.

11. See respectively I. H., *This World's Folly, or a Warning-Peece Discharged upon the Wickednesse thereof* (1615); John Dickenson, *Arisbas, Euphues Amidst his Slumbers; Or, Cupid's Iourney to Hell* (London, 1594), sig. D2; Robert Daborne, *A Christian Turn'd Turk* (1612), 13.52–55, in *Three Turk Plays from Early Modern England*, ed. Daniel J. Vitkus (New York: Columbia University Press, 2000), which includes "a barber" (13.60–72) and multiple references to the barbarous. In relation to wordplay on barbers, balls, and barbarisms, see Jonson's *Magnetic Lady* (2.7.51–52) and Dekker, *Noble Spanish Soldier* (c. 1626) 5.4.143 ("Shee loves no Barbars washing . . . My Balls are sav'd then"); with other examples in Williams, *Dictionary*, 1:62–63.

12. See *Twelfth Night* 3.2.7 ("a very renegado"), and 2.5.86–88, 130–38. On Illyria and the Turk, see Samuel Chew, *The Crescent and Rose* (1937 rprt; New York: Octagon Books, 1965), 132, citing John Foxe, *A Sermon of Christ Crucified, preached at Paules Crosse the Friday before Easter commonly called Goodfryday* (London, 1570), on the growing empire of the Turk, including "the Empire of Constantinople, Greece, Illyria, with almost all Hungary and much of Austria"; and the Second Part of *Tamburlaine* (3.1.1–4), where the territories of "Callapinus, Emperor of Turkey" include Illyria, here cited from Christopher Marlowe, *Tamburlaine the Great, Parts 1 and 2*, ed. J. W. Harper (New York: Hill and Wang, 1973), 122. On *caesus*/cut, *castrati*, and eunuchry in *Twelfth Night*, see Keir Elam, "The Fertile Eunuch: *Twelfth Night*, Early Modern Intercourse, and the Fruits of Castration," *Shakespeare Quarterly* 47, no. 1 (Spring 1996): 1–36; Stephen Orgel, *Impersonations* (Cambridge: Cambridge University Press, 1996), 53–57. See also my forthcoming Norton Critical Edition of *Twelfth Night* on the "eunuch" as a musical instrument, with no sound of its own.

13. On this aspect of the Diet of Worms, see Dorothy M. Vaughan, *Europe and the Turk: A Pattern of Alliances 1350–1700* (New York: AMS Press, 1976), 108.

14. On Steevens's emendation of "Muliteus" to "Muly" (familiar from Peele's *Battle of Alcazar*), see Bate, *Titus*, 222, with Jack D'Amico, *The Moor in English Renaissance Drama* (Tampa, FL: University of South Florida Press, 1991), 141. On "Mulatto" and mule, below, see Margo Hendricks, " 'Obscured by dreams': Race, Empire, and Shakespeare's *A Midsummer Night's Dream*," *Shakespeare Quarterly* 47 (1996): 37–60, esp. 56–60. For the variant spellings in *Titus Andronicus* and *Two Noble Kinsmen*, see the corresponding passages in the Arden 3 editions of those plays by Jonathan Bate and Lois Potter respectively.

15. Jerry Brotton, " 'This Tunis, sir, was Carthage': Contesting Colonialism in *The Tempest*," in *Post-colonial Shakespeares*, ed. Ania Loomba and Martin Orkin (London: Routledge, 1998) 23–42, 41.

16. David Quint, *Epic and Empire* (Princeton, NJ: Princeton University Press, 1993), 24.

17. See 4.377 (p. 80) and 4.377 (p. 82) of *The Aeneid of Thomas Phaer and Thomas Twyne*, ed. Steven Lally (New York: Garland Publishing, 1987).

18. See both here and in relation to what follows, the discussion of echoes of the *Aeneid* and of Cleopatra's Islamic counterparts in Quint, *Epic and Empire*, 21ff., 49, 157–58.

19. Both Arden editions of the play and David Bevington's New Cambridge edition (124) note the echoes of Edward Fairfax's translation of Tasso's *Jerusalem Delivered*, under

the English title *Godfrey of Bulloigne* (1600), 16.4 ("The waters burnt about their vessels good, / Such flames the god therein enchased threw").

20. See Jonson's *The Gypsies Metamorphosed;* and the texts of Daborne and Massinger in Vitkus, *Three Turk Plays.*

21. See the commentary in the New Variorum edition of the play (which cites among other glosses Hanmer's 1744 derivation of "reneages" here from Spanish *renegar*) and Nicholas de Nicholay, in *Navigations, Peregrinations and Voyages Made into Turkie,* trans. T. Washington (London,1585), book 1, 8.

22. See the New Variorum edition commentary on each of these passages.

23. See *The Battell of Alcazar, Fought in Barbarie, betweene Sebastian king of Portugall, and Abdelmelec king of Marocco. With the death of Captaine Stukeley* (1594), which begins with the summary title "The Tragical battell of Alcazar in Barbarie. with the death of three Kings, and Captaine Stukley an Englishman."

24. Lois Potter, "Pirates and 'turning Turk' in Renaissance drama," in *Travel and Drama in Shakespeare's Time,* ed. Jean-Pierre Maquerlot and Michele Willems (Cambridge: Cambridge University Press, 1996), 125–140.

25. See 4.377 (p. 80) and 4.377 (p. 82) of the *Aeneid,* trans. Phaer and Twyne.

26. See *OED,* "tire" and "attire" (noun and verb); the Globe Quartos edition of *2 Honest Whore,* p. 129; and Spenser, *Faerie Queene* (1590) 1.10.31.

27. See John Wilders's Arden 3 edition of *Antony and Cleopatra* (London: Routledge, 1995); the New Variorum glosses on 1.1.22ff for Upton (1748, p. 89) on Antony's "Asiatic manner of speaking" as "a very rodomontade." See Mary Nyquist, "'Profuse, Proud Cleopatra': 'Barbarism' and Female Rule in Early Modern English Republicanism," in *The Representation of Gender in the English Revolution, 1640–1660,* ed. Sharon Achinstein, *Women's Studies* 24 (1994), 85–130, who cites "motifs from the discourse of barbarism that are frequently voiced by Roman characters" including Caesar, who refers to Antony as "a mere soft Purple Asian Prince (4.1.51), from *The Poetical and Dramatic Works of Sir Charles Sedley,* ed. V. de Sola Pinto (London: Constable, 1928), 1:105.

28. See Bate, *Titus,* 226, with D'Amico, *Moor in English Renaissance Drama,* 141, on "Muly" and Muliteus.

29. For "Caesario" as spelling of Caesarion, see Suetonius, *History of Twelve Caesars,* trans. Philemon Holland (1606), ed. Charles Whibley, 2 vols. (London: David Nutt, 1899), vol. 1 (*Life of Octavius Caesar Augustus*), 94; and the 1594 play *Cleopatra* by Samuel Daniel, long acknowledged as an influence on *Antony and Cleopatra* (where Caesarion appears as "Caesario," for example, throughout act 4, scene 1).

30. See Maurice Charney, *Shakespeare's Roman Plays* (Cambridge, MA: Harvard University Press, 1961), 131.

31. See the New Variorum glosses on "nickt" (3.13.1–8), including for the nicking of "the hair of Fools" and Theobald (ed. 1733) on "three-nook'd world" as "Europe, Asia, and Africk making . . . the three Angles of the Globe . . . the American Parts not being then discover'd"; for contemporary Jacobean resonances for this division, H. Neville Davies, "Jacobean Antony and Cleopatra" (pp. 126–65), 133–34, in John Drakakis, ed., New Casebooks volume on *Antony and Cleopatra; Henry IV, Part 1,* 2.4.69–119; *Henry V,* 3.5.14; *Comedy of Errors,* 5.1.175, cited in David Bevington's New Cambridge edition; Michael Neill's Oxford edition, which observes (of "nicked") that "Various senses of the verb are possible: (1) cut, damage, cut short; (2) catch, take unawares; (3) to win against a competitor (as in the game of hazard); (4) cheat, defraud"; Wilders's Arden 3 gloss (212); Barbara Fuchs, *Passing for Spain* (Urbana: University of Illinois Press, 2003), 2–30, on the importance of Cervantes' barber named Nicolas, with *Don Quijote,* part 1, esp. chapters 21–22, 27, 29, 32, 39–43; *The Knight of the Burning Pestle,* ed. Andrew Gurr (Berkeley and Los Angeles:

University of California Press, 1968), 3.2.78 ("Nick the Barbor") and 1.192 (on a "double gelding" Barbary horse).

32. See Elkin Calhoun Wilson, "Shakespeare's Enobarbus," in *Joseph Quincy Adams: Memorial Studies,* ed. James G. McManaway, Giles E. Dawson, and Edwin E. Willoughby (Washington, DC: Folger Shakespeare Library, 1948), 391–408, 391: "There is no trace of Enobarbus in any of the French, Italian, German, and English plays about Antony and Cleopatra—Estienne Jodelle's *Cléopâtre Captive* (1552), Robert Garnier's *Marc-Antoine* (1578), Nicolas de Montreux's *Tragédie de Cléopatre* (1595), Alessandro Spinello's *Cleopatra* (1540), Cesare De' Cesari's *Cleopatra* (1552), Celso Pistorelli's *Marc'Antonio e Cleopatra* (1576), Battista Giraldi Cinthio's *Cleopatra* (1583), Hans Sach's *Tragedi* (1560), the Countess of Pembroke's *Antoine* (1592), Samuel Daniel's *Cleopatra* (1594), and Samuel Brandon's *The Vertuous Octavia* (1598)."

33. R. MacG. Dawson, "But Why Enobarbus?," *Notes and Queries* (June 1987): 216–17, which also points out the stress on the beard through the shortened "Enobarbe" and the fact that Shakespeare uses Enobarbus more often than "Domitius." The association of red beards with Judas and Jews has been well documented. See, for example, Ruth Mellinkoff, *Outcasts* (Berkeley and Los Angeles: University of California Press, 1993).

34. Arthur M. Z. Norman, "Source Material in *Antony and Cleopatra,*" *Notes and Queries* 201 (1956): 59–61, introduced several such confusions into criticism of the play, which continue to be repeated in Wilders's 1995 Arden 3 edition (e.g. p. 87).

35. See *Plutarch's Lives, Englished by Sir Thomas North in Ten Volumes* (London: J.M. Dent, 1899), 56; 77–78; 86–87; 117–18; the entry on "Domitius Ahenobarbus, Gnaeus," in the *Oxford Classical Dictionary;* and for glosses on the appearances of Domitius Enobarbus in this source for the play, Plutarch, *Life of Antony,* ed. C. B. R. Pelling (Cambridge: Cambridge University Press, 1988), which also comments on its striking ending, which goes out of its way to connect Antony, Enobarbus, and the line of Octavius to the ultimate Domitius Enobarbus, Nero (323–27). Pelling (325) points out that this concluding connection with Nero suggests that Octavius's defeat of Antony was "not total," since Antony's descendants became Octavius's "successors" as emperors of Rome; that it links Antony with Nero via two family lines; and that it implicates Octavius himself in the ancestry of Nero, through the marriage of the only son of Antony's Enobarbus to the daughter of Antony and Octavia. It is ironically thus the lawful race of Antony (not the unlawful relationship with Cleopatra) that produces the ultimate Domitius Enobarbus, Nero, who brought Alexandrian revels into the imperial seat of Rome itself. I am grateful for these references, as well as information on other textual sources for Enobarbus, to classicists Anthony Corbeill and Brendon Reay.

36. See the Loeb edition of *Suetonius,* trans. J. C. Rolfe, 2 vols. (London: William Heinemann, 1914), 2: 86. Suetonius also provides other details about Antony's Enobarbus and his line—beyond the *Life of Nero*—including in texts consulted by Shakespeare, before *Antony and Cleopatra.* Most important, in relation to Antony's Enobarbus, Suetonius's *Life of Octavius Caesar Augustus* (a more negative view of Octavius than Virgil or his encomiasts) provides a much fuller account than Plutarch's of the return of Enobarbus (here "T. Domitius") with Sosia from Rome to Antony in Egypt, as the triumvirate disintegrates and the collision course is set for Actium. Here it is made very clear that this "Domitius" is very close to Antony, of "his neerest acquaintance and inward friendes." Even before Holland's English translation of Suetonius in 1606, Matthew Gwynne's Latin play *Nero* (1603)—whose preface acknowledges Suetonius, Tacitus, Dio Cassius, and Seneca among its sources—made clear Nero's Ahenobarbus family origins, while Jonson's *Sejanus* (in that same year), in which not only Burbage but Shakespeare played a role (possibly Tiberius), focused on the Roman history known from Suetonius and other classical writings. Thomas May—whose 1626 *Cleopatra* is frequently cited in relation to *Antony and Cleopatra*—signalled precisely such an awareness of the "Enobarbus" connection in his later play on Nero's mother

(*Julia Agrippina* of 1639), which cites Dio Cassius as well as Plutarch among its authorities and echoes Suetonius's *Nero* directly in the scene in act 1 in which the adopted Nero is taunted by his new "brother" Brittanicus (as "Domitius Aenobarbus").

37. On the red-beard Enobarbus name, see also Thomas Cooper, *Thesaurus linguae Romanae & Britannicae* (London, 1565), cited in *A New Variorum Edition of Shakespeare, Antony and Cleopatra,* ed. Marvin Spevack (New York: The Modern Language Association of America, 1990). For speculations on the name (Ahenobarbus) as also combining the attributes of Bacchus and Hercules, wine-bibbing (*oeno-*) and manly valor (*-barbus*), see Donald Cheney, " 'A very Antony': Patterns of Antonomasia in Shakespeare," *Connotations* 4, no. 1–2 (1994/5): 8–24.

38. See Holland trans. *Suetonius,* 2:101–2; Jonson, *Poetaster* (1601), 3.4.283, on p. 254 of the Herford and Simpson edition.

39. For this "dauncer" (*saltator*) and "Barber," see Holland, *Suetonius,* 2:103.

40. *Saltator* (related to "leap," hence also French "sault") was—with its vernacular variants—well known as the term for dancer, in sixteenth-century manuals on dancing, as well as from condemnations of dancing, including Philip Stubbes. In addition to the possible resonances of the Roman *saltator* or wanton transvestite dancer (known from Plautus and other sources) in "Salt Cleopatra" (the queen who in Shakespeare's play famously reveals herself to be a transvestite English boy player), see also in the Shakespeare canon the dancing "Saltiers" of *The Winter's Tale* 4.4.327.

41. On the complication of these binaries in the play, see inter alia Jonathan Gil Harris, " 'Narcissus in thy face': Roman Desire and the Difference It Fakes in *Antony and Cleopatra,*" *Shakespeare Quarterly* 45 (1994): 408–25.

42. On the prosthetic as opposed to the allegedly "natural" beard as masculine index, see Fisher, "Renaissance Beard," *Renaissance Quarterly* 54, no. 1 (2001), 155–87; and " 'His Majesty the Beard': Facial Hair and Masculinity on the Early Modern Stage," in *Staged Properties,* ed. Natasha Korda and Jonathan Gil Harris (Cambridge: Cambridge University Press, 2002); and Gleason, *Making Men,* 73, for the complication of this binary in Roman and classical texts.

43. It is difficult to read the accounts (in Florus, Appian, and other well-known histories) of Roman pirates on the Mediterranean, Adriatic, and Ionian seas without thinking of the "Barbary" pirates on those same seas. In Plutarch's *Life of Antony,* the very passage that inspired the scene of *Antony and Cleopatra* where Menas offers to "cut" the "cable" (and the throats of their guests) registers in both temporal frames, evoking the early modern threat of pirates to European fortunes on the "seas": "Sextus Pompeius at that time kept in Sicily, and so made many an inroad into Italy with a great number of pinnaces and other pirates' ships, of the which were captains two notable pirates, Menas and Menecrates, who so scoured all the sea thereabouts, that none durst peep out with a sail." Menas (like Antony and the "master-leaver" Enobarbus) was not only a pirate, but a renegade, who repeatedly changed sides, capturing Sardinia for Sextus Pompeius (son of Pompey the Great), then turning it over to Octavius, and finally returning to the service of Pompey.

44. See Camden, *Remains Concerning Britain* (1605). Perhaps thinking in the same associational fashion, Barnabe Barnes, in *The Devil's Charter* (1607)—the play used to date *Antony and Cleopatra* because it echoes Cleopatra's asps—used "Barbarossa" for the first time, as the name of an actual character in early modern English drama.

45. On Barbarossa and the new Battle of Actium at Prevesa, see Fernand Braudel, *The Mediterranean and the Mediterranean World in the Age of Philip II* (New York: Harper and Row, 1972), 1: 116; 2: 884–85, 1242 (on "the age of Barbarossa, the golden age of the Turkish armadas"); S. Soucek, "The Rise of the Barbarossas in North Africa," *Archivum Ottomanicum* 3 (1971), 238–50; John F. Guilmartin, Jr., *Gunpower and Galleys* (Cambridge: Cambridge University Press, 1974), esp. 20–26, 42–56; Palmira Brummett, *Ottoman*

Seapower and Levantine Diplomacy in the Age of Discovery (Albany: State University of New York Press, 1994); *The copye of the goyng away of the chefe Captayne of the Turke called Barbarossa, oute of Fraunce* (London, ca. 1545), where he is alternately called *Barbarus;* the account in Richard Knolles, *The Generall Historie of the Turkes* (London, 1603), 686–92, which, as Guilmartin notes (47), was written "almost within living memory of Prevesa." For Minsheu, see *A Dictionarie in Spanish and English, first published into the English tongue by R. Perciuale Gent. . . . Now enlarged and amplified . . . by Iohn Minsheu Professor of Languages in London* (London, 1599).

46. The Folio and all three Quartos of *The Knight of the Burning Pestle* have "Barbarossa" (rather than the "Barberoso" it is sometimes editorially emended to) for the lines on "Barbarossa's cell, / Where no man comes but leaves his fleece behind" (3.3.28). For the reprise of the barber's "barba roja" in the allusion to the renegade corsair Barbaroja in the Captive's Tale, in relation to Cervantes' exploitation of the discursive nexus that includes barbers and beards, see Fuchs, *Passing for Spain,* 23–30.

47. See the masterful discussion of the echoes in *Antony and Cleopatra* of the tradition of Alexander and the pirate and its critique of empire itself as a form of pillaging or theft, in J. Leeds Barroll's book-length study of this play.

Part II
Researching the Renaissance

(Title of Graduate Seminars Led by Leeds Barroll
at the Folger Shakespeare Library, 1991–1999)

Our Canon, Ourselves

Phyllis Rackin

FOR MODERN SCHOLARS, SHAKESPEARE'S PLAYS have often constituted a notable site of women's repression—evidence of women's subordinate place in his own world and an influential means of validating that subordination for future generations. Women's roles in Shakespeare's plays are far more limited than men's, both in size and in number, and female power is repeatedly characterized as threatening or even demonic. In fact, Shakespeare's representations of women often seem less sympathetic than those of other playwrights working at the same time. The figure of the witch, for instance, memorably demonized in *Macbeth*, appears as an amiable charlatan in Thomas Heywood's *The Wise Woman of Hogsdon*, where the title character, although denounced as a witch by dissolute young gallants, turns out to be the agent for effecting their reform and bringing about the desired resolution of the plot. In Dekker, Ford, and Rowley's *The Witch of Edmonton,* the witch is a tragic figure, driven to witchcraft by need and persecution and explicitly stated to be far less guilty than the respectable gentleman who occupies the highest social rank of all the characters in the play.

These are only two of many possible examples. It is interesting, for instance, to compare Shakespeare's treatment of warlike women in his early history plays with their far more sympathetic treatment in the anonymous contemporary play *Edward III*. This play is sometimes attributed to Shakespeare, and it even appears in recent editions of his collected works, but it has yet to achieve a secure place in the Shakespearean canon, and its female characters are depicted in strikingly different terms from those in the canonical Shakespearean history plays. In Shakespeare's *Henry VI, Part 1,* Joan is both the chief enemy to the English kingdom and a witch as well. In *Parts 2* and *3,* Margaret is a bloodthirsty adulteress. The more sympathetically depicted female characters in Shakespeare's history plays, such as the victimized women in *Richard III* and the Duchess of Gloucester and the Queen in *Richard II*, never go to war, they play no part in the affairs of state, and they seem to spend most of their limited time on stage in tears. Helplessness seems to be an essential component of female virtue in most of Shakespeare's English histories. *Edward III*, by contrast, depicts courageous women warriors who are also models of feminine virtue. The Countess of Salisbury resists the Scots king's siege of her castle and the English king's assault on her virtue with equal courage and resolution. The English queen, equally virtuous, leads her army to victory over the Scots at Newcastle, "big with child" but still "every day in arms" (4.2.40–46).[1] In *Edward III*, warlike English women defend their country against foreign threats. In Shakespeare's English history plays, warlike women *embody* those threats. Both Joan's French nationality and Margaret's are repeatedly emphasized, and both are depicted as threatening to the well-being and stability of the English kingdom. Similarly, in *Henry IV, Part 1,* where the foreign enemies are Welsh, the opening scene describes the Welsh women's mutilation of the corpses of the English soldiers killed in battle against Owen Glendower. No women fight on the side of the English.

Comparisons between Shakespeare's representations of women and those of his fellow playwrights suggest that a too-exclusive focus on Shakespeare may produce a misleading picture of the assumptions about women's roles that early modern English playgoers were prepared to accept. But even within the Shakespearean canon, there are indications of a more generous view of women's place than the examples typically cited in recent scholarship have seemed to suggest. In fact, the plays that modern scholars have chosen to emphasize may tell us more about our own assumptions regarding women than about the beliefs that informed the responses of Shakespeare's first audiences. Among the history plays, for example, the one that is most frequently taught and probably most admired is *Henry IV, Part 1*. This is also the one in which female characters are most marginalized, speaking fewer than 3.5 percent of the words in the script. Female characters are much more prominent in the Henry VI plays, *King John,* and *Henry VIII*. In Shakespeare's better-known history plays, women's roles are severely limited, both in size and in scope. The places where history is made—the royal court, the council chamber, and the field of battle—are overwhelmingly male preserves, and the business of the main historical plots is conducted entirely by men. However, the picture changes if we look at the other plays I have named. All three parts of *Henry VI*, as well as *King John*, feature women in what are now considered "untraditional" roles—as generals leading victorious armies on the battlefield and as political actors who exercise significant power in the conduct of state affairs. Unlike Shakespeare's better-known history plays, these plays feature active, energetic female characters. Their roles may be unsympathetic, but they are real players in the theater of history. These plays, however, are much less frequently performed or taught. In fact, there is an almost perfect inverse correlation between the prominence of women's roles in a history play and the play's current reputation. In the most highly esteemed of Shakespeare's history plays—*Richard II*, the two parts of *Henry IV*, and *Henry V*, the percentage of words assigned to female characters never reaches 10 percent of the script, and the women who do appear are typically confined, either to enclosed domestic settings or to the fictional lowlife world of Mistress Quickly's tavern in Eastcheap. Often designated by modern scholars as "The Henriad," these plays are the ones most admired by scholars and critics, and they are also most frequently produced on stage and best known by the general public.

The responses of Shakespeare's earliest audiences may have been strikingly different.[2] In the case of *Henry VI, Part 1*, for instance, Thomas Nashe wrote in 1592 that "ten thousand spectators (at least)" had seen that play, and Philip Henslowe's records of the receipts for its initial run suggest a figure closer to twenty thousand, more than all but one of the many other plays that Henslowe produced.[3] It may very well be that we, much more than Shakespeare's original audience, prefer the plays that minimize the roles of women and depict female characters in stereotypically "feminine" roles and settings. If that is the case, our negative estimation of these early plays—and also of women's place in Shakespeare's English histories—may tell us more about our own limitations than about those of Shakespeare and his original audiences.

A similar argument can be made for whatever genre of Shakespearean plays we choose to compare. The patriarchal fantasy played out in *The Tempest* has proved much more attractive to modern scholars and theater audiences than any of the other late romances, all of which include more, and more powerful, roles for female characters. The paradigmatic Shakespearean tragedy is *Hamlet*; it is interesting to contemplate the ways our picture of women's place in Shakespeare's plays would be altered if it were *Antony and Cleopatra*. Probably the best illustration of this effect, however, can be found in the comedies, because comedy was the genre that focused most frequently on women, sex, and gender.

Two comedies that illustrate with remarkable clarity the modern preference for stories in which women are put in their (subordinate) place are *The Taming of the Shrew* and *The Merry Wives of Windsor*. *The Taming of the Shrew* has enjoyed exceptional popularity in recent years, while *The Merry Wives of Windsor*, which offers a much more benign view of women's place in marriage (and also seems to have been modeled much more closely on the world that Shakespeare and his audiences actually knew), has been relatively neglected. During the years between 1979 and 1993, for instance, the Royal Shakespeare Company staged *The Taming of the Shrew* twice as often as *The Merry Wives of Windsor* (twelve times vs. six).[4] *The Taming of the Shrew* has also been favored by scholars. *The MLA International Bibliography of Books and Articles on the Modern Languages and Literatures* for the years since 1963 has 359 entries for that play, far more than for any other of Shakespeare's early comedies (for *The Two Gentlemen of Verona*, for instance, there are 131; for *The Comedy of Errors* 189). The *Shrew* has been equally popular with the general public. One of the most frequently produced of all Shakespeare's plays, it also became, in 1929, the first to be presented in a talking film.[5] Since then, it has provided the basis for innumerable other films, stage productions, and spinoffs. The hit musical *Kiss Me Kate* is the best known, but there have been many others as well.

There is no evidence that the play enjoyed a comparable popularity when it was first performed. Although it is usually dated in the early 1590s, it does not appear among the titles cited in 1598 in Francis Meres's *Palladis Tamia* as examples of Shakespeare's excellence as a playwright. Meres lists five early comedies—*The Two Gentlemen of Verona, The Comedy of Errors, Love's Labor's Lost, A Midsummer Night's Dream,* and *The Merchant of Venice.* Unless *The Taming of the Shrew* is the unidentified play Meres called "Love's Labour's Won," it was not included in his list, even though it is generally believed to have appeared during or before the 1593–94 theatrical season. Another indication that the play may not have been much admired—or even noticed—in Shakespeare's time is the fact that there are only three recorded references to it before 1649.[6] The performance history is equally skimpy: only three were recorded before the end of the seventeenth century.[7] The first of these dates from 1633, when it was followed two days later by *The Woman's Prize, or The Tamer Tamed,* a sequel written around 1611 by John Fletcher, Shakespeare's successor as the leading playwright for the King's Men. In Fletcher's play, the tables are turned, and Petruchio gets his comeuppance. Ann Thompson notes that this was the only case in which one of Shakespeare's plays "provoked a theatrical 'reply'" during his own lifetime (*Taming,* 17–18).

In *The Tamer Tamed*, Petruchio, now widowed, marries a spirited young woman named Maria who resolves to tame the notorious shrewtamer. Although Maria admits that she freely chose Petruchio for her husband and would choose him again "before the best man living" (1.3.155), she locks and barricades the house against him and refuses to let him enter or consummate the marriage until he has been properly tamed. Clearly designed as a response to Shakespeare's play, *The Tamer Tamed* opens with a scene in which three men debate Petruchio's merits as a husband. Two of them—Tranio, who bears the name of the sympathetic character from the earlier play, and Sophocles, whose name suggests wisdom—condemn his rough, domineering ways. His only defender is Moroso, who places the blame on Kate; but Moroso is clearly identified as an unsympathetic character—an old man who wants to marry the romantic heroine Livia, who is herself in love with Rowland. The scene ends with both of the other men expressing their hopes that Moroso will never marry Livia. The Livia/Rowland/Moroso subplot also offers an implicit rebuttal to the earlier play, with its auction for Bianca's hand and the monetary bargaining over Katherine's marriage to Petruchio. The undesirable match between Moroso and Livia is based on mercenary motives and paternal choice, while the desirable marriage between Livia and Rowland is based on Livia's own free choice. In the second scene of the play, Livia assures her lover, "no man shall make use of me; / My beauty was born free, and free Ile give it / To him that loves, not buys me" (1.2.37–39). Throughout *The Tamer Tamed*, love is repeatedly opposed to mercenary considerations: Maria proclaims that she'd take Petruchio "In's shirt, with one ten Groats to pay the Priest, / Before the best man living" (2.3.154–55), and Petruchio declares that he married Maria for her wit (4.2.26)—a statement that offers a direct contrast to Shakespeare's Petruchio's declaration that he will marry any woman who is "rich enough to be Petruchio's wife," regardless of her age, appearance or temperament (1.2.63–73). At the end of Fletcher's play, Rowland is overjoyed to learn he will lose the money he has bet Tranio because it means he will have Livia (5.3.36). At the end of Shakespeare's play, by contrast, Petruchio wins both his bet and an increased dowry. At the court of Charles I, where Fletcher's play was presented along with Shakespeare's, *The Taming of the Shrew* was "liked," but *The Tamer Tamed* was "very well liked."[8]

Despite the lack of evidence that *The Taming of the Shrew* was well received in its own time, recent scholarship has often proceeded on the assumption that the story it tells exemplifies beliefs that governed the attitudes of Shakespeare and his contemporaries regarding women's place in marriage. It may very well be, however, that our preoccupation with this crudely misogynist story tells us more about our own biases than about those of Shakespeare's original audience. The same anxieties that made Laura Doyle's guidebook for women *The Surrendered Wife: A Practical Guide to Finding Intimacy, Passion, and Peace with Your Man* a best-seller in the year 2001 seem to have made Kate's taming a deeply satisfying fantasy to audiences ranging from Harold Bloom to the many filmgoers who paid to see the more than eighteen movies that have made *Shrew* one of the most popular of all Shakespeare's plays for production on the modern screen.[9] Women have also bought into the fantasy. They are, after all, the primary audience for *The Surrendered Wife*. Deirdre Donahue wrote in *USA Today* that the book's author, "a self-described 'former shrew,' offers a surprisingly honest recipe for getting along with the man you married." Bloom describes his admiration for *The Taming of the Shrew* in strikingly similar terms: "One would have to be tone deaf (or ideologically crazed) not to hear in this [the dialogue between Kate and Petruchio at 5.1.122–31] a subtly exquisite music of marriage at its happiest."[10] Meryl Streep, who played the part of Katherine for Joseph Papp, seems to have

heard the same music: "Really what matters," she has said, "is that they
have an incredible passion and love; it's not something that Katherine
admits to right away but it does provide the source of her change" (Henderson, "Shrew for the Times," 161).

Seen in the context of current anxieties, desires, and beliefs, Shakespeare's play seems to prefigure the most oppressive modern assumptions
about women and to validate those assumptions as timeless truths, already
present in a sixteenth-century text and already apparent to Shakespeare's
original audiences. However, the play would have looked very different
when it was first performed. One telling indication of that difference is the
fact that modern productions of *The Taming of the Shrew* often cut or
rewrite the Induction, which frames the action as a play within a play.
Katherine's final speech of submission relies heavily on the fiction of a
woman's body beneath her costume, arguing, as it does, that women's
subjugation to men is required by their embodied weakness:

> Why are our bodies soft, and weak, and smooth,
> Unapt to toil and trouble in the world,
> But that our soft conditions and our hearts
> Should well agree with our external parts? (5.2.169–72)

This speech, which naturalizes women's subordination, works well in a modern production, where the actor who plays Kate really is a woman. The ideological work it accomplishes is less assured if it is performed (as it often is
not, especially in film versions) with the old Induction framing the action.
For there, in the page's cross-dressed disguise as Christopher Sly's wife, feminine submission is staged as a theatrical show designed and performed by
men in order to trick a drunken tinker with delusions of grandeur.

Sly is "wrapped in sweet clothes," with rings on his fingers, "a most
delicious banquet by his bed, / And brave attendants near him when he
wakes," but he is still not convinced that he really is a nobleman who has
lost his memory until he is told that he has a beautiful lady who has been
weeping about his affliction. The page Bartholomew, disguised in a lady's
clothes and weeping with the help of an onion concealed in a napkin, is
needed to complete the illusion. "My husband and my lord, my lord and
husband," Bartholomew says: "I am your wife in all obedience" (Induction
2.203–4). Bartholomew's act parodically foreshadows Kate's declarations of
submission to Petruchio at the end of the play. Whether or not the same
actor played the parts of Bartholomew and Kate, the page's performance of
femininity in the Induction implicitly destabilizes the performance of femininity by the boy actor who played Kate's part in the taming plot.

Spoken by a woman actor, the implications of Kate's final speech are
radically transformed. As George Bernard Shaw noted at the end of the

nineteenth century, "No man with any decency of feeling can sit it out in
the company of a woman without being extremely ashamed of the lord-of-
creation moral implied in the wager and the speech put into the woman's
own mouth" (quoted in Thompson, *Taming*, 21). Presented by a cross-
dressed boy, however, Katherine's proclamation can be seen as a male
performance of female compliance, especially if the play is performed
with the Induction, in which the cross-dressed page persuades a drunken
tinker that he is truly a lord by obsequiously performing the role of his
obedient wife. Thus, although the marriage plot affirms the authority of
patriarchy, the repressive implications of the action it represents are
undermined by the initial reminder to the audience that what they are
watching is a performance of theatrical shapeshifting. This effect would be
intensified if the play were performed—as it probably was—as farce, for the
action is replete with slapstick comedy, and the characters are portrayed
in one-dimensional stereotypes.

Framed by the Induction, the taming plot comes to the audience as a
farcical theatrical performance rather than a representation of actual life.
Similar farcical stories would have been familiar to Shakespeare's original
audience from widely circulated folktales and ballads. This version,
explicitly set in Italy, might also have recalled the fantastic travelers' tales
that were popular at the time the play was written, for the taming plot
begins with the arrival of two travelers—Lucentio, who has come to Padua
from Florence; and Petruchio, who has come from Verona. The only part
of the play that is set in a recognizable contemporary England is the
Induction; and the only female character who appears there is the Hostess, who ejects Sly from her tavern and threatens to fetch the constable to
punish him.

As short as it is, the Induction is studded with specific details that set the
action in the here-and-now of the world that Shakespeare and his audience
actually inhabited. Sly identifies the home of his father as "Burton-heath";
Barton-on-the-Heath was a village about sixteen miles south of Stratford,
where Shakespeare's aunt lived. The Hostess who threatens Sly in the
opening lines of the Induction is "Marian Hacket, the fat ale-wife of Wincot"; there was, in the sixteenth century, a Hacket family living in Wincot,
a hamlet about four miles south of Stratford.[11] These specific references
may have provided in-jokes for Shakespeare's fellow actors and for the
members of the audience who knew the countryside around Stratford; but
even for those who did not catch the specific allusions, the setting of the
Induction would have recalled the familiar features of English village life,
where the trade of alewife traditionally belonged to women and drunken
tinkers were a far more familiar sight than Italian gentlemen.[12] In the taming plot none of the women have any trade at all or any means of economic support that is not provided by their fathers or husbands. Given

what we know about the widespread economic activity of women in six-teenth-century England, the roles of women in the taming plot look much more like a wistful fantasy than a recognizable representation of the kind of women that Shakespeare and his first audiences would have been likely to encounter in their daily lives.

Recent scholars have often interpreted this fantasy as a response to the anxious desires of Shakespeare's countrymen, confronted by various man-ifestations of female power, ranging from the monarchy of Queen Eliza-beth at the top of the social hierarchy to the railings of village scolds and the riots of unruly women at its lower reaches protesting the rising prices of food. Certainly, the shrew-taming story has served a similar function for modern admirers of the play who are manifestly unhappy with the grow-ing assertiveness of women in their own world. However, it is probably a mistake to read the place of that fantasy in the cultural imagination of Shakespeare's contemporaries as if it were identical to its impact in a world where women's power and assertiveness are visibly increasing. The prominence of women in the twentieth-century academy, for instance, is a new phenomenon; in Shakespeare's England, what was new were the increased calls for the domestication of women and women's increasing exclusion from many trades where they had formerly been active. More-over, there is no evidence that the taming plot attracted as much attention in Shakespeare's time as it has done in our own. A mid-sixteenth-century English ballad, "A Merry Jest of a Shrewd and Curst Wife Lapped in Morel's Skin for Her Good Behavior" is often cited by modern scholars both as a possible source for Shakespeare's taming plot and as evidence that such stories were extremely popular in the period, but, as Frances E. Dolan reminds us, the ballad was printed only once.[13] Moreover, early allusions to Shakespeare's play tend to focus not on the taming plot but on the frame story, where the butt of the joke is not an unruly woman but an unruly poor man.

The trick the Lord plays on Sly depends for its shock value on the pre-tense that the poor tinker is a nobleman: what is in question is not the dis-tinctions that separate men from women but those that separate people who occupy disparate ranks in the social hierarchy. Those distinctions, which were a matter of persistent and compelling interest in Shake-speare's world, surface again in the taming plot when the clever servant Tranio impersonates his master; but in the Induction, they are the only distinctions that seem to matter. At the end of the first scene of the Induc-tion, for instance, the Lord declares,

> I know the boy will well usurp the grace,
> Voice, gait, and action of a gentlewoman.
> I long to hear him call the drunkard husband,

> And how my men will stay themselves from laughter
> When they do homage to this simple peasant.

What threatens to provoke uncontrollable laughter in the participants is not the boy's disguise as a gentlewoman but the pretense that a simple peasant is a nobleman. Since this is also the point of the entire charade, it was presumably also what was designed to titillate and amuse the playgoers.

And amuse them it did. There is considerable evidence that early audiences favored the Sly plot. A version of the play called *The Taming of a Shrew,* in which Sly reappeared at various points of the play and at the end as well to offer his comments upon the action, was printed in various quarto editions, the first of which, published in 1594, stated on its title page that the play had been "sundry times acted." It is also noteworthy that this play was less stridently male supremacist than the version that appeared in the First Folio edition of Shakespeare's plays (Marcus, "Shakespearean Editor," 177–200). The fact that *The Taming of the Shrew* did not appear in print until the First Folio suggests that it may have been less popular than the other version, since quarto editions may have been produced to capitalize upon a demand for printed copies of plays that had been popular in performance.[14] In any event, it was Sly's story, not the taming plot, that featured in several early recorded comments on the play. John Dryden, in fact, compared Sly to Shakespeare himself, when he wrote in 1672, "Thus like the drunken Tinker in his play, / He grew a Prince, and never knew which way" (*Allusion-Book* 2: 172). The Induction material was also expanded to form the basis of two eighteenth-century plays, both called *The Cobbler of Preston.* One of these was so popular that it was reprinted in eight editions.[15]

This is not to say that the taming plot was forgotten. It formed the basis of David Garrick's popular three-act farce, *Catharine and Petruchio,* which was virtually the only version staged from the time it was written in 1754 until the middle of the following century.[16] In fact, of all Shakespeare's plays, *The Taming of the Shrew* was the last to be restored to its original form on stage (Thompson, *Taming,* 20). It is easy to see why eighteenth- and nineteenth-century playgoers found Garrick's version of the taming plot more palatable than its Shakespearean prototype. In Garrick's final scene, when Baptista offers to give Petruchio an additional dowry for his newly reformed daughter, Petruchio, now as indifferent to mercenary advantage as the faithful lovers in Fletcher's play, immediately refuses, declaring:

> My Fortune is sufficient. Here's my Wealth:
> Kiss me, my *Kate*; and since thou art become
> So prudent, kind, and dutiful a Wife,
> *Petruchio* here shall doff the lordly Husband;
> An honest Mask, which I throw off with Pleasure.

> Far hence all Rudeness, Wilfulness, and Noise,
> And be our future Lives one gentle Stream
> Of mutual Love, Compliance and Regard.[17]

Garrick's revisions of the play are revealing, not only because they display the impact of a changing gender ideology but also because they anticipate the celebratory modern readings that have made the play so popular in our own time. Not only our preferences among the Shakespearean canon, but also our interpretations of the plays we prefer are clearly shaped by the pressures of our own time and place. Garrick's Petruchio prefigures the recurrent plot motif identified by Janice Radway in twentieth-century popular romance novels when he makes it clear at the end of the play (as Shakespeare's Petruchio does not) that his loveless behavior was a mere screen for his true feelings, easily thrown aside once his wife has learned to be dutifully obedient. This is not to say that he promises an equal relationship. Garrick makes sure that it is Petruchio rather than Catharine who has the last word, and in his very next speech—the final speech in the play—he recites the lines Shakespeare had given his Katherine to authorize wifely subordination by analogy to the subordination of subjects to monarchs.

Like Garrick's play, the romances Radway studied end in the promise of a happy, loving marriage, when, despite the apparent cruelty of their hypermasculine, aggressive heroes, it turns out that they really care for the heroines. The heroines, in turn, abandon their own defiant and inappropriately masculine behavior because, "Like all romances, these novels eventually recommend the usual sexual division of labor that dictates that women take charge of the domestic and purely personal spheres of human endeavor."[18] Many other features of Garrick's play—and of Shakespeare's as well—also prefigure those novels, and Radway's analysis of the cultural work the novels perform helps to explain the widespread appeal Shakespeare's play has acquired in recent years—years when one out of every six mass-market paperbacks sold in North America is a Harlequin or Silhouette romance novel.[19] Katherine, like the heroines preferred by the late twentieth-century women readers Radway surveyed, "is differentiated . . . by an extraordinarily fiery disposition" and "the particularly exaggerated quality of her early rebelliousness against parental strictures." Like them, Katherine also "explicitly refuse[s] to be silenced by the male desire to control women through the eradication of their individual voices." "[S]peak I will," she insists:

> My tongue will tell the anger of my heart,
> Or else my heart concealing it will break,
> And rather than it shall, I will be free,
> Even to the uttermost, as I please, in words.
>   (4.3.74–80)

Even the fact that most of Katherine's ordeal takes place at Petruchio's house in the country has a counterpart in the modern romances Radway studied, where the heroine is typically removed from the familiar realm associated with her childhood and family (*Reading the Romance,* 123–24). These novels, in Radway's analysis, express and assuage their readers' ambivalences about the constraints that define their roles as women in our own culture. Specifically, the novels place the blame for men's "rigid indifference and their mistreatment of women" not on the men's own "indifference, competitiveness, or ambition," but instead on the "women's own insufficiency as perfect wife-mothers" (128). Only after the heroine has learned to behave like a true woman will the hero be transformed into an ideal figure who, while retaining his masculine power, will also be able to care for her in a tender, solicitous way that satisfies the readers' desires (127–28).

This is not to say that all of the features preferred by the romance readers Radway studied are present in *The Taming of the Shrew*. Significantly, a crucial characteristic of the modern romance hero is the fact that "the terrorizing effect of his exemplary masculinity is always tempered by the presence of a small feature that introduces an important element of softness into the overall picture" (128). No such feature appears in Shakespeare's characterization of Petruchio, but it is revealing that modern readers of the play have been at great pains to discover it. According to an early twentieth-century editor, for instance, "there is a delicacy in the man underlying his boisterousness throughout. . . . He has to tame this termagant bride of his, and he does it in action with a very harsh severity. But while he storms and raves among servants and tailors, showing off for her benefit, to her his speech remains courteous and restrained—well restrained and, with its ironical excess, elaborately courteous. It is observable through all the trials he imposes on her, he never says the sort of misprising word that hurts a high-mettled woman more than any rough deed."[20] Quiller-Couch is clearly an apologist for Petruchio and for the taming plot. Like a number of recent critics, he waxes sentimental about the play's conclusion, declaring that "there are truly few prettier conclusions in Shakespeare than [Katherine's] final submission" (43); but because he is less guarded than they are in expressing the reasons for his admiration, his remarks are worth quoting in some detail:

> It is not discreet perhaps for an editor to discuss, save historically, the effective way of dealing with [shrews]. Petruchio's was undoubtedly drastic and has gone out of fashion. But avoiding the present times and recalling . . . Dickens's long gallery of middle-aged wives who make household life intolerable by various and odious methods, one cannot help thinking a little wistfully that the Petruchian discipline had something to say for itself. It may be that these

curses on the hearth are an inheritance of our middle-class, exacerbating wives by deserting them, most of the day, for desks and professional routine; that the high feudal lord would have none of it, and as little would the rough serf or labourer with an unrestrained hand. Let it suffice to say that *The Taming of the Shrew* belongs to a period and is not ungallant, even so. The works of our author do not enforce set lessons in morals. . . . He is nowhere the expositor of creed or dogma, but simply always an exhorter, by quiet catholic influence, to valiancy and noble conduct of life (43).

Clearly, this early twentieth-century editor's response to the play is fueled by his own longing for a world where wives can be tamed by whatever means it takes. Apparently embarrassed by his self-revelation, however, he immediately retreats into historicism, disavowing his very personal and contemporary response by "avoiding the present times" and reminding his readers that "*The Taming of the Shrew* belongs to a period." Quiller-Couch's essay is itself a period piece, and the period to which it belongs is his own. His reading of the play tells us much more about the early twentieth-century social milieu in which he wrote than it does about the world in which the play was originally produced. Both the nakedness of his self-revelation and the historical veil with which he quickly attempts to conceal it prefigure in the simplest possible terms and with amazing clarity the social and psychological mechanisms that went into the construction of the twentieth-century image of a patriarchal bard.[21] For readers like Quiller-Couch, that image has been the object of wistful desire; for feminist critics it has produced a set of texts so inimical to feminist reading that "feminist criticism. . . is restricted to exposing its own exclusion" (McLuskie, "Patriarchal Bard," 97).

Quiller-Couch and many of his successors have attempted to whitewash the oppressiveness of Katherine's taming. More recently, feminist scholars, such as Lynda E. Boose and Frances E. Dolan, have refuted their arguments by exposing both the brutality of the represented action and its dreadful historical implications. The stakes in these critical debates have been high, but one unfortunate consequence of the interest they have attracted is that despite the lack of evidence that the play was popular in its own time, it has taken on, not only in the popular imagination but also in feminist scholarship, the status of the paradigmatic Shakespearean representation of women's place in marriage.

THE MERRY WIVES OF WINDSOR

The play that probably should occupy that status is *The Merry Wives of Windsor* both because of the unequaled prominence of married women and marital relationships in the action and because it is the only Shake-spearean comedy set in a recognizable, contemporary England. With its location in an actual town situated not far from London, its characters taken from the middle ranks of society, and its representation of the homely details of everyday life, it comes closest in characterization and setting to the actual world that Shakespeare and his original audiences inhabited. The script is laced with references to specific locations in and around Windsor, such as Frogmore, a nearby village (2.3.65) and Datchet Mead (3.3.11), a meadow situated between Windsor Little Park and the Thames.[22] Instead of romantic adventures in far-off places, the audience hears about the familiar activities of everyday life. There are whitsters (i.e., linen bleachers) in Datchet Mead; Mistress Ford has a buck-basket for her laundry and a cowl-staff for her servants to carry it; Mistress Quickly com-plains that she has to "wash, wring, brew, bake, scour, dress meat and drink, [and] make the beds" (1.4. 84-85). Here, unlike *Macbeth*, perfumes are identified not as coming from Arabia but as having been purchased in Bucklesbury, a London street where herbs were sold (3.3.61). Here, unlike *A Midsummer Night's Dream*, the fairies who appear in the woods outside the town are town children in masquerade.

In this recognizably contemporary English town, women are gainfully employed, run households, supervise servants, and arrange marriages. The only husband who attempts to exercise the kind of patriarchal sur-veillance that recent critics have assumed as the historical norm is Ford; but instead of being taken seriously, Ford's anxiety about his wife's fidelity makes him the object of his neighbors' ridicule. To at least one seventeenth-century Englishwoman, the roles and representations of women in *The Merry Wives of Windsor* rang remarkably true. Margaret Cavendish, the author of the first critical essay ever published on Shake-speare, regarded Shakespeare's representations of female characters as one of his greatest strengths. Among the eight characters she cited as examples, four are from *The Merry Wives of Windsor*. "[O]ne would think," she wrote, "he had been Metamorphosed from a Man to a Woman, for who could Describe *Cleopatra* Better than he hath done, and many other Females of his own Creating, as *Nan Page, Mrs. Page, Mrs. Ford*, the Doctors Maid, *Bettrice*, Mrs. *Quickly, Doll Tearsheet*, and others, too many to Relate?"[23]

In the vastly different England of the turn of the twentieth century another woman recorded a similar response. In 1902, Rosa Grindon, the President of the Manchester Ladies Literary and Scientific Club, pub-lished her monograph *In Praise of Shakespeare's "Merry Wives of Wind-sor": An Essay in Exposition and Appreciation.* Grindon's argument is worth noting because by the time she wrote, *The Merry Wives* was rarely per-formed and almost universally disparaged as a second- or third-rate play, and her monograph was an attempt to defend the play against the by-then-prevailing judgment that it was vastly inferior to Shakespeare's other works. Grindon explained and answered the criticisms by invoking the tradition that the play had been written at Queen Elizabeth's command. Since the play had been written for a woman, she argued, women were best suited to understand and judge it.[24]

The eighteenth-century tradition that *The Merry Wives* was originally written at the request of Queen Elizabeth has never been verified, but it has had a remarkable persistence, often as an explanation for what seemed to be the play's inferiority as the result both of hasty composition and of Shakespeare's lack of interest in the project. Perhaps, however, there is something to be said for Rosa Grindon's argument—not her assumption that the story about Queen Elizabeth was true, but her sense that it expressed something essential about the curiously negative reputation the play had acquired by the time she wrote. The tradition connecting the play to Queen Elizabeth may very well owe its persistence to the critics' sense that this play was in fact designed to address the interests of women—an intuition that may also help to explain the play's lack of interest and esteem in a scholarly tradition that has been overwhelmingly shaped by men. What is more difficult to explain, however, is the fact that until very recently the play has also been surprisingly absent from most of the twentieth-century feminist scholarship that examined women's place in Shakespeare's plays and its relation to their place in the historical world he inhabited.[25] Following the mainstream of popular and scholarly interest, feminist criticism often focused instead on the extravagant stories in the other comedies, which (perhaps not incidentally) tend to depict women in much less empowered—and much less familiar—roles. The fact that the history of *The Merry Wives'* reputation can be plotted on a trajectory almost exactly opposite to that of *The Taming of the Shrew* suggests that some of the same cultural forces have been involved. Throughout the twentieth century, as *The Taming of the Shrew* received more and more attention, *The Merry Wives* was dismissed or ignored in virtually every study of Shakespeare's comedies.[26] Both the dismissal of *The Merry Wives* and the current interest in *The Taming of the Shrew* appear to be the products of a distinctively modern taste, because—again in direct contrast to the *Shrew*—*The Merry Wives* was extremely popular throughout most of its earlier history. When the theaters reopened after the Restoration, it was one of the first of Shakespeare's plays to be revived on stage, and was one of the most popular plays in the new repertory.[27] Its supremacy continued well into the eighteenth century. During the years 1701–50, in fact, it was produced over two hundred times, more than any of Shakespeare's other comedies.[28] Moreover, the play's critical reputation equalled its popularity on stage. John Dryden praised it both in his essay *Of Dramatic Poesie* and in his Preface to the revised version of *Troilus and Cressida* as the most "regular" and "exactly form'd" of all Shakespeare's compositions (Taylor, *Reinventing Shakespeare,* 30). Charles Gildon wrote in 1702 that it was Shakespeare's only "true comedy," and Joseph Warton declared in 1778 that it was "the most complete specimen of Shakespeare's comic powers." Samuel Johnson noted in 1773 that "its general power, that power by which all works of genius shall finally be tried, is such, that perhaps it never yet had reader or spectator, who did not think it too soon at an end."[29]

Even in the nineteenth century, when the play's reputation was in decline, it could still evoke enthusiastic responses from editors. In 1820, William Oxberry wrote, "this delightful comedy is perfect"; and Samuel William Singer declared in 1826 that "the incidents, characters, and plot of this delightful comedy are unrivalled in any drama, ancient or modern" (quoted in Roberts, *Shakespeare's English Comedy,* 62–63). It was also valued for its representation of sixteenth-century English life, as in this nostalgic encomium from one late-nineteenth-century admirer: "The whirligig of time and death must run its round, ere ever they bring back Shakespeare's England out of the dust of years. . . . But in the enchanted pages the old world dwells secure . . . [It lies] in Shakespeare's pages, and you have but to throw down the . . . newspapers, to open the volume, and your life is that you would gladlier have lived in the larger, airer, more kindly and congenial days, 'the spacious days of great Elizabeth.'"[30] Friedrich Engels declared that "the first act of the *Merry Wives* alone contains more life and reality than all German literature."[31] To the Shakespeare scholar Felix Schelling, there was "no play of Shakespeare's which draws so unmistakably on his own experience of English life as this, and the dramatist's real source here is undoubtedly the life of the Elizabethans."[32]

That very realism, however, probably helped to marginalize the play in the mainstream of post-Romantic criticism, with its veneration for poetry and imaginative flights of fancy. Instead of encouraging its audiences to imagine a timeless, ideal world, it imitates the very specific world of late sixteenth-century England. As Frederick Wedmore wrote in 1874, "Here then, perhaps more than elsewhere as a whole has Shakspere. . . [drawn] from just the common life about" him, but the result is that the play depicts "usages we do not recognize, types we have forgotten."[33] A striking anomaly in the canon of Shakespeare's comedies, the play had no place in the universe of marvelous invention and fine poetry they seemed to inhabit. There are brief glimpses of similarly down-to-earth, contemporary settings in the Gloucestershire scenes in *Henry IV, Part 2* and the Induction to *The Taming of the Shrew,* both of which depict scenes and characters that are based on the life Shakespeare and many of the members of his audience must have known; but the setting for the typical Shakespearean comedy is a distant or imaginary place, where the leading characters have no visible means of support and no business more serious than falling in and out of love and pursuing the objects of their romantic desire. In *The Merry Wives*, Fenton's courtship of Anne, which would have been the main plot in a standard Shakespearean romantic comedy, is given very little time on stage. The main business of this play is Falstaff's inept, mercenary pursuit of the Windsor wives, which, as Arthur F. Kinney has observed, serves as a parody of the traditional business of romantic comedy.[34] Even the language of *The Merry Wives of Windsor* is peculiar. Written predominantly in prose—more prose, in fact, than in any other Shakespearean playscript—it seems much closer to the language of actual, everyday life. All these anomalies probably contributed to the failure of *The Merry Wives of Windsor* to find a place in twentieth-century studies of Shakespeare's comedies, where it was either ignored or dismissed as distinctly inferior to the others (Roberts, *Shakespeare's English Comedy,* 65–66).

The striking differences between the here and now of Shakespeare's familiar, contemporary Windsor and the glamorous, remote worlds his other plays evoked for the imagination often seemed a terrible disappointment to the playwright's romantically minded admirers. The fairies who torment Falstaff are actually town children in masquerade, and their queen is none other than Mistress Quickly. Male sexual insecurity is equally subject to commonsense demystification. Instead of being taken seriously as a motive for tragic action, the irrational jealousy that threatens to kill Hermione and does kill Desdemona does no harm at all to Ford's merry wife: its only consequence is to make Ford the object of his neighbors' ridicule. What was most disappointing, however, was the effect of this new environment on Falstaff.

From Maurice Morgann to Harold Bloom, male critics have fallen in love with the Falstaff of the history plays and identified with him. To them, he has been far more than a character in a play: pulsating with vivid life, he seemed to transcend both the historical moment of his creation and the historical world in which Shakespeare originally installed him to take his place in their imaginations as a kindred spirit. In the context of the history plays, the fact that Falstaff was a fictional character gave him a unique place in the historical action. The fact that the predominant language of those plays was blank verse meant that Falstaff's witty irreverent prose had the effect of spontaneous, unpredictable present speech. His irrepressible, transgressive eloquence enabled him to debunk the conventional pieties that defined the limits of historical representation. He seemed to break through the frame of the represented action to join the audience in an eternal theatrical present. In *The Merry Wives of Windsor,* by contrast, while Falstaff is still an outsider in the world of the play, he no longer enjoys a privileged relationship either with the play's original audience or with its later readers. Here, he speaks the same language and occupies the same frame of representation as the other characters in a setting that recalls the here-and-now of the original, late sixteenth-century audience's experience.

In the Henry IV plays, Falstaff could talk his way out of paying for his misdeeds. In the mundane, physically grounded setting of *The Merry Wives of Windsor*, verbal facility is no longer privileged. Mistress Quickly's speech is still riddled with malapropisms, but while they made her the butt of Falstaff's jokes in the Henry IV plays, where she was easily victimized by his empty promises of marriage and unpaid debts, it is now equally easy for her to outwit Falstaff as she repeatedly lures him into the traps set by the wives. And at the end of the play, she supervises his punishments as Falstaff is made to "stand at the taunt of [another verbally inept character, the Welsh parson] who makes fritters of English" (5.5.135–36). In the history plays, Falstaff's theatrical power is supreme: he even upstages the future king of England. In the familiar, contemporary world of the Windsor wives, he is a beached whale, helplessly gasping on a shore where he cannot navigate (2.1.56–57). He is repeatedly humiliated by the town wives who arrange for him to be buried in dirty laundry, dunked in a muddy stream, convinced to disguise himself as a fat woman, beaten with a cudgel, and tormented by little children, whom he is gullible enough to take for fairies.

To Falstaff's critical admirers, the transformation was intolerable. To William Hazlitt, the Falstaff of *The Merry Wives* "is like a person recalled to the stage to perform an unaccustomed and ungracious part": he "is not the man he was in the two parts of *Henry IV*."[35] To Edward Dowden, Shakespeare "dressed up a fat rogue, brought forward for the occasion from the back premises of the poet's imagination, in Falstaff's clothes."[36] In our own time, Harold Bloom echoes the judgments of numerous predecessors when he calls the Falstaff of *The Merry Wives* "a rank impostor." In fact, both Hartley Coleridge and A. C. Bradley had used exactly the same term: to Coleridge, he was a "big-bellied impostor," to Bradley simply "the impostor." The play, Bradley thought, showed evidence of hasty composition, and the spectacle of a "disreputable fat old knight called Falstaff" "baffled, duped, treated like dirty linen, beaten, burnt, pricked, mocked, insulted, and, worst of all, repentant and didactic" was "horrible."[37] Perhaps most "horrible" was the fact that Falstaff's humiliations are devised by women. Like Fletcher's sequel to *The Taming of the Shrew*, *The Merry Wives of Windsor* turns the tables in a conflict that resonates with modern conflicts between the sexes.[38]

In the Henry IV plays female characters were confined to the margins of the action. They make brief appearances at the homes of the rebels in

Part 1, but no women ever appear at the court of Henry IV, and although Mistress Quickly is the Hostess of the Boar's Head Tavern, she is powerless in the homosocial historical world imagined in the Henry IV plays and *Henry V*, while in *Merry Wives of Windsor*, she is empowered by her membership in the social network of the Windsor community, which includes wives as well as husbands, daughters as well as sons. In the Henry IV plays, although the tavern is designated as hers, it is Falstaff who dominates the tavern scenes and embodies its effeminating pleasures. In these plays, Falstaff is able to appropriate the "woman's part." Threatening to corrupt the prince with the temptations of idleness and debauchery, he takes on the role of the amoral, sensual seductress. His contempt for military honor and valor, his loquacity, his lying, his inconstancy, his sensual self-indulgence, his unruly behavior, and his gross corpulence all implied effeminacy within the system of analogies that opposed spirit to body, aristocrat to plebeian, and man to woman.[39] He even refers to his fat belly as a "womb" (*Henry IV, Part 2,* 4.2.19–20) and compares himself to a "sow that hath o'erwhelmed all her litter but one" (*Henry IV, Part 2,* 1.2.9). In *Henry IV, Part 1* Falstaff even appropriates what is often considered the most powerful and dangerous of the threats associated with women—that of emasculation. That threat is briefly invoked at the beginning of that play, when Westmoreland reports that the corpses of the English soldiers killed in battle have been abused by Welsh women in a way that "may not be / Without much shame retold or spoken of" (1.1.43–46). At the end of the play, Falstaff performs on stage what looks like a reenactment of that reported mutilation when he stabs Hotspur's corpse in the thigh. In Windsor, by contrast, it is Falstaff who suffers a series of symbolic emasculations, all contrived by the women. To cool his lust, he is drenched in a muddy stream. Next, he is dressed in women's clothes and beaten. Finally, he is persuaded to wear the emasculating horns of a cuckold, horns that he intended to plant on the head of Master Ford.

In *The Merry Wives,* the women also acquire what was undoubtedly the most important basis of Falstaff's power in the history plays—his theatrical preeminence. Here, the characters most closely identified with theatricality are the wives themselves. As the Epilogue to *Henry IV, Part 2* acknowledges, the chief function of any commercial play was entertainment, and in the Henry IV plays, Falstaff was the most entertaining figure on stage. "My fear," the Epilogue begins, "is your displeasure," and it concludes with a promise to "continue the story with Sir John in it." Falstaff is also among the theatrical pleasures promised in the title page of the quarto edition of *The Merry Wives of Windsor*, which begins by advertising "A Most pleasaunt and excellent conceited Comedie, of Syr *John Falstaffe*, and the merrie Wives of *Windsor*." However, the title page also promises to depict the "pleasing humors" of many other characters: Sir Hugh, the

Welsh Knight, Justice Shallow, his wise cousin Master Slender, Ancient Pistol, and Corporal Nym. Here, Falstaff is only one of the many attractions promised by the play. And in the running title—"*A pleasant Comedie, of the merry Wives of Windsor*"—Falstaff disappears. Moreover, in the playscript itself, the characters who are most closely identified with theatrical entertainment are the merry wives, who devise and perform a series of skits for Falstaff's humiliation. Falstaff is featured in these skits, but he does not contrive them, and, unlike the wives, he does not enjoy their performance at all. Although the women offer conventional moral rationales for their actions—that Falstaff needs to be punished, that they want to prove that "wives may be merry, and yet honest [i.e., chaste] too" (4.2.88-89)—their main purpose is their own entertainment, which, not so incidentally, is the audience's entertainment, too.

One crucial difference between a play read and a play seen in the theater is that the audience in a theater, having gone there for entertainment, shares a communal endeavor and a community of interest and purpose with the characters who are entertainers or enjoying entertainment. Characters like Richard III, Iago, and the witches in *Macbeth* are all attractive on stage. Despite their destructive roles in the represented action, their roles in the production of an entertaining performance are entirely constructive. A novel or a play experienced in solitary reading encourages its readers to imagine themselves into the represented action: their own presence and participation are occluded. A play experienced in the theater is designed to enlist playgoers in a communal project, which involves the actors who are there to entertain them as well as the characters those actors represent. Clearly, this complicity in the production of theatrical pleasure is part of the appeal of characters who disguise themselves, especially the cross-dressed heroines, such as Rosalind and Viola, who take the audience into their confidence as they deceive the other characters on stage. The women in *The Merry Wives of Windsor* do not themselves adopt male disguise, but they provide a similar pleasure for the audience when they persuade Falstaff to disguise himself from Ford by wearing the clothes of the old woman of Brentford. However, in direct antithesis to the cross-dressed heroines in Shakespeare's other comedies, Falstaff takes no pleasure in his disguise: that privilege is reserved for the wives and for the audience, joined together in a community of laughter from which Falstaff is excluded. At the very end of *The Merry Wives*, Mistress Page includes Falstaff in a general invitation to "go home, / And laugh this sport o'er by a country fire." The implication is that he is finally to be included, at least temporarily, in the Windsor community. But for most of the play, he is represented as an isolated figure, betrayed by his followers, scorned by the townspeople, and the solitary butt of their practical jokes.

It is significant that the merry wives, unlike Falstaff, and unlike the heroines of a number of other Shakespearean comedies, do not cross-dress. In
plays like *As You Like It*, cross-dressing provides a theatrical holiday for the
heroines, temporarily freed from the constraints that define their roles as
women in a male-dominated society. In *The Merry Wives of Windsor*, the
female characters exercise considerable power in their own persons as
women. As such, they provide a striking contrast to what we have come to
think of as the paradigmatic Shakespearean heroine, who inhabits a homosocial world where women are isolated and confined within households controlled by fathers and husbands. The merry wives are central figures in the
community that Shakespeare placed in the English town of Windsor, and
they are empowered by the fact that it includes women as well as men. It
may very well be that the oppression and constraints that define the roles of
women in the plays we have come to assume as normative were actually
counterfactual fantasies rather than reflections of the life that the majority of
Shakespeare's original audience knew outside the theater.

In the everyday world of Windsor, the only female figure who resembles the heroines of the romantic comedies is Anne Page. She constitutes
the center of a romantic courtship plot, which is conducted in conventional verse rather than the colloquial prose that makes up the dominant
language of the play. Significantly, Anne is characterized from the first as
a *representation*. Even before she enters, Slender tells us that "She has
brown hair, and speaks small *like* a woman" (1.1.40–41; my italics). Even
her name—Anne Page (an page)—identifies her origins in literary and theatrical convention. The romantic heroine disguised as a boy page was a
familiar figure to readers and playgoers in Shakespeare's England, and in
a few notorious cases actual women followed their example; but it is
doubtful that many of the playgoers in Shakespeare's original audiences
had ever encountered such a creature in their own lives. Merry wives,
however, must have been everywhere.

NOTES

This essay is taken from my book *Shakespeare and Women* (Oxford: Oxford University
Press, 2005).

1. My quotations from *Edward III* come from G. Blakemore Evans and J. J. M. Tobin,
eds., *The Riverside Shakespeare,* 2nd ed. (Boston: Houghton Mifflin, 1997). My Shakespeare
quotations come from Stephen Greenblatt and others, eds., *The Norton Shakespeare* (New
York: W. W. Norton, 1997).

2. Jean E. Howard and Phyllis Rackin, *Engendering a Nation: A Feminist Account of
Shakespeare's English Histories* (London: Routledge, 1997), 21–26, 217–18.

3. Alfred Harbage, *Shakespeare's Audience* (New York: Columbia University Press,
1941).

4. *Theater at Stratford-upon-Avon, First Supplement to A Catalogue-Index to Productions of the Royal Shakespeare Company, 1979–1993,* ed. Michael Mullin (London: Greenwood Press, 1994), 140–42, 214–17.

5. Ann Thompson, ed., *The Taming of the Shrew* (Cambridge: Cambridge University Press, 1984), 22.

6. C. M. Ingleby, L. Toulmin Smith, F. J. Furnivall, and John Munro, *The Shakspere Allusion-Book: A Collection of Allusions to Shakspere from 1591 to 1700* (London: Oxford University Press, 1932), 2:540.

7. Dana E. Aspinall, "The Play and the Critics," in *The Taming of the Shrew: Critical Essays,* ed. Dana E. Aspinall (New York: Routledge, 2002), 20.

8. Leah Marcus, "The Shakespearean Editor as Shrew-Tamer," *English Literary Renaissance* 22, no. 2 (1992): 199–200.

9. Diana E. Henderson, "A Shrew for the Times," in *Shakespeare the Movie: Popularizing the Plays on Film, TV, and Video,* ed. Lynda E. Boose and Richard Burt (London: Routledge, 1997), 148.

10. Harold Bloom, *Shakespeare: The Invention of the Human* (New York: Riverhead Books, 1998), 33.

11. The references to Burton-heath and Wincot come from the second scene of the Induction. Their identifications come from the notes to that scene in Brian Morris's Arden edition of the play (London: Methuen, 1981).

12. On alewives in early modern England, see Judith M. Bennett, "The Village Ale-Wife: Women and Brewing in Fourteenth-Century England," in *Women and Work in Preindustrial Europe,* ed. Barbara A. Hanawalt (Bloomington: Indiana University Press, 1986).

13. *The Taming of the Shrew: Texts and Contexts* (Boston: Bedford Books of St. Martin's Press, 1996), 254.

14. The evidence for the relative popularity of the two plays is not clear, however, since early records do not make a clear distinction between the two titles. For instance, Henslowe's reference to a June 1594 performance of "the tamynge of A Shrowe" that netted only nine shillings may be further evidence of *The Taming of the Shrew's* early lack of success if, as H. J. Oliver argued, the play in question was *The Taming of the Shrew* (Oxford ed., p. 32).

15. Katherine West Scheil, "Early Georgian Politics and Shakespeare," *Shakespeare Survey* 51 (1998): 48.

16. Tori Haring-Smith, *From Farce to Metadrama: A Stage History of "The Taming of the Shrew," 1594–1983* (Westport, CT: Greenwood Press, 1985), 15.

17. *Catharine and Petruchio* (London: J. and R. Tonson, and S. Draper, 1756).

18. Janice A. Radway, *Reading the Romance: Women, Patriarchy, and Popular Literature* (Chapel Hill: University of North Carolina Press, 1984), 123.

19. These statistics come from a talk entitled "The Substance of Romance, " presented by Isabel Swift, the editorial head of Harlequin Enterprises, at the University of Pennsylvania in October, 2002.

20. Introduction to *The Taming of the Shrew* (1928), in *The Taming of the Shrew: Critical Essays,* ed. Dana E. Aspinall (New York: Routledge, 2002), 42–43.

21. This phrase comes from Kathleen McLuskie's important and influential article, "The Patriarchal Bard: Feminist Criticism and Shakespeare: *King Lear* and *Measure for Measure,"* in *Political Shakespeare: Essays in Cultural Materialism,* ed. Jonathan Dollimore and Alan Sinfield, 2nd ed. (Ithaca, NY: Cornell University Press, 1994).

22. Although, as Leah Marcus points out, the locations in the Quarto are more generalized, allowing for the audience to imagine them in London rather than Windsor, both scripts seem clearly designed to evoke a familiar setting for their audiences. See "Levelling Shakespeare: Local Customs and Local Texts," *Shakespeare Quarterly* 42 (1991): 173–75.

23. Letter 122 in *Sociable Letters* (London: William Wilson, 1664).

24. Rosa Leo Grindon, *In Praise of Shakespeare's "Merry Wives of Windsor": An Essay in Exposition and Appreciation* (Manchester, UK: Sherratt and Hughes, 1902).

25. The index in Philip Kolin's *Shakespeare and Feminist Criticism: An Annotated Bibliography and Commentary* (New York: Garland, 1991), which covers the years 1975–88, has fifty-one entries for *The Taming of the Shrew* but only twenty-three for *The Merry Wives of Windsor.* In the last few years, however, there have been a number of excellent studies: Rosemary Kegl, "'The adoption of abominable terms': Middle Classes, Merry Wives, and the Insults That Shape Windsor," in *The Rhetoric of Concealment: Figuring Gender and Class in Renaissance Literature* (Ithaca, NY: Cornell University Press, 1994), 77–125; Richard Helgerson, "The Buck Basket, the Witch, and the Queen of Fairies: The Women's World of Shakespeare's Windsor," in *Adulterous Alliances: Home, State, and History in Early Modern European Drama and Painting* (Chicago: University of Chicago Press, 2000), 57–76; Wendy Wall, "Why Does Puck Sweep?: Shakespearean Fairies and the Politics of Cleaning," in *Staging Domesticity: Household Work and English Identity in Early Modern Drama* (Cambridge: Cambridge University Press, 2002), 94–126, and *"The Merry Wives of Windsor:* Unhusbanding Desires in Windsor," in *A Companion to Shakespeare's Works, Volume III, The Comedies,* ed. Richard Dutton and Jean E. Howard (Oxford: Blackwell, 2003), 376–92; Natasha Korda, "Judicious Oeillades: Supervising Marital Property in *The Merry Wives of Windsor,"* in *Shakespeare's Domestic Economies: Gender and Property in Early Modern England* (Philadelphia: University of Pennsylvania Press, 2002), 76–110; and Lena Cowen Orlin, "Shakespearean Comedy and Material Life," in *A Companion to Shakespeare's Works, Volume III,* ed. Dutton and Howard, 159–81.

26. Jeanne Addison Roberts, *Shakespeare's English Comedy: "The Merry Wives of Windsor" in Context* (Lincoln: University of Nebraska Press, 1979), xi–xii, 65–66.

27. Gary Taylor, *Reinventing Shakespeare: A Cultural History from the Restoration to the Present* (Oxford: Oxford University Press, 1989), 28.

28. Charles Beecher Hogan, *Shakespeare in the Theater* (Oxford: Clarendon Press, 1952), 460.

29. Bertrand H. Bronson, ed., *Selections from Johnson on Shakespeare* (New Haven, CT: Yale University Press, 1986), 129.

30. Andrew Lang, writing in *Harper's New Monthly Magazine,* 80 (December 1889).

31. Quoted by Walter Cohen in his introduction to the play in *The Norton Shakespeare,* 1225.

32. Felix Schelling, *Elizabethan Drama 1588–1642* (Boston: Houghton Mifflin, 1908), 1: 324.

33. Frederick Wedmore, *The Academy,* December 26, 1874.

34. Arthur F. Kinney, "Textual Signs in *The Merry Wives of Windsor," Yearbook of Shakespeare Studies* 3 (1993): 209.

35. William Hazlitt, *Characters of Shakespeare's Plays* (London: Oxford University Press, 1955), 257–58.

36. Edward Dowden, *Shakspere: A Critical Study of His Mind and Art* (New York: Harper and Brothers, 1905), 329.

37. Hartley Coleridge, qtd. in Dowden, *Shakspere,* 330. Bloom, *Shakespeare,* 317. A. C. Bradley, "The Rejection of Falstaff," *Fortnightly Review* 77 (May 1902): 849.

38. This reversal is of a piece with what seems to be the governing principle of Falstaff's characterization in *The Merry Wives;* for if the play was indeed designed as a showcase for Falstaff, it seems to have been conceived in a spirit of contradiction, as the very forces that provided the basis of Falstaff's power in the history plays are now mobilized against him. There he invoked material, physical life as the the ultimate reality and *summum bonum.* Honor, he declared, was worthless, because it was a mere "word," that could not "set to a

leg . . . or an arm . . . Or take away the grief of a wound" (*Henry IV, Part 1*, 5.1.127–39). In Windsor, he is confronted with the material world he opposed to the pieties of history and made to suffer a series of punishments that are all physical.

39. Valerie Traub, *Desire and Anxiety: Circulations of Sexuality in Shakespearean Drama* (London: Routledge, 1992), 50–70; Phyllis Rackin, "Historical Difference/Sexual Difference," in *Privileging Gender in Early Modern Britain,* ed. J. Brink (Kirksville, MO: Sixteenth Century Journal Publishers, 1992), 37–63 .

Artificial Couples:
The Apprehensive Household
in Dutch Pendants and *Othello*

Harry Berger, Jr.

> Whatever made us think of marriage as closure . . . ?
> The family is a place of passion.
> —Catherine Belsey, *Shakespeare and the Loss of Eden*

THE THEATRICALIZATION OF RENAISSANCE culture has been endlessly discussed by commentators from Burckhardt to the present. This discourse took a major turn in the 1950s and 1960s when Erving Goffman and his followers developed theatrical models of social role enactment to explore "the presentation of self in everyday life." It took another major turn in 1980 with Stephen Greenblatt's activation of the term "self-fashioning." Although I have trouble with the conceptualizations of both Goffman and Greenblatt, their abiding value for me lies in their insistence on linking theatricalization to performance anxiety, and in the sensitivity, the persuasive power, the reflexive eloquence and wit, with which they stage their own interpretive performances and attendant anxieties.[1]

The link to performance anxiety is the subject of the present essay, but in recent years my understanding of theatricalization has been both modified and broadened. It has been modified by my encounter with Leeds Barroll's 1992 critique of New Historicist methodology in *Politics, Plague, and Shakespeare's Theater,* which I discuss below. It has been broadened by my encounter with the work of many scholars who, in recent decades, have expressly or tacitly extended the concept to the artificiality, and therefore the lability, the express performativity, of identities, genders, and social positions.

For me, the most important contributions are those that explore the lability and performativity produced by such tectonic changes of institutional structure as the emergence of new forms of state and family organization. In the three-part essay that follows, aspects of these developments will be viewed in the comparative context of the English monarchy and the Dutch Republic. The first part begins with an account of changing perspectives on the new roles and anxieties associated with the emergence of the nuclear family; it then shifts to an account of changing perspectives on the political roles and anxieties associated with the theater-state nexus. The second and third sections explore the dramatization of performance anxiety in examples drawn from two representational genres, examples of the depiction of marital relations in seventeenth-century Dutch pendants and in Shakespeare's *Othello*. My principle of selection is entirely illegitimate: these happen to be topics I'm currently working on. The challenge will be to see if I can bring them together in a way that lets them speak to each other without too much strain.

NUCLEAR WARFARE

"The dignity of marriage is . . . not based on the satisfaction accruing to the couple; rather it derives from the vital social function marriage fulfills in bringing kin groups together and in preserving peace among them." So David Herlihy and Christiane Klapisch-Zuber paraphrase the view stated in 1053 by Peter Damian in "De parentelae gradibus."[2] Expressly organized in terms of this rationale, "ancestor-focused patrilineage organized around agnatic lines of descent" became a kind of fellowship of males stretching backward and forward over time.[3] This doesn't mean that the social and economic value of women was insignificant. On the contrary, their importance to the alliance strategies of oligarchic or aristocratic lineages was acknowledged in the ritualization of finicky attention to the details of dotal arrangements and in constant attempts to refine or revise or simply circumvent inheritance law. In Renaissance Italy, the nuisance value both of existing female members of the lineage and of those newly inducted through marriage was cleverly defused by a convention in which the former were enlisted to socialize the latter.[4] Such practices were deployed to protect lineal investments in the marriage market because, from the standpoint of dotal strategies if not of personal sentiment, the wifely embodiments of the investments unfortunately had wills and desires and kinfolk of their own—properties that were often caricatured or scapegoated in literature and defended against in the admonitory genres of *cassone* and boudoir decoration.

Although controls of this sort involved moral exhortation, they were installed and practiced at the level of behavioral *technai*. Partly because they presupposed the resources and culture of the extended household, they were less available to the general run of householders in Reformation England and Holland and less adapted to the needs of a new model of domesticity protected by the moral sanction of the state religion. Of course the most striking difference was the difference in size: "The predominance of the nuclear family, a household shorn of a coresident older generation or coresident siblings and other relations of the married couple, had established itself in much of western Europe, certainly by the late sixteenth century."[5]

An obvious consequence of this development was the increase of social responsibility and moral authority accorded to the individual male householder: "During the sixteenth century [in England] . . . the phrase 'A man's house is his castle' became proverbial. . . . The state designated the individual household, in the absence of the old authoritarian church and of a national police, as the primary unit of social control. It identified the householder as responsible for the maintenance of moral order in his immediate sphere."[6] Lena Cowen Orlin's emphasis is on the householder in this passage, but she goes on to discuss at length the faultlines this shift of responsibility produced in all domestic roles and relations. The effect of this structural shift is that, as Catherine Belsey puts it, the nuclear family built on "the institution of permanent marriage . . . becomes quite explicitly an ideological apparatus" through which the state strives to organize, control, and maintain surveillance over its population.[7] In the same period the Reformation clergy—taking advantage of the disseminability of scriptural and priestly power made possible by printed Bibles—seized on "the ideal of the affective nuclear family" as "a new way of perfection" that would "replace the now discredited monastic celibacy. Family values became the object of intense propaganda, and of the anxiety that the reconstruction of any value system necessarily creates."[8]

We today, Belsey continues, "are the direct heirs" to this reconstruction and to the anxieties structurally built into it—anxieties partly fueled by the specious "proposition that there is only one proper ['natural'] way to arrange our sexual relations."[9] In the "absolutist" or medieval model, conjugal love was not an article in the constitution of dynastic marriage, which served primarily as the motor of patrilineal/agnatic continuity. The shift to the nuclear family model introduced conjugal love into the equation. It also involved a change in which the position of woman/wife/mother as a kind of *secunda inter pares* became formally and structurally (if not actually) central.[10] "Part of the project of the early modern romance of marriage," therefore, was "to bring desire in from the cold: to moralize and domesticate a destabilizing passion, confining it within the safety of the loving family. Dynastic marriage must have been an anxious business, especially with so many adulterous love stories in circulation idealizing unfaithfulness."[11]

Although there has never been sexual equality in any regime, the inequality of women to men and of wives to husbands becomes more conspicuous and thus more problematic in a model that promises or demands a measure of equality because it makes the reciprocity of desire, affection, and romantic love normative. In this "liberal-humanist" version of marriage women are represented as "autonomous subjects freely exercising their power to choose a husband"—an exercise putatively conducted "on the basis of romantic love"—"and becoming partners in the affective family." But, Belsey styptically continues, the plays and the domestic conduct books of the Restoration period show "women as free to choose to the extent that they are free to acquiesce," and the price they pay for the apparent upgrading of their position in the family "is their exclusion from the political," since, after 1660, "the family progressively becomes a privileged private realm of retreat from a public world increasingly experienced as hostile and alien."[12]

They are not, however, excluded from the male imaginary. For it seems that only when desire in the guise of romantic love was co-opted as the affective guarantor of family values, only when the state designated and registered the individual male householder as a local site of its authority, only when women were formally allocated their proper place and unequal rights "in the bosom of the family"—only then were they structurally placed in the position to function in cultural fantasy as "dangerous familiars." Belsey thus sees "a direct connection between the emergence of family values and the increasing perception of the loving family as a place of danger."[13]

Such ironies of structural change were not restricted to northwest Europe. In her landmark essay on early modern Italian family portraits by Van Dyck and others, Diane Owens Hughes confronts Philippe Ariès's argument that while the links between the conjugal family and the lineage were weakening, "a new structure of authority" emerged "within the reduced family, as husbands seized authority to become domestic monarchs."[14] For Hughes the situation is more complicated than Ariès represents it. On the one hand, she deduces from the Genoese family portraits she examines that the positive ways in which women were represented did not reflect a new access to power by wives in more nucleated forms of domesticity but were, on the contrary, a compensatory response to "a steady erosion of their right to an equal share in the family [i.e., lineal] estate." On the other hand, she finds "hints in the paintings of the seventeenth and eighteenth centuries not only that the domestic world was a creation of women, but also that men may have viewed it as a threat to their former authority."[15]

The threat is familiar to historians of the Dutch Republic: "Customary male markers of patriarchal dynasticism, the residue of a feudal warrior ethos or the accumulation of a territorial estate all being less important in the Republic, the aura and status of a family household assumed correspondingly more significance. And within that household, it was the wife that was held responsible for the contentment or disarray of the domestic regime."[16] Lacking the internal resources furnished in the older system by

the elders and women of the lineage, the responsibility for policing the
new faultlines has to devolve onto extradomestic cultural agencies. Thus
in Holland, Jacob Cats's influential book on marriage, *Houwelyck* (1625),
was addressed to women and told them how to comport themselves
through the six stages of life (maiden, sweetheart, bride, housewife,
mother, widow), a sequence of roles defined in terms of their relations
and responsibilities to men, family, and household. Behind the injunctions
of Cats and other Protestant moralists "lies more than pious moralizing
alone." Theirs was "a deep concern for the character of a couple's relationship that would be merely incidental if dynastic interests were . . .
[their] main concern."[17] But as Cats's rhetorical focus on women indicates, it was primarily women who needed to be policed, in part perhaps
because they "exercised enormous power within the home, with or without their husband's consent. Their authority was reinforced by legal protections that greatly exceeded those accorded women outside the Dutch
Republic."[18] Commenting on the stereotype of the "obedient Dutchman,
who allowed himself to be ruled by his wife," A. Th. van Deursen
remarks that Cats offered his work "as a corrective for both spouses, but
especially [for] wives."[19]

The power women exerted *with* their husbands' wholehearted consent
was noticed in 1673 by Sir William Temple, who wrote that whether it
was owing to the dullness of the air in the United Provinces or that of the
inhabitants' "Appetites and Passions," their "Married Women" were reliable household managers. They were trusted with "the whole care and
absolute management of all their Domestick," and they justified that
trust.[20] Other observers devote less attention to a woman's powers of hus-
bandry than to her worrisome ability to influence the selection of a husband.[21]

Cats's awareness of and approach to this problem have been characterized by Agnes Sneller as those of the worried male strategist. For example,
in one of the narratives in his *Touchstone of the Wedding Ring* the "action
seems to be originated by Hipparchia" and in the end "she gets what she
wants, for she can marry the man of her choice."[22] Nevertheless, her ritual-
ized assertions of acceptance reestablish her subservience: "The headstrong
female . . . is no longer there. The strong young woman will disappear as
soon as the marriage takes place." Her independence "only meant that she
was allowed to choose . . . to whom she should become subordinate." So
Cats's moral is not only that the wife "will be the servant of her husband" but
also that "she herself is the one who formulates this as her wish."[23]

"To make the strong young woman disappear" expresses the reaction to
a fantasy of male impotence that is at the source of the anxiety and precau-
tion inscribed in the structure and routine of wed-lock. "Cats used the
authority of the Bible" to support the idea that "if women [are] inferior to

men," it is "not because men wanted it so, but because . . . it is women's own choice": "The moral attitude of women is shaped in such a way, that women themselves formulate their oppression . . . [by] men, especially their husbands, as the most desirable state of life."[24] Sneller's "deconstruction" (her term) of Cats shows how a classic defense mechanism drives his argument and rhetoric: men imagine what women desire and then displace these fantasies onto women as *their* fantasies and desires.[25]

Recent studies of Dutch genre painting and domestic ideology have explored this move with great sophistication. In the course of a stimulating study of gender and genre painting, Elizabeth Honig remarks of "the space that genre painting defines as 'domestic'" that it "is more intensely feminine than the home was in reality. . . . [T]he 'home' as pictured in Dutch art is—like the female body—an internal, enclosed entity, possessed by one man, whose precarious entrances must be protected against (other) male invasion, yet which, precisely because of this nature, provokes a desire to penetrate, to know that which is hidden within." Hence the question posed by "much Dutch painting": "Is the bourgeois woman failing to guard the purity of her sacrosanct world from male penetration as she invites the entrance of his gaze?" Genre painting thus "plays with the anxieties of its male beholders."[26]

English analogues of this kind of play have been brilliantly theorized and explored by Wendy Wall in *Staging Domesticity.* Wall reads domestic guides and manuals as male-authored fantasies "about fantasies devised by women"—for example, "an imagined moment when housewives, busy . . . [doing what they're supposed to be doing] mask their production of invisible delights." "Once housework is imagined as a site of fantasy," Wall asks, "might it not have unexpected resonances for a culture where domesticity provided the template for political order?"[27] And she goes on to argue that "the fear of a libidinal domestic space begins to speak to more than female sexuality in isolation."[28] Citing Elizabeth's 1561 proclamation aimed at institutionalizing "the divide between the cross-gendered world of domesticity and the scholarly world of men," Wall insists that it is "cross-gendered domestic life rather than sexuality *per se* that threatens the order of university students and faculty. . . . Elizabeth's order cordons off universities not from the influence of women, generally, but from the domestic practices of 'particular households.'"[29]

Similar suspicions have been entertained by students of Dutch culture about the disinterestedness or "realism" with which domestic interiors were depicted in genre paintings and family portraits. It isn't inconsequential that "nearly all paintings of domestic interiors were done by men."[30] In addition, the fictiveness of such items as fancy floors and tapestries, sequences of rooms *en enfilade,* and radiance that ignores—or, to put it more forcefully, that conspicuously excludes—the limitations of indoor illumination, have

often been noted.[31] "These striking illusions of a domestic actuality," Mariët Westermann observes, "can be highly tendentious" because they play
an "active role in echoing, reinforcing, and even shaping powerful ideals
of the family and its perfectly designed shelter."[32]

The foregoing discussion suggests that students of Dutch culture and
society during the Eighty Years' War—a period roughly coinciding with
the time span from the birth of Shakespeare to the death of Charles I—
draw conclusions from their data that strongly resemble those drawn by
students of Tudor-Stuart culture and society. Their conclusions may not
fully reflect the view of "the emergence of family values" Belsey finds in
Reformation England, that is, that it entails "the increasing perception
of the loving family as a place of danger."[33] But they are equally interested in the increasing perception of the family as a place of theater. In
presenting the sphere of domestic practices as a critical site of sociocul-
tural reorganization, Dutch historians emphasize the need for expressly
prescriptive curricula vitae (like those of Jacob Cats) to define or control institutional role performances. However, the political contexts in
which these parallel developments occur are superficially very different, and in the discussion that follows emphasis falls first on the obvious
differences between the English and Dutch states, and then on the less
obvious superficiality of that difference. For my point of entry, I turn to
the important revisionist account of historical methodology in which
Leeds Barroll challenges not merely the New-Historical picture of theater-state relations but also the procedures by which the picture was
produced.

One of the important accomplishments of Barroll's *Politics, Plague, and
Shakespeare's Theater* is its identification and critique of a narrative common to both old and new historicist ideologies. The narrative is itself a
second story built on an archival foundation, an "assemblage of favored
historical narratives" that have "overstated the power and significance of
Shakespeare and also of plays in general at the royal Stuart court."[34] Such
"traditional recensions" encourage the view that "the performance of
Shakespeare's works at court" expresses "a particular relationship in
which the Stuart crown desires to use drama for its own political purposes
to contain subversive forces attempting to employ the stage against the
interest of the state."[35] This view also overstates the power of the Crown,
an overstatement Barroll attributes in part to a theoretical misdescription
of the political context. The historicist narrative mistakenly "envisions
early Stuart society not as a state" but as an empire.[36] A state is a body
politic in which there is relative mobility of power between the crown and
such constituencies as "the peerage, Parliament, and the city guilds,"
while in an empire "the crown possesses all organized power" and uses it
primarily to control "the single large mass of the populace."[37]

The imperial misdescription of course goes back to the Tudor ideology of sacralized kingship reflected in the first book of homilies and paradigmatically expressed in the *Homily on Obedience,* which proclaims the principle of nonresistance in ringing tones. Among the familiar reasons why these fervid asseverations were reprinted eleven times between 1559 and 1595 are the recurrent threats of resistance motivated by the plague, crop failures, socioeconomic dislocations, and religious dissent: food riots, antienclosure riots, insurrections of artisans, the persistent threat to order posed by masterless men. During the second half of the sixteenth century these problems were coupled to a long-term drop in living standards and inflations in rent.

Barroll takes this environment into account in his rejoinder to the imperial, regiocentric, and theatrocentric character of the historicist narratives. He develops a darker picture of Shakespeare's and the theater's interlocking careers during the early Stuart period. The picture emphasizes the marginality of players, and, as a consequence, their vulnerability to the disruptive effects of the plague and inclement weather. Barroll's book manages, without straying from its theme, to hint persistently at an ulterior inclemency: the rain "that raineth every day" on the unprotected player is seldom the "gentle rain" of mercy; rather it tends to be the downpour of social, political, and economic contingencies that mark the statist climate—a climate in which the thunderstorms of power flash about in more labile and unpredictable patterns than those depicted by Barroll's historicist predecessors.

The effects of this climate on the Elizabethan theater and its players, and the reciprocal effect of theater on the climate of cultural politics, have subsequently been explored in greater detail by Meredith Skura and Louis Montrose respectively. In different ways, both Skura and Montrose also take up the complex of themes Barroll treats in more intellectual-historical terms in his earlier study, *Artificial Persons.*[38] Although Skura's study of the conditions of playing reflected in Shakespeare's texts doesn't mention *Politics, Plague, and Shakespeare's Theater,* it chimes with and reinforces Barroll's dark counternarrative in two ways: first, she extends the sources of anxiety to the quotidian uncertainties of the professional player's life; second, she shows how Shakespeare models the experiences and anxieties of characters on those of players, especially the anxiety of self-representation that "the dynamics of spectatorship" produces when it continuously subjects players to the fickleness of popular and aristocratic audiences.[39]

Montrose attends to the vicissitudes of players in *The Purpose of Playing,* but his emphasis falls on the surprisingly effective ideological power exercised by the institution of professional and commercial theater—a power it wielded in spite of its embattled status as an "unofficial and marginal site of performative authority" situated at "the unstable conjunction of patronage-based and market-based models of cultural production."[40] The new accent that distinguishes his critical revision of New-Historicist regiocentrism is an insistence on the "reciprocal" or "dialectical" relation between "formal innovation" in the theater and "social and ideological changes" in its cultural context.[41] During his sustained analysis of this reciprocity he picks out three overlapping striations of the theater's power.

First, the playhouse was "a new kind of social and cognitive space" because it was "a material realization of the *theatrum mundi* metaphor" (210). The express theatricality of Elizabethan drama had potentially profound implications "for the construction and manipulation of social rules and interpersonal relations," especially those involving "issues of causality and legitimacy, identity and agency" (104). Its metatheatrical power lay in the facility with which playwrights could use this quality to foreground the theatricality of the rest of the world—as when, for example, the playwright uses the conventions of the stage to boy the greatness of a queen.

Second, "the increasing concern of [Elizabethan] players and dramatists with individual characterization in the motivation of dramatic action" encouraged the "conceptual and practical development" of "the power of [dramatic] personation" (92–93). Montrose explores the consonance of this development with others grounded in "the emergence of capitalism and modernity in England," among them the interest of "the late Elizabethan sociopolitical and intellectual elites" in potentially seditious "Tacitean/Machiavellian views" of power, legitimacy, agency, and subjectivity (ibid.). As subjects of an early modern state, "Shakespeare, his company, and his audience . . . collaborated in producing . . . theatrical anatomies of the political processes to which they were subjected" (77–78). During the course of this collaboration they not only demonstrated "a serious concern with the 'problematics' of their own 'subjecthood'" (78) but also contributed to elite society's sharpened awareness of the role personation could play in identity formation.[42] A "theory of characterization" is, incidentally, the subject of Barroll's *Artificial Persons,* which centers on the search for a protocol that would elucidate the means by which, and the criteria in terms of which, Shakespeare and his contemporaries created the "artificial persons" of the drama.[43] Though Barroll and Montrose approach the development of personation in very different ways—one through historical psychology and intellectual history, the other through the analysis of cultural politics—neither considers it a free-floating aesthetic development. Both link its importance as an emergent cultural practice to its capacity for producing performance anxiety.

Third, the power of the "theatrical anatomies" Montrose mentions lay not "in the explicit advocacy of specific political positions but rather in the implicit but pervasive suggestion . . . that all such positions are relationally located and circumstantially shaped and that they are motivated by the passions and interests of their advocates" (105). He cites the worries famously expressed by Elizabeth and Essex and notes that since "the performativity of power is a mystery of state, . . . the prospect of losing control over one's self-presentation arouses palpable alarm" (82) in those who are privileged or forced to be the observed of all observers. For to assert "theatricality as a universal condition of social life" ("All the world's a stage") while performing the "'absolutist theatricality' of the state . . . in the public and professional playhouse" is to expose even the "royal actor" and the theater state to the perils of "appropriation and destabilization" (210). Implicit in Montrose's narrative is the idea that the process of theatricalization operating across several discursive areas contributed to a sharper perception of the artificiality linking individual identities ("persons") to sociopolitical positions. The perception was sharpened even more by the reforms in schooling introduced early in the sixteenth century when Colet, with the help of Erasmus and others, promoted the study of grammar, rhetoric, and translation as the instruments by which their pupils could master the ethical skills of mimesis.

I call these skills "ethical" in a specific sense. The term is normally used to mean something like "moral," "virtuous," "principled," and so on. But "ethical" and "ethics" ultimately derive from the Greek word *ēthos,* which had a range of meanings that include custom, usage, character, disposition, bearing, manner. Aristotle uses *ēthos* in the *Poetics* to designate characters in drama and their moral quality as inferred or constructed by audiences. When a playwright (Aeschylus, Sophocles, Euripides) borrows a character from epic or other sources and remodels it, in Aristotelian parlance he "imitates" that character, as does the actor who plays the role. Aristotle uses the term *ēthos* again in the *Rhetoric* to designate the "character" a speaker assumes—performs, or imitates—in order to persuade his audience of his moral authority. The peculiar consequence of this overlapping usage has been articulated with great force by Keir Elam, who makes the important point that in both cases moral character is depicted as an effect rather than as the cause of dramatic or rhetorical speech—as the product of art rather than nature. And in both cases, an act of personation, that is, the production of a convincing "character," is treated as the fictive effect of a performance and closely identified with acts of imitation.[44]

During the sixteenth century, when the classical rhetorical tradition was assimilated into humanist pedagogy, this Aristotelian association of ethos with mimesis dominated the rationale of the grammar school curriculum in England. The effects of assimilation, along with Shakespeare's critique of them, have been trenchantly analyzed in a brilliant new study by Lynn Enterline, who argues that humanist schooling gave the practice of rhetorical imitation a performative or theatrical edge, thereby insuring that rhetoric and subjectivity or character would remain intimately intertwined. Erasmus and other humanists founded their pedagogical programs on the premise that learning by imitation was superior to the medieval method of learning by rule. They argued that one best cultivated one's own voice and manners by taking a detour through the voices and manners of others. Because the humanist schoolmasters based their curricula on this premise, the theory and practice of rhetorical imitation in the grammar school implicitly endorsed a view of subjectivity as something that is produced, and then refined, through its symbolic relations with others.[45]

At the same time, the all-male grammar school installed in its curriculum a culturally significant engendering of the difference between a Latin "father" tongue and an English "mother" tongue. Enterline is among a handful of scholars who, in recent years, have questioned the hypothesis about the bracing effects on masculine identity formation of Latin language study as a rite of passage into manhood—a hypothesis first put forth by Walter Ong in 1959, restated with pseudo-Lacanian variations by William Kerrigan in 1980, and accepted by Bruce R. Smith in 1991.[46] This accords with a longstanding conventional view of the work done by humanist pedagogy, with its "fidelity to the ancients and to the principles exemplified in classical literature," a veneration that was "essentially conservative" and androcentric in its injunctions to imitate the *mos maiores*.[47] In Kerrigan's words, "Latin was the gift of a severe, if ultimately forthcoming, father. It was an initiation into the mysteries of his ways, and the ardors of . . . imitation . . . finally yielded to possession. . . . Veneration was rewarded by a new and male articulation of the ego."[48] This opinion, oddly hoisted up the flagpole of Lacanian theory, was easy to demystify when scholars looked more closely at the pedagogical scene of such mimetic ardors and at the archival accounts of or by the humanist masters who supposedly stood in as models of patriarchal authority.

The revised story generated from the more context-sensitive standpoint of queer theory is that in the theater of pedagogy the performance of masculine ethos is learned through an art of personation, a disciplinary practice that works at cross-purposes because its latent effect is to introject as its boundary condition the gynephobia of gender, or castration anxiety— that is, fear of the woman within the man.[49] As Alan Stewart puts it, "the value of the educational experience of a young man as a rite of passage or an act of institution—the making of the man—is fundamentally threatened by that experience itself." Stewart supports this generalization with the following example: "The 'breeching' of a boy was not only the entry into his education, but also his institution as a man. . . . For this major psychological event . . . to be temporarily reversed by the schoolmaster in a new form of breeching, to expose the boy for beating, can therefore be seen as a radical form of 'unmanning.'"[50]

This brief survey of studies by Barroll, Skura, Montrose, and Enterline indicates that in addition to their diverse critical projects they share a common concern. Their inquiries into the problems and effects of "personation" as an emergent theatrical practice in early modern England have illuminated the part it plays in the more general theatricalization of the Renaissance hypothesized from Burckhardt on. But I haven't yet made it clear how they help us cross the channel from one polity and culture to the other, and in order to do this I want to return to Barroll's distinction between empire and state. The historicist misdescription he criticizes—that the English Crown "possesses all organized [and organizing] power"—was obviously a cardinal tenet of royalist ideology in its struggles with the church and Parliament. This interpretation was recognized as "contentious" early in the sixteenth century; that it continued to be upheld was in part symptomatic of the opposing pressures of and toward limited decentralization exerted throughout this century and into the next—the establishment, for example, of provincial councils manifestly set up to increase the power of the Crown but latently empowering the upholders of local and regional interests.[51]

In *The Purpose of Playing,* Montrose gives several brief but finely nuanced accounts of the conflicts of interest over the status of plays and players among aristocratic patrons, merchants, the clergy, the city authorities, and the Privy Council. Structured by his attention to the dialectical interplay between "patronage-based" and "market-based" forces, these accounts elucidate the complex micropolitical negotiations necessary to keep things going behind the ceremonial facades of the Two-Body constitution. Although such conflicts are peculiar to London, they are dense and condensed versions that display *in parvo* the consequences of the mobility of power characteristic of states rather than empires. More recently, Montrose has refined his analysis of Elizabethan micropolitics in a manner that further accentuates the tension between imperial or royalist ideology and statist reality.[52] The analysis generates an odd thought in the febrile brain of someone who has been reading Dutch history. It is as if the tissue of "ideological instability and contradiction" (*The Purpose of Playing,* xii) by which the centralized Tudor state was sustained resembles nothing so much as that decentralized Rube Goldberg contraption, that wonderfully elastic and disorderly and successful system of checks and unbalances, that repressed bad dream of constitutional monarchy, the Dutch Republic.

This is only my fantasy. Nevertheless, the idea that Elizabeth I may not have been insensitive to the subterranean resemblance has been broached in a debate among historians about her part in the Anglo-Dutch fiasco of 1585–87. Some have claimed that England's disastrous adventure was all Leicester's fault. Their view was, in my opinion, decisively contravened by Charles Wilson, who redirected attention to flaws in the Queen's policy, flaws he attributes to the "[o]bstinate, obsessive conservatism" that was "the key to her attitude to the Netherlands."[53] This attitude was partly fueled by snobbery. Like many of her courtiers and subjects, she both wondered and puckered at the phenomenon of an urban patriciate whose members, throughout most of the sixteenth century, were fishers of herring, brewers of beer, makers of cheese, and traders of salt. She sneered at them as upstart merchants, and English contempt for the Dutch was pithily expressed in 1586 by someone in the Earl of Leicester's entourage, who called the regents "'Sovereign Lords Millers and Cheesemen. . . . ' The jibe was supercilious but near the knuckle: this contempt for a meritocracy of tradesmen always hardening into an oligarchy, an oligarchy based not on the nation or even the region but on the individual town—this contempt lay at the root of the hesitation, anxiety and repulsion that Elizabeth, Burghley, Leicester and others felt towards any equal alliance with the northern rebels."[54] But the final word of this passage reminds us that Elizabeth's snobbery coexisted with another reaction, one that was more troubling because of its resonances with homebred evil: "The Netherlanders were first and foremost rebels. Elizabeth Tudor was heir to an England still deeply divided. She was no less heir to that traumatic horror of civil war and rebellion which was the legacy of the Wars of the Roses. . . . If the rebels were heretics too, that only made it worse."[55] The conspicuous decentralization of the Dutch Republic together with the mobility of its social order may have presented a caricature of disorders that threatened Elizabeth's realm, but they nevertheless spoke to ever-present dangers and sources of anxiety. The response in both cases was structurally parallel. It consisted of meeting the threat of uncontrolled decentralization with strategies of controlled decentralization.

Decentralization is both horizontal and vertical. It is horizontal in the sense that power is shared or divided among several spatially as well as politically related entities: the Orangist court and the Provinces, the English monarchy and the provincial councils. It is vertical in that power devolves or is, so to speak, delegated from higher to lower forms of jurisdiction, from the church or state to the parish and household. The pressures confronted by the putatively centralized monarchy may differ from those confronted by the decentralized republic, but they produce the same effect in both contexts: both cultures acknowledge the political importance of domestic ethos. In both, the nuclear family came to be viewed as the object of acts of collective personation and the household was its stage.

Among the genres of Dutch portraiture, the structural tensions that beset "the cross-gendered world of domesticity" discussed by Wendy Wall are most strikingly and consistently manifested by the poses of wives and husbands in the paired marriage portraits called pendants. In the following parts I explore different representations and inflections of the family as "a place of danger" in Dutch pendants and Shakespeare's *Othello*. We'll see that pendants give us an essentially comedic view of spousal competition while in *Othello* the representation of Emilia and Iago leads us into its darker corners. My emphasis will fall on the wife's performance in pendants but on the husband's anxiety in *Othello*.

Women with Elbows: Offsetting Personation[s] in Some Seventeenth-Century Dutch Pendants

Middle-class women exercised enormous power within the home, with or without their husband's consent. Their authority was reinforced by legal protections that greatly exceeded those accorded women outside the Dutch Republic. . . . Both women and children in seventeenth-century Holland were viewed by foreigners as "overly outspoken and independent."[56]

Simple and restrained as pair portraits [pendants] tend to be, each one reflects choices of pose, gesture, format, and setting that tie the pendants to the viewer and to one another in ways that often differ significantly from other, seemingly similar works. . . . Not only do paired portraits of husbands and wives implicitly relate to the larger theme of marriage, but the contrasts between the sitters often help to define further the character of each. The imagined interplay of two personalities and, on a broader plane, the dialectic of masculinity and femininity itself play a crucial role in the meaning of the companion piece.[57]

The two portraits reproduced in figures 1 and 2 belong together because they represent a married couple. Dated 1641 (his) and 1640 (hers), they were painted by the Haarlem portraitist, Johannes Verspronck. Such coupled images are called pendants and are related to but different from another genre, the single-pair portrait, in which the two sitters are depicted within a single frame. In pendants, which were very popular in seventeenth-century Holland, a limited repertory of poses or pose conventions reflects—reasserts, rather—the assumptions, laws, and interests of gender, class or rank, and status:

The paintings would have faced one another, perhaps on either side of a chimneypiece. Almost invariably, the woman's portrait would hang at right, the man's at left. From the perspective of the sitters, this convention placed the woman on the man's *sinister* (left-hand) or lesser side, according to theological and social formulas which valued the *dexter* (right-hand) position more highly. This rule conformed to seventeenth-century Dutch views of marriage as a partnership based on mutual affection but steered by the man.[58]

The repertory of poses gains or maintains its authority by being constantly repeated, albeit with variations. Sitters, painters, and images imitate prior sitters, painters, and images, and this sameness, this redundancy, by itself reinforces the genre's power of political correctness. These may be trite observations, but they take on special meaning when applied to the portrait genre of pendants. The word *pendant,* whatever its actual etymology, suggests that the ideal relation between any pair of figures is achieved when each figure is shown to depend on and lean toward the other. The

Figure 2. Johannes Verspronck, Portrait of a Woman, 1640. Oil on canvas, 81.3 x 66 cm. Rijksmuseum Twenthe, Enschede.

Figure 1. Johannes Verspronck, Portrait of a Man, 1641. Oil on canvas, 81.3 x 66 cm. Rijksmuseum Twenthe, Enschede.

space between the frames is part of this relation: a marker of separateness, of relative independence, of confinement, but also (as we'll see) the marker of a site of public scrutiny, of exposure, and therefore of vulnerability; a reminder that the two sitters are never merely a dyad. The space marks the interruption of each partner's turn toward the other as both their bodies follow faces that rotate out toward the indispensable third party, the observer who completes—and who disrupts—their symmetrical acts of self-presentation.

Whether in public or private installations, pendants on display create behind and around themselves a mural area that represents the domestic setting in which the images first hung and their subjects lived. It is as if they carry a section of the original household interior with them wherever they wander—and so long as they aren't separated. Since the portraits are separate they're separable, and this means their future is uncertain. Many pendant pairs end up divorced, in different domiciles of display. No wonder the occasional sitter looks a little tense.

Pendants generally, and generically, advertise two things: harmonious domestic life and comfortable social standing. Once again, the force of this advertisement is amplified by the sameness manifested at two levels: first, the family resemblances among all pendants that constitute them as a genre, and, second, those between the partners in the individual pair of pendants. Redundancy produces ideological and rhetorical reinforcement, broadcasting a consistent message about *burgerlijk* style and virtues. The great majority of sitters wear roughly the same clothes and strike roughly similar poses. In any pair, for example, both partners turn inward toward the center and toward each other, with the outer arm (his right, her left) closer to the observer than the inner arm. In spite of variations and different angles of pose their figures tend to mirror one other.

Obviously, not every sitter wears only white on black. When you draw closer, you find aggressive emulations as well as deferential imitations, and you also find variations and attempts at novelty—new inventions, new departures—by sitters and painters alike. Nevertheless, these only testify to the *need* for difference in the face of the repetitiveness imposed by a relatively restricted code of class self-definition. Predictably, an important feature of the code is the failure of pendants to advertise the harmony and well-being of married life under the rule of equal rights. The husband's dominance is marked not only by position but also by size and proximity: in addition to occupying the right side, his body tends either to be larger or else to be closer to the picture plane. It may project more aggressively than hers toward the observer, as when Verspronck's husband thrusts an elbow through the picture plane. Sometimes, when his relation to the observer is more oblique and hers more frontal, he may appear to be presenting her as his prize and pride. A coyly muffled or restrained version of this gesture is often produced by the mere direction of the husband's hand, which may seem to point toward his partner while actually being used to hold a glove or hat. By such means the painter presents him as mediator between his wife and the world. Her part is graciously—and gratefully—to acknowledge her place and, in effect, to all but curtsy. If the pair's symmetrically mirroring poses express domestic harmony, they also express the normative difference between the authority he gets from his role as male spouse and the obeisance, the obedience, inscribed in the role she's expected to perform. He claims responsibility for the domestic harmony he bought and supervises; she maintains it, exercising a separate role within whatever he claims for himself.

These comments apply to the majority of examples in what Mariët Westermann calls "a voluminous genre, which did not change significantly over the first three quarters of the 17th century." She describes pendants as the portrait painter's "bread and butter," and she uses the Verspronck pendants reproduced in figures 1 and 2 to exemplify the standard emphasis on the way "the man's active stance and the woman's physical reticence" contribute to "the harmonious balance of their union" as the partners produce an impression of "effortless concord by conforming to their preferred roles."[59]

Westermann's is a good translation of the visual signs that reinforce the domestic ideology. But traces of resistance to "effortless concord" begin to make themselves felt as soon as you notice the effect produced both on the relation of the figures and on the positioning of the observer by a phenomenon these sitters share with many others: exotropy, or walleyedness. The man's right eye wanders toward his right, the woman's left eye toward her left. In her case this reinforces an effect already produced by the turn of her head and body: she seems to be viewing the observer over her shoulder, and the shoulder itself, resplendent in its layered collars, demands your attention. If the husband's aggressive elbow keeps you centered—prevents you from following his wandering eye to your left—her stance pulls you to the right, away from him. And something vaguer but more interesting happens when you try to read the ensemble of her facial expression and bodily gesture. The ensemble delivers an impertinently pertinent message about the wifely prerogative: "It's not my role to talk. Therefore, although I have something to say, I won't say a word." Notice also how the background lighting increases the projective or aggressive thrust of his body, while she is drawn by the lower intensity of ambient lighting into the shadows as a more withheld, I'd even say more mysterious, figure. His pose is contorted and affected by its concentration on the performing elbow and seems even more affected and strained in the neighborhood of her quietly self-assured composure.

The elbow is a famous bone (or joint) of contention. In her fine and funny essay on "The Renaissance Elbow," Joaneath Spicer explains that the arm akimbo came close "to achieving the status of a national attribute" in the Dutch Republic, where it adorned the poses of countless members of the regent class, "who managed so successfully to inform the values of seventeenth-century Holland."[60] Like the sword, the codpiece, and the plume, the Renaissance elbow is a symptom of the dis-ease, the anxiety, the representational pathology of status and gender, especially in the members of a nonmilitary, nonaristocratic, lately arrived class like the regents. From an array of male sitters in the different portrait genres, one could easily assemble a manual of elbows whose function would nicely reinforce or supplement that of a manual of arms.

Verspronck predictably equips his male sitter with the mark of manliness, but it takes a Rembrandt to imagine women with elbows. Figures 3 and 4 are his 1634 portraits of a Calvinist preacher and his wife. Both place their right hands on their chair arms and their left hands on their bodies. Her hand rests on her bodice with fingers closed or loosely cupped but positionally it follows his and points across the divide toward his manual profession of faith or avowal. David Smith notes that the angle of the chair forces the male sitter to turn his head more sharply to face the viewer, lending the image "a slightly restless angularity, a theme . . . also picked up in the clutter of books on his desk."[61] To this I add that the same details register a touch of impatience with the work of posing that takes the scholar away from his research.

They might also register something else. The preacher's chair is angled toward his wife in a manner that conforms to a conventional feature of the genre: the husband mediates between his wife and the world as her presenter. This places him closer to the picture plane. But here the convention is invoked only to be violated. Although his hand with its fingers spread apart may signify marital or religious faithfulness, it is also a gesture of emphatic self-identification. And even as he leans more toward her than she does toward him, his leaning becomes assimilated to the self-identifying gesture, which is secured by the way his compact and defended form coils tensely about itself. Because his gaze is slightly diffused rather than direct—one eye wanders leftward—he begins to appear self-consciously dutiful. I don't mean he looks like a dutiful husband, though. I mean he looks like someone dutifully holding a pose.

The accent in this pair of pendants is mainly on him. His space is so busy with the signs of his calling that it makes hers by contrast seem vacant. They pose in separate rooms, yet, although she is excluded from his work space, everything in her pendant slips downward and leftward toward him and reinforces the visual crossing that reaches its climax in his expressive hand. Similarly, the folds of her gown flowing loosely down

Figure 3. Rembrandt, Portrait of Rev. Johannes Elison, 1634. Oil on canvas, 174.0 x 124.5 cm. Photograph ©2004 Museum of Fine Arts, Boston.

Figure 4. Rembrandt, Portrait of Mevr. Johannes Elison, Maria Bockenolle, 1634. Oil on canvas, 174.9 x 124.1 cm. Photograph © 2004 Museum of Fine Arts, Boston.

and fanning out indicate that her knees and lower body are positioned closer to his pendant than her head and upper body. So far, then, the signifiers of male dominance seem to be doing their conventional Thing, and she, at first glance, is predictably both cooperative and deferential. More frontal and open, calmer and less dynamic, her figure sits farther back, an effect enhanced by the broadbrimmed hat that shadows her eyes.

Nevertheless, the very openness and frontality of her pose contribute to a countermovement that subversively resists her subordinate role. The resistance centers on the subdued but noticeable contrapposto produced by the tilt and shading of her collar, which accentuates the turn of her upper body away from him and toward the observer. This conflicts with the angle of a chair that seems to have been aimed in his direction, in accordance with the standard scenario of mirroring poses. She now appears awkwardly positioned in the chair, as if she had departed from the standard plan in order to stake a claim to equal rights and compete with her husband for the observer's attention. Of the supporting props, the use of the curtain is the most important contributor to this seditious effect: the curtain framing him and looping over the books directs attention not only to them but also toward her. The echoing direction of her curtain, drawn aside as if to display her, completes that movement. My sense of the sitter builds on Smith's comment that the play of horizontals culminating in the hat works "to turn passivity into deep, quiet stability. The shadow cast over her eyes by . . . the hat and her calm enigmatic smile suggest that the outward conventionality of her pose veils inner resources of strength and will. Rembrandt may even have wanted to suggest that she was the stronger of the two."[62] Her hat, which is essentially a man's hat, contributes to this effect. She is one of a very few women in pendants and pair portraits who wears one (Rubens's wife is the only other example I know).[63]

In 1641, Rembrandt produced his intricate and haunting pendants of Nicolaes van Bambeeck and Agatha Bas (figures 5 and 6), pendants famous for the illusionistic trick produced by the painted ebony frames beyond which both sitters project (her thumb and fan, his right elbow). Simon Schama's sensitive reading of these pendants takes into account the fact that van Bambeeck's social standing was inferior to that of his wife's family, and that this "made the concern to balance display and reticence within the portraits of the married couple an even trickier calculation than usual. The husband had to appear the authority figure, but Agatha Bas's illustrious pedigree made it imperative that she should show off the splendor of her fortune and rank, yet without going beyond the bounds of wifely duty."[64] Having noted this, Schama goes on to describe the subtle devices by which Rembrandt visualizes the harmonious interaction between husband and wife:

Figure 6. Rembrandt, Portrait of Agatha Bas, 1641. Oil on canvas, 104 x 82 cm. London, Buckingham Palace, The Royal Collection © 2005, Her Majesty Queen Elizabeth II.

Figure 5. Rembrandt. Portrait of Nicolaes van Bambeeck, 1641. Oil on canvas, 105.5 x 84 cm. Musées Royaux des Beaux-Art de Belgique, Brussels. Photo Speltdoorn.

[T]he fact that van Bambeeck stands within the framed space but still in front of another wooden door behind him gives a sense, simultaneously, that he is both master of his house and yet hospitably approachable. . . . His wife's portrait . . . retains this strong sense of a figure both inside and outside the domestic space. . . . Both her hands, like those of her husband, protrude through the frame, and they too carry simultaneous messages of modesty and show.[65]

It's true that the vectors drawing the eye from the viewer's left toward the right, from the husband toward the wife, accentuate a conventional pattern in pendants: he is turned toward her more than she toward him to signify that he is the mediator and superior who presents his wife as his property, and who claims the credit for the splendor in which she's attired. Even though she is placed higher in her frame than he in his, suggesting that he is either seated or shorter, the formal triangle that has its base in her head and fan converges on his head and thus maintains at least his compositional primacy. Schama's benign emphasis on analogy and complementarity nevertheless underplays another set of effects that accord equally well with the logic of the social disparity he reports. For the harmony he ascribes to the couple is no sooner registered than it's challenged.

Look first at the significant difference in the rendering of detail. On the one hand, his arms and hands encircle a deeply shadowed area. You may be inclined to peer into the shadow but since you can't make anything out you keep your distance—especially because of the stiff manner in which he looks you off and fences himself in while demanding your respect. She, on the other hand, more directly and even invitingly engages the viewer with her unfolded fan, giving herself to be seen and watching herself being watched. David Smith comments on the ambivalence with which she leans against the frame as if "buttressing herself from the audience" while at the same time she extends the fan in a quietly discreet and delicately understated but still obvious gesture of "feminine appeal."[66] He seems closer to the viewer than she is but her presence is more tangible.[67] The finely painted and textured surfaces of her fan, bodice, sleeves, and collar may at first give off an effect of armor, but they pull the viewer in close to admire the detail, which means to admire both the painter's skill and the sitter's sartorial panache. She seems on the verge of stepping into the observer's space and threatens to monopolize your gaze, and when you become aware of this and look back toward him, he too starts to edge nervously forward and push his nose through the picture plane. His pose modulates into a more intense and tight-lipped effort to reclaim priority of place. The contrast further accentuates the oddest feature of his pose. The hand that tightly holds the glove is a discernible feint toward the conventional gesture of presentation. But because the glove points stubbornly downward and his other arm and hand swing around to obstruct the presentational path, the gesture—like the sitter—seems blocked, as if he can't quite force himself to display the courtesy he knows he's expected to perform. Maybe this is why the pendants have separated. He now languishes in Brussels, while she's appropriately domiciled in Buckingham Palace.

Sitters wouldn't be satisfied if their poses were carbon copies of the pendants already in their neighbors' houses. Painters can add this motive to their own desire to overgo their peers and predecessors. No doubt, the differences within sameness only reassert and multiply the power of generic conventions to produce new examples of the old genre. This holds true of all forms of production, but within the pendant genre the play of antithetical forces resonates with special intensity. More often than not, pendants register the pull between the two sitters' positional reciprocity and their performative competition. On the one hand, within the limits of a differentiated gender hierarchy, there is the scenario of cooperation in which husband and wife present themselves as companions, as company for each other. They also form a company in another sense: they're members of a legal and contractual partnership—a limited corporation. On the other hand, this companionate scenario opens up the possibility of resistance, difference, competition, challenge. It opens up the possibility that the wife will pose so as to perform resistance to her place, will pose so as to assert her presence and demand more attention from the observer, will lay a subversive claim to equal rights. She may, for example, insist on your undivided attention by turning her body and arranging her gestures in a manner you can't ignore. Every time she makes a claim for equal performative rights she challenges the terms of the marriage contract. The paired pendants may well have turned out to be more separable than the couples they represent, but the separability of the material images itself underlines a structural danger in their sitters' coupleness.

The foregoing comments on pendants may be viewed as just another application of the subversion-containment pattern, but this thought interests me less than another, which will serve to introduce the theme of castration more central to *Othello:* Bryan Wolf speculates that since painters normally worked at home they were in the feminized position of domestic workers, and he applies the premise with brilliant effect in several close readings of genre scenes.[68] I think of this speculation when I find myself wondering whether male painters of pendants may at some level have been motivated to take the wife's part. In the case of Shakespeare's domestic tragedy the roles assigned both wives, Desdemona and Emilia, reveal the author's sensitivity to the institutional effects of seriously divided spousal power. The division is exacerbated because *Othello* depicts a Venetian culture dominated by a misogynist discourse governing relations between men and women, fathers and daughters, wives and husbands, in and out of marriage. Both the kind of trouble Desdemona makes for Othello and Iago's tacit but real dependence on Emilia for the success of his project presuppose the institutional stabilization of wifely power. Since I've discussed Desdemona and Othello elsewhere, I'll focus on Emilia and Iago here.[69]

IAGO'S ELBOW

From the start Iago performs like a needy actor who hogs the *platea* (the downstage area) and continuously solicits the audience's admiration.[70] But which audience? Does he perform *like* an actor or *as* an actor? Brian Vickers misses the point by taking the direct address of Shakespearean villains personally and then getting huffy about it: Iago, he grumbles, thrusts his intentions on us, and this makes Vickers nervous because it "leads to an intimacy which we would willingly avoid, if we could. There is no one in the world whose confidence I would rather less share than Iago's."[71] But, first, the audience constituted by the soliloquy of a character preexists—and thus can't be identical to—any particular theater audience addressed by the actor who plays the character. Iago is not forcing himself on Vickers any more than on me. And second, I, for one, very much enjoy Iago's confidential nasties and can't get enough of them. I would be tickled to be a member of the ideal audience he addresses, and, in addressing, constructs—especially the audience at whom he beams his first soliloquy.

In 1.3, after Iago and Roderigo had heard Othello and Desdemona proclaim their love for each other in the presence of the assembled Duke and senators, the lovelorn Roderigo threatens to drown himself. This draws from Iago a series of contemptuous harangues spanning some sixty lines and filled with the clichés of misanthropic discourse. While trying to restore Roderigo's self-confidence and hope, he seems at the same time to take pleasure in rubbing Roderigo's unmanliness in his face and increasing the sense of impotence that binds him to his diabolical savior. Since the threat of suicide seems little more than a melodramatic whine, the energy and volume of Iago's swash are gratuitous. This he all but acknowledges just after Roderigo's exit, as he steps forward and delivers his first soliloquy:

> Thus do I ever make my fool my purse:
> For I mine own gained knowledge should profane
> If I would time expend with such a snipe
> But for my sport and profit: I hate the Moor
> And it is thought abroad, that 'twixt my sheets
> He's done my office; I know not if't be true,
> But I for mere suspicion in that kind

Will do as if for surety. He holds me well,
The better shall my purpose work on him
Cassio's a proper man: let me see now,
To get this place, and to make up my will
In double knavery. How? How? let's see:
After some time to abuse Othello's ear
That he is too familiar with his wife.
He hath a person and a smooth dispose
To be suspected, fram'd to make women false.
The Moor is of a free and open nature
That thinks men honest that but seem to be so,
And will as tenderly be led by th' nose
As asses are.
I have't, it is engender'd! Hell and night
Must bring this monstrous birth to the world's light.
(1.3.382–403)[72]

The opening word, "Thus," points back to the preceding eighty lines of dialogue with Roderigo, and the words that follow make Iago sound apologetic. He speaks as one who has been and still is performing before an audience that was present throughout the scene. This must be a discriminating audience, since he defends against the imagined charge that his man-of-the-world outburst (312–73) was sententious overkill, wasted on "such a snipe" as his only onstage auditor.

The suspicion that he performs for another and better audience than Roderigo carries back to the first sixty-five lines of 1.1, which also featured the temptation to rhetorical overkill. There, Iago monopolizes the conversation with blather about himself and with generous dollops of cynicism that seem excessive to Roderigo's interlocutory demands. He is clearly enchanted with the rhetoric of villainy, with a discourse whose basic theme is not that of the victim, as in Lear's "I am a man / More sinned against than sinning," but that of the villain, "I am a man / More sinning than sinned against." Something else, however, is going on in this performance. Iago is not only running the show but putting on a show, and since he treats Roderigo with a certain amount of impatience and disdain, you begin to wonder why he confides in him and what pleasure he gets in pushing him around. It isn't until the first soliloquy that we get some purchase on this question. Was it for Roderigo alone that Iago, in the first scene, pumped up his wickedness with the rhetorical verve of someone impersonating the stage villain?—

For when my outward action does demonstrate
The native act, and figure of my heart
In complement extern, 'tis not long after

But I will wear my heart upon my sleeve
For doves to peck at: I am not what I am.[73]
(1.1.60–64)

It is as if he has been using Roderigo not only as a factor in his revenge but also as a kind of stand-in or dummy against which to bounce a performance of the villain's discourse destined for an invisible gallery of discerning spectators, whom, from now on, I'll refer to as "supervisors," borrowing a term Iago himself uses later in the etymological sense of "onlookers," or, more accurately, spectators looking down from above.[74]

What Iago bestows on this audience in his first soliloquy is unexpected. It has nothing to do with motiveless malignancy. As A. D. Nuttall well expresses it, Iago "is not just motivated, like other people. Instead, he *decides* to be motivated."[75] The very arbitrariness of the decision puts his manliness and autonomy on parade even as it mischievously airs a possible threat to it in the suspicion of cuckoldry. He dares the imaginary audience to accuse him of defeating his "favor with an usurp'd beard" (341–42) and then proceeds to disarm the threat by converting the mere suspicion to a sufficient motive for revenge. With Roderigo alone among his onstage interlocutors, Iago had honestly flaunted his dishonesty, taking the calculated risk that he might at some point be exposed by the poor snipe. Now, in soliloquy, he appears to have staged this risk for the approval of the audience that could appreciate his intrepidity, his masterful control, and, above all, the suave dishonesty of his frank avowals to Roderigo. He represents himself as a plainspeaking, disenchanted, resentful, satirical rogue—a "me-firster" who "tells it as it is." But can this be any more honest as a confession of knavery than his pledge of friendship to Roderigo? Iago's audience is encouraged to giggle along with Iago at everyone's stupid persistence in enlisting him as a trusty mediator and pinning medals of honesty on his chest.

Such moves make you wonder whether Iago's self-disclosure to the supervisors is any more reliable, genuine, or disinterested than his self-disclosure to Roderigo. Suppose it is just another conspicuously dishonest pretense of honesty, which he puts on to remind the supervisors that they're dealing with a consummate actor, and villain. To be thought of as honest in Venice serves his purposes but may also be a little humiliating. He wants more respect, more appreciation, for the rogue he knows himself to be. Perhaps he's looking for an audience he can shock and awe in frontal assault; or an audience of superior wit and judgment capable of rewarding him with the applause and execration he deserves.

"I am not what I am": Iago protects his absence—his freedom—from the honest Iago that confines him in Venice by pretending he is like an actor on a stage (which, of course, he isn't), escaping to the *platea,* clinging parasitically to the fantasy that he performs his villainies before the imaginary gallery of supervisors whose hero is dishonest Iago. But if it is possible to be dishonestly honest in Venice, is it equally possible to be honestly dishonest in Iago's imaginary theater? In 1.1, he confides that he hates the Moor because Othello passed him over and gave Cassio the military office for which he himself is more qualified. In 1.3, he confides to the supervisors that he has disingenuously taken Roderigo into his confidence only for the "sport and profit" connected with his hatred of the Moor, who is rumored to have usurped his sexual office. Is the second confidence any less disingenuous than the first? Immediately after having suggested that so far as hatred and revenge are concerned the truth of the rumor is irrelevant—the mere fantasy "Will do, as if for surety"—he notes that he expects to succeed because Othello "holds him well."

This casual remark doesn't square with the story of being passed over for Cassio, and Othello's subsequent displays of confidence in Iago hardly substantiate the truth of the story.[76] Maybe, then, the story he tells Roderigo in 1.1 has the same doubtful status as the story of cuckoldry. If so, he leaves it up to the supervisors to make that determination. He doesn't tell them much more than he discloses to Roderigo about his villainy, and his teasing obfuscations tend to diminish the implied contrast between taking the poor snipe into his confidence and confiding in the supervisors.

Iago exults in the power of soliloquy. He delivers nine soliloquies in verse in addition to the two prose asides in act 2, scene 1.[77] Four occur before, and five after, the fateful disclosure in 3.3 that Cassio was the go-between who helped Othello woo Desdemona. The first four, which vary in length from sixteen to thirty-two lines, stand out as rhetorical performances because each follows and precedes passages of prose. The remaining five are shorter—they vary from thirteen to one and a half lines—and with one exception they are surrounded by verse, and thus not so clearly set off. They differ tonally from the first four in that they show him spinning his wheels: redundantly preparing new snares for an Othello already trapped, nervously keeping the supervisors up to date on his plans and progress. They are less consistently performative, less expansive, and more hurried, partly because Iago is trying hard to keep up with the different plots he has going, and partly because he gets interrupted by other characters (Cassio in three instances, Othello in two).

The soliloquies delivered before the disclosure in 3.3 are both more sustained and more conclusive. Three of them end scenes, four terminate in couplets, and all have more rhetorical juice and spirit in them than the last five. The speaker seems to be in performative heaven. He coaxes, cajoles, confides, confesses, gloats, and sneers. The soliloquy is his verbal elbow. Nevertheless, even if, following Nuttall, we choose not to attribute his often tortuous deployment of its rhetorical posture to "motiveless malignancy," his repeated references to his wickedness in the first four soliloquies still betray an apparently motiveless anxiety of self-representation. It is an anxiety that subsequent events justify, and of course the most significant of these events is the reference to something that happened before the play began, something that retroactively changes the complexion of all that preceded the reference. Iago's belated discovery of Cassio's role in the courtship casts a long and deep shadow over his tendency in previous scenes to strut his villainy. The discovery and Iago's response to it make it embarrassingly clear that of the four major characters, he was the only one who was out of the loop up to the moment of disclosure in 3.3, and that during the time he was out of the loop, he was playing the villain in the most outrageous and engaging manner.

This is one source of Iago's anxiety. There are two others, less melodramatic but more important because they are ongoing rather than punctual. The first is a function of what I call the redistribution of complicities. I've argued elsewhere that Iago doesn't merely do things *to* Desdemona and Othello; the things he does *to* them he does with their help. If this is true, it jeopardizes his autonomy as he construes and expresses it, for if what he does *to* them he also does *for* them, it follows that what they do *for* him they also do *to* him. What they do *to* him is reflected in the sequence of his soliloquies. In the first two, his worries about being cuckolded are so obviously off the wall that I find it hard to take them as personal complaints rather than as mimicry of the structure of suspicion and castration known in Venice as manhood. At this point, Iago isn't airing his own suspicion so much as making fun of the insecurity of Venetian males in general—the sexual and proprietary insecurity of husbands and fathers in a culture that promotes the distrust of wives and women.

Things change after the fateful disclosure in 3.3. Iago begins to question Othello about this shortly after Desdemona mentions it. By the time he leaves the stage some 150 lines later, Othello shows himself ready to supplant him by stepping up to the *platea* and batting out the first of *his* three soliloquies. But Iago now faces more than one competitor in this practice. Othello's soliloquy segues into the handkerchief episode that leaves Emilia standing alone on the *platea* armed with the power of soliloquy, with the handkerchief, and with knowledge of its meaning. The second source of Iago's anxiety is that he depends, and will continue to depend, more on Emilia's complicity than he knows. Her soliloquy introduces a new element that changes and complicates the representation of Iago's power during the second half of the play. Beginning with Emilia's handkerchief soliloquy, the remainder of this essay explores her wifely power and its implications.

Having just accompanied Desdemona onstage, where Othello, newly shaken by Iago's first campaign, stands muttering to himself, Emilia listens as Desdemona worriedly asks, "Are you not well?" and Othello complains of "a pain upon my forehead." She hears Desdemona respond to this portentously allusive remark by offering to "bind" his forehead with her handkerchief. She then hears Othello reject the offer with an ambiguous command, "Your napkin is too little. / Let it alone" ("it": his forehead or the handkerchief?). Finally, she watches as Desdemona drops the handkerchief, and after Othello escorts Desdemona offstage, she snatches it up with these words:

> I am glad I have found this napkin,
> This was her first remembrance from the Moor.
> My wayward husband hath a hundred times
> Wooed me to steal it, but she so loves the token
> —For he conjured her she should ever keep it—
> That she reserves it evermore about her
> To kiss and talk to. I'll have the work ta'en out
> And give't Iago: what he will do with it
> Heaven knows, not I,
> I nothing but to please his fantasy.
>
> (3.3.294–302)

This utterance continues the method of preposterous disclosure because—not for the last time—it tells us something that belatedly but drastically alters the meaning of the episode it follows.[78] (Information about the handkerchief could have been given before the episode occurred.) To hear that the handkerchief has special value as a keepsake is to realize that something momentous may have flown across the field of vision, no sooner glimpsed than gone. Desdemona has just chosen to interpret "Let it alone" as a command to drop what Othello had conjured her she should ever keep about her. She responds defiantly by taking him at his word. For one moment they flare up into a fury of mutual rejection.

Emilia's soliloquy has been characterized as thoughtless and mindless.[79] Yet she speaks as if she understands something important has just occurred, and also as if she feels a conflict between the token's value to Desdemona and Iago's importunate demands. He has either been after it for a longer period of time than seems plausible, or else her "a hundred times," like her subsequent "That which so often you did bid me steal" (3.3.313), is an exaggeration that registers his importunity.[80] During her final confession, she acknowledges that she noticed this and thought it was odd: "often, with a solemn earnestness / —More than indeed belonged to such a trifle— / He begged of me to steal't" (5.2.225–27). In her soliloquy she attributes this to his waywardness. But "wayward" is a term with a broad range of meanings (mischievous, wrongheaded, perverse, weird), and Emilia's usage is extenuative: her husband is a practical joker, a trickster, and although he's probably up to no good, she prefers to remain in the dark about his intentions. But she is also curious enough about the possible effect of those intentions to act as his accomplice not only by giving him the handkerchief but also by her willingness to keep Othello and Desdemona in the dark about its whereabouts.[81]

What sort of soliloquizing is this? Does it resemble Iago's in performative intention? Is it merely an informational aside? A voicing of her thought process as in the convention we now call a voice-over? Her proposal to have "the work ta'en out"—that is, copied—before giving it to Iago suggests a more complex function.[82] Why have it copied unless to return either the original or the copy to Desdemona? And why do that if not to hide the theft? Granted, she doesn't get around to copying it because at that moment Iago enters and in her effort both to please and to tease him, she dangles it before him. When he snatches it away she gives voice to the scruple behind her intention to have "this napkin" copied: "Poor lady, she'll run mad / When she shall lack it." His response, "Be not acknown on't, / I have use for it. Go, leave me" (3.3.321–23), is enough to overcome the scruple: she promptly, obediently, and wordlessly leaves the stage.

Pechter thinks that in passing the handkerchief to Iago Emilia "doesn't know what she is doing."[83] But of course she does. To answer the question asked at the beginning of the preceding paragraph, this kind of soliloquizing is a theatrical device for representing acts of ethical self-representation. It expresses a desire for an assurance the speaker can't give herself and needs others to confer on her: justification rather than judgment. She soliloquizes to get off the hook: "what he will do with it / Heaven knows, not I, / I nothing but to please his fantasy." In other words, she acknowledges that she doesn't want to know (that she wants not to know) what he'll do with it. But she has a suspicion. If she plans to have it copied so the theft or loss won't be noticed, that means she doesn't expect the handkerchief to be returned right away. The very phrase Pechter cites as evidence for his opinion, "I nothing, but to please his fantasy," enacts in its noticeably syncopated or stifled syntax the more complex discursive behavior Iago urges on Emilia twenty lines later: "Be not acknown on't."[84] Honigmann is more mindful of the tonal diffidence of Emilia's phrase: "Emilia . . . prefers not to ask too many questions, fearing to discover things as they really are."[85]

"Be not acknown on't": "Forget about it. Disremember it." Honigmann notes that this occurrence of "acknown" is "unique in Shakespeare," but its resonance is familiar. Both in form and meaning, the usage resembles Thomas More's in a passage of *The History of King Richard III* that deeply impressed the author of Shakespeare's *Richard III*. Describing the bad faith of London's citizens in acquiescing to Richard's seizure of the crown, More writes that "menne must sommetime for the manner sake not bee a knowen what they knowe."[86] Emilia's "Heaven knows, not I," marks her soliloquy as an example of this technique, the technique of ethical evasion Cavell calls "disowning knowledge." The soliloquy has illocutionary force as a speech act, an act of preemptive self-auscultation by which a speaker who undertakes morally dubious action positions herself in a manner that will minimize the effect of this undertaking on her self-respect. The awareness of collusion and of divided loyalties nevertheless vibrates uneasily in Emilia's utterance. She uses her words to soothe a ruffled conscience while in the scenes that follow she continues in the course of action that ruffles it, refusing to tell the beleaguered couple what she knows as she voyeuristically watches their relation disintegrate. "Where should I lose that handkerchief, Emilia? / I know not, madam" (3.4.23–24).[87]

But we know she knows. And we can follow the path the handkerchief takes down the Emilian trail marked by a chain of echoing signifiers:

3.3.300–301:   I'll have the work ta'en out
    And give't Iago.

3.3.326–27: I will in Cassio's lodging lose this napkin
    And let him find it.

3.3.437–42: Have you not sometimes seen a handkerchief
    Spotted with strawberries, in your wife's hand?
    . . . .
    . . . . such a handkerchief,
    I am sure it was your wife's, did I today
    See Cassio wipe his beard with.

3.4.179–91:

Cassio.   Take me this work out.
. . . .

Bianca.   Why, whose is it?

Cassio.   I know not neither, I found it in my chamber.
    I like the work well enough: ere it be demanded,
    As like enough it will, I'd have it copied.
    Take it, and do't, and leave me for this time.

4.1.147–54:

[Bianca to Cassio:]   I must take out the work! . . . I must take
    out the work? . . . I'll take out no work on't.

The Emilian trail is a series of recurrent echoes of the act that enabled Iago to secure the ocular proof Othello demanded, and of the silence that remains the necessary condition of his success. The most interesting of these is the hand-in-glove relation of Emilia's and Cassio's motives for having the work copied: hers, unstated, is to keep it from being missed; his is to have it copied because he assumes the original will sooner or later be missed and "demanded." Honigmann thinks Cassio "might be expected to recognize it" as Desdemona's.[88] What makes this thought compelling is that it highlights Cassio's diffidence: like Emilia, he in effect follows Iago's advice: "Be not acknown on't." The Emilian trail of silent complicities winds through this and the next Cassio-Bianca episode in 4.1, episodes that show Cassio at his worst. The chamberer in him comes out, and once again we wonder about Othello's taste in go-betweens and his sense of what would impress Desdemona. Cassio's hurried command to Bianca to take the handkerchief is part of his effort to get rid of her because he doesn't want Othello to see him "womaned" (3.4.192–94). Her spirited refusal to copy the work in 4.1 provides a parodic commentary on the more deeply infolded double rejection signified by Desdemona's dropping the handkerchief.

Emilia might well apply to herself and Iago what she heard the Clown say about Cassio: "To tell you where he lodges is to tell you where I lie" (3.4.8–9). On this point, Honigmann's reflections on Emilia are consistently enlightening. He thinks she "should have suspected her 'wayward husband,'" judges from her discussion with Desdemona and Iago in 4.2 that by then she probably did suspect him, and notes in support of this opinion her subsequent reference back to this scene at 5.2.188–89: "I think I smell't it, O villainy! / I thought so then." Acknowledging her complicity, Honigmann wonders how guilty she is "of acting as a passive accomplice in Iago's plot? The question arises when Desdemona asks 'Where should I lose that handkerchief, Emilia?' and she lies, 'I know not, madam' (3.4.23–4). Just four words, yet momentous in their implications. Had she not been afraid of Iago the truth might have come out and Iago's plot would have collapsed."[89]

There's a difference, however, between "fearing to discover things as they really are" and fearing Iago.[90] Honigmann's decision to focus on the latter throws too much away. It ignores Emilia's prolonged investment in the strategy of bad faith described above. It keeps us from appreciating the extent to which her refusal to enlighten Desdemona and Othello is a source of her power over Iago inasmuch as it ratifies and preserves his power over them. At the end of the play she belatedly exercises this power in the accusation that undoes Iago and leads to her death at his hands. But there is an earlier episode in which the power struggle between them flashes briefly into view. It occurs in 4.2, the scene that follows the embarrassing clash witnessed by Lodovico.

In this scene, Emilia seems as truly upset and perplexed by Othello's behavior as she is concerned about and protective of Desdemona. But the incompatibility between her loyalties to Iago and to Desdemona presses insistently up to the surface in her outburst against whomever Desdemona was slandered by. The outburst activates the full range of the word she had previously applied to Iago, "wayward": "some eternal villain, / Some busy and insinuating rogue, / Some cogging, cozening slave" (4.2.132–34; see also 141–42). "Emilia *senses* that someone like Iago is responsible, and may suspect him" (Honigmann, *Othello,* 282, my italics). Honigmann's is a psychological speculation, but since Iago is present along with Desdemona, a rhetorical and dialogical gloss would be more relevant: "Emilia *hints* that . . . ," or, more precisely, "Iago *hears* Emilia hinting, in Desdemona's presence, that. . . ." Regardless of what we think the speaker of Emilia's language means to say, the language itself seeks out Iago like a guided projectile to remind him of something she knows and of the power over him that knowledge guarantees. The projectile grazes Iago; he reacts curtly: "Speak within doors" (146). As if to oblige, Emilia redirects her accusation toward an unidentified third person, and aims a safer, more conventional, reproach at Iago: "some such squire he was / That turned your wit the seamy side without / And made you to suspect me with the Moor" (147–49). Iago lightens up. She has capitulated. He is relieved. His rejoinder is more relaxed: "You are a fool, go to" (150).

But after the murder capitulation is no longer possible. Emilia implores Iago to disprove Othello's charge that he had slandered Desdemona: "I know thou didst not, thou'rt not such a villain. / Speak, for my heart is full." Iago's dogged refusal to satisfy her compels her, she says, "to speak: / My mistress here lies murdered in her bed," and, she adds, "your reports have set the murder on" (5.2.170–83). She then fixes everybody's attention on Iago's culpability, recalls her earlier suspicion ("I thought so then"), and joins the chorus of his accusers only to learn the one fact that could make the terrible deed more terrible. She hears Othello confess that what drove him over the brink was "the pledge of love / . . . I saw . . . in his hand" (212–13); the "ocular proof" made possible, first, by her provision of the handkerchief and, second, by her silence about it:

> *Emilia.*   O God, O heavenly God!
>
> *Iago.*   Zounds, hold your peace!
>
> *Emilia.*   'Twill out, 'twill out! I peace?
>   No, I will speak as liberal as the north.
>   Let heaven and men and devils, let them all,

    All, all cry shame against me, yet I'll speak.

Iago.   Be wise, and get you home.

Emilia. I will not.

Gratiano. Fie! Your sword upon a woman?

Emilia. O thou dull Moor, that handkerchief thou speak'st of
    I found by fortune and did give my husband,
    For often, with a solemn earnestness
    —More than indeed belong'd to such a trifle—
    He begged of me to steal't.

Iago.   Villainous whore!

Emilia. She give it Cassio? No, alas, I found it
    And I did give't my husband.

Iago.   Filth, thou liest!

Emilia. By heaven, I do not, I do not, gentlemen!
    O murderous coxcomb, what should such a fool
    Do with so good a wife?
           (5.2.216–32)

 "Let them . . . cry shame against me": why? Because "what I did and
didn't do made me an accessory to murder"? That message flashes briefly
across the listener's mind before being pushed aside by the next clause,
"yet I'll speak." Now the message slides from "I am guilty" to "I am
brave": "let them cry shame against me for not holding my peace and disobeying my husband, or worse, for accusing him. But I will speak out at
all costs"—as she had just done a few minutes earlier, "You told a lie, an
odious, damned lie!" (5.2.176)—"and I will tell the truth." And the truth
she tells, "fearing," as Honigmann puts it, "to discover things as they really
are," is that she found the handkerchief and gave it to Iago, who put it to
deadly use. End of truth.

 I can be expected to keep Emilia from getting off the hook, to insist
that she fudges a little, that it's less than the whole story to say she "found
[it] by fortune," that "shame" may be more, or less, than she deserves. But
even in my bitter book this moment is too sad for moral casuistry. If she
fudges, it must be because she perceives and acknowledges what she

helped happen, because she anticipates my criticism enough to stand up to it and brave this moment out the best she can. She owes me less than she owes Desdemona. Why shouldn't she drown her silence in the music at the close and draw as close to Desdemona as she'll ever get?

> What did thy song bode, Lady?
> Hark, canst thou hear me? I will play the swan
> And die in music. . . . Willow, willow, willow.
> —Moor, she was chaste, she loved thee, cruel Moor,
> So come my soul to bliss as I speak true!
> So speaking as I think, alas, I die.
>   (5.2.246–49)

She speaks as she thinks at last (alas) and not in time. The act of silence remains deafening.

Emilia's protracted silence, her protracted lie, is the power behind Iago's throne from 3.3 to the play's last scene, at which point, as we've seen, he is defeated by her refusal to be silent, and reduced to the figure of castration he had initially mocked. He threatens her with his sword, but if we follow the Quarto stage direction a few lines later— "*The Moore runnes at* Iago. Iago *kils his wife*"—the prescribed action is fuzzy enough to make Honigmann think Iago stabs Emilia while trying to avoid Othello, which is a marvelous literalization, a caricature, of the redistribution of power as well as complicity.[91] Iago's subsequent "I bleed, sir, but not killed" (5.2.285) is taunting but tinny, pert but puerile: he sticks out his tongue ("you missed"). But rustling within that retort is the shade of the wounded Cassio, the shade of Desdemona's desire to bleed and live. He declines into the position of the morality Vice, but with a difference. The Vice is not merely a maverick individual but the embodiment of cultural norms of evil. The wickedness this figure represents is not his own but everyone else's. Shakespeare inserts the villain into this position in such a way as to set up an ironic structure of agency. He transforms the idea that the Vice *represents* everyone else's evil desires and purposes into the idea that the villain *is empowered* by them, but empowered in a such a way as to be disempowered. He is undone, his claim to autonomy compromised, not only by the efficiency with which his victims have used him to undo themselves, but also by his reliance on Emilia's wifely silence and thus his vulnerability to her wifely power. And even his last defiant stand undoes itself: "Demand me nothing. What you know, you know. / From this time forth I never will speak word." Mum's the model housewife's word.[92]

Notes

1. On the limits of the concept of self-fashioning, see *Fictions of the Pose: Rembrandt Against the Italian Renaissance* (Stanford, CA: Stanford University Press, 2000), 18–20. My doubts about the viability of Goffman's work as a model for the interpretation of early modern culture are recorded in ibid., 543–44. I find his "reports" of the unreflective performativity encouraged in modern Anglo-American society darkly illuminating, as hilarious as they are insightful, full of brilliantly mordant and epigrammatic observations about the relations of performers to their roles or selves. But I also find them ahistorical, limited to hypotheses about performance before others (as opposed to those about performance before oneself), and marked by the skeptico-cynical verve of the Inside Dopester: as he opens our eyes to the truth of what we've always done (play roles) but never knew we were doing, he treats all representation as misrepresentation.

2. David Herlihy and Christiane Klapisch-Zuber, *Tuscans and their Families: A Study of the Florentine Catasto of 1427* (New Haven, CT: Yale University Press, 1985), 339.

3. David Herlihy, *Medieval Households* (Cambridge, MA: Harvard University Press, 1985), 82.

4. This topic has been exhaustively studied by Christiane Klapisch-Zuber and many others. See Klapisch-Zuber's *Women, Family, and Ritual in Renaissance Italy,* trans. Lydia G. Cochrane (Chicago: University of Chicago Press, 1985), especially 231–36 on the induction of new wives into the lineage. See also Diane Owen Hughes, "From Brideprice to Dowry in Mediterranean Europe," *Journal of Family History* 3 (1978): 262–96 and Julius Kirshner and Anthony Molho, "The Dowry Fund and the Marriage Market in Early *Quattrocento* Florence," *Journal of Modern History* 50 (1978): 403–38. For a more recent revisionary study, see Anthony Molho, Roberto Barducci, Gabriella Battista, and Francesco Donnini, "Genealogy and Marriage Alliance: Memories of Power in Late Medieval Florence," in *Portraits of Medieval and Renaissance Living: Essays in Honor of David Herlihy,* ed. Samuel K. Cohn, Jr., and Steven A. Epstein (Ann Arbor: University of Michigan Press, 1996), 39–89.

5. Jan de Vries and Ad van der Woude, *The First Modern Economy: Success, Failure, and Perseverance of the Dutch Economy, 1500–1815* (Cambridge: Cambridge University Press, 1997), 163.

6. Lena Cowen Orlin, *Private Matters and Public Culture in Post-Reformation England* (Ithaca, NY: Cornell University Press, 1994), 3.

7. Belsey, *The Subject of Tragedy: Identity and Difference in Renaissance Drama* (London: Methuen, 1985), 144–45. See also *Desire: Love Stories in Western Culture* (Oxford: Blackwell, 1994), 6, 134–35, 146–49, 158.

In *Private Matters and Public Culture,* Orlin explores what happens at the interface of the domestic and political orders when the taxonomies and dichotomies of ideological prescription are skewed by their embeddedness in household "stuff," which includes not only goods and possessions but also architecture and domestic spaces. *Shakespeare and the Loss of Eden* complements Orlin's account by attending to what happens when similar prescriptive structures are skewed by their embeddedness in visual and verbal texts. It also complements Richard Helgerson's study, in *Adulterous Alliances,* of the ways in which conflicts between the literary genres of domestic drama and history (or tragedy) represent and interact with conflicts between the institutions of the household and the state. See Helgerson, *Adulterous Alliances: Home, State, and History in Early Modern European Drama and Painting* (Chicago: University of Chicago Press, 2000). For Helgerson's responses to the work of Orlin and Belsey, inter alia, see "Murder in Faversham: Holinshed's Impertinent History," in *The Historical Imagination in Early Modern Britain: History, Rhetoric, and Fiction, 1500–1800,* ed. Donald R. Kelley and David Harris Sacks (Cambridge: Cambridge University Press, 1997), 133–58.

8. Catherine Belsey, *Shakespeare and the Loss of Eden* (New Brunswick, NJ: Rutgers University Press, 1999), xiii–xiv. This is not only a book about early modern domestic ideology but also a book that expressly intervenes in a current debate: Belsey's "essay in cultural history . . . is put forward as a reservation about the call for the restoration of family values in our own society" (176).

9. Ibid., xiii.

10. In the "absolutist version of marriage" depicted in twelfth-century romances, women were formally and structurally (if not actually) marginalized, expressly reduced to "objects of exchange and the guarantee of dynastic continuity" (Belsey, *Subject of Tragedy,* 192).

11. Belsey, *Shakespeare and the Loss of Eden,* 81.

12. Belsey, *Subject of Tragedy,* 192–93.

13. Belsey, *Shakespeare and the Loss of Eden,* 23; *Subject of Tragedy,* 192. "Dangerous familiars" is the title of an important study cited by Belsey during this discussion: Frances E. Dolan, *Dangerous Familiars: Representations of Domestic Crime in England, 1550–1700* (Ithaca, NY: Cornell University Press, 1994). Dolan's account of "stories of women who plot against their husbands" centers on the ways in which these stories "articulate and shape fears of the danger lurking within the home," and connect these fears to "the instability of masculine privilege and power" (58).

14. Diane Owen Hughes, "Representing the Family: Portraits and Purposes in Early Modern Italy," *Journal of Interdisciplinary History* 17 (1986): 7.

15. Ibid., 25, 32. Barbara Correll has analyzed evidence of the same threat in England and on the Continent during the Tudor period. See "Malleable Material, Models of Power: Woman in Erasmus's 'Marriage Group' and *Civility in Boys,*" *English Literary History* 57 (1990): 242. See also the fuller development of this argument in Correll's remarkable *The End of Conduct: "Grobianus" and the Renaissance Text of the Subject* (Ithaca, NY: Cornell University Press, 1996).

A similar argument has been mounted by Keith Moxey in his discussion of illustrated broadsheets that depicted various versions of the battle of the sexes produced in sixteenth-century Nuremberg during the Reformation. He attributes the popularity of the motif to the effects of the long-term change from the medieval pattern in which women were married at puberty to a system "in which partners married when both were in their late twenties or early thirties—the man usually being older than the wife." Moxey oddly speculates that "[t]his change . . . would have enhanced the husband's authority at the expense of the wife's," but as his subsequent comment and general argument indicate, he probably means that because the change structurally produces greater equality between partners it creates the need for the husband to reinforce his authority at the wife's expense. See Keith Moxey, *Peasants, Warriors, and Wives: Popular Imagery in the Reformation* (Chicago: University of Chicago Press, 1989), 125.

16. Simon Schama, *The Embarrassment of Riches: An Interpretation of Dutch Culture in the Golden Age* (New York: Alfred A. Knopf, 1987), 400. De Vries and van der Woude similarly comment on the "explicitly central" role of women in "the domestic sphere," the increasing emphasis on the distinction between adult and child, and the selectivity of representation in which the "male head of the household appears seldom in his primary role of provider. . . . This stands to reason, in a culture increasingly inclined to see the home as an enclosed, feminine sphere" (*First Modern Economy,* 58–59). J. L. Price notes that there is "a deal of anecdotal evidence regarding the dominant role of women within the Dutch household but not much other evidence." He goes on to identify "one semi-political area of Dutch social life where women did have a significant part to play, and this was in demonstrations, riot, and disorder. . . . [W]omen were prominent in all aspects and phases of public disturbances in the towns of Holland in the seventeenth century, including the more violent episodes. This was the reverse side of the denigratory image held about them by society in general": J. L. Price, *Holland and the Dutch*

Republic in the Seventeenth Century: The Politics of Particularism (Oxford: Oxford University Press, 1994), 106–8.

17. David R. Smith, *Masks of Wedlock: Seventeenth-Century Dutch Marriage Portraiture* (Ann Arbor, MI: UMI Research Press, 1982), 26.

18. Bryan Jay Wolf, *Vermeer and the Invention of Seeing* (Chicago: University of Chicago Press, 2001), 49. The normative assignment of domestic authority to women was partly necessitated by the fact that provincial or state matters and the demands of the maritime economy made regular travelers of so many husbands—as Cats acknowledges when he denounces the double standard and advises men to reject the temptations to unfaithfulness they encounter in their travels.

19. A. Th. van Deursen, *Plain Lives in a Golden Age: Popular Culture, Religion and Society in Seventeenth-Century Holland,* trans. Maarten Ultee (Cambridge: Cambridge University Press, 1991), 83.

20. William Temple, *Observations upon the United Provinces of the Netherlands,* ed. George Clark (Oxford: Clarendon Press, 1972), 105–6.

21. As Perry Chapman points out, although marriage choices in seventeenth-century Holland were constrained by criteria of "social and religious compatibility," matches "were made more for love and friendship than was the case in other and earlier societies where marriage remained primarily an economic and political contract between families": H. Perry Chapman, "Home and the Display of Privacy," in *Art and Home: Dutch Interiors in the Age of Rembrandt,* ed. Mariët Westermann (Zwolle, Netherlands: Waanders, 2000), 145.

22. A. Agnes Sneller, "Reading Jacob Cats," in *Women of the Golden Age: An International Debate on Women in Seventeenth-Century Holland, England, and Italy,* ed. Els Kloek, Nicole Teeuwen, and Marijke Huisman (Hilversum, Netherlands: Verlorn, 1994), 23.

23. Ibid., 26.

24. Ibid., 31. Similarly, A. Th. van Deursen has remarked on the way an ideology of blame based on male anxiety was characterized by proverbs that "made the girl the butt of ridicule" and thus revealed the extent to which "the norms and standards of good moral behavior were defined by men." "The man could not help it if woman drove him crazy; she would have to learn to control herself." See van Deursen, *Plain Lives in a Golden Age,* 89.

25. Ibid., 30–31. The redundancy of Cats's narratives is itself a symptom of anxiety.

26. Elizabeth Alice Honig, "The Space of Gender in Seventeenth-Century Dutch Painting," in *Looking at Seventeenth-Century Dutch Art: Realism Reconsidered,* ed. Wayne E. Franits (Cambridge: Cambridge University Press, 1997), 195–97.

27. Wendy Wall, *Staging Domesticity: Household Work and English Identity in Early Modern Drama* (Cambridge: Cambridge University Press, 2002), 13–14.

28. Ibid., 14.

29. Ibid., 61–62.

30. Klaske Muizelaar and Derek Phillips, *Picturing Men and Women in the Dutch Golden Age: Paintings and People in Historical Perspective* (New Haven, CT: Yale University Press, 2003), 54.

31. See, for example, ibid., 54–60, Mariët Westermann, "'Costly and Curious, Full of pleasure and home contentment': Making Home in the Dutch Republic," in Westermann, ed., *Art and Home* 46–47, and especially C. Willemijn Fock, "The Domestic Interior in Seventeenth-Century Dutch Genre Painting," in Westermann, ed., *Art and Home,* 83–101. For an attempt to describe the less idyllic aspects of everyday life and domesticity see Witold Rybczynski, *Home: A Short History of an Idea* (New York: Viking Penguin Books, 1986), 51–75.

32. Westermann, "Making Home," 46–47.

33. *Shakespeare and the Loss of Eden,* 23.

34. Leeds Barroll, *Politics, Plague, and Shakespeare's Theater: The Stuart Years* (Ithaca, NY: Cornell University Press, 1991), 24. Barroll's basic move is brilliant in its simplicity and polemical force: he demonstrates how the "countermovements" attempted by self-styled revisionist approaches to early modern literature and culture—cultural materialism, cultural poetics (or the New Historicism), and "the new history"—are disabled by their proponents' uncritical reliance on the traditional historical accounts they claim to be superseding. Methodologically, they tend, in his formulation, to direct their energies to "received *readings* of historical documents rather than the documents themselves" (6). Substantively, this leads them to dust off accounts of Shakespeare's career based on antiquated principles of artistic development—narratives, for example, about "the sequence of a dramatist's works" (21). His revisionist antidote is to replace historicist narratives with an "*annaliste*" counternarrative that draws often radically different conclusions from the same documents.

35. Ibid., 23.

36. For the sources of this distinction, see ibid., 24n.2.

37. Ibid., 23–24.

38. Barroll, *Artificial Persons: The Formation of Character in the Tragedies of Shakespeare* (Columbia: University of South Carolina Press, 1974); Meredith Anne Skura, *Shakespeare the Actor and the Purposes of Playing* (Chicago: University of Chicago Press, 1993); Louis Montrose, *The Purpose of Playing: Shakespeare and the Cultural Politics of the Elizabethan Theatre* (Chicago: University of Chicago Press, 1996).

39. Skura, *Shakespeare the Actor,* 4–8 and passim.

40. Montrose, *Purpose of Playing*, xi, 75. On the vicissitudes of players, see chapters 2–4. On the cultural importance of Shakespeare's theater, see 104–5, 203, and Montrose's critique of Paul Yachnin's thesis on 86–98.

41. Ibid., 92. Montrose expressly draws his inspiration for this new accent from the work of Raymond Williams.

42. "Problematics" and "subjecthood" are in scare quotes because Montrose borrows them from Richard Helgerson during a criticism of the latter's argument that in the history plays Shakespeare did not problematize subjecthood.

43. Barroll, *Artificial Persons,* 3–4 and passim. In this protocol, "the study of cultural presuppositions about personality in a specific historical period" precedes and frames "the study of characterization" as "artistic process" (101). For some exemplary reflections on the former, see chapter 3, especially 77–81 and 90–91. The relation between the two projects is epitomized in the following statement: "While perfection was the ideal, the dramatist's problem was to portray men who could not, by nature, live up to the philosophical purities proposed by various ethical codes" (127). Perhaps it was not only the dramatist's problem but also his desire and intention. At any rate, this formulation guarantees that whatever the typology of dispositions and desires artificial persons may be constructed in accordance with, they will always be portrayed as subject to incompatible or contradictory transcendental imperatives: Shakespeare's tragic protagonists necessarily aspire, and necessarily fail, to transcend or escape from themselves by assuming the armor of an alienating identity: on this, see chapters 3 and 4 of *Artificial Persons,* especially 78–81 and 84–88.

Barroll's view is entirely compatible with more recent accounts that proclaim their poststructuralist pedigree. "Assuming the armor of an alienating identity" is a Lacanian phrase frequently cited in a variety of psychoanalytic and poststructural venues. It is one of several passages in the early mirror-stage essay in which Lacan pointedly uses terms of art to describe primary processes of mimesis that conventional Freudian theory depicts in biological or epigenetic rhetoric: see Jacques Lacan, *Écrits: A Selection,* trans. Alan Sheridan (New York: Norton, 1977), 1–7. The phrase has been criticized because, as a figure for the narcissistic process of identity formation, it betrays its restrictive orientation: "Narcissus presents the static image of a man looking at a man and turning away from a woman" (Kathryn

Schwarz, *Tough Love: Amazon Encounters in the English Renaissance* [Durham, NC: Duke University Press, 2000], 143). This wonderfully deadpan understatement appears during an account of Spenser's Britomart, who literally assumes the armor of an alienating identity in the third book of *The Faerie Queene.* But at the same time Schwarz casually if wickedly captures—or caricatures—the androcentric and misogynist narcissism of identity formation as depicted in such narratives as Lacan's. (Why not don the dress, or gown, or, more neutrally, the robe of an alienating identity?) Nevertheless, I find the Lacanian narrative useful in directing readers toward the foundational importance both of the theory of personation as ethos-formation and of the phenomenon of performance anxiety entailed by the Lacanian assumption that identities, *ēthoi,* subjects, are artificial persons. On the express affinity of Lacanian theory with Renaissance accounts of subjectivity as self-representation, see my *Fictions of the Pose,* 155–69. I note in passing that the very association of masculine identity formation with the donning of armor characterizes the process as involving a threat, and so brings castration anxiety into play.

44. Keir Elam, *Shakespeare's Universe of Discourse: Language-Games in the Comedies* (Cambridge: Cambridge University Press, 1984), 219–26.

45. This brief paraphrase, which contains a pastiche of phrases from Enterline's prospectus, doesn't do justice to the subtlety and originality of her treatment.

46. Walter J. Ong, "Latin Language as a Renaissance Puberty Rite," *Studies in Philology* 56 (1959): 103–24, reprinted in *Rhetoric, Romance and Technology: Studies in the Interaction of Expression and Culture* (Ithaca, NY: Cornell University Press, 1981), 113–41; Ong, *Fighting for Life: Contest, Sexuality and Consciousness* (Ithaca, NY: Cornell University Press, 1981), 126–39; William Kerrigan, "The Articulation of the Ego in the English Renaissance," in *The Literary Freud: Mechanisms of Defense and the Poetic Will,* ed. Joseph H. Smith (New Haven: Yale University Press, 1980), 262–308; Bruce R. Smith, *Homosexual Desire in Shakespeare's England: A Cultural Poetics* (Chicago: University of Chicago Press, 1991), 82–86.

47. J. L. Price, *The Dutch Republic in the Seventeenth Century* (New York: St. Martin's Press, 1998), 134–35.

48. Kerrigan, "Articulation of the Ego," 285–86.

49. On the gynephobia of gender see my "Gynephobia and Culture Change: An Irigarayan Just-So Story," in *Irigaray and Premodern Culture,* ed. T. Krier and E. Harvey (London: Routledge, 2004), 138–45.

50. Alan Stewart, *Close Readers: Humanism and Sodomy in Early Modern England* (Princeton, NJ: Princeton University Press, 1997), 102. See also Richard Halpern, *The Poetics of Primitive Accumulation: English Renaissance Culture and the Genealogy of Capital* (Ithaca, NY: Cornell University Press, 1991), 21–60; Mary Thomas Crane, *Framing Authority: Sayings, Self, and Society in Sixteenth-Century England* (Princeton, NJ: Princeton University Press, 1993), 77–92 and passim. In her work in progress entitled "Imitating Schoolboys," Enterline takes issue with the Ong/Kerrigan thesis and argues that Lacan's mirror-stage account of emulation has much in common with Shakespeare's critique of subject and gender formation in humanist pedagogy, and therefore that Lacanian theory can illuminate the perils of emulation and imitation in humanist pedagogy more accurately, more fully, than does the theory advanced by Ong and Kerrigan. Once again, my attention was directed to these texts by Enterline's study.

51. See John Guy, *Tudor England* (New York: Oxford University Press, 1988), 355, 371, and chapter 13 passim. See also Montrose, *Purpose of Playing,* 21: "During the course of the sixteenth century, English society experienced the dislocations of rapid change. And in the means by which it established and sought to consolidate its authority, the arriviste Tudor dynasty itself became a major agent or catalyst of such change. The Tudor state sought to legitimate itself by means of its integration into a providentially ordered cosmos. But it could not effectively contain the ideologically anomalous realities of heterodoxy, nor arrest the social flux, that it had helped to set in motion."

52. Specifically, in "O Queene, the matter of my song," the plenary lecture Montrose delivered at Cambridge in 2001 during the conference of the International Spenser Society. In this rethinking of his earlier work, he directed attention to "quasi-republican" tendencies of resistance that complicated and threatened to destabilize the "Elizabethan political imaginary."

53. Charles Wilson, *Queen Elizabeth and the Revolt of the Netherlands* (Berkeley and Los Angeles: University of California Press, 1970), 127.

54. Ibid., 23.

55. Ibid., 127–28.

56. Wolf, *Vermeer and the Invention of Seeing,* 49.

57. Smith, *Masks of Wedlock,* 37, 41. Most of Smith's book is devoted to lucid, informative, perceptive, and original—*and* persuasive—discussions of pendants and double portraits. I consider it by far the best study of the subject, and my debt to it runs very deep.

58. Mariët Westermann, *The Art of the Dutch Republic, 1585–1718* (London: George Weidenfeld and Nicolson, 1996), 133.

59. Ibid., 132–33.

60. Joaneath Spicer, "The Renaissance Elbow," in *A Cultural History of Gesture,* ed. Jan Bremmer and Herman Roodenburg (Ithaca, NY: Cornell University Press, 1991), 86. See also Marjorie Garber, "Out of Joint," in *The Body in Parts: Fantasies of Corporeality in Early Modern Europe,* ed. David Hillman and Carla Mazzio (New York: Routledge, 1997), 23–51.

61. Smith, *Masks of Wedlock,* 44.

62. Ibid.

63. Thanks to H. Perry Chapman for help on the question of women and hats in pendants.

64. Simon Schama, *Rembrandt's Eyes* (New York: Alfred A. Knopf, 1999), 473–74.

65. Ibid., 474.

66. Smith, *Masks of Wedlock,* 85.

67. On this, see Mariët Westermann, *Rembrandt* (London: Phaidon Press, 2000), 157.

68. A *fijnschilder* like Vermeer "allied himself with the cultural production of the household, took refuge in the world of women, and sought redress for his feminized position by reclaiming, if not his manhood, then his agency within the world": Wolf, *Vermeer and the Invention of Seeing,* 15–16. Using Vermeer as his example, Wolf associates this position—sometimes too literally, but often with sophisticated indirection—with castration and performance anxiety. See chapters 6 and 7 passim, and 248–50.

69. See "Impertinent Trifling: On Desdemona's Handkerchief," *Shakespeare Quarterly* 47 (1996): 235–50.

70. On the needy actor as a model, see in general Meredith Skura's remarkable *Shakespeare the Actor and the Purposes of Playing.* On the meaning and significance of the *platea* and the *locus* as, respectively, a downstage area reserved for interactions between characters and the audience and an upstage area where self-contained action among fictional characters occurs, see Robert Weimann, *Shakespeare and the Popular Tradition in the Theater: Studies in the Social Dimension of Dramatic Form and Function,* ed. Robert Schwartz (Baltimore, MD: Johns Hopkins University Press, 1978), 73–85 and passim. Weimann correlates these two stage areas with the different orientations of stage presence ("Figurenpositionen") by which the actor connects with "his fellow actors, the play, or the audience, even when direct address has been abandoned" (230). But he goes on to insist that in moments of direct audience contact the character and the actor both address the same audience, the one consisting of the actual spectators in the actual theater. This means that the character at least intermittently behaves as if he or she knows he or she is in a theater performing before an audience (and if the character is a "she" does she know she is a "he"?). I want to modify this premise, not reject it. In my version, if such participatory episodes as prologues, epilogues, and soliloquies are scripted, the audience they

engage must be a fiction. It's a virtual audience constituted by the direction and express motivation of address. The main difference between Weimann's notion and mine is this: For Weimann, when characters like Hamlet, Iago, and Richard III address the audience, they function *as* actors. For me, they function *like* actors. See my "The Prince's Dog: Falstaff and the Perils of Speech-Prefixity," *Shakespeare Quarterly* 49 (1998): 40–73, especially 47–50.

71. Brian Vickers, *Appropriating Shakespeare: Contemporary Critical Quarrels* (New Haven, CT: Yale University Press, 1993), 79.

72. The text of Shakespeare's *Othello* cited in this essay is E. A. J. Honigmann's Arden[3] edition: The Arden Shakespeare, Third Series (Walton-on-Thames, Surrey: Thomas Nelson & Sons, 1997).

73. Since one expects "I am not what I seem," "I am not what I am" doesn't merely replace it but is defined by it: "what I seem *is* what I am."

74. "Would you, the supervisor, grossly gape on, / Behold her topp'd?" (3.3.398–99). This is the term in the first Quarto and it is preferable to the Folio's "super-vision." I use "gallery" in the Elizabethan sense of "lords' rooms" in the upper level of the public stage, not in the demotic sense of the peanut gallery or space for groundlings. Edward Snow remarks that the Quarto term "neatly condenses the watching, controlling, and judging functions that Freud defines as the superego's three attributes" ("Sexual Anxiety and the Male Order of Things in *Othello*," *English Literary Renaissance* 10 [1980]: 396). Later in the essay Snow claims that Iago fulfills the function "within Othello's psyche . . . [of] the punitive, sex-hating superego" (409). Although the Freudian spin tends to diminish the context-specific force of the way Shakespeare uses the ethical discourses to redistribute complicities, the idea of an imaginary audience fulfilling that function in Iago's fantasy makes good sense. On ethical discourses see my *Making Trifles of Terrors: Redistributing Complicities in Shakespeare* (Stanford, CA: Stanford University Press, 1997).

75. A. D. Nuttall, *A New Mimesis: Shakespeare and the Representation of Reality* (London: Methuen, 1983), 143.

76. See Marvin Rosenberg, *The Masks of Othello: The Search for the Identity of Othello, Iago, and Desdemona by Three Centuries of Actors and Critics* (Berkeley and Los Angeles: University of California Press, 1961), 168–69.

77. Verse soliloquies: 1.3.381–403, 2.1.284–310, 2.3.45–60, 2.3.331–57 and 377–83, 3.3.324–36, 4.1.44–48, 4.1.94–104, 5.1.11–22, 5.1.129–30. The two prose asides occur at 2.1.167–78 and 2.1.198–200. Arden[3] and the 1622 Quarto format the second aside as verse but I follow the Folio in treating it as prose. Of the two verse versions, which differ from each other, Q makes more sense both metrically and rhetorically because its line divisions (a hendecasyllable sandwiched between two iambic trimeters) accentuate the phrasal structure: "O, you are well tun'd now, / But I'll set down the pegs, that make this music, / As honest as I am." I prefer the prose version on situational grounds: this and the preceding aside differ from the soliloquies in being more spontaneous outbursts directly triggered by actions taking place onstage and in being partly or wholly addressed to participants in those actions. The longer first aside begins as a commentary to the supervisors but after two sentences it changes into a threat aimed at Cassio. All the speeches I call "soliloquy" are characterized by direct and formalized address to the supervisors that interrupts the action.

Neither the Quarto nor the Folio text of *Othello* uses the words "aside" and "solus" (or such alternative indicators as "Manet") to distinguish these performances. Consult the discussions of those terms in Alan Dessen and Leslie Thomson's invaluable *A Dictionary of Stage Directions in English Drama, 1580–1642* (Cambridge: Cambridge University Press, 1999).

78. I'd be tempted to borrow Karen Newman's wonderful characterization of the hand-kerchief as a "snowballing signifier," but it doesn't accumulate its meanings so much as

renew and alter them. See Newman, *Fashioning Femininity and English Renaissance Drama* (Chicago: University of Chicago Press, 1991), 91.

On the implications of preposterous disclosure, which demands reinterpretation of all events that preceded the event of disclosure (in this case, the disclosure, in 3.3., of Cassio's role in the courtship), and on preposterity in general, see the brilliant discussions by Joel Altman and Patricia Parker: Joel B. Altman, "'Preposterous Conclusions': Eros, *Enargeia*, and the Composition of *Othello*," *Representations* 18 (Spring, 1987): 129–57; Patricia Parker, *Shakespeare from the Margins: Language, Culture, Context* (Chicago: University of Chicago Press, 1996), chapter 1, especially 48–52. See also the related discussion of "dilation" in *Othello* in Chapter 7, especially 248–52 and 268–70, and the earlier more expanded version of these pages in "Shakespeare and Rhetoric: 'Dilation' and 'Delation' in *Othello*," in *Shakespeare and the Question of Theory*, ed. Parker and Geoffrey Hartman (New York: Methuen, 1985), 54–74.

79. "The thoughtfulness [of her utterances in 5.2] . . . is directly opposed to the thoughtlessness—indeed, mindlessness: 'I nothing, but to please his fantasy'—at the beginning of her story": Edward Pechter, *"Othello" and Interpretive Traditions* (Iowa City: University of Iowa Press, 1998), 119.

80. The first alternative has narrative force and presupposes the "long time" interval hypothesized by the double-time theory. The second alternative has rhetorical force and registers the speaker's reaction to the pressure of a persistent demand. Many of the dilemmas that get resolved by resorting to double time would disappear if expressions were treated as rhetorical and reflexive signifiers of *pathos* in discourse time rather than as narrative and objective signifiers of *mythos* in story time.

81. On this episode, see "Impertinent Trifling," 245–48.

82. Ridley's Arden² gloss suggests that "ta'en out" could also mean "removed," but both in Cinthio's novella and in the other occurrences of the idiom at 3.4.180 and 4.1.153, "copied" is clearly the intended meaning.

83. Pechter, *"Othello" and Interpretive Traditions*, 116.

84. Pechter cites the syncopated Folio variant. The First Quarto reads, "I nothing know, but for his fantasy." Russ McDonald's New Pelican gloss, "I *do* nothing but please his whims" (my italics), is a possible expansion of the Folio line. I prefer the constrictedness of the Folio line because it makes more vivid the difficulty of the move Emilia is trying to negotiate. But both versions equally convey a touch of moral embarrassment, an apologetic nuance, that reflects anything but mindlessness or thoughtlessness.

85. Honigmann, *Othello*, 47.

86. Thomas More, *The History of King Richard III*, ed. Richard S. Sylvester (New Haven, CT: Yale University Press, 1963), 80.

87. This is the Lie Direct. Later in the scene we encounter the Lie Indirect. "Sure there's some wonder in this handkerchief," Desdemona muses after Othello's Egyptic parable, "I am most unhappy in the loss of it." Emilia continues to stonewall, responding with a non sequitur, a standard wisecrack about male appetites: "They are all but stomachs, and we all but food" (3.4.102–5).

88. Honigmann, *Othello*, 71.

89. Ibid., 46, 44. Honigmann simply adopts the motivation mentioned by Cinthio: "The Ensign's wife . . . did not dare, for fear of her husband, to tell her anything" (381).

90. Ibid., 47.

91. Honigmann, *Othello*, 5.2.223–32; 322.

92. Except for a few minor variations, most of this final paragraph is identical with the final paragraph of my "Acts of Silence, Acts of Speech: How to Do Things with Othello and Desdemona," forthcoming in *Renaissance Drama* 33 (2004): 1–33.

Spaces of Treason in Tudor England

Lena Cowen Orlin

THIS CHAPTER REVISITS A FAMILIAR NARRATIVE, one of the most famous of the rebellions that punctuated Elizabeth I's long reign. It led directly to the execution of Thomas Howard, fourth Duke of Norfolk (in 1572) and, eventually, to that of Mary Stuart, Queen of Scots (in 1587). An account of William Cecil's investigation into the so-called "Ridolfi Plot" emerges from State Papers and from Cecil's own papers, preserved at Salisbury House. These documents testify to the multiple interrogations that were conducted, many under torture, to compile evidence of a plan for Mary to take the English throne with Norfolk as her consort and for the new Queen and King to make the country Catholic again. Norfolk's man Lawrence Bannister was examined ten times; his confidential secretary and cryptographer Robert Higford, twelve times; his junior secretary William Barker, twenty-one times. There were also depositions from the Earl of Moray, Regent of Scotland; Mary's ally John Leslie, Bishop of Ross; and others, including the Florentine merchant Roberto Ridolfi himself. As transcribed, the statements of these witnesses represent a massive accumulation of detail about political conspiracy. It is also possible to recover from them a subtext that cannot be fully extricated from this dominant narrative of national crisis but that has other imports for our understanding of sixteenth-century England. The story in the margins is a spatial history of treason.

THE TUDOR LONG GALLERY

For this story to reveal itself, it is necessary first to review some of the circumstances of household space in Tudor England and, in particular, to remark the fad for a new room called the "long gallery" (see figure 7). If the great hall dominated the medieval castle, the long gallery was the most distinctive innovation of the Elizabethan stately home. It represented one of many changes to the ways people related to their domestic environments in the sixteenth century.

At the intersections of demographic, social, and architectural history, for instance, we discover widespread transformations in Elizabethan living

158

Figure 7. The long gallery at Albyns Hall, Essex. From M. Jourdain,
English Decoration and Furniture of the Early Renaissance **(London: B. T. Batsford,**
1924).

conditions: domestic arrangements that were less communal, as households were increasingly organized around nuclear families; a heightened
level of investment in personal comfort by persons of all classes, as documented in probate inventories and by contemporary commentators like
William Harrison; significant developments in design and ornamentation,
especially as inspired by Continental ideas about rationalized spatial
arrangements and use of the classical orders; and a move away from
large, multipurpose areas to a greater number of small, function-specific
rooms. What gave a sense of identity to chambers that were indistinguish-
able in their contours? We tend to have clear expectations for the signifying capacity of elevation, because we assume that public or shared areas
will be encountered at ground level and that private bedchambers require
vertical separation from them. We also imagine that we can recognize a
room by its place in a floorplan, associating presentational spaces like foy-
ers and lounges with the front of the house and imagining workrooms like
kitchens and laundries tucked inconspicuously behind them. And, perhaps most importantly, we divine a room's meaning from its contents.
Furnishings are the primary mechanisms for communicating to us the
behavior that is appropriately engaged in a given space, whether this is to

Figure 8. Chastleton House, Oxfordshire. Photographed by the author.

gather with others to eat, to lie down to sleep, or to sit in seclusion to read or think. Long galleries, however, demonstrate how anachronistic all these assumptions can be. They were public rooms located at the tops of houses and generally at the back, to afford views over gardens and orchards. Uniquely in the Renaissance home, they were not given definition by objects. Built long and narrow to afford walking space in inclement weather, they were kept more or less bare of any obstacles. Instead, their purpose was communicated by their unusual shape and vast size. The length of the gallery at Buckhurst was 254 feet; at Ampthill, 245 feet; at Worksop, 212 feet; at Bridewell Palace, 200 feet; at Audley End, 190 feet; at Montacute, 170 feet; at Parham, 166 feet; at Aston and Holdenby, 140 feet; at Haddon and Littlecote, 110 feet. Even in a small house like Chastleton (see figure 8), the long gallery was impressive at 72 feet (see figure 9). At Burton Constable the room was measured out so that if one walked up and back twenty-four times one had traveled precisely a mile.[1]

The medieval great hall, too, had occupied a large footprint. The archetypal example, at Penshurst Place, was 62 feet long, 39 feet wide, and 60 feet tall at the peak of its exposed roofbeams (see figure 10). Great halls were essentially feudal spaces; the larger a hall was, the more retainers it could shelter (or could make claim to shelter). Because medieval construction required height to achieve breadth, all the measurements of a hall gave

Figure 9. The long gallery at Chastleton House. Photographed by the author.

Figure 10. Looking from the dais toward the screen in the medieval great hall at Penshurst Place, Kent. From *Famous Homes of Great Britain and Their Stories*, ed. A. H. Malan (New York: G. P. Putnam's Sons, 1899).

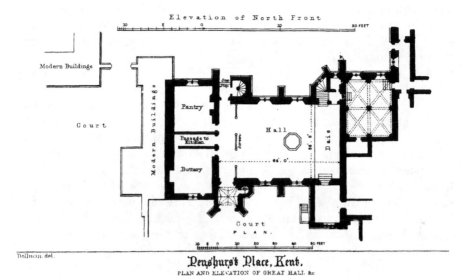

Figure 11. Floorplan of Penshurst Place, showing the entrance porch, screens passage, great hall, central hearth, and dais. From E. T. Doll-man and L. R. Jobbins, *An Analysis of Ancient Domestic Achitecture in Great Britain* (London: B. T. Batsford, 1890).

off important connotations about power and command. The system of spatial organization that evolved around the hall extended these public meanings (see figure 11). Buildings of any status were entered by means of a wide corridor known as the "screens passage," so named for the screen, or partial wall, that subdivided the main living area to define both the corridor and the hall. Typically, two doors opened off the screens passage, one into the pantry and one into the buttery, reassuring any welcome newcomer of his immediate access to sustenance and hospitality. These doors were balanced across the passage by two openings in the screen. To reach the hall, a visitor was required to enter the screens passage, take a few steps forward, and then turn sharply to proceed through one of these openings. Thus the screen constricted access for any unwelcome intruders. In a further security measure, the high table for the lord of the medieval manor was located at the far end of the hall, a room's length and a small army away. By 1500, though, with no bands of feudal retainers to harbor, these spatial strategies had little functional purpose. William Cecil built a hall at Burghley House that was nearly Penshurst's match at 68 feet long, 30 feet wide, and 60 feet high, but it was designed mainly to overawe its visitors with its double hammerbeam roof, soaring stone chimneypiece, and carved family arms. His son Robert, lavishing £38,000 on renovations at Hatfield House, was one of many who redecorated an old hall in the sixteenth and seventeenth centuries. Rather than filtering traffic as a defensive strategy, screens openings now more often framed impressive domestic vistas. The new Renaissance vocabulary for power and status was an ornamental one.[2]

The domestication of great houses had other consequences for the medieval hall, as well. While the hall had long before become obsolete in function, it was newly and perhaps even more importantly discovered to be incompatible with current fashions in design. A principal feature of European architecture was a symmetrical exterior. Running across the front of a house but with its entrance to one far side (at the site of the screens passage), any great hall that honored the old, medieval syntax for space also imposed its asymmetry upon the façade. Some Elizabethans invented ingenious ways of camouflaging the presence of a hall and a screens passage behind a balanced elevation. At Burton Agnes, for example, the entrance porch was disguised to look like a bay window, the two projections positioned to create a false equilibrium (see figure 12). But such techniques grew increasingly strained and artificial. Finally, English ideas of interior organization were revolutionized by the architect Robert Smythson and his patron and "aedificatrix," Elizabeth Hardwick (whose married names included Barlow, Cavendish, St. Loe, and Talbot, and who, though titled Countess of Shrewsbury in her last match, is better known as "Bess of Hardwick"). Hardwick Hall had an immaculately symmetrical façade created by placing the main entrance at dead center, rather than to one side (see figure 13). Hardwick and Smythson then turned the great hall on end, so that its length extended through the building, from front to back, rather than across the front, from side to side. They retained an allusion to a screens passage in the form of a narrow foyer that ran the width of the hall. But they abandoned all the old medieval drama of delayed disclosure, encounter with buttery and pantry, enforced turn, and withheld view. The theater of spatial experience at Hardwick Hall was concentrated instead in rooms on the upper stories, reached by what has been called her great "river of stairs." The hall became little more than an overbuilt passageway to this medium for transit to preferred spaces. At Hardwick Hall, significance was still communicated by size, but the large room which eclipsed the great hall in importance was a long gallery (see figure 14). Positioned at the uppermost level of the house, the gallery was 162 feet long, as wide as 40 feet at some points, and 26 feet high. It was hung with tapestries depicting the story of Gideon and featured two chimney pieces incorporating alabaster statues of Justice and Mercy. There was also one major piece of furniture, a large throne-like chair with its own imperial canopy.[3]

Figure 12. The symmetrical façade of Burton Agnes Hall, Yorkshire. From J. Alfred Gotch, *Architecture of the Renaissance in England* (London: B. T. Batsford, 1890)

Figure 13. The symmetrical façade of Hardwick Hall, Derbyshire. Photographed by the author.

When Hardwick learned in January 1603 that an emissary of Elizabeth I had called upon her, she received him in what she thus considered to be the most impressive of her presentational spaces.[4] Sir Henry Brounker subsequently reported to the Queen that Hardwick "sent for me into her gallery." She had obliged him to process through the house and up two long flights of stairs to reach her as, in a feigned show of unconcern, "she was walking with [her granddaughter] the Lady Arbella and her son William Cavendish." Brounker recognized signs of anxiety that, in fact, were not misplaced. As the great-great-granddaughter of Henry VII, Lady Arbella Stuart had been instilled since birth with the very highest ambitions.[5] Now, at the age of twenty-seven, recognizing that Elizabeth I was in failing health, and knowing also that no successor had been named to the throne, Stuart had finally grown impatient with nearly three decades of royal hopes and strict supervision. Unbeknownst to Hardwick, Stuart had dispatched a servant, John Dodderidge, to make an offer of matrimony to Edward Seymour, who was kin to the third wife of Henry VIII.[6] A statute of 1536 prohibited any person of royal blood from marrying without the reigning monarch's approval, and, to compound this intended act of treason, Stuart also sought to strengthen her own princely status by joining two formidable pedigrees. The proposal had been brought to the attention of the Queen.

Figure 14. The long gallery at Hardwick Hall in the late nineteenth century. From *Famous Homes of Great Britain and Their Stories.*

Seymour, then just sixteen, lived in Hampshire with his grandfather, the Earl of Hertford. In 1560, Hertford had secretly wed Katherine Grey, herself a great-granddaughter of Henry VII and tenth in the line of succession established by the dying Henry VIII.[7] For lack of proof, the marriage was invalidated; even so, Hertford and Grey were punished for having made a match without Elizabeth's permission. They were confined to the Tower for two years (and conceived two children) before being transferred to house arrests which kept them separate until Grey's death in 1568. Only then was Hertford allowed to return to court, but he was assessed heavy fines and, forty years on, still had not succeeded in legitimating his descendants, including the young Edward Seymour. In 1595, he had been reminded of the royal will in these matters when it was discovered that his second son had sought to have the marriage reinstated; Hertford was returned to the Tower for several months. Stuart may have imagined that this personal history would dispose Hertford to fall in with her dangerous scheme, but in fact the opposite was true. He sought immediately to dissociate himself from it.[8] Dodderidge had arrived at Hertford's house on December 30, 1602; Hertford sent him to Robert Cecil for questioning on January 1; Cecil referred Dodderidge to the Privy Council for further interrogation on January 2; and Elizabeth personally commissioned Sir Henry Brounker to investigate the affair on January 3. By January 7, Brounker had traveled 145 miles from London to Derbyshire to examine Arbella Stuart.

In the long gallery at Hardwick Hall, Brounker made certain that Stuart knew from whence he had come and on whose authority: "I told her Ladyship [that is, Hardwick], in the hearing of her grandchild, that your Highness . . . commanded me." Next, he expressed the Queen's "gracious favor," at which point, he observed wryly, Hardwick was so relieved that "I could hardly keep her from kneeling." Then, Brounker led Hardwick aside: "Drawing her on with other compliments towards the further end of the gallery to free her from the young lady, I delivered your Majesty's letter." With Stuart out of earshot, Brounker told Hardwick that it was Elizabeth's "pleasure" that "I might speak privately with the Lady Arbella." Finally, "leaving her there," recounted Brounker, "I led the Lady Arbella to the other end of the long gallery." Stuart at first "denied all" but, under questioning, eventually offered to "deal plainly and sincerely so I would promise to conceal it from her grandmother"—this as Hardwick watched helplessly, out of hearing range, from the other end of the gallery. While Stuart's scheme was not to succeed, she had the fleeting pleasures of having outfoxed the older woman in sending Dodderidge to Hampshire and now for the length of this private conference. She did not have many such opportunities, for she not only lived in her grandmother's house, she was required to sleep in her grandmother's bedchamber.

Brounker was finally persuaded that Hardwick, Seymour, and Hertford were guiltless in the matter, and he wrote Elizabeth from Derbyshire that he "found the house without any strange company"—that is, without any sign of political conspiracy or armed rebellion. There was only Stuart's secretly conceived plot. Hardwick, who forty years earlier had herself spent thirty-one weeks in the Tower for having been Katherine Grey's confidante in the matter of the unauthorized marriage to Hertford, wrote Elizabeth at once. "I did in my heart most humbly thank your Majesty for commanding that course to be taken," she said, referring to Brounker's orchestration of events in her long gallery. At first, she admits, his strategy "did make me doubtful that your Majesty had some suspicion in me," because of "his preciseness at his first coming to keep the offense from me till he had privately talked with Arbell."

Given what was revealed in the long gallery at Hardwick Hall, it was clear that Hardwick's hopes for her granddaughter would not be realized; in 1603, she disinherited the unfortunate "Arbell." In 1610, with James VI of Scotland fully secured as Elizabeth's successor on the English throne, Stuart finally made a clandestine marriage with Edward Seymour's younger brother, William. The union was even then so politically fraught that Hertford was summoned for interrogation by the Privy Council, and Stuart was imprisoned. She died in the Tower in 1615. The room that Hardwick had designed as a fit setting for a royal aspirant had not achieved its end. Moreover, in the matter of the Brounker investigation, it had betrayed its designer. Its size and its acoustics had had the unintended consequence of making Hardwick a distant witness to, not an active participant in, the examination in which Stuart's potentially treasonous ambition was so momentously confessed. As the Arbella Stuart affair suggests, an accidental effect of the long gallery was its surprising facility for sheltering private conversations.

Private Talking/Private Walking

When we search for privacy in history, we tend to look first for the privacies on which we ourselves place most value. These we often define in terms of the spaces which, we imagine, permitted or protected them. There are intellectual privacies, those of the study; bodily privacies, those of the bathroom; and sexual privacies, those of the bedchamber. All were fairly uncommon in the sixteenth century, and few were widely remarked. As the living arrangements at Hardwick Hall suggest, for example, shared bedchambers were as much matters of social convention and personal choice as of economic imperative and physical comfort.[9] Indeed, it is difficult to determine whether Bess of Hardwick simply observed general custom in her household organization or whether she was more personally motivated by the specific suspicion that, in the interest of Stuart's royal prospects, her grand-daughter could not be trusted to be private. Even in families without so much immediately at stake there would have been known value in the inhibiting effects of collectivity. But if the privacies which interest us seem rarely to have been explicit objects of desire in the public discourse of the sixteenth century, one early modern anxiety that *did* leave a considerable documentary trace, by contrast, was a social privacy. My thesis is that the first interior space to be associated with conversational privacy was that six-teenth-century innovation, the long gallery.[10]

Elsewhere, Elizabethans seem to have been convinced, "the walls have ears." And, researching the Renaissance, one can come to believe that there were very few secrets in this society. In the royal residences, women who shared Elizabeth's bedchamber reported on her moods to courtiers and emissaries. Her laundress was bribed by Spanish ambassadors who wished to chart her menstrual cycles. When it was rumored that Elizabeth was having an affair with Robert Dudley, she told one diplomat that "My life is in the open, and I have so many witnesses that I cannot understand how so bad a judgment can have been formed of me." At the other end of the social scale, trial depositions taken from private citizens expose all manner of intimate details about the behavior, possessions, housekeeping practices, sleeping arrangements, dangerous liaisons, and private conver-sations of near neighbors.[11]

The stage plays of the period, a sure guide to cultural constructions in these matters, are full of witnessings, overhearings, and eavesdroppings. We might think of Polonius behind the arras in Gertrude's closet, or of Volpone on a stool, behind a curtain, "hearkening" to the parade of his potential heirs. In John Marston's *The Dutch Courtesan* (1604), eaves-droppers are described in a contemporary stage direction, tellingly, as "those in ambush." George Gascoigne's *Supposes* (1566) opens with the nurse Balia warning her young charge, "Let us look about, to be sure lest any man hear our talk; for I think within the house the tables, the planks, the beds, the portals, yea, and the cupboards themselves have ears." Even though two lords in the anonymous *Nobody and Somebody* (1606) have reminded themselves that "walls have ears and eyes," they attempt a "word in private." Inevitably, their "secret conference" is "betrayed and overheard." But they, in turn, observe the observers and speak words to their hearing, in a multiple regression of the clandestine listenings that characterized the early modern interior, on stage and off. The attentiveness of the Renaissance household was also a main theme in Thomas Heywood's *The Wise Woman of Hogsdon* (1604). Described as sitting inside a closet near the entrance of her home, the "wise" woman overhears the conversations of visitors and then, coming forth, can tell back to them every word they thought they had spoken "in private."

Hers is a house dedicated to eavesdropping, for she also has a central chamber surrounded by several rooms that look into it. In the play's denouement, she places five characters in four of the encompassing rooms so that they can overhear the supposedly confidential conversation of Young Chartley and Luce, at the center. From the eavesdroppers, we hear in sequence Gratiana, recognizing the voice of "My husband!"; Sir Harry, remarking, "What, young Chartley!"; Old Chartley, crying, "How! my son!"; and Boyster, marveling, "My grannam is a witch." The proverbial ears of a house materialize in the form of parody in this play.[12] While scenes of intercepted knowledge are both fodder for comedy and necessary engines of drama, they are also revelatory of larger social meanings and suspicions.

For private conference, as it was called in the sixteenth and seventeenth centuries, a principal strategy was to go outdoors, away from the listening walls, as Overreach suggests in Philip Massinger's *A New Way to Pay Old Debts* (1620): "Let's quit the house," to "[ex]change / Six words in private." Most often, conversants sought the nearby garden or orchard, like Bel-Imperia in Thomas Kyd's *The Spanish Tragedy* (1590), bidding Horatio to join her in a "pleasant bower" because, while "The court were dangerous, that place is safe." In John Ford's *The Broken Heart* (1629), Ithocles has "some secret" to share with Penthea. So he proposes: "Let me an hour hence / Meet you alone, within the palace grove."[13] There are resonances of these associations in the archives, too. In the diplomatic correspondence of the period, one has the sense of an operative, now lost code, a shorthand language of place. It meant one thing when an envoy was received in chambers, always crowded with courtiers, but something else again when he was invited into the royal garden for a private hearing. Ambassadors made a point of informing their superiors when they were favored with such privileged communication. Similarly, in order to emphasize the confidentiality of a conversation with Sir Thomas More, More's son-in-law William Roper specified its outdoor setting. The occasion was More's return home to Chelsea after having been brought before Parliament on a charge of misprision of treason in 1534. "Then walked we twain alone into his garden together," Roper described. In the garden, Roper was able to put questions more directly than he might have dared had he been in an enclosed space within hearing of More's wife and daughters.[14]

If private conversation was an occasion for concern among those who feared that they could not speak without being overheard, it was also, as for Bess of Hardwick, a source of anxiety for those who feared that there might be speech they were not overhearing. Elizabeth Tudor learned this lesson when she was imprisoned during the reign of her sister Mary I.[15] As John Foxe recounts at length, a five-year-old boy made daily visits to Elizabeth's Tower lodgings to bring her flowers. However, it was known that the child also had regular contact with a past participant in Wyatt's Rebellion against Mary, the Earl of Devonshire, and suspicion mounted that the child was conveying messages between the two; some thought it may have been Robert Dudley who used the child as an intermediary. Elizabeth's interior accommodations surrendered fully to the surveillance of Mary's Privy Councillors when "the child's father was commanded to permit the boy no more to come up into their chambers." But the Queen's men were less effective with respect to the "little garden" in which, after a month's repeated requests, Elizabeth had been given leave to walk for the sake of her health. There, Tower keepers were charged with monitoring other prisoners for the duration of her recreation, specifically to ensure that no one spoke to her. Elizabeth herself was always accompanied by two officials of the court and three of her own gentlewomen, a party of six to prevent any collusion of two—that is, to preclude private exchange. Nonetheless, it was in the garden that the five-year-old boy managed one last covert exchange with the imprisoned princess. "The next day," as Elizabeth "was walking" in the garden, "the child, peeping in at a hole in the door, cried unto her, saying, 'Mistress, I can bring you no more flowers.' Whereat she smiled, but said nothing, understanding thereby what they had done." On the face of it, this incident seems an unlikely subject for Foxe's project to heroize the Protestant princess. But Elizabeth's access to the outdoors, like the boy's semiotic identification with flowers, established a plausible context for resistant private knowledge in a period of persecution. The anecdote developed from and depended upon cultural conditions in which surreptitious communication was rarely associated with interior spaces.

It may seem self-evident that the best strategy for the pursuit of private conversation was to step into the garden, the area immediately beyond betraying internal walls. What must additionally be emphasized, however, is that the place was inseparably associated with a behavior, which was walking. Paths were essential to the strict geometry of Renaissance garden design. In his 1625 essay on "Gardens," Francis Bacon called for "Alleys, Spacious and Faire. . . . enough for four to walk a breast." Even in describing the scents of flowers, Bacon specified that they were to be planted so "you may walk by a whole row of them." The significance of the activity in this context can be indicated by the companion proverb to "the walls have ears": "hedges have ears." If any structure of sufficient size could conceal eavesdroppers, then what was reassuring about the garden was not only its acoustical inefficiency, as sound dissipated in open air, but also its spatial range, so that confidences could be exchanged elusively, in motion, rather than captured in stasis. Thus, in Ford's *'Tis Pity She's a Whore* (1632) Giovanni prepares to tell his sister he is incestuously in love with her by taking her outside, dismissing her attendant, saying "I would be private with you," and coaxing, "Come, sister, lend your hand, let's walk together. / I hope you need not blush to walk with me." In *Measure for Measure,* when Isabella is prevailed upon by Duke Vincentio to tell Mariana of his proposed bed trick, Mariana is called forth from "within" so that Isabella can ask, "Will't please you walk aside?"[16]

In part this is a dramaturgic technique to take a problematic conversation offstage or out of our hearing, but to this end Isabella could as easily have exited herself, as if to join Mariana "inside." Instead she enacts a dominant cultural convention regarding privacy, which in this superbly metadramatic moment is preserved against a theatrical audience as well as against the play's larger cast of characters. That this construct was sufficiently prevalent to have been thoroughly internalized is suggested by the notorious 1597 dream of Simon Forman. Forman imagines jesting to the aging Elizabeth, "I mean to wait *upon* you and not under you, that I might make this belly a little bigger to carry up this smock and coats out of the dirt." His fantasy takes him not into her bedchamber, as might seem at once more appropriate and more titillating to us, but instead outside. He remembers having delivered his scurrilous remarks as "she and I walked up and down through lanes and closes."[17] Even in his unconscious imagination, the license of space and motion were required for spoken intimacies.

Walking was a highly popular form of exercise in the sixteenth century, especially after dining, when it served, as one commentator wrote, to "send [meat] down to the bottom of [the] stomach." Elizabeth, however, preferred the mornings, and she walked at a sufficient pace "to get up a heat." In 1581, the educator Richard Mulcaster analyzed in detail the differing health benefits of walking swiftly or slowly, uphill or downhill, on even or uneven ground, over long distances or short, in sun or in shade, before midday or in the evening. He concluded that the benefits of walking were no respecters of person, age, or gender. It was "not only the most excellent exercise," he wrote, "but almost alone worthy to bear the name of an exercise."[18] This was the excellency to which the long gallery was explicitly dedicated. The 1620 will of John Wilson specified that his widow was to be permitted to "walk and recreate herself at all times in the gallery" at Charlton House. In Massinger's *A New Way to Pay Old Debts* a character describes "walking, for health sake, in the gallery."[19] A gallery at Knole still retains a pulley contraption so that those stretching their legs could also strengthen their arms. In the known physical benefits of walking, the makers of long galleries had an irreproachable pretext for their extravagance. The vast square footage and protracted extent of Tudor long galleries were deemed essential to their active purposes.

While walking was the behavior that characterized both gardens and galleries, the two had always shared other sorts of material and conceptual space, as well. Long galleries were most often built in intimate relationship to gardens, either running alongside them, providing private entrance to them, or offering overviews of them (see figure 15). The standard definition of the space is "a long room which leads nowhere [that is, it is not a corridor] but exists in its own right as a place of recreation overlooking the garden." The first known reference to a long gallery in England is from 1509, when Edmund Dudley's London house was described as having a "long gallery against the garden." A Venetian visitor to Whitehall in 1531 referred to long galleries when he described "three so-called galleries which are long porticos or halls without chambers, with windows on each side looking on rivers and gardens."[20] The paucity of goods and furnishings in a long gallery further exaggerated its kinship with the garden because, while within the dominion of the householder, it was nonetheless less marked by personality and possession than other enclosed spaces. As was also contributory to its conversational virtues, it was thus comparatively neutral territory. Through their close associations and shared activities, therefore, at least one difference between interior and exterior was deconstructed in the early modern period, until there occurred a sort of conceptual merge. By the time Francis Bacon wrote his essay "Of Gardens" in 1625, the chief aspect of the long gallery was so thoroughly established that he could read it back into the garden: there, he said, "You are to form [alleys] likewise for shelter, that when the wind blows sharp, you may walk, as in a gallery."[21]

No interior structure could seem more unnatural on first acquaintance, more transformational, more a flight from what we suppose to be rational

Figure 15. The long gallery wing at Haddon Hall, Derbyshire, overlooking the garden. Photographed by the author.

architectural organization. This was space thinly interiorized, wrapped to the extent possible in sheets of glass, often tethered to the house merely by one long shared wall, sometimes only by an end wall. Frequently, the gallery went "without chambers," that is, without the proximity to other spaces adjoining it or beyond it that characterized all other architectural experience. Its main connection with the rest of the house was not a room but a staircase, which through its own vertical shaft also worked its way free of the horizontal map of interrelated household spaces. The near-perfect autonomy of some long galleries was part of their almost magical affiliation with the outside world, with gardens. Hardwick was designed from the first to culminate in its long gallery, but many houses had to be retrofitted to accommodate the Tudor craze for the space. It was easy enough to create new parlors and private dining chambers in old buildings, for these rooms were boxy, interchangeable, and adaptable. But at The Vyne, for example, where the first long gallery in a private home was built in the early 1520s, a whole new wing had to be constructed. Little Moreton Hall in Cheshire was a rambling fifteenth-century house of two stories throughout until 1570 or so, when a third floor was superimposed on a gatehouse wing for a gallery with ornamental plasterwork and with windows on both long sides (see figure 16). At Penshurst in Kent, a new two-storied wing was constructed in 1599, linking one section of the house with a freestanding tower, the long gallery on the upper level and a "nether gallery" below letting out into the garden (see figure 17). At Burton Agnes, in Humberside, frontal symmetry was ingeniously executed. But the mounting of a third story along the entrance façade, only for the sake of a long gallery running the entire width of the building, rendered the side façades oddly asymmetrical (see figure 12). Astley Hall in Lancashire was significantly remodeled as late as 1656, but it was a curious throwback, thoroughly Elizabethan in design, with another third story added only across the front to allow for a glass-walled long gallery (see figure 18). In imperfectly integrated spaces such as these, the free-floating autonomy of the long gallery realized its purest form. Its nature was to be hospitable to private conversation.

The network of associations between garden, gallery, walking, and intimacy can be traced in an investigation conducted by Elizabeth's Privy Council in December 1580. Edward de Vere, seventeenth Earl of Oxford, had accused Charles Arundel, Henry Howard, and Francis Southwell of treason. Arundel counterclaimed that he had incurred Oxford's anger by refusing to falsely name the two others papists. The attempted solicitation was made, according to Arundel, "On Sunday last, being Christmas Day," when Oxford "desired secret conference with me." Their appointed rendezvous was outside "the Maids' chamber door" at Whitehall Palace, where Anne Vavasor, then six months pregnant by Oxford, "was the mean of our meeting." Together, the two men "departed thence

Figure 16. The gatehouse wing at Little Moreton Hall, Cheshire. Photographed by the author.

Figure 17. The long gallery wing at Penshurst Place. Photographed by the author.

Figure 18. Astley Hall, Lancashire. Photographed by the author.

to have gone to the garden. But the door being double locked or bolted, we could not get in. Then we returned to the terrace and there, in the farther part of the low gallery," the private conversation that was in search of a secure location finally took place. Oxford and Arundel had moved uneasily from the eavesdropping household out toward a garden but, finding it inaccessible, had sought its domestic cognate. The "low gallery" at Whitehall ran along the east side of the Privy Garden and may have been named for its proximity to the Thames.[22] If Arundel's anecdote goes to confirm the related uses of gardens and galleries, another report from Guzman de Silva suggests that on some occasions the gallery could be even more facilitative of private conversation. In July 1564, the Spanish ambassador wrote Philip II that he had called on Elizabeth where she visited in a courtier's house. She was walking in a garden at the time with her noblemen and ladies, and de Silva was shown into a room while his arrival was announced. She then honored him by sending for him to join her, and bid him "forget that the Queen was there and look upon her as a private lady." He indicated his awareness of others about her, and "answered that wherever monarchs were there was their regal state, as I perceived in this case." Elizabeth rose to the implicit challenge. "We then went into a very large gallery, where she took me aside for nearly an hour."[23] In the long gallery, Elizabeth was able to be as "private" a lady as was possible for her.

Walking is mentioned so often in these accounts that it must have come to serve as a sort of mnemonic device, a conditioned response to the stimulus of the site. The behavior, walking, was itself capable of inciting the state of being, privacy. But in some cases walking seemed to be no more than a necessary prologue to private conversation. It actively reassured discussants that they were taking themselves out of the overhearing range of others, especially as they reached the "farther part" of a gallery. With their conversational intents established, however, they might then step "aside" into one or another of the long gallery's bay windows, each the size of a small room and containing any meager furnishings the gallery might have (see figure 19). The bay represented a distinct advance over the garden in nurturing conversational privacy. It was a structural paradox: a defined, interior space that had no interior walls at all. It projected out into empty air at the second or third story, was wrapped in glass on three sides, and for a fourth opened into the long gallery, itself nearly free-floating. A space without walls was a space miraculously incapable of sustaining the proverbial listening "ears" of the treacherous house. The sound of private conversation was contained in the bay and protected, for there was no chance that any other walker could approach unnoticed. Francis Bacon called "inbowed windows" "pretty retiring places for conferences," and that was precisely how Sir Piers Legh used his bay window at Lyme Park in the late sixteenth century. Seated there, he met with members of his household, gave them

Figure 19. The long gallery bay at Haddon Hall. Photographed by the author.

their wages, and heard their complaints.[24] In the bay, each could be assured that these discussions took place in confidence.

Inevitably, other meanings were to attach to galleries; Bess of Hardwick's tapestries, for example, were symptoms of an impulse to provide the walker with visual diversion. The paintings and portraits that were also hung were eventually to transform the very idea of the space, so that by the late seventeenth century the "gallery" had accrued its modern connotation as an exhibition area.[25] And even in the sixteenth century, galleries lived active, signifying lives in status rivalries, as François I inquired jealously after the length of Henry VIII's gallery, or as the builder of Berwick vowed that "Worksop gallery was but a garret in respect of the gallery that would there be" (that is, at Berwick).[26] It would be a mistake, though, to think that elite competitions and private conversations had entirely disparate histories; the contrary is proved true for one of the earliest English builders of long galleries, Thomas Wolsey.

All evidences are that the long gallery was a French invention, and it was in France that Wolsey encountered the space. His man George Cavendish describes a diplomatic mission in which the English cardinal met with the French king at a castle in Compiègne. Making a subtle testimony to Wolsey's standing, Cavendish says that the lodging space at Compiègne was strictly distributed. Even the long gallery was "divided between them, wherein was made in the middest thereof a strong wall with a door and window." According to Cavendish, "the king and my lord would many times meet at the same window and secretly talk togethers." Cavendish's means of visual access to these unheard conversations was probably as described in Wolsey's own long gallery at York Place. There, Wolsey placed a form (or bench) at one end so that his attendants could "take their ease" as he conducted negotiations further along, out of overhearing range. Wolsey had strategic uses for his large household, as also for his vast space. When Henry VIII confided his "secret affection" and "secret intendment" for Anne Boleyn, it was because the king required Wolsey's intervention in the matter of a competing "secret love," the private understanding between Boleyn and Henry Percy. To end the affair, Wolsey sought to expose it. Although he summoned Percy to his long gallery, he spoke within earshot of all the "servants of his chamber": "I marvel not a little . . . of thy peevish folly that thou wouldst tangle and ensure thyself with a foolish girl." Wolsey also called Percy's formidable father, the Earl of Northumberland, to London. The two men had "secret communication" at the far end of the gallery. Northumberland then replicated Wolsey's strategy, walking to the bench-sitters to say distinctly, "Son . . . thou hast always been a proud, presumptious, disdainful, and a very unthrifty waster." The process of taking this private matter to a private space but then exposing it in a publicly humiliating way had the desired, coercive effect; Percy broke off with Anne Boleyn.[27] Like Henry Brounker, who did Bess of Hardwick one better in exploiting the uses of her long gallery, Wolsey took thorough advantage of the psychological impacts of his domestic environment. At the same time, it is apparent from Cavendish's reports that Wolsey himself enjoyed the frisson associated with his power to achieve privacy, especially when he could stage it as a public event. It is scarcely surprising that as the long gallery achieved its full range of private meanings, it was also eroticized.

In 1572 George Gascoigne published his notoriously pornographic *Adventures of Master F. J.,* in which all the attributes of the long gallery—its conversational intimacy, its ambulatory range, its structural autonomy, its spatial neutrality, its outdoor analogies—took on a sexual charge.[28] The fictional F. J.'s infatuation for the married Dame Elinor is represented as having first been encouraged in a garden (146). Their relationship advances, however, when "his chance was to meet her alone in a gallery of the same house," where "they walked and talked traversing divers ways" and where, as he offers to kiss her hand, she instead kisses his lips (148–49). The intimacy of this scene is set in high relief by subsequent action in Elinor's bedchamber, which is always shown to be crowded with a "company" of other gentlemen and women (151–52). F. J. then "counsel[s] his Mistress by little and little to walk abroad, saying that the gallery near adjoining was so pleasant, as if he were half dead he thought that by walking therein he might be half and more revived" (156). The next night, "taking him apart from the rest" who clutter the chamber-landscape, Elinor suggests that "she would talk with him more at large in the gallery" (167). F. J. waits until the servant sharing his own chamber is safely asleep. Then, with his nightgown concealing his "naked sword," he steals "to the gallery, where he finds his good Mistress walking in her night gown." There follows a vivid depiction of their lovemaking on the "hard floor" (167–68).

C. T. Prouty, long Gascoigne's chief editor, calls these markers of "the physical environment" "added details which have no direct connection with the action of the love story."[29] This of course goes against the grain of all this chapter would argue regarding material structures and how they shaped early modern social and secret relations. In fact, nearly every stage of F. J.'s love story has a totemic point of intersection with the long gallery, including its unhappy conclusion. The affair is made known to Elinor's sister, and F. J. thereafter grows suspicious that Elinor has lost interest in him. He haunts "the gallery near adjoining unto his mistress' chamber," wishing that it might work its magic yet one more time (167). But, walking there, he overhears Dame Elinor and her "secretary" exchanging ominously "kind words." With the secretary wielding the phallic pen, F. J. becomes all ears, listening surreptitiously near the threshold (214).[30] The long gallery is not implicated in the sister's discovery of the affair; other spaces are, and now the easily eavesdropped bedchamber betrays Elinor's newer secrets and dashes F. J.'s forlorn hopes. This pattern of associations with both bedchambers and long galleries had been observable only the year before, in another discursive realm, among the interrogations into the Duke of Norfolk's treason.

The Ridolfi Plot

In Shakespeare's dramaturgy, famously, locations are identified only when they have significance. The same cannot be said for archival records, and especially witness depositions, where the questions prepared in advance, or interrogatories, often ask for reports of events to be grounded in specific times and places. But there may nonetheless have been larger connotations to the fact that in the Brounker investigation and the Arundel allegation, both of which were concerned with possible treason, long galleries featured so strongly. Locational mappings in the Ridolfi plot suggest as much. The events of 1568 through 1571 included schemes that were variously diplomatic, military, and subversive: to free Mary Queen of Scots from imprisonment in England, to raise funds for her in Catholic countries in Europe, to place her on the throne of England (if necessary with the aid of Spanish forces in the Netherlands), and to restore the Catholic religion in England. To advance Mary's claim on the crown, it was proposed that she should be married to the most elevated of England's aristocrats, the only living possessor of a dukedom and, as such, "the second person in this realm."[31] Thomas Howard, fourth Duke of Norfolk was implicated in a complex, shifting series of plots that were developed in gardens, parks, and, repeatedly, long galleries.[32]

Norfolk had a long personal history with Elizabeth, being kin to her through her Boleyn connections, and a significant public involvement with Scotland, having served the Queen as Lieutenant General of the North from 1559. In this role he became an ally of Cecil's, and, in 1562, he was made a member of the Privy Council. In 1564, he joined in anxious discussions of "the Mary problem." At the time, Mary Stewart represented trouble primarily within Scotland, to which she had returned following the death of her first husband, François II, in 1560. Having come of age, she assumed a personal rule in her birth country despite the opposition of powerful Scottish lords. Her principal allies included William Maitland of Lethington and her illegitimate half-brother, Lord James Stewart, whom she created first Earl of Moray. Within two months of her arrival in Scotland, Mary had commissioned Maitland to represent her to Elizabeth in requesting that she be named next in line of succession to the English throne. This, Elizabeth declined to do; instead, in 1564, Elizabeth suggested that Mary might be matched with Robert Dudley, recently made a more suitable partner through his elevation to Earl of Leicester. The idea was that "the Mary problem" would be best contained were she married not to a Catholic foreign prince but instead to a Protestant English nobleman. Later, with the Leicester match tabled, both Henry Fitzalan, twelfth Earl of Arundel, and also the newly widowed Norfolk were put forward as possible husbands, but Mary made the independent decision to wed her cousin Henry Stewart, Lord Darnley. Though his own initiatives were betrayed by this marriage, Maitland remained loyal to Mary. Moray, by contrast, was sufficiently opposed to the Darnley match that he broke with his sister irrevocably. Following the ignominious failure of his rebellion, the so-called "Chase about Raid," he retreated to France. In 1567, however, Moray was called back to Scotland. That year, Darnley was murdered; Mary was abducted by James Hepburn, fourth Earl of Bothwell, and then married him; Mary relinquished the throne to her infant son; and Moray, a committed Protestant, became Regent of Scotland during the minority of James VI. Meanwhile, in England, the succession issue was again urgently pressed. At this point, Norfolk favored the candidacy of Katherine Grey and not, as Leicester did, Mary Stewart. The pieces came together differently beginning in 1568.

In May of that year, the dethroned Scottish Queen sought refuge in England. Elizabeth authorized an October commission on her future. Mary agreed to the summit on the understanding that the subjects in arbitration should be the conditions for her return to power in Scotland. She was herself unable to attend the negotiations in York, being domiciled at Bolton not quite under house arrest but not entirely at her free choice, either; Maitland represented her interests, as did John Leslie, Bishop of Ross. Moray appeared in opposition to her. Elizabeth appointed as mediators Thomas Radcliffe, third Earl of Sussex, Sir Ralph Sadler, and, as chief commissioner, Norfolk. Although Norfolk seems not to have been enthusiastic, he accepted a charge that was to prove so fateful that allies subsequently suggested that his enemies had intended to entrap him by means of this assignment. In York, he went hawking privately with Maitland, and outdoors, alone, Maitland raised anew the possibility of a match between Norfolk and Mary. The alliance would advance Maitland's own goals to secure Mary's position and unite the two kingdoms, and it now achieved a more favorable reception from Norfolk. With some prospects for Elizabeth's marriage newly abandoned, with Katherine Grey recently dead, and with Mary auspiciously furnished with a male heir, Mary's claim to the English succession suddenly appeared significantly stronger. Norfolk could anticipate that the normal course of events, which at some point would include Elizabeth's natural death, would bring him to the throne of England.

Thus encouraged, Maitland advised Moray and Ross to undertake "familiar conference" with Norfolk, each to "speak with the Duke secretly alone, without the [other] commissioners." Ross and Norfolk "talked alone in a gallery," cautiously acknowledging common interests. And Moray, who by this point regarded Maitland as a "necessary evil," also agreed to meet Norfolk at a "time and place convenient in the gallery of the house where the Duke was lodged." In the private exchange that the long gallery admitted, the two men concluded that they themselves, each so powerful and so esteemed in his own country, represented the best hope for amity between England and Scotland.[33] At Norfolk's later trial for treason, his accusers traced the origins of his misplaced ambition and suspicious behavior back to York: "If you meant directly, then needed you not to have dealt so secretly in conference with Lethington without the rest of the commissioners." Both Ross and Moray, it was said, had confirmed "your practicing with them to the same intent."[34]

Norfolk and his fellows were abruptly summoned south for a new commission, the Westminster Conference. The climate had changed, and Mary's reinstatement in Scotland was no longer at issue. Instead, Moray, who had been promised that Mary would not be restored were she proved guilty of murder, displayed the "Casket Letters." These have since been proved fraudulent, but at the time they had the sensational effect of seeming to show that Mary had committed adultery with Bothwell and had conspired with him to kill Darnley. Before Mary's allies adjourned the commission, admitting defeat, Moray and Norfolk again met independently. In the park at Hampton Court, Norfolk carefully deplored the events of Mary's recent past, but he said that he might nonetheless "find in [his] heart to love" her if she repented her ill-advised behavior and divorced Bothwell.[35] The eventual charges against Norfolk emphasized not the substance of this discussion with Moray but the fact that the two men "secretly confer[red] in the park."

The next spring, at Easter time 1569, Norfolk tested the idea of marriage with Mary on his man Lawrence Bannister, this time in the garden of his own London residence, Howard House.[36] Cecil, who may originally have approved the notion, withdrew his support after quarrelling with Norfolk in May or June. Leicester and William Herbert, first Earl of Pembroke, rallied to the proposed union; their motives included opposition to the man whose increasing power had not long before been celebrated in his creation as Lord Burghley. Other supporters of the marriage included strange bedfellows Moray and Maitland, the English agent Sir Nicholas Throckmorton, and the Scottish go-between Ross. In June 1569, Mary herself agreed to wed Norfolk, though she raised the crucial question of how

Elizabeth's approval was to be obtained. It was one thing for Elizabeth herself to have matched one of her noblemen with her Scottish "sister," but, as the Earl of Hertford knew, it was another thing entirely for plans to go forward without the English Queen's knowledge and consent. Norfolk had already discussed the issue with Leicester as Leicester sat fishing at Thames-side near Kew.

Leicester insisted that he should broach the subject with Elizabeth himself. It was nearly a year before the time seemed right to him. On September 6, 1569, Leicester spoke with the Queen while she was on progress, at the Earl of Southampton's house in Titchfield. Elizabeth immediately summoned Norfolk to the Titchfield gallery for a private confrontation. She "commanded and charged him that he should not deal any further with the Queen of Scots, nor any other person in that matter." Later, she said she had charged him "upon his allegiance," which meant that to defy her was treason. Norfolk professed at first not to remember this stricture. He may have been emboldened in his denial by the knowledge that the long gallery would yield up no third parties to contradict him. If so, this was another mark of the arrogance he is said to have displayed throughout, because the principal witness against him was an incontrovertible one. He was to be asked sarcastically if he could name a single occasion on which he had in fact honored his Titchfield pledge: "I pray you, at what time . . . *did* you forbear to deal with the Scottish queen?" (emphasis added). Under the duress of his trial, he finally admitted that Elizabeth had indeed engaged his allegiance.[37]

Ten days later, Norfolk angrily left Titchfield without Elizabeth's permission to do so. He traveled to London to meet with Pembroke. It could be argued that at this point Norfolk still imagined only a politic marriage and an orderly succession, and that he did not countenance the plots of others to secure the help of Spain, to rally a force to free Mary from her current captivity, and to revolt against Elizabeth. But it also seems increasingly unlikely that he was entirely ignorant of these plans. Hugh Owen, a servant of Norfolk's father-in-law the Earl of Arundel, later reported that he joined Norfolk on the road to London and there told him of a scheme to seize the Tower of London. Its treasures were to be used to fund Mary's cause. Ross confirmed that the "device" of the Tower had been concocted in the long gallery at Arundel House, where he, Arundel, Norfolk's man Liggons, and also Roberto Ridolfi met. At Norfolk's trial much was made of the fact that his knowledge of the device proved an "intention to pursue the marriage with force."[38]

Norfolk was himself in London for less than a week in the fall of 1569, but in that time Ross was secretly smuggled into Howard House. Liggons met Ross at about seven o'clock in the evening at Norfolk's great gate, showed him to the Back Court, and led him into the gallery. The secretary

William Barker did not see or hear the meeting, but he observed that Ross came "privily" and "closely," through the "backside," rather than openly as in the past. He later remembered speculating with his fellows as to why Norfolk and Ross "dare[d] not be seen in their business"—in other words, why the meeting and their conversation were so private.[39]

Norfolk was warned by Leicester that there was talk of his imprisonment and, in late September 1569, he hastily left London for his country estate, Kenninghall. Within two weeks, however, he was placed under house arrest in the custody of Sir Francis Knollys and Sir Henry Neville, who were advised that the duke was to be held "without conference with any person without your knowledge." On October 8, Norfolk was returned to London, interrogated, and confined in the Tower so that he could be watched and, again, so that "no conference [could] be had" with him. Except for one reported discussion between Norfolk and his secretary Robert Higford on the leads (the Tower roof), Norfolk's part in the Ridolfi plot temporarily ceased to operate by means of secret conversations in walking spaces.[40] The correspondence of the conspirators continued actively, however. Norfolk himself wrote to Mary in cipher and sent her tokens of courtship.[41] And Ridolfi smuggled news from the Continent into England. When his encrypted papers were intercepted, Sir Henry Cobham, Lord Warden of the Cinque Ports, was persuaded to protect his friends by substituting innocent letters in the packet sent on to Cecil. In subsequent months, Cobham required multiple meetings in his long gallery, demanding reassurance that his part in the plot would not be revealed.[42] Meanwhile, Ross met with the Earl of Shrewsbury's man, John Hall, in Ross's gallery in Islington. Shrewsbury, fourth husband to Bess of Hardwick, was now Mary's jailor in his houses at Tutbury and Sheffield. Ross persuaded Hall to smuggle out letters from Mary to her followers; Hall was to be intercepted with the incriminating documents.

Cecil, said to be "always upon the watch," had "bent his mind diligently to sift out the matter" of Norfolk's "secret conferences." Ridolfi was called in at the same time Norfolk was; some have speculated that because he was held in Sir Francis Walsingham's house rather than the Tower there may have been an attempt to "turn" him into a double agent, and even that the attempt may have been successful (though from the course of subsequent events this seems unlikely).[43] Governmental concern escalated in the wake of the Northern Rising, also known as the Revolt of the Northern Earls, which was launched on November 14, 1569. Tracing the trajectories of the various plots that had revealed themselves to him, Cecil also questioned the Earl of Moray. He received the Scottish regent's account of the York and Westminster conferences before Moray was assassinated in January 1570.

Norfolk had known that the Northern Rising would endanger him by seeming to implicate him, and indeed it was two months before Elizabeth accepted his letter denying any part in or sympathy with the insurgency. Many more months passed before he wrote a humble letter of "submission," promising "upon his faith and allegiance" never again "to deal with that marriage nor with any other matter touching the Scottish Queen." Thus he implicitly admitted that he had violated the pledge already made at Titchfield; he also, duplicitously, sent a copy of the letter to Mary by way of Ross. It was said that Norfolk was permitted to leave the Tower on August 3, 1570 for fear of plague, but there was subsequent speculation that this represented another strategic attempt to give him enough space to fatally incriminate himself. Although Norfolk continued under supervision at Howard House, Ridolfi met with him there less than a week after his release, and Ross made a clandestine visit in December. Norfolk's man Bannister testified that "he left the door open of his own lodging, which hath a back-door in the duke's house . . . for the Bishop of Ross to come to the duke secretly."[44] The usual pattern was for secret meetings to be held in the long gallery. As Barker later deposed, Ridolfi met with Norfolk in the gallery at Howard House twice more in the spring of 1571, each time around eight or nine o'clock, after Norfolk's keeper Neville was safely in bed. Barker was so specific, describing the differing surreptitious routes used on each occasion, that it was prejudicial to Norfolk when, at his trial, he disputed the report of a second assignation. With respect to the first, he claimed to have met with Ridolfi only to negotiate a personal loan. His prosecutor asked rhetorically, "What needeth that secret coming in the night time about a private cause?"[45]

Norfolk subsequently consulted again with Bannister. Mary was restless and eager to flee to the Continent, and a plan had been evolved for her escape from a window in Shrewsbury's long gallery. Ross had measured the casement in preparation. But Norfolk dispatched Bannister to persuade Ross that England was the safest place for her. By this time, Ross was lodging near Paul's Wharf. The meeting between Bannister and Ross took place "in the gallery alone." Bannister reported back to Norfolk "in the gallery over the gate" at Howard House, carrying three letters that Ross had prepared for Norfolk's signature. The plot now centered more certainly on the removal of Elizabeth and restoration of the Roman church, and the conspirators sought monetary and military support from Pope Pius V, Philip II of Spain, and Philip's governor in the Netherlands, the Duke of Alva. Norfolk refused to sign the letters, however: "if I should set my hand to this, I shall commit treason." In a second meeting between Ross and Bannister, a compromise was reached. Norfolk's name would appear on the documents, if not his autograph. Norfolk's man Barker would "affirm" the duke's support of the letters to the Spanish ambassador in London. And Barker would travel to Europe with Ridolfi, as Norfolk's public surrogate in the fundraising efforts. In the gallery at Howard House, Norfolk gave instructions to Barker privately.[46]

Ross's servant Charles Bailly was taken with damaging letters in April 1571. Within a few months more, other aspects of the scheme were fully exposed. In Italy, Ridolfi had confided too much to Cosimo de Medici, who promptly sent a warning to Elizabeth. In England, it was said, the plot "was opened by God himself."[47] The authentic originals of the letters switched by Cobham found their way into Cecil's hands. And a draper named Thomas Browne came to Cecil with a suspicious package. Barker and Higford had asked Browne to carry a bag to Bannister, then in the north; they told him it contained £50 in silver. Instead, Cecil discovered £600 in gold meant for Mary, along with some letters written in cipher. He had Howard House searched, and the key to the cipher was found there. With this and with information gathered in multiple interrogations, Cecil ordered Norfolk confined to his chamber in early September 1571. On November 22, 1571 a preliminary hearing on Norfolk's case was held, and on January 16, 1572 his trial opened. That night he was found to have committed treason by seeking to deprive Elizabeth of her crown and her life, by giving aid to the rebels of the Northern Rising, and by assisting others of the Queen's enemies. Those who ruled him guilty included the earls of Leicester, Hertford, Pembroke, and Sussex. Before his execution, there were attempts to cause uprisings in the north as a distraction, so that he might be broken out of the Tower by loyal Londoners, but these came to nothing. Norfolk was beheaded on Tower Hill on June 2, 1572.

Cecil, largely silent during the trial, had interrupted at one point to ask why Norfolk produced no witnesses in his own behalf and brought forward no evidence of his innocence. This was to suggest that the case against him was so strong that it was incontestable, but the question went also to the continuing mystery of Norfolk's motivation in the matter of the Ridolfi plot. Though he had fallen in with the conspiracy against Elizabeth and had withheld information about it from her and from her government, he seems not to have been sufficiently moved to devise any aspect of it himself. He vehemently denied that his objective was to restore the Roman church, claiming always to have been a loyal Protestant, insisting in his last letters to his children that they should give no credence to false rumors of his papistry, and declaring his Anglican orthodoxy on the scaffold, too. His prosecutors suggested an overreaching ambition. In consequence of the Casket Letters, they said, he must necessarily have had "an evil opinion" of Mary Stewart. Thus, it was impossible to believe that he might "seek the marriage in respect of her person"—that is, for love. It must have been "in respect of her false title, and that not to the kingdom of Scotland, which she had not, and which [he] despised, but to the Crown of England."

Only one witness claimed to understand Norfolk rather than to interpret him, and that was Higford. On the leads of the Tower, he said, Norfolk had confided that his chief motivation was grievance, because he was not in the Queen's favor. In fact, his behavior at trial seemed consistent with Higford's image of a man full of self-importance and resentment. As Cecil remarked, Norfolk mounted no defense. He confined himself to what his prosecutor called "a bare denying." He leaned heavily on his stature. He derogated the standing of those whose depositions were read into the record: Ridolfi was absent, he said, in Europe; Ross was a foreigner and a Scot; Barker was an admitted traitor himself. Others he dismissed contemptuously as men whose spending money amounted to fewer than five marks a year. He spoke more often to the alleged illegitimacy of the investigation and trial than to the matter of the charges, demanding legal counsel, asking to see his accusers face-to-face, and raising challenges to readings of the applicable statutes. These were, in fact, legitimate.[48]

Norfolk's most cogent substantive complaint may have been that "the indictment containeth sundry points and matters to touch me by circumstance and so to draw me into matter of treason, which are not treasons themselves." Indeed, Cecil and his agents had set out to prove "how the design was continued by secret conferences and messages . . . and by other indirect means of dissimulation and falsehood on the part of the Duke."[49] The circumstantial evidence to which Norfolk referred was the long roster of clandestine meetings that included encounters held safely out of doors, while hawking at York, in a park at Hampton Court, in the garden at Howard House, while fishing in the Thames, and on the road to London. There was also the string of secret conferences in the long galleries at York, at Titchfield, at Arundel House, at Cobham's house, in Ross's residences in Islington and near Paul's Wharf, and, over and over again, at Howard House.

All information about the consultations held in these long galleries proceeded from the principals, not any observers. There were no reports of eavesdropping in these vast and curiously configured Tudor spaces. By contrast, the bedchambers of the Ridolfi plot again revealed their unreliable nature. In the early spring of 1571, for example, William Barker was summoned to Ross's lodgings one morning. Ross had not yet risen, and Barker "sat by him on the further side of his bed next the wall. . . . While we were talking, one of his men came to him, and told him, there was one would speak with him." It was Hugh Owen. Ross advised Barker he would "hear more of the matter." Ross drew the bed curtain "so that [Barker] was not seen" behind it. At Ross's bedside and in Barker's hearing, Owen reported that Sir Henry Percy had enlisted in their cause. A related spatial dynamic is operative in the deposition of a go-between named Edmund Powell. Powell would visit Ross secretly in the night and then convey news to Sir Thomas Stanley. After one session with Ross, Powell went to Stanley's "own chamber at Cannon Row." Powell deposed that "Sir Edward Stanley was by in the chamber, but heard no part of our talk. There was none else present with me, nor heard anything."[50] No one describing a conference in a gallery needed to say, "There was none else present, nor heard anything." In the Ridolfi plot, this may have been the most important of the long gallery's meanings: it was generally understood to perpetuate an impenetrable privacy.

As is true for any case with this sort of import and level of scandal, and especially one relying primarily on witness testimonies, the textual record is far from trustworthy. The interrogations necessarily produced self-serving lies, evasions, omissions, and exaggerations. But whether or not all the secret meetings of the Ridolfi plot took place as reported, or had the agendas described, is not at issue here. My subject is the signifying capacity of space. In cases like the Brounker investigation at Hardwick Hall, the preclusive nature of the gallery was, clearly, material. On other occasions, though, the room may have created an effect of privacy rather than its actual experience, and this was equally powerful. The gallery's chief virtues were less auditory than visual, in that no conversants could approach unseen or listen at a nearby threshold unknown. In fact the rooms may have been quite "live" acoustically; in later years some would earn the name "whispering galleries" for the fact that words spoken at one end could be heard at the other. Thus, Brounker may have relied on age-related impairment to Bess of Hardwick's hearing when he staged his inaudible interview in her gallery. What seems incontrovertible in the Ridolfi case, however, is that a deponent who said that he had witnessed a meeting that took place in a gallery was in effect declaring that it could not be overheard. And his examiners accepted this investigative dead-end. Indeed the gallery seems to have provided a legitimate way for some on the fringes of the plot to state, "I could not overhear; I cannot testify." The history of privacy is a history of perception and convention, and the Ridolfi plot charts the development of a cultural construct in which conversational privacy was mediated through the specific space of the long gallery.

The primary significance of the spatial history that Cecil compiled was what it revealed to him about the intent of those who resorted to their long galleries. They sought to exploit its accidental effects to traitorous ends. Norfolk could not be accused of a literal act of treason: Elizabeth was still alive on the throne, he was not married to Mary Stewart, the Scottish Queen was still in custody, Spanish troops had not invaded from the Netherlands, the country was not in liege to Rome. Norfolk was condemned largely for having demonstrated in historically specific ways a suspicious intent to be private. While an earlier Scots ruler, King Duncan, was imagined by Shakespeare to have puzzled over the surprising treason of his thane of Cawdor, Cecil and his agents believed that in the matter of Thomas Howard, fourth Duke of Norfolk, they had found a mind's construction in his space.

NOTES

This paper developed out of my experience of walking in surviving long galleries; the first of several tours was conducted with the help of a Summer Stipend from the National Endowment for the Humanities. I am particularly grateful to the National Trust, private and municipal owners, and the staffs at Astley Hall (Lancashire), Aston Hall (West Midlands), Audley End (Essex), Blakesley Hall (West Midlands), Burghley House (Lincolnshire), Burton Agnes Hall (Yorkshire), Charterhouse (London), Chastleton House (Oxfordshire), Gosfield Hall (Essex), Haddon Hall (Derbyshire), Hardwick Hall (Derbyshire), Hatfield House (Hertfordshire), Holdenby House (Northamptonshire), Knole (Kent), Little Moreton Hall (Cheshire), Lyme Park (Cheshire), Montacute House (Somerset), Parham House (Sussex), Penshurst Place (Kent), and The Vyne (Hampshire). Further research was completed while on fellowship at the Center for Advanced Study in the Visual Arts at the National Gallery of Art; I am indebted to Henry Millon, Stephen Mansbach, and Therese O'Malley. At the Folger Shakespeare Library I would like to thank especially Betsy Walsh, Rosalind Larry, LuEllen DeHaven, Harold Beattie, and Camille Seeratan. Conversations with Sheila ffolliott, Pamela Tudor-Craig, and Alan H. Nelson were critical to the development of the argument. I am also grateful for those audiences who heard the paper in its various stages: at the Modern Language Association (thanks to Patricia Fumerton and Don Wayne), at the University of Delaware (thanks to Lois Potter), at the Renaissance Society of America (thanks to Linda Charnes), at the University of Houston (thanks to Ann Christensen, Lois Zamora, and Laura Oren), at the University of Maryland, College Park (thanks to William Sherman and Theodore Leinwand), and at the University of Nebraska School of Architecture (thanks to Mark Hinchman, Benjamin Kroll, Kate Saroka, and Carole Levin). An early version of the chapter has appeared in print in *InForm: The Journal of Architecture, Design, and Material Culture* 2 (2001): 84–98. Batsford publishers kindly authorized reproduction of many of the illustrations.

1. Demographic, social, and architectural change is treated more fully in my *Elizabethan Households: An Anthology* (Washington, DC: Folger Shakespeare Library, 1995). Some long gallery measurements come from *The History of the King's Works, Volume 4, 1485–1660 (Part II)*, ed. H. M. Colvin et al. (London: Her Majesty's Stationery Office, 1982); others, from guidebooks to the individual houses listed (as is also the case for other material, below, when not specifically documented). In a 1650 survey, a gallery in Whitehall only 55 feet long and 11 1/2 feet wide was described as being "large and spacious"; see gen. eds. Montagu H. Cox and Philip Norman, *The Survey of London, Vol. 13: The Parish of St. Margaret, Westminster, Part II (Neighbourhood of Whitehall, Vol. 1)* (London: B. T. Batsford for London City Council, 1930), 232. It seems also as if there were even more modest versions of the space. At Blakesley Hall in Birmingham, for example, there is a large open area on the upper level, occupying the main front of the house, with two bay windows—all features of a long gallery—but just 35 feet long. The house was built in 1590 by Richard Smalbroke, a merchant and farmer. The space is termed a "long gallery" in the Department of Local History Information Sheet 15 compiled by the Birmingham Museums and Art Gallery.

2. For more on this, see my "'Causes and Reasons of all Artificial Things' in the Eliza-bethan Domestic Environment," *Medieval and Renaissance Drama in England* 7 (1995): 19–75.

3. See Mark Girouard, *Robert Smythson and the Elizabethan Country House* (New Haven, CT: Yale University Press, 1983), 143–60, and also Girouard's National Trust guidebook to *Hardwick Hall* (1976 and revised ed., 1989).

4. The incident recounted below has become familiar in recent years through work on women writers. See especially Sara Jayne Steen, ed., *The Letters of Lady Arbella Stuart,* Women Writers in English, 1350–1850 (New York: Oxford University Press, 1994), 28–44 and 120–76; and also Barbara Kiefer Lewalski, "Writing Resistance in Letters: Arbella Stuart and the Rhetoric of Disguise and Defiance," in *Writing Women in Jacobean England* (Cambridge, MA: Harvard University Press, 1993), 71–77. For this spatial analysis of the story, I have also consulted the *Calendar of the Manuscripts of . . . Salisbury, Preserved at Hatfield House,* 24 vols. (London: His/Her Majesty's Stationery Office, 1883–1976), 12: 593–97 and 12: 681–96 (Series of letters from or connected with Lady Arbella Stuart); David N. Durant, *Bess of Hardwick: Portrait of an Elizabethan Dynast* (New York: Atheneum, 1978), 202–8; Durant, *Arbella Stuart, a Rival to the Queen* (London: Weidenfeld and Nicolson, 1978); Sarah Gristwood, *Arbella: England's Lost Queen* (London: Bantam, 2003); and *Oxford DNB* entries for Elizabeth Talbot (by Elizabeth Goldring) and Arbella Stuart (by Rosalind K. Marshall).

5. Henry VII's daughter Margaret Tudor had three husbands. Mary of Scotland was Margaret's granddaughter by her first marriage to James IV of Scotland. Arbella Stuart was Margaret's great-granddaughter by her second marriage to Archibald Douglas. The Hard-wick connection came with the marriage of Margaret's grandson Charles Stuart to Bess of Hardwick's daughter (by her second marriage) Elizabeth Cavendish; Charles Stuart and Elizabeth Cavendish were Arbella Stuart's parents.

6. Steen is skeptical that the throne was Arbella's principal goal; she notes that Stuart's "consistently stated objectives were freedom from her grandmother's domination, the right to live where she chose, and the opportunity to marry" (*Letters,* 30). Brounker's view was that she sought mainly to draw attention to a situation that she found intolerable.

7. Henry VIII's Act of Succession of 1544 listed his three children, then the four descendants of his older sister Margaret (including James V and Mary of Scotland), and finally the four descendants of his younger sister Mary (with Katherine Grey preceded by her older sister Jane).

8. Steen suggests that Hertford refused to see Dodderidge without witnesses and that, once Dodderidge's mission was made public, Hertford had no choice but to "exonerate himself" (*Letters,* 31).

9. There were studies, but only in the wealthiest houses. Although the watercloset or flush toilet was invented at the very end of the century by Elizabeth's godson Sir John Harington, it was regarded as a fantastic contraption and was not to replace the chamber-pot and the privy for decades.

10. The definitive work on the long gallery is that of Rosalys Coope in "The 'Long Gallery': Its Origins, Development, Use, and Decoration," *Architectural History* 29 (1986): 43–72, and in this splendid study she has preceded me in many conclusions. Citing the Hardwick incident and the long-gallery conversations reported in George Cavendish's *Life and Death of Cardinal Wolsey* (discussed more fully below), she suggests that the long gallery was "an excellent place in which to conduct difficult diplomatic interviews" (60). See also Maurice Howard, who, in his admirable *The Early Tudor Country House: Architecture and Politics, 1490–1550* (London: George Philip, 1987), refers to Cavendish in suggesting "the long gallery's usefulness as a place for private conversation" (116). And see Coope's "The Gallery in England: Names and Meanings," in *Design and Practice in British Architec-ture: Studies in Architectural History Presented to Howard Colvin,* a special issue of *Architectural*

History 27 (1984): 446–55. In understanding the meanings of the long gallery, a complicating factor is that the documentary trail is not always clear; the term "gallery" could also signify lobbies or anterooms, corridors, and what we would call "minstrels' galleries." When associated with recreational walking, however, the space indicated is usually that which is the subject of this chapter.

11. Robert Beale, Clerk of the Council, advised counselors to "Learn before your access her Majesty's disposition by some of the Privy Chamber" (quoted in Paul Johnson, *Elizabeth I* [New York: Holt, Rinehart and Winston, 1974], 198). For the laundry reports, see 109. For Elizabeth's complaint to Spanish ambassador Guzman de Silva about the Dudley rumors, see Carole Levin, *The Heart and Stomach of a King: Elizabeth I and the Politics of Sex and Power* (Philadelphia: University of Pennsylvania Press, 1994), 77. For church-court reports, see Laura Gowing, *Domestic Dangers: Women, Words, and Sex in Early Modern London* (Oxford: Clarendon Press, 1996); Martin Ingram, *Church Courts, Sex and Marriage in England, 1570–1640* (Cambridge: Cambridge University Press, 1987); and the work of Loreen Giese forthcoming from Palgrave/Macmillan.

12. Ben Jonson, *Volpone, or The Fox*, ed. Alvin B. Kernan for The Yale Ben Jonson (New Haven, CT: Yale University Press, 1962), 5.2.83–85. John Marston, *The Dutch Courtesan*, ed. David Crane for New Mermaids (London: A. C. Black, 1997), 5.1.10sd, 44sd. (The stage directions "She conceals them behind the curtain" and "Those in ambush rusheth forth and takes him" are original to the 1604 quarto, STC 17475.) George Gascoigne, *Supposes*, in *Drama of the English Renaissance, vol. 1: The Tudor Period*, ed. Russell A. Fraser and Norman Rabkin (New York: Macmillan, 1976), 1.1.1–5. *Nobody and Somebody*, ed. David L. Hay for Renaissance Drama (New York: Garland Publishing, 1980), 1.191–256. Thomas Heywood, *The Wise Woman of Hogsdon*, ed. Michael Leonard for Garland Critical Editions (New York: Garland, 1980), 3.1.890–900; 5.1–4.

13. Philip Massinger, *A New Way to Pay Old Debts*, ed. T. W. Craik for New Mermaids (London: Ernest Benn, 1964), 5.1.303–4. Thomas Kyd, *The Spanish Tragedy*, ed. Philip Edwards for The Revels Plays (London: Methuen, 1959), 2.2.42–44. John Ford, *The Broken Heart*, ed. T. J. B. Spencer for The Revels Plays (Manchester, UK: Manchester University Press, 1980), 2.2.108–12. It may be that the eavesdropping scenes in the gardens of *Much Ado about Nothing* and *Twelfth Night* derive some of their humor from the fact that a cultural convention is turned on its head. In *The Winter's Tale*, by contrast, the exit of Hermione and Polixenes to the garden is a contributing factor in fueling Leontes' suspicions.

14. See, for example, the first reports of Sir Thomas Smith as a junior ambassador to France in 1571, reprinted in Sir Dudley Digges, *The Compleat Ambassador: or Two Treaties of the Intended Marriage of Qu: Elizabeth . . . Comprised in Letters of Negotiation* (London: 1655; Wing STC D1453). For an audience in the King's Chamber, he listed the presence of the Duke of Alençon and other nobles; in the Queen Mother's Chamber, there were the Lady Margaret and a "great number" of other ladies (Thomas Smith and Francis Walsingham to Elizabeth, March 1, 1571, 169–70). But in the King's Garden the conference included only Smith; his senior, Francis Walsingham; the King; and the King's man Malvosire (Thomas Smith to Burleigh, March 22, 1571, 196–97). William Roper, *The Life of Sir Thomas More*, in *Two Early Tudor Lives*, ed. Richard S. Sylvester and Davis P. Harding (New Haven, CT: Yale University Press, 1962), 235.

15. This account is taken from *The Acts and Monuments of John Foxe*, 4th ed., rev. Rev. Josiah Pratt (London, 1877), 8: 612–13.

16. Francis Bacon, "Of Gardens," in *Sir Francis Bacon: The Essayes or Counsels, Civill and Morall*, ed. Michael Kiernan (Cambridge, MA: Harvard University Press, 1985), 142, 140. See Morris Palmer Tilley, *A Dictionary of the Proverbs in England in the Sixteenth and Seventeenth Centuries* (Ann Arbor: University of Michigan Press, 1950), for proverb W19: "Walls (Hedges) have ears (eyes)." John Ford, *'Tis Pity She's a Whore*, ed. Brian Morris for New

Mermaids (London: Ernest Benn, 1968), 1.1.166, 171–72. The scene makes clear its out-door location: it opens with Grimaldi and Vasques fighting and Florio complaining at "broils so near my doors"; and Annabella watches from an upper-level "window" until she exits to reemerge "outside" at ground level. William Shakespeare, *Measure for Measure,* ed. J. W. Lever for the Arden Shakespeare (New York: Vintage Books, 1965), 4.1.50, 59.

17. For Forman's dream, see especially Louis Montrose, "Shaping Fantasies: Figurations of Gender and Power in Elizabethan Culture," *Representations* 1, no. 2 (Spring 1983): 61–94.

18. In his *Heptameron of Civil Discourses,* George Whetstone depicts a party who "pause[d] a little after their dinner, observing therein an old health rule: 'After dinner, talk a while, After supper, walk a mile.'" See *A Critical Edition of George Whetstone's 1582 An Heptameron of Civill Discourses,* ed. Diana Shklanka, The Renaissance Imagination vol. 35 (New York: Garland, 1987), sig. E4^r. On Elizabeth, see Johnson, *Elizabeth I,* 432; as late as September 26, 1602 the Queen was reported to walk in the garden at Oaklands "as briskly as though she were 18 years old." In Richard Mulcaster's *Positions* (London: 1581; STC 18253), see chapter 20, "Of Walking," sigs. L1^r–L4^v.

19. M. Jourdain cites the will of John Wilson in *English Decoration and Furniture of the Early Renaissance* (London: B. T. Batsford, 1924), 5. For Lady Alworth in *A New Way to Pay Old Debts,* see 4.1.166–67.

20. For the definition of the long gallery, see *History of the King's Works,* 4: 17. For Dudley's gallery and the Whitehall visitor, see Coope's "Gallery in England," 448 and 446–57, respectively.

21. Bacon, "Of Gardens," 144.

22. I am grateful to Alan H. Nelson for introducing me to this episode and for sharing his facsimiles of PRO MS SP15/27A[/46], fols. 81–82. Arundel's deposition is also reported in the Calendar of the Bath manuscripts at Longleat, vol. 5, pp. 204–5. I have also relied upon Nelson's since-published version of the episode, in *Monstrous Adversary: The Life of Edward de Vere, 17th Earl of Oxford* (Liverpool: Liverpool University Press, 2003), 249–58. For more on accusations against Oxford, see also Conyers Read, *Lord Burghley and Queen Elizabeth* (New York: Knopf, 1960), Chapter 9: "Theobalds and the Oxford Marriage," and especially 129–30. On the "low gallery" (and other Whitehall galleries), see *The History of the King's Works, The Survey of London,* and Simon Thurley, *Whitehall Palace: An Architectural History of the Royal Apartments 1240–1698* (New Haven, CT: Yale University Press, 1999).

23. See *CSP Spanish,* vol. 1, no. 256: Guzman de Silva to the King, July 10, 1564, 367–68.

24. For Bacon, see "Of Building," 137. Coope also cites Sir Roger North, who wrote in the late seventeenth century that "these recesses are for select companies to converse in" ("Long Gallery," 59). For Sir Piers Legh, see the Lyme Park guidebook prepared for the National Trust in 1981, 12 (the more recent guidebook omits the report of staff received in the bay window). Cavendish also portrays Wolsey conducting private conversations through frequent recourse to the bay windows of his long gallery (61, 168, and 175), presence chamber (99), and dining chamber (143); my argument is that the bays associated with galleries were doubly private.

25. While conversational privacy dominates most sixteenth-century associations with the long gallery, and while the exhibition of paintings and maps features most strongly in the seventeenth century, both functions were current in both centuries, as Coope and Howard make clear. The dominant cultural constructs were, however, periodized as indicated.

26. Girouard, *Robert Smythson,* 113.

27. George Cavendish, *The Life and Death of Cardinal Wolsey* in *Two Early Tudor Lives,* 61, 32–36. Wolsey's palace at York was to be renamed Whitehall by Henry VIII.

28. Although references below are to *George Gascoigne: A Hundreth Sundrie Flowers,* ed. G. W. Pigman III (Oxford: Clarendon Press, 2000), I have modernized more fully. For an excellent review of the criticism, especially regarding genre and textual revision, see 658–55.

29. C. T. Prouty, ed., *George Gascoigne's A Hundreth Sundrie Flowers* (Columbia: University of Missouri Press, 1942), 199.

30. Gascoigne describes a long gallery that did not go "without chambers," as Elinor's room opens off it.

31. Thomas Norton, "A Discourse Touching the Pretended Match between the Duke of Norfolk and the Queen of Scots." There are many contemporary copies of this tract; I consulted Folger MS. V.b. 41.

32. For the following discussion of the Ridolfi plot, principal sources include: *A Collection of State Papers Relating to Affairs in the Reigns of King Henry VIII, King Edward VI, Queen Mary, and Queen Elizabeth. . . . 1542 to 1570,* ed. Samuel Haynes (London: William Bowyer, 1740) (hereafter, "Haynes"); *A Collection of State Papers Relating to Affairs in the Reign of Queen Elizabeth from . . . 1571 to 1596,* ed. William Murdin (London: William Bowyer, 1759) (hereafter, "Murdin"); *The Trial of Thomas Duke of Norfolk by his Peers, for High Treason against the Queen* (London: J. Morphew, 1709) (hereafter, *Trial*); CSPD; and *A Compleat Collection of State-Tryals . . . From the Reign of King Henry the Fourth, to The End of the Reign of Queen Anne,* 4 vols. (London: Timothy Goodwin et al., 1719) (hereafter, "*State Trials*"). Especially helpful in establishing a chronology for the examinations is Neville Williams, *Thomas Howard, Fourth Duke of Norfolk* (London: Barrie and Rockliff, 1964) (hereafter, "Williams"). I am also indebted to Francis Edwards, *The Marvellous Chance: Thomas Howard, Fourth Duke of Norfolk and the Ridolphi Plot, 1570–1572* (London: Hart-Davis, 1968) and the following entries in the *Oxford DNB:* Charles Baillie (by Peter Holmes), William Barker (by Kenneth R. Bartlett), William Brooke, tenth Baron Cobham (by Julian Lock), William Cecil, first Baron Burghley (by Wallace T. MacCaffrey), Henry Fitzalan, twelfth Earl of Arundel (by Julian Lock), William Herle (by David Lewis Jones), Thomas Howard, fourth Duke of Norfolk (by Michael A. R. Graves), John Lesley, Bishop of Ross (by Rosalind K. Marshall), Sir Richard Lowther (by C. H. H. Owen), John Lumley, first Baron Lumley (by Kathryn Barron), William Maitland of Lethington (by Mark Loughlin), Thomas Morgan (by Alison Plowden), Charles Neville, sixth Earl of Westmoreland (by Roger N. McDermott), Thomas Percy, seventh Earl of Northumberland (by Julian Lock), Roberto di Ridolfi (by L. E. Hunt), Sir Ralph Sadler (by Gervase Phillips), James Stewart, first Earl of Moray (by Mark Loughlin), Mary Stewart, Queen of Scots (by Julian Goodare), and John Story (by Julian Lock).

33. For Moray, see *State Trials,* 75–76. For Ross, see Murdin, "The Examination of the Bishop of Ross," November 6, 1571, 53; *State Trials,* 73–74; and Williams, 139.

34. *Trial,* 49.

35. For Moray, see *State Trials,* 76; and Haynes, "A Summary of Matters wherewith the Duke of Norfolk hath been charged for the Attempt to marry with the Scots Queen," January 20, 1569, 574.

36. For Bannister, see Murdin, "Banister's [sic] Declaration," September 29, 1571, 134; and Williams, 222.

37. See *State Trials,* 80; Williams, 159; *Trial,* 69, 57.

38. For Owen, see Williams, 160. For Arundel, see Murdin, "The Bishop of Ross's Examination touching Sir Henry Percy and Diverse Others," October 26, 1571, 25; the *Calendar of the Manuscripts . . . Preserved at Hatfield House,* 1: 458; and *Trial,* 59.

39. For Ross, see Murdin, "The Examination of the Bishop of Ross," November 6, 1571, 50. For Barker, see Murdin, "The Examination of William Barker," November 7, 1571, 125–26.

40. See Williams, 161–62 and 190. For Norfolk at Kenninghall, see Haynes, 640; for the Tower, CSPD (October 1569), 345. After little more than a week in the Tower, Norfolk petitioned for liberty to walk on the walls or in the gallery, because his health was suffering. Permission was granted to him to be moved to lodgings near the long gallery, so that he could walk there, so long as one of his jailers was always in his company. Later, a man at the Tower was disciplined because his seven-year-old daughter came almost daily to bring Norfolk flowers. The similarity of this story to that of the imprisoned Elizabeth is striking and suggests some imaginative intervention at work in at least one instance. Notably, what was a garden in Elizabeth's story is a gallery in Norfolk's.

41. Higford detailed how communications among the conspirators continued even with Norfolk in the Tower: letters were put into wine bottles with crosses marked on their corks; letters were held up in the window of an adjoining house; voice messages were exchanged through a shared privy shaft; and Lawrence Bannister left letters wrapped in black paper in a dark privy (Murdin, "The Most Humble and True Answer of me Robert Higford," October 1, 1571, 80).

42. See Williams, 202–3, 205–6, and 221; Murdin, 85 and 78–79. For Cecil, see *Trial*, sig. A1ᵛ.

43. The principal source for this speculation, as also for such other suggestions as that Cecil sought to entrap Norfolk by assigning him to the York Conference and releasing him from his first imprisonment in the Tower, is Edwards.

44. See Murdin, "Banester's [sic] Examination," September 18 and 19, 1571, 133.

45. See Murdin, "William Barker's last Confession," September 19, 1571: "Upon this, I brought him [Ridolfi] to my Lord in Lent last, between eight and nine of the clock (Sir Henry Neville being in bed) and he talked with my Lord about three quarters of an hour" (99). See also Murdin, "Answer of William Barker to the Interrogatories," October 10, 1571: "and so this Examinate, about eight or nine of the clock the night in Lent last, did bring Ridolphi [sic] secretly to the Duke; where Ridolphi [sic] did talk with the Duke in his Gallery half an hour and more" (111). Finally, see Murdin, "Barker's Last Answer upon Interrogatories," October 11, 1571: "Ridolphi [sic] came to the Duke of Norfolk the second time, and about nine of the clock at night, and this examinate did bring him thither; and in the Gallery they talked together about half an hour" (115). Barker described how the gate was left open for Ridolfi (120), and how "The first time I brought him up on the back side, by the long workhouse, at the further end of the Lavendry Court, and so up a new pair of stairs that goeth up to the old Wardrobe, and so through the Chamber where my Lady Lestrange used to dine and sup. The second time I brought him up at the stairs of the entry that goeth to Sir Henry Nevill's Chamber, and down again that way" (121). See also Murdin, "The Duke of Norfolk's Answers," October 13, 1571: "that Night Barker brought Ridolphi [sic] to this Examinate into the long Gallery, next the Duke's Bed-chamber, where the Duke walked with Ridolphi [sic], and Barker stood in the Window" (161). See also *Trial*, 95–96, 106.

46. For Bannister at Paul's Wharf, see Murdin, "To Lawrence Banester [sic]," October 11, 1571, 142. For the letters to Alva, see Murdin, "The Examination of the Bishop of Ross," November 6, 1571, 46. For Norfolk's desire to help Mary, see Murdin, "Examination of Barker," October 31, 1571, 123. For Norfolk refusing treason, see Murdin, "Laurence Banester [sic]," October 13, 1571, 144.

47. *Trial*, 84.

48. For Cecil, see *Trial*, 69; for Norfolk's motivation, 62; for his denying, 110. Norfolk was tried by the terms of the Treason Statute of 1571, which added the "stirring of foreigners to invade the realm" to the lengthening list of activities with treasonous import. However, the offenses with which he was charged were committed between September 23, 1569 and July 16, 1571, all but one predating the new statute. His prosecutors therefore claimed

to try him by the Treason Statute of 1532, even though they laid great emphasis on activities not covered by that act. See John Bellamy, *The Tudor Law of Treason: An Introduction* (London: Routledge & Kegan Paul, 1979), 65.

49. *Trial,* 15; David Jardine, *Criminal Trials: Supplying Copious Illustrations of the Important Periods of English History during the Reigns of Queen Elizabeth and James I* (London: M. A. Nattali, 1847), 150.

50. For Owen, see Murdin, "William Barker's Answer to Articles," October 14, 1571, 119. For Powell, see *Calendar of the Manuscripts . . . Preserved at Hatfield House* for October 19, 1571, 1: 546.

Part III
The Human Figure on the Stage

(Title of Chapter Ten in Leeds Barroll's *Shakespearean Tragedy: Genre, Tradition, and Change in* Antony and Cleopatra, 1984*)

Stage Masculinities, National History, and the Making of London Theatrical Culture

Jean E. Howard

SHAKESPEARE'S FIRST FOUR HISTORY PLAYS, NOW popularly known as *Henry VI, Parts 1, 2,* and *3* and *Richard III,*[1] stage spectacular failures of the male-dominated social order. At their symbolic center is the poignant figure of Henry VI, a king so weak that he loses control of his wife, Margaret; of the French lands won by his father; of the army he supposedly commands; and of the succession to the English throne. In theatrical terms, he also often loses control of center stage. In fact, in the three Henry VI plays, Henry often seems peripheral to much of the action: absent, passive, increasingly isolated. Initiating energy emanates from Margaret, but not from him. But Henry's are not the only masculine failures these texts outline. *Parts 2* and *3*, which follow the loss of France and the death of England's chivalric hero, Talbot, take place on English soil and dramatize the chaos of civil war as England's male nobility destroys itself. Even the Yorkist faction, at first powerful precisely because of the tight bonds between father, sons, and brothers, splinters as Richard, the hunchback, grows fratricidal.[2]

Yet in exploring the dynamics of civil war and the chaos occasioned by a weak king, Shakespeare, and those who perhaps collaborated with him, were experimenting with stagecraft, with the business of making good plays, as surely as they were anatomizing a diseased social order.[3] In the first tetralogy, one can discern experiments with the soliloquy, with emblem scenes, and with the interweaving of multiple actions and subplots. I want to suggest that in these plays one can also see Shakespeare learning to delineate styles of stagable masculinity, learning to work with the raw material of his actors to create riveting stage images—not of the collapse of an abstract, patriarchal social order—but of individual men who hack, weep, or strut their way through the falling timbers of that larger edifice. In short, one of the tasks I see Shakespeare facing, representationally, was how to differentiate, not just one line of action from another, but also one man from another; and, moreover, how to create interesting fits between the thing represented and the man, presentationally, impersonating the stage character. That remains, of course, a problem for every director of these plays, how to match play to available personnel. It was clearly a problem easier for Shakespeare to address after, rather than before, 1594, when the relative stability of the Chamberlain's Men, and his long association with them, gave him unique opportunities to write plays in which he could capitalize on the particular capabilities of members of his acting troupe.[4] But in these early history plays I will argue that Shakespeare was already learning how to differentiate styles of masculinity and, moreover, that in doing so he helped to generate the excitement that surrounded theatrical culture in the theatrically explosive decade of the 1590s.

In making this argument, I am mindful that the commercial theater was still a relatively fledgling institution as the 1590s began and that it faced a number of challenges to its growth and stability including the ire of the antitheatricalists, enforced closings due to visitations of the plague, and the economic burden of maintaining functioning theater companies in difficult and uncertain times. In many ways, the commercial theater was a marginal institution, marginal in a geographical sense, since a number of its playhouses were located in the suburbs, and marginal in terms of the social status of the majority of its actors and playwrights, often men of low estate who, except for aristocratic patronage, would have fallen prey to charges of vagrancy or masterlessness.[5] Yet there were a number of signs of this theater's popularity: the size of audiences relative to the city's population, the enthusiastic reports of foreign visitors, the rapid evolution of a diverse theatrical repertoire.[6] It is my contention that, in his first set of history plays, Shakespeare and those who collaborated with him were learning how to become successful participants in this evolving industry in which Shakespeare would rapidly become a leader, subject both to the envy and to the admiration of his peers. His apprenticeship within this theater culture included, at this early stage, learning how to create compelling and diverse stage masculinities under the special conditions of early modern theatrical performance.

It is important to recall—and in a new way—one of the central facts about early modern London stages, namely, that they were populated *only* by male actors, and not by women. Critics have quite often written about what that meant for how femininity was constructed on this stage,[7] but it also bears on this theater's capacity for representing masculinity and distinguishing man from man. In almost every genre of early modern play, men characters wildly outnumber women characters. This is certainly true for these early histories. In terms of significant characters, *Henry VI, Part 1* has 32 men and 3 women; *Henry VI, Part 2* has 50 men and 4 women; *Henry VI, Part 3* has 42 men and 3 women; *Richard III* has 37 men and 5 women.[8] This is astonishing when one actually registers the numbers, and it gives material purchase to Coppélia Kahn's claim that the history plays are about men and a male-dominated social order, with a few spectacular,

though extremely important, women added in, especially in the first tetralogy.[9] And it makes clear a central theatrical dilemma: how to distinguish—
by clothing, rhetoric, physical differences—one male character from
another, especially when the relative size of casts and of acting troupes
made doubling inevitable. Not every character, of course, needs to be
memorable or distinctive. Sometimes the generic nature of lords, attendants, and citizens is the point. But for *Henry VI, Part 2,* for example, to
be theatrically intelligible, let alone compelling, some of the fifty-odd male
characters need to achieve singular definition if only as the most compelling exemplars of a specific social group or stage type.[10]

I am suggesting, therefore, that it is important to think about the implications for performance of these male-saturated dramas, including the
problems and opportunities they created for the histrionic display of competing styles of masculinity. We know that certain male characters in these
early histories *did* make lasting impressions on audiences. Thomas Nashe,
Shakespeare's contemporary, writing about *Henry VI, Part 1* in *Pierce Penniless His Supplication to the Devil,* records the powerful effect created by
the figure of Talbot—over time, ten thousand spectators wept, Nashe
claims, at the hero's stage death.[11] We do not know for certain who
played Talbot in the first productions, but clearly the role was a memorable one, and may have been memorably embodied by a particular
actor. In March of 1592, Henslowe recorded a performance of *Henry VI*
at the Rose, and many scholars feel that the entry refers to *Part 1* and puts
the play in the repertory of Strange's Men.[12] If so, could the actor playing
Talbot have been Edward Alleyn, the then star of Strange's Men who
made his reputation performing such memorable roles as Tamburlaine,
Barabas, Faustus, Muly Mohamet, and Tamar Cam?[13] In *Pierce Penniless,*
soon after he has remarked on the power of the figure of Talbot to move
stage audiences, Nashe also lavishes praise on Alleyn's skills as an actor.
"Not *Roscius* nor *Aesope,* those admyred tragedians that have lived ever
since before Christ was borne, could ever performe more in action than
famous *Ned Allen*" (215).[14] In 1592, Alleyn was arguably the leading
tragic actor on the public stage, and it is tempting to think that the memorable nature of Talbot's affecting death may have been due, in part, to the
productive synergy between Shakespeare's increasing rhetorical skills and
the charismatic acting of Strange's star performer.[15]

On the other hand, it is not clear that Shakespeare wrote the part with
Alleyn in mind, since Shakespeare's company affiliations were obscure
before 1594, nor is it certain that even in 1592 Alleyn was playing the role.
Several lines in the play raise interesting questions about alternate casting
possibilities. Recall the terms in which the Countess of Auvergne
describes Talbot when she invites him to her castle so she can see with
her own eyes the man whose army has wreaked so much havoc on her

country. Looking at Talbot's physical body, she surprisingly proclaims him a "child, a seely dwarf . . . this weak and writhled shrimp" (2.3.21–22).[16] Her picture of a dwarfish shrimp accords with nothing we know of the historical Ned Alleyn. There are, however, many ways to interpret the Countess's words. She may be maliciously and wrongly insulting Talbot just because he is the enemy of France. She may be revealing her own inability to judge a man by his deeds, rather than by his looks. But she may also perhaps be calling attention to the body of a specific actor who, if Nashe is to be believed, might have made a powerful and affecting impression despite—or, perhaps, because of—his unimposing size? Is this a case of a mighty heart ennobling the incongruously frail container in which it is housed? Is the *point* the gap between martial accomplishments and the physical instrument that enacted them?

Another possibility exists, and that is that in this scene Talbot is not wearing his customary armor. I can find no textual evidence to indicate how he is dressed, but it is an occasion when he has been summoned from the battlefield to appear before a lady. If he comes before the Countess in robes, not armor, her words may call attention to the gap between the physical reality of Talbot's body and the metallic carapace which customarily gives the "shadow" a particular form or "substance."[17] It is such language, of course, which Talbot evokes when he extricates himself from the Countess's trap by summoning his "substance," a band of armed English soldiers, the prosthetic enhancement of his own shadowy self (*Part 1,* 2.3.50–51, 61–66).

The questions raised by this scene suggest both the representational and presentational challenges posed by these early histories and by the all-male casts who performed them. Because of the state of theatrical records, we do not know who played most of the parts in Shakespeare's early plays. Nonetheless, in thinking about styles of masculinity in these histories, I want to keep in mind that Shakespeare, himself an actor as well as a playwright, wrote for real actors and their bodies. How much that influenced the way particular roles were written we can only guess, though I want to return at the end of the paper to two figures, Will Kemp and Richard Burbage, some of whose Shakespearean roles, even in the early histories, we can identify or about which we can profitably speculate.

Initially, however, I want to explore further the general proposition that the first tetralogy can be viewed in part as a sustained experiment in differentiating styles of stage masculinity. Ideologically speaking, the story of England's fall into civil war depends on making palpable the particular failures or excesses to which those in power are prone. In this project, the figure of Henry VI is absolutely crucial. All three Henry VI plays pivot around the figure of the king who fails to rule, to be the head, either in the family or state. Henry's masculinity is compromised from the beginning.

He cannot quell the fighting among his nobles and so fails to get reinforcements to Talbot in France. And in *Parts 2* and *3,* he certainly cannot control the French wife whom Suffolk brings home to him. The most poignant aspect of his characterization arises from the perfect coincidence of his political and domestic failures. Overwhelmed by his passion for Margaret, he grows effeminate, that is, he becomes like a woman in putting passion before reason.[18] This abdication of reason, the prerequisite for rule, makes him fail as a king, as well as a husband and father. In *Part 3,* he even allows the crown to pass away from his son by granting it at his death to the Yorkist line.[19] A study in feckless masculinity, Henry VI must, on the stage, have provided a striking contrast to the virile Talbot, nostalgic embodiment of English chivalric masculinity. Typically clothed in the armor of a warrior, Talbot's signature actions, except for his meeting with the Countess of Auvergne, involve siege warfare and hand-to-hand combat. By contrast, Henry never actually engages in battle, and in *Part 3* he sneaks back to his country, as early stage directions indicate, "disguised, with a prayer-book" (*Part 3,* s.d. following 3.1.12). A hollow imitation of effective kingship, Henry here has even shed his robe and crown.

As the prayerbook suggests, moreover, Henry is further distinguished from those around him by an iconically rendered piety that, unfortunately, fails to coexist with courage or skill in leading men. Of her husband Margaret contemptuously says: "All his mind is bent to holiness, / To number Ave-Maries on his beads. / His champions are the prophets and apostles, / His weapons holy saws of sacred writ, / His study is his tilt-yard, and his loves / Are brazen images of canonized saints" (*Part 2,* 1.3.59–64). Not bad in and of themselves, Henry's devotional inclinations are rendered suspect because they so clearly substitute for the tasks of rule to which his position as king has destined him. It is quite likely that on the stage the suspect Catholic rosary beads, along with the prayer-book, would have been among the stage props that most clearly defined Henry in the eyes of the audience. In *Part 3,* when Margaret is leading Henry's army against the Yorkist faction, Henry memorably sits on a molehill far from the battle, lamenting that he cannot live the life of a simple shepherd (2.5.1–54). In the most effective version of the Henry VI plays I have seen to date, Henry was played by a man who looked, and sounded, remarkably like the Mr. Rogers of early morning children's TV fame.[20] It was an extremely good casting choice for a character whose identity as the weak but saintly king stands in stark contrast not only to the warriors who do his fighting for him but also to the masculine femininity of the wife, Margaret, who leads them into battle.

If Henry VI serves as an umbrella figure who through his decline into complete impotence provides one kind of link among the three plays that now bear his name, each play also contains other male figures who attain a signature "style," often in contrast to the feckless masculinity of Henry. In *Part 1,* as we have seen, that man is Talbot. As England plunges into a civil war largely caused by the selfishness of its own aristocracy, Talbot fights unsupported in France, upholding the king's cause when the king himself cannot. A warrior whose very name frightens the enemy, he is absolute in his fidelity to his king and to the traditional values of his class. Outwitting the Countess of Auvergne and pitting himself against the feminine leader of the French forces, Joan of Arc, Talbot represents an English masculinity untainted by effeminacy, a masculinity the more nostalgically compelling because doomed. One of the most moving scenes in *Part 1* occurs when Talbot and his young son, overwhelmingly outnumbered, die together on the battlefield of France. By their code of honor, should they fly they would be bastards and traitors, marked by the stain of women's frailty and unfaithful to the cause of the English king (4.5.1–55). They do not fly, of course, and their double deaths determine that the kind of old-fashioned integrity they represent will have no lineage into the future.

Part 2 has no Talbot in the picture, therefore, but with the ensuing descent into civil war, several interestingly different kinds of masculinity for a time hold center stage, the first of which I would call the masculinity of modernity represented by the Duke of Suffolk. At the end of *Part 1,* Suffolk wooed Margaret in the name of Henry VI. In *Part 2,* he brings her back from France, sans dowry, to be Henry's wife, but also to be his own mistress. Suffolk is a new type of stage man, invested with the glamour of one of the characters from Castiglione's *The Book of the Courtier.*[21] This and other sixteenth-century conduct books taught ambitious men how to behave in courtly contexts, that is, how to be graceful conversationalists, skilled at horsemanship, and elegant in deportment. Shakespeare endows Suffolk with just such courtly skills. He can praise Margaret in terms appropriate to a Petrarchan mistress and describe her to King Henry in poetry so ravishing that the young king rashly forgoes his planned marriage with a French princess to wed the newly penniless Margaret (*Part 1,* 5.5.2–6, 9–27 and 5.7.1–9). Moreover, when Margaret later describes her disappointment with Henry as husband, she does so by way of a flattering comparison to Suffolk's courtly skills:

> I tell thee, Pole, when in the city Tours
> Thou rann'st a-tilt in honour of my love
> And stol'st away the ladies' hearts of France,
> I thought King Henry had resembled thee
> In courage, courtship, and proportion.
> (*Part 2,* 1.3.54–58)

Instead, she finds Henry busy with his rosary beads, not at all a man who would take part in a courtly tournament or steal women's hearts with his sophisticated courtship rituals. In staging Suffolk, Shakespeare decided, I think, for a satiric, but also a seductive portrait of a "new man," a man whose courtier masculinity is founded not, as with Talbot, primarily on his martial prowess and his fidelity to the king and to his own family lineage, but rather on his performative skills as a smooth-tongued wooer and self-serving courtier.

Though titled like Talbot, Suffolk reveals the fissures and differences within aristocratic masculinity. If Talbot is a nostalgic figure, Suffolk represents courtly modernity. If Talbot embraces the manly comradery of battle, Suffolk embraces a fatal and adulterous liaison with his King's wife. His death scene contrasts starkly with Talbot's. Outraged that he is called to account by men he considers beneath him in rank, Suffolk spends his last minutes vilifying members of the ship's crew as "obscure and lousy swain" (4.1.51), "base slave" (68), "paltry, servile, abject drudges" (105), and "villain" (106). His contemptuous response to his captors heightens the class antagonism that erupts elsewhere in the play, especially in the Jack Cade rebellion. It is an antagonism exacerbated by the failings of the ruling class, including Suffolk, who in 3.1 had spurned the petitions of the common people and had later conspired to murder their champion, Duke Humphrey. Talbot, too, has a sense of his own honor, but it expresses itself not in contempt for his social inferiors, but in fidelity to a code of conduct based on mutual obligation. In creating the glamorous, but haughty, woman-besotted Suffolk, Shakespeare not only constructed an aristocratic masculinity markedly distinct from that of the pious Henry and the warrior hero, Talbot; he also made it possible to see the link between this "new man" and the implosion of the traditional social order.

Part 2 yields, however, an even more distinctive masculine type, one exemplifying not aristocratic masculinity but that of the lower classes. I am referring, of course, to the character of Jack Cade. Cade, the rebel, sticks out memorably amid the aristocratic warriors, counselors, and courtiers who dominate these early histories. He, like the men who kill Suffolk, is a commoner, and Shakespeare makes much, theatrically speaking, of Cade's class origins and affiliations. Ironically, Cade is suborned by Richard Duke of York to impersonate the figure of Edmund Mortimer, Richard II's designated heir to the throne, in order to stir up rebellion against Henry VI. Yet Cade's most notable attributes are an artisanal physical vigor and raw, class-based anger at the nobility. For example, when he initially describes Cade, York tells how he once saw him fighting in Ireland against the Irish kerns, his thighs impaled with so many arrows that Cade looked like a porcupine. But instead of being weakened by the darts, Cade capered about like a Morris dancer, shaking the arrows like a dancer's bells (*Part 2*, 3.1.360–66).

This memorable image, associating Cade both with animality and with popular pastimes, tellingly foreshadows the brutal energy he will embody as leader of a group of rebellious artisans who march on London. Cade's promises to these followers turn largely on the fulfillment of their physical needs. He declares that when he is king bread will be cheap, beer of the highest quality, and all goods held in common. "There shall be in England seven halfpenny loaves sold for a penny, the three-hooped pot shall have ten hoops, and I will make it felony to drink small beer. All the realm shall be in common" (*Part 2*, 4.2.58–61). He and his followers represent the desires and the power of the lower-class body as well as the terror it could inspire. Cade is nothing if not class-conscious. He rails against the privileges of the rich, "these silken-coated slaves" (4.2.115), with their knowledge of French (4.2.151) and their associations with grammar schools, printing presses, paper mills, and their "talk of a noun and a verb and such abominable words" (4.7.28–34, esp. 33). Cade and his followers have needs that the nobility have not met; they have strengths and skills that England requires to butcher its cattle, weave its cloth, make its shoes. But it is the genius of this play to show that the productive power and strength of the artisanal body can equally be a source of fear. Part of the threat to social order these artisans represent lies in their ability to turn the tools of their trade to the tasks of murder and mayhem. The axe with which a butcher slaughters a calf can also behead a nobleman or cut out his tongue. In an uncanny transformation, instruments of labor become refunctioned as weapons of human slaughter.[22] Jesting among themselves, the rebels, armed with rough staves, not with aristocratic swords, talk about the nobles' scorn for honest labor and about how they can turn the skills of their trades from production to violence against class enemies.

> *Second Rebel.*   The nobility think scorn to go in leather aprons.
>
> *First Rebel.*   Nay more, the King's Council are no good workmen.
>
> *Second Rebel.*   True; and yet it is said "Labour in thy vocation," which is as much as to say as "Let the magistrates be labouring men"; and therefore should we be magistrates.
>
> *First Rebel.*   Thou hast hit it; for there's no better sign of a brave mind than a hard hand.
>
> *Second Rebel.*   I see them! I see them! There's Best's son, the tanner of Wingham—

First Rebel.	He shall have the skins of our enemies to make dog's leather of.
Second Rebel.	And Dick the butcher—
First Rebel.	Then is sin struck down like an ox, and iniquity's throat cut like a calf.
Second Rebel.	And Smith the weaver—
First Rebel.	Argo, their thread of life is spun.

(4.2.10–26)

Just as Cade knights himself, usurping the King's prerogative, so his followers imagine themselves in the roles of magistrates and executioners, tanning noble hides and slitting noble throats, rather than laboring to produce the food and the clothing that will feed and adorn noble bodies. At one and the same time, such scenes embody—depending on one's class commitments— the nightmare of the aristocratic class or the savage Saturnalia of the oppressed. There is no doubt that part of the ideological purpose of the Cade scenes is to provide a warning against popular rebellion and the delivery of the state into the hands of the common people.[23] And yet, these scenes are among the most theatrically riveting and energetic in *Part 2*. The rebels are terrifying, but also funny. They rib Cade about his pretensions to be Mortimer, and they are masters of the pun. If these portraits of artisanal masculinity warn against plebeian rebellion and the political enfranchisement of the lower classes, they are strangely ambivalent warnings, giving theatrical pleasure and inciting admiration even while also inciting terror.

There is no certain evidence as to what actor played Cade in the first stage productions of the play, partly because, as noted above, its date of composition remains a matter of debate. What we know for certain is that the title page of the first printed quartos of *Part 3* and of *Richard III* say that these two plays were performed by Pembroke's Men, with which Shakespeare may have had an association before his definite affiliation with the Chamberlain's Men in 1594. Most scholars assume that *Part 2* was also in the possession of Pembroke's Men before all of the plays of the first tetralogy became part of the repertoire of the Chamberlain's Men in 1594.[24] After 1594, the part of Cade may well have been assumed by Will Kemp, the famous acrobat, dancer, and actor who was a member of the Chamberlain's Men between 1594 and 1599 and played such roles as Peter in *Romeo and Juliet*, Dogberry in *Much Ado about Nothing*, and probably a number of others such as Bottom in *Midsummer Night's Dream*, Costard in *Love's Labor's Lost*, and Falstaff in *Henry IV, Parts 1* and *2*.[25]

Kemp was one of the most famous stage clowns of the 1590s, and before he joined the Lord Chamberlain's Men, he already had an independent reputation as an improvisational entertainer who could play instruments, perform jigs, as well as act, often in parts requiring an emphasis on physicality and the assumption of a rustic or lower-class persona. He was associated with several companies in the shifting theatrical world of 1588–94 before becoming a sharer, with Shakespeare, in the Chamberlain's Men.[26] In 1599, when he left the Chamberlain's Men, Kemp did a celebrated morris dance from London to Norwich which was commemorated in an illustrated pamphlet entitled *Kemp's Nine Daies Wonder.*

Even if Shakespeare did not *create* the Cade part for Kemp, it is clear that Kemp, like Tarlton before him, represented a distinctive and highly popular kind of stage entertainer. Shakespeare would have been familiar both with the type and with Kemp in particular. In fact, in the early 1590s, performers such as Kemp would have had a notoriety no playwright could have rivaled. It is possible, therefore, that in creating the part of Cade, the dramatist might have incorporated aspects of the famous performer's skills and persona into the role. Cade's distinctive characteristics include many of the stage traits for which Kemp was notorious: athleticism, a bluff and often rustic physicality, earthy humor. If he performed the part of Cade after 1594, Kemp would have infused the role with a theatrically pleasurable athleticism. Moreover, because actors themselves were usually drawn from the artisan class from which Cade derives, in the fused person of Cade/Kemp, the theater would have been showcasing the bodily skills of its own artisan performers. If Cade, who is beheaded in act 5, returned to the stage at the end of the play to dance a jig as many scholars surmise was common practice in the theater of the 1590s,[27] then Cade would be the only decapitated character—and there are many in *Part 2*—to undergo an onstage resurrection (an uncanny anticipation, as it would turn out, of Falstaff's "resurrection" in *Henry IV, Part 1,* a part also arguably performed by Kemp). As so often in the Elizabethan theater, the presentational elements of performance clearly had the capacity to disrupt and complicate the ideological thrust of representation as the character, Cade, dies, while the actor, Kemp, lives to dance again.[28]

Speculations about a jig aside, however, and whether or not Kemp ever performed the role, what remains indisputable is the striking masculine *difference* Cade embodied in a play focused predominantly on the tribulations of aristocratic masculinity. Scorning, parodying, and appropriating the privileges of his "betters," Cade affords an ideological and theatrically compelling alternative both to warrior and to "silken-coated" masculinities.

My final example, however, of Shakespeare's experimentation with styles of masculinity involves another aristocratic figure, his first great stage villain, the hunchback, Richard, Duke of Gloucester. Richard comes to prominence in *Part 3* where he begins to speak the soliloquies that become the signature of Shakespeare's future tragic heroes. As early as act 3, he is given a soliloquy in which he describes the Machiavellian tricks he will employ to carve his way to the throne:

> I'll drown more sailors than the mermaid shall;
> I'll slay more gazers than the basilisk;
> I'll play the orator as well as Nestor,
> Deceive more slyly than Ulysses could,
> And, like a Sinon, take another Troy.
> I can add colours to the chameleon,
> Change shapes with Proteus for advantages,
> And set the murderous Machiavel to school.
> Can I do this, and cannot get a crown?
> Tut, were it farther off, I'll pluck it down.
> (3.2.186–95)

Several things are striking here. One is the engaging confidence with which Richard speaks, boasting of future villainies. The other is how he couches his plans in terms of the theatrical roles he will play. Richard's is, in fact, an overwhelmingly theatrical masculinity. As Phyllis Rackin has demonstrated, Richard assumes at will both masculine and feminine subject positions, as in his wooing of Henry's widow, Ann; and he constantly manipulates his public face.[29] Feeling no ties of kinship or fellowship with other men, he boldly proclaims "I am myself alone" (*Henry VI, Part 3,* 5.6.84). What he is, at least until his spectacular downfall at Bosworth Field, is a series of spectacular poses.

We are certain who became famous playing Richard for the Chamberlain's Men. It was Richard Burbage, one of the two famous tragedians, along with his rival Edward Alleyn, of the Elizabethan stage. Burbage was probably with Shakespeare in Pembroke's Men in the early 1590s and was certainly a charter member of the Lord Chamberlain's Men when they were formed in 1594. Several contemporary anecdotes connect him to the role and suggest the inseparability of the actor and the part. In 1635, Bishop Corbet wrote of a visit he made to the battlefield of Bosworth where Richard died. He recounts how his guide, in telling him of the battle and Richard's part in it, conflated historical fact and theatrical representation, historical king and early modern actor. He reports of this guide:

> Besides what of his knowledge he could say,
> He had authenticke notice from the Play;
> Which I might guesse, by's mustring up the ghosts,
> And polycyes, not incident to hosts,
> But chiefly by that one perspicuous thing,

> Where he mistook a player for a king,
> For when he would have said King Richard dyed,
> And called—a horse! a horse! he Burbidge cryed.[30]

Another anecdote, this one attesting not only to the inseparability of actor and role, but also to the particular sexual charisma with which both role and actor were endowed, was related by John Manningham, a London law student, in a diary entry dated March 1601. "Upon a tyme when Burbidge played Rich[ard] 3. there was a Citizen grewe soe farr in liking with him, that before shee went from the play shee appointed him to come that night unto hir by the name of Ri[chard] the 3. Shakespeare, overhearing their conclusion, went before, was entertained and at his game ere Burbidge came. Then message being brought that Richard the 3. was at the doore, Shakespeare caused returne to be made that William the Conquerour was before Rich[ard] the 3."[31] This sexist anecdote, recording men's competitiveness at sexual conquest, is interesting in terms of what it says about Burbage's glamour in the role of Richard III and about the synergy between the role and the theatrical culture forming in Elizabethan London. In the anecdote, who is attractive: Richard III or the Burbage who impersonated him? And might the figure of the charismatic actor, a choice chameleon, have affected Shakespeare's very conception of this part? If Talbot is an idealized version of a residual masculinity, Suffolk an image of a new, fashionable, and fashion-conscious type of courtliness, then what is Richard but the medieval vice refashioned to encompass the skills and the glamour of the modern tragedian?

The very circulation of these anecdotes suggests that the stage, its players, and its playwrights had fairly early on become objects of cultural interest and even the focus of gossip. Might they also have been objects of emulation? A final anecdote gives a suggestive glimpse into the possible cultural impact these masculine roles may have had on men who saw them. In 1600, Samuel Rowlands in *The Letting of Humour's Blood in the Head-Vaine,* a critique of fashion-conscious gallants, says that there are young men who "like Richard, the usurper, swagger, / That had his hand continual on his dagger."[32] What we may be hearing in these words is evidence both of one of the stage gestures Burbage employed in creating the part of Richard III and also of the emulation it inspired in attentive young playgoers. Swaggering about London, hands on daggers, were these young gallants imagining they were Richard III or Burbage?

I have been suggesting throughout this essay that we look at the early history plays as experiments: experiments in staging history and adapting chronicle sources, experiments in dramatic construction, and experiments in character creation and the management of male bodies and the differentiation of competing masculine styles. When I use the word *experiment,* of course, I do not mean to suggest that these plays are in any way second-rate. I simply mean that they have about them the energy of discovery, of problems perceived and mastered in the real time of theatrical enactment. And one of the things I find most interesting is how, in dramatizing the collapse of a patriarchal culture into chaos, Shakespeare found ways to differentiate his men as they fell before the axe, the lance, or the sword; found ways to capitalize on the particular skills of his fellow actors, and ways to capture the glamour of the emerging entertainment industry and make it part of his creation of characters such as Richard III and Jack Cade.

In the early 1590s, the English history play afforded Shakespeare, at least, an occasion for such experimentation. In dramatizing his nation's past, he was helping to create a vigorous contemporary institution, the London public theater, a theater that from marginal status was quickly to assume a central place in the city's cultural life. In the early moments of this burgeoning theater industry, the extraordinary skills of performers such as Will Kemp and Richard Burbage could spur the creation of particular characters even as the sharp delineation of masculine roles within these histories made the complexities of chronicle history theatrically intelligible and gave actors materials with which to develop their craft further and to achieve the levels of notoriety to which the Burbage anecdotes attest.

For his participation in this emerging theatrical culture, it is only fitting that Shakespeare himself should have been enrolled in the discursive network of anecdotes and narratives that grew up around it. Manningham's story makes Shakespeare the sexual rival of Burbage and through the name William the Conqueror aggrandizes Shakespeare's accomplishments and victories in that arena. As William the Conqueror ruled England before Richard III, so Shakespeare came before the charismatic Burbage in sexual achievement. There is another narrative, however, which connects Shakespeare to one of the characters he had created in this first tetralogy. In 1592 in *Groats-worth of Wit,* Robert Greene, a university-educated writer envious of Shakespeare's growing theatrical successes, described Shakespeare thus: "There is an upstart Crow, beautified with our feathers, that with his *Tygers heart wrapt in a Players hide,* supposes he is as well able to bumbast out a blanke verse as the best of you: and being an absolute *Johannes fac totum,* is in his own conceit the onely Shake-scene in a countrie."[33] This anecdote suggests the impression even the young Shakespeare must have been making as actor/writer/man of the theater—at least in the eyes of a rival writer. The line about "his Tygers heart wrapt in a Players hide" is, of course, a reference to *Henry VI, Part 3* (1.4.138), in which Queen Margaret is described as having a "tiger's heart wrapped in a woman's hide." In the gender-bending world of the early modern theater, it is a nice touch that in its narratives Shakespeare should figure both as William the Conqueror and also as his own creation, the Amazonian Queen Margaret. The one anecdote, stressing Shakespeare's victory over Burbage in a sexual conquest, allies both theater practitioners with a world of entrepreneurial and sexually attractive masculinity. The other anecdote associates Shakespeare with the demonized ambition of his own Amazonian character. Together, these two brief stories suggest popular images of the evolving theater world—a place of glamorous opportunity or a site of monstrous and socially destabilizing ambition. Both, moreover, suggest that this world, while it could endanger masculine identity, was also a socially influential showcase for its dazzlingly new or powerfully seductive embodiments.

NOTES

1. The Folio of 1623 is the first printed version of what it calls *The First Part of Henry the Sixt.* What it calls *The Second Part of Henry the Sixt* was printed in a shorter quarto version in 1594 entitled *The First Part of the Contention of the Two Famous Houses of York and Lancaster.* What the Folio called *The Third Part of Henry the Sixt* was also printed in a shorter version in 1595 entitled *The True Tragedy of Richard Duke of York and the Good King Henry the Sixth.* These shorter texts are now widely assumed to be memorial reconstructions of abridged versions of the plays prepared from the authorial foul papers that stand behind the Folio text. As acting texts, they are particularly interesting as they contain very full stage directions indicative of playhouse practice of the period. In this paper, I will use the names employed in the 1623 Folio simply because they are the most readily familiar to modern critics and theatergoers.

2. See Ronald Berman, "Fathers and Sons in the *Henry VI* Plays," *Shakespeare Quarterly* 13 (1962): 487–97, and Jean E. Howard and Phyllis Rackin, *Engendering a Nation: A Feminist Account of Shakespeare's English Histories* (London: Routledge, 1997), esp. 83–118.

3. Whether Shakespeare was the sole creator of these early history plays remains in dispute. He may have collaborated with other playwrights, but the extent and nature of that collaboration is not clear. Consequently, throughout this paper, I will for convenience use "Shakespeare" to refer to the writer(s) who alone or together conceived of these plays for the stage.

4. For a brief introduction to London theatrical companies, see Andrew Gurr, "The Companies," chapter 2 of *The Shakespearean Stage 1574–1642* 3rd ed. (Cambridge: Cambridge University Press, 1992), 27–79. For a much fuller account see his *The Shakespearian Playing Companies* (Oxford: Clarendon Press, 1996).

5. Steven Mullaney's important book, *The Place of the Stage* (Chicago: University of Chicago Press, 1988) did perhaps the most to cement the idea of the public stage as a socially marginal institution which nonetheless played a central role in the cultural life of London. His book has been criticized for misunderstanding the place of the suburbs in urban life in the late sixteenth century (the suburbs were, among other things, full of new and thriving business ventures and not just the site of brothels and other disreputable institutions) and for underestimating the amount of theatrical life that occurred within the walls of the city. Nonetheless, Mullaney's study remains a useful account of the cultural importance of an institution that in crucial ways had to struggle for legitimacy, especially prior to 1603 when King James and his family extended their patronage to the major acting companies.

6. Gurr in *Shakespearean Stage 1574–1642* provides a good account of the gradual rise in the players' fortunes and social standing, particularly after 1603 when members of the royal household became direct patrons of particular theater companies (see especially 27–79). Critics who stress that the theater was one of London's most profitable new business ventures include Douglas Bruster in *Drama and the Market in the Age of Shakespeare* (Cambridge: Cambridge University Press, 1992) and Roslyn Lander Knutson in *Playing Companies and Commerce in Shakespeare's Time* (Cambridge: Cambridge University Press, 2001).

7. The critical literature on cross-dressing is by now quite voluminous. I summarize a good deal of it in *The Stage and Social Struggle in Early Modern England* (London: Routledge, 1994), esp. 93–128.

8. These numbers, especially for the men, are approximations taken from the cast of characters placed before each play in *The Norton Shakespeare*. It excludes generic figures such as "attendants," "citizens," and "messengers" who appear only at the margins of the text, most of whom were also probably male and nearly all of whom would have been played by actors doubling in several roles.

9. Coppélia Kahn, *Man's Estate: Masculine Identity in Shakespeare* (Berkeley and Los Angeles: University of California Press, 1981), 47–81.

10. I am not here making the claim that Shakespeare was instrumental in creating either the modern individual or modern forms of interiority and subjectivity. Instead, I am making the more modest argument that in these plays he was experimenting with the stage as a venue for displaying distinctive masculine styles in ways that helped to make large casts of male figures intelligible to a theater audience and that could capitalize on the distinctive physical instruments and talents of the performers with whom he, both as actor and playwright, worked.

11. *Pierce Penniless His Supplication to the Devil*, in *The Works of Thomas Nashe*, ed. Ronald B. McKerrow (Oxford: Basil Blackwell, 1958), 1: 212.

12. See Michael Hattaway, ed., *The First Part of King Henry VI* (Cambridge: Cambridge University Press, 1990), 36, and Stanley Wells, Gary Taylor, et al., eds. *William Shakespeare: A Textual Companion* (Oxford: Clarendon Press, 1987), 113.

13. For a concise description of Alleyn's parts and his acting style see Gurr, *Shakespearean Stage 1564–1642*, 90–94.

14. Andrew Gurr in *Shakespearian Playing Companies*, 261, seems to assume on the basis of Nashe's remarks that Alleyn definitely played Talbot.

15. Even those such as Gary Taylor who assume that *Henry VI, Part 1* was collaboratively written, believe that the death scenes of Talbot and his son were Shakespeare's creation. See *William Shakespeare: A Textual Companion*, 217.

16. All quotations from Shakespeare's plays are taken from *The Norton Shakespeare*, ed. Stephen Greenblatt, Katharine Eisaman Maus, Jean E. Howard, and Walter Cohen (New York: Norton, 1997), here cited at 462.

17. For a discussion of the role of armor in creating nostalgic masculine warrior identity, see Peter Stallybrass and Ann Rosalind Jones, *Renaissance Clothing and the Materials of Memory* (Cambridge: Cambridge University Press, 2000), 245–68.

18. Phyllis Rackin offers an important analysis of how early modern notions of effeminacy differ from our contemporary ideas in "Historical Difference/Sexual Difference," in *Privileging Gender in Early Modern England*, ed. Jean R. Brink (Kirksville, MO: Sixteenth-Century Journal Publishers, 1993), 37–63. See also Alan Sinfield, *Faultlines: Cultural Materialism and the Politics of Dissident Reading* (Berkeley and Los Angeles: University of California Press, 1992), 127–42.

19. Kathryn Schwarz in *Tough Love: Amazon Encounters in the English Renaissance* (Durham, NC: Duke University Press, 2000), esp. 103–5, makes the interesting argument that Henry's failings as a father simply highlight how effectively Margaret fills the maternal

role of advocate for her son. She is the parent who is committed to preserving his rights as Henry's heir, though her masculine fierceness in the maternal role contributes to the demonization of her within the play.

20. The plays, which could be seen in two parts in one day, were directed by Barry Kyle in 1995 for Theatre for a New Audience in New York City.

21. For a longer discussion of Suffolk see Jean E. Howard and Phyllis Rackin's *Engendering a Nation,* esp. 65–74.

22. I owe this insight to my former student, Ronda Arab, whose dissertation on the bodies of working men dealt not only with Jack Cade but with Bottom and other dramatic characters whose physical strength and artisanal skills define a masculinity in competition with aristocratic bodies.

23. A nuanced investigation of the ambivalence surrounding the Cade figure is provided by Thomas Cartelli in "Jack Cade in the Garden: Class Consciousness and Class Conflict in *2 Henry VI,*" in *Enclosure Acts: Sexuality, Property, and Culture in Early Modern England,* ed. Richard Burt and John Michael Archer (Ithaca, NY: Cornell University Press, 1994), 48–67.

24. For discussion of the theatrical provenance of these plays before 1594 see Michael Hattaway, ed., *The First Part of King Henry VI,* 36–38 and Gurr, *Shakespearian Playing Companies,* 261–62.

25. For the fullest account of Kemp's life and his probable theatrical parts see David Wiles, *Shakespeare's Clown: Actor and Text in the Elizabethan Playhouse* (Cambridge: Cambridge University Press, 1987). See also David Grote who, in *The Best Actors in the World: Shakespeare and His Acting Company* (Westport, CT: Greenwood Press, 2002), argues that Kemp definitely played Cade during the Chamberlain's revival of *Part 2* (31 and 231).

26. See Wiles, *Shakespeare's Clown,* 31–34, and Edwin Nungezer, *A Dictionary of Actors* (New Haven, CT: Yale University Press, 1929), 216–22, for accounts of Kemp's theatrical affiliations. The case for Shakespeare's early affiliation with Strange's Men, where Kemp definitely served, has been made most extensively by E. A. J. Honigmann, *Shakespeare: The Lost Years* (Manchester, UK: Manchester University Press, 1985), chapter 6.

27. Wiles, *Shakespeare's Clown,* 43–60.

28. For a discussion of the many consequences of this gap between the representational and the presentational levels of performance, especially in regard to gender issues on the early modern stage, see my *Stage and Social Struggle in Early Modern England.* For sophisticated discussion of how the actor's body, his stage positioning, and performative skills affected early modern theatrical meaning, see also the work of Robert Weimann, especially *Shakespeare and the Popular Tradition: Studies in the Social Dimension of Dramatic Form and Function,* ed. Robert Schwartz (Baltimore, MD: Johns Hopkins University Press, 1978) and *Author's Pen and Actor's Voice: Playing and Writing in Shakespeare's Theatre,* ed. Helen Higbee and William West (Cambridge: Cambridge University Press, 2000).

29. Phyllis Rackin, "History into Tragedy: The Case of *Richard III,*" in *Shakespearean Tragedy and Gender,* ed. Shirley Nelson Garner and Madelon Sprengnether (Bloomington: Indiana University Press, 1996), 31–53.

30. Quoted in Judith Cook's *Shakespeare's Players* (London: Harrap Limited, 1983), 36–37.

31. *The Diary of John Manningham of the Middle Temple 1602–03,* ed. Robert Parker Sorlien (Hanover, NH: University Press of New England, 1976), 75.

32. Quoted in Judith Cook's *Shakespeare's Players,* 37.

33. Robert Greene, *Greens Groats-worth of Wit,* in *The Life and Complete Works in Prose and Verse of Robert Greene,* 15 vols., ed. Alexander B. Grosart (London: Hazell, Watson, and Viney, 1881–86), 12: 144.

Charisma and Institution-Building in Shakespeare's Second Tetralogy

Raphael Falco

I

IN THE PRESENT ESSAY I WOULD LIKE TO speculate on how charismatic authority affects the representation of group experience in Shakespeare's histories in the second tetralogy.[1] I borrowed the title "Charisma and Institution-building" from S. F. Eisenstadt's collection of Max Weber's writing on charisma because it links the near-opposites of charismatic authority and institutional authority while anticipating the stages of the group relationship found in the tetralogy.[2] But the relationship between charisma and institution-building is not so neat as to produce a facile polarization. Consequently, in the present paper I am interested in those near-opposites for their nearness, rather than as opposites per se, specifically in terms of the degrees of authority calibrating the gap between charisma and institutions.

I would like to concentrate, in so far as possible, on group relations in the tetralogy, somewhat bucking the critical trend. Henry and Hal (later himself King Henry) have usually been discussed as individuals. Critics have charted their development in terms of personal ambition, individual needs, and emotional maturity, citing such militating factors as Machiavellianism, theatrical role-playing, Elizabethan ideology, and martial idealism in the shaping of the stage figures. Even policy decisions have been seen as subordinate to the construction of the individual.[3] I do not mean to suggest that these emphases—or these critics—are wrong to call our attention to individual vicissitudes. But there's something to be gained, I think, in shifting emphasis from the personal or individual experiences of Henry and Hal to the group experiences by which they achieve and maintain their ascendancy.

Max Weber identified three kinds of authority: charismatic, traditional, and legal-bureaucratic. The tetralogy is concerned chiefly with the first two of these, although there is an interesting progression of the status of law beginning with Bolingbroke's return from exile and Hal's striking of the Chief Justice, through the Archbishop of Canterbury's speech on Salic law, and culminating in the hanging of Bardolph. But legal authority is best described as an undercurrent in the plays, which are dominated by the conflict between traditional and charismatic authority, and particularly between kinds or degrees of charisma.

Charismatic authority depends on a shared experience, an interdependence of leader and followers. It is worth reviewing here the origins of the term *charisma* as background to the charismatic group dynamics of the second tetralogy. Weber took over and secularized the concept as he found it in Rudolph Sohm's nineteenth-century history of the church. The word originates in the Greek New Testament, in 1 Corinthians 12, where Paul names the nine charisms or gifts of grace available to the Christian congregation. And, while Weber never acknowledges the fact, it is crucial to recognize that Paul introduces his term as a means of suppressing the dissent of the rebellious church at Corinth where certain members had threatened Paul's leadership by proclaiming their gift of speaking in tongues as superior to his supposed divine charge to form a church (he demotes the speaking in tongues to the bottom of the supposedly egalitarian list). The irony of the Corinthian situation is that, although Paul's ecclesiological movement was nurtured in dissent from traditional religious practices at the time, he unambiguously suppresses dissent from his own dissenting movement.[4] This is clearly an institutionalizing methodology, an extension of Jesus's revolutionary and charismatic conservatism: Jesus says that he has come, not to overturn the Torah, but to fulfill it.

Weber enlarged and retaxonomized Paul's (and Sohm's) basic charisms, all of which would probably fit in his first category. The kinds of charisma, according to Weber, are pure or personal charisma, lineage charisma, and office charisma. The latter two represent a depersonalization of pure or personal charisma and (in the Weberian scheme) tend to result when an original, disruptive charismatic authority is controlled and reduced in force through compromises with either traditional or legal-bureaucratic authority. Weber spoke of this sort of compromise as the "routinization" of charismatic authority, by which he meant that an original (and personal) charismatic force increasingly becomes part of the everyday routine of, for example, governing, rulership, and church leadership. He recognized that the ideal type of pure charisma is always bound to fail. It simply cannot last in its pure disruptive state and can only actually survive in diluted form, in a kind of compromise with other forms of authority—a compromise often engineered by members of a charismatic group who want to continue to enjoy the privileges of the revolutionary movement after the death of the original charismatic figure, or after the revolution.

In tragedies, where we often find examples to match Weber's ideal type of pure charisma, the sudden end of a pure charismatic movement can foster an utterly destructive isolation for the protagonist, a Niet-zschean sort of *sparagmos* at the heart of the catastrophe. In the history plays of the second tetralogy, on the other hand, the compromise between pure charisma and other forms of authority often signals quite the oppo-site. It is in fact the sign of a newfound stability, a new ideological hege-mony, and a new genealogical line. The sense of loss may remain, but more as a bittersweet remembrance than as a tragic inevitability, while the emphasis of the dramatic development is on the solidifying union of charismatic and traditional authority.

No doubt, if we were to apply Weber dogmatically, we would con-clude that this union of the traditional and the charismatic in the second tetralogy constitutes a routinization of pure Bolingbrokean charisma. But it is hard to be satisfied with that conclusion. Routinization suggests a loss of charismatic force, a dilution of that magical heterogeneous power which Weber termed charisma, and which, he claimed, satisfied all extraordinary demands by breaking the routine constraints of society.[5] Perhaps a pattern of dilution works for Henry IV. But if the second tetral-ogy reflects chiefly a downward graph of charisma, a gradual domestica-tion of the more disruptive elements of the charismatic movement that deposed Richard, then what do we say about Henry V? How do we account for Henry V's obvious personal charisma (and group depend-ency) in Weberian terms when it seems counterintuitive to call his charis-matic mission disruptive or revolutionary?

As it turns out, this question has been partly answered by Weber's revi-sionists who continue to refine the concept of charisma nearly a century after Weber advanced his theory. Critics such as Edward Shils, Charles Camic, Liah Greenfeld (and others) have voiced uneasiness about the prominence of the revolutionary mission—or of social disruptiveness—as a necessary feature of every charismatic movement.[6] Edward Shils, for instance, amplified Weber's contention, noting that "charisma not only disrupts social order; it also maintains or conserves it."[7] He argued that Weber's concentrated, mission-driven form of charisma was very rare and, instead, what he termed "attenuated and dispersed charisma" was "normal" charisma: "In this form," he maintained, "[charisma] is attrib-uted in a context of routine actions to the rules, norms, offices, institutions, and strata of any society."[8] This is a powerful revision and to some extent contradicts Weber because the notions of the charismatic and the routine are linked.

Yet this linking can be very useful in working out the degrees of charis-matic authority in Shakespeare's histories. In particular, as we try to recon-cile our understanding of both Henry IV and Henry V as charismatic figures, it is invaluable to have at our disposal the theory that some form of charismatic attenuation—rather than merely the draining-off of charisma—

can foster and sustain all institutions. Moreover, the notion of attenuated and dispersed charisma should help us to avoid viewing authority as either charismatic or not, as if charisma were itself a single force. There are degrees of charismatic authority by which we can effectively describe the status of power. Shakespeare's *Henry V* is a proof-text of this theory, I think, just as the two parts of *Henry IV* provide an excruciating illustration of the failure of charismatic authority to achieve the kind of attenuation with which social order might be conserved and institutions sustained.

Unfortunately, literary critics have tended to see charismatic authority as an either/or proposition, as if, for example, a kingship is either charismatic or not. This practice probably stems from a lack of familiarity with the sociological literature, which is, as I have noted, fairly explicit on the stages and variations of charismatic authority. And of course there is also the temptation to use the words *charisma* and *charismatic* in their less rigorous vernacular sense to mean something like "magnetism" or "heightened appeal." As a result, much of the reference to charisma by literary critics reflects a general overpolarization of causes, too arbitrarily eliminating group experience from the analysis of social authority. But literary critics are not the only ones guilty of this overpolarization. Even the redoubtable Quentin Skinner seems inclined to reduce charismatic kingship to a pure or personal category, leaving little room for such degrees of charismatic authority as lineage or office charisma, let alone such subtleties as dispersed and attenuated charisma. In prefacing his remarks on Hobbes's use of the word "state," he notes that Hobbes's declaration that the duties of subjects are owed to the state "announces the end of an era in which the concept of public power had been treated in far more personal and charismatic terms."[9] Skinner is undoubtedly right about the opposition of state and person, even if it might be difficult to separate the obligations of subjects marked for the state from those marked for, say, the Crown. The reason for this difficulty is that, as we have seen, "personal" and "charismatic" do not necessarily mean the same thing, and therefore public power might well be considered simultaneously charismatic *and* less personal. For, while pure or personal charisma might sanction the early stages of a movement, the later transformations of charismatic authority are much more common and long-lasting. Skinner goes on to remark that "underlying the suggestion that a distinctive quality of stateliness 'belongs' to kings was the prevailing belief that sovereignty is intimately connected with display, that the presence of majesty serves in itself as an ordering force." He adds that "[t]his was to prove the most enduring of the many features of charismatic leadership eventually subverted by the emergence of the modern concept of an impersonal state."[10] Certainly the impersonal state "subverts"—that may not be the appropriate concept—the purest forms of charismatic leadership. But those pure forms never last in any case, and it is probably just as accurate to say that less pure forms of charismatic authority are the agents of subversion as to invoke the so-called impersonal state.

But Skinner's yoking of display and charisma has resonance with, indeed might well have been derived from, literary criticism. Stephen Greenblatt in "Invisible Bullets" sees a necessary connection between charisma and a form of theatrical force sustained by ambiguity. According to Greenblatt, it is precisely in the threat to hegemonic rulership in *Henry V* that Henry's charismatic authority is manifest: "the play's central figure seems to feed on the doubts he provokes. For the enhancement of royal power is not only a matter of the deferral of doubt: the very doubts that Shakespeare raises serve not to rob the king of his charisma but to heighten it, precisely as they heighten the theatrical interest of the play; the unequivocal, unambiguous celebrations of royal power with which the period abounds have no theatrical force and have long since fallen into oblivion. The charismatic authority of the king, like that of the stage, depends on falsification."[11] Greenblatt's assessment is very astute in its recognition of the uses of instability (here manifest as doubt) for charismatic leadership.[12] Henry V's charismatic authority "like that of the stage, depends on falsification" because it is the result of a continuing process of invention and reinvention. Just as the stage requires such a process in the audience, Henry requires his followers—and perhaps the audience too—to participate in his constant self-falsifying. But it should be noted that his legitimacy does not depend exclusively on a stage-play falsification any more than it depends exclusively on the putative truth of his lineage claim or on the evidence of his martial prowess. A juggler's combination of these elements produces Henry's authority.

In a brilliant chapter from *Shakespeare After Theory*, David Kastan addresses the precise nature of Henry V's charismatic claim of kingship, and Henry's deployment of that claim: "Lacan notoriously asserted that the man who believes himself king is no more mad than the *king* who believes himself king; that is, it is madness to believe that kingship resides magically in the person of the king rather than in the political relations that bind, even create, king and subject. But this is precisely Hal's enabling knowledge, the authorization of his impressive improvisations. He never confuses the charismatic claims of kingship with the political relations they would accomplish."[13] Kastan has brought together three signal concepts: improvisation, charisma, and political relations. The blending of these concepts is what allows Hal not only to establish himself as a genealogical (and therefore charismatically endowed) king, but also to make the transition from improvisatory leader to institutional head.

Curiously, for a critic so attuned to the improvisations of charisma, Kastan proceeds to pit charismatic leadership against comic misrule without considering the possibility of something like Greenblatt's suggestion that the doubts Shakespeare introduces might serve to heighten Henry V's charisma rather than merely threaten it. He sets up an irreconcilable contrast between the comic voice of the clown at the end of *Henry IV, Part 2* and a somewhat vague, or maybe too generous, notion of charismatic kingship: the clown's speech, he says, "exuberantly undermines both the unifying fantasies of charismatic kingship and the coherence and closure of the represented history that such kingship appropriates for its authorization."[14] The problem with this analysis, placing comic misrule against charismatic kingship, is that it requires us to see the latter as static, at least to the degree that it constitutes an opposition to the Falstaff stand-in of Kastan's argument. But such a conception misrepresents the transformations and flexibilities of charisma, even of charismatic kingship. Kastan concludes with this statement: "The play [*Henry V*] literally brings [Falstaff] back, declaring Hal's victory to be limited and temporary, insisting on the social, ideological, linguistic, and aesthetic multiplicity that both the well-ordered play and the well-ordered state would deny, insisting, that is, precisely on an image of the political nation 'compromising high and low,' however more various and unruly than its charismatic king would have it."[15] Kastan here captures the rigidity of certain charismatic movements, the inherent resistance to dissent fostered by certain leaders, and in this his reading shows an uncommon sensitivity to charismatic group dynamics—uncommon among literary critics, that is. But Kastan nonetheless neglects the likelihood that, of all the various components of kingship, charisma is in fact the most flexible, the most likely to be able to embrace and deploy Falstaff's unruliness. All kingship is after all charismatic, as Shakespeare seems to intuit; it is just a matter of determining what stage of charismatic transformation a particular lineage has reached. In my view, Kastan here—in contrast to his earlier suggestions regarding improvisation—proposes too advanced a charismatic transformation for Henry V, too petrified a set of charismatic symbols.

There is no question that the historical Henrys IV and V long predated the advent of what Skinner refers to as the impersonal state, presumably a monarchy in which the ruler stands above the law.[16] Nevertheless, Shakespeare's kings in the tetralogy all suffer from the conflict between an impersonal institution of rule and the personal charismatic qualities that seem at times to sustain their royal legitimacy; we can track the establishment of institutionalized authority through the formation and breakdown of their charismatic group relationships. But it is easy to fall into anachronism when dealing with these subjects, especially when trying to disentangle the Elizabethan milieu from Shakespeare's distortions of fifteenth-century political myth. The best course is probably a robust skepticism about seeing in Shakespeare's kings some sort of prototype of the conflict between the charismatic and the impersonal state. Analyzing the struggle between kinds of charisma offers a useful means of avoiding that overpolarized prototype and has the added advantage of historical pertinence: both the York-Lancaster conflict and the Elizabethan succession were marked by such a struggle.

The charismatic conditions of the plays may or may not be reflective of political realities, but the best way to read those conditions, as primarily literary representations, is in a kind of triangulation with the source material and Weberian theory. Weber's theories were built around what he termed ideal types, and these types are sometimes best sought in literary rather than real contexts. Tragedies in particular supply ideal types of charismatic authority. But tragedies are scarcely the real world and in tragic dénouements it often seems that there is an utterly unrealistic dichotomy between pure charismatic authority and the less pure, less personal forms of authority. Such stark contrasts are not to be found in daily life, of course, and, curiously, tend to be less manifest in Shakespeare's history plays, where degrees of charismatic authority are much more prevalent than its absolute presence or absence. Indeed, if Shakespeare and other writers seem to anticipate Weber's subtleties regarding the transformations of charisma, that is in part because Weber derives his theories from those very writers' representations (as did Freud for his sphere of interests). As a matter of fact, one might argue that, even if he probably would not have known the word, Shakespeare would have had considerable knowledge of charisma because the concept was so much a part of sixteenth-century religious idealism.

II

Earlier I called attention to the charismatic conservatism of Jesus's claim that he had come not to overturn the Torah, but to fulfill it. This is a provocative notion of the relationship between charisma and law to apply to the second tetralogy. For instance, we might imagine Henry V making the same sort of claim as Jesus in regard to English law (or tradition), but it is difficult to imagine Henry IV making such a claim with any conviction, and it is impossible to imagine Hotspur taking such a position. I bring up this last figure because Shakespeare opens *Henry IV, Part 2* with a description of him, offering the picture of a palpably charismatic figure and the shambles of his movement. Morton (a minor character) is retelling the end of the battle of Shrewsbury, ostensibly for the nobles who were not there but of course also as a summary for the audience. His sudden appearance as an eyewitness to a scene supposedly only witnessed by Hal and Falstaff allows us to glimpse the breakdown of Hotspur's group:

> In few, his death, whose spirit lent a fire
> Even to the dullest peasant in his camp,
> Being bruited once, took fire and heat away
> From the best-temper'd courage of his troops:
> For from his metal was his party steel'd,
> Which once in him abated, all the rest
> Turn'd on themselves, like dull and heavy lead:
> And the thing that's heavy in itself
> Upon enforcement flies with greatest speed,
> So did our men, heavy in Hotspur's loss,
> Lend to his weight such lightness with their fear
> That arrows fled not swifter toward their aim
> Than did our soldiers, aiming at their safety,
> Fly from the field
>
> (2.1.1.112–25)[17]

The metaphor of the arrows has great proleptic significance in the tetralogy, as if, by the time we get to *Henry V,* the fearful fleeing rebel soldiers were transformed into the victorious arrows of Agincourt which Shakespeare would have read about in Edward Hall or in Holinshed.[18] Still, the breakdown of group cohesion, the obvious chaos brought on by the death of a pure charismatic leader, is a curious way to open *Henry IV, Part 2.* It might be seen as a kind of cautionary tale for Hal and as a warning to King Henry regarding the necessity to transform his own authority into a full-fledged institution to survive. The obvious interdependence between Hotspur's band and Hotspur calls attention to the fragility of the charismatic bond, and his death, recounted where it is, clearly indicates the inappropriateness of that kind of mission-driven movement in a stability-hungry political milieu.

Henry's embrace of traditional and even legal resources to preserve his kingship must be seen in contrast to the failure of Hotspur's pure charismatic rebellion. In *Richard II,* Henry's own rebellion, despite its dependence on his personal charisma, relied on a conflicting mixture of traditional claims and dissent against the crown. He sought to overthrow Richard, or at least to resist Richard, in the very name of tradition—a paradox that eventually lands him in some difficulty as he attempts to suppress the personal charismatic attributes of his kingship in favor of the traditional and legal attributes of a cobbled-together lineage charismatic claim.

The last three plays of the tetralogy allow us to watch the two Henrys in their gradual reestablishment of two related institutions: the traditional kingship and the genealogical legitimacy of Henry's lineage. This reestablishment is no small feat in so far as genealogical custom, governmental organization, and law itself undergo a ruinous harrowing in *Richard II.*

Although, as Bolingbroke, Henry never entirely rejects traditional authority and never denies the validity of monarchy per se, he and his charismatic cohort come to power on a wave of dissent.[19] His task after his own coronation is to transform his charismatic group of dissenters into a traditional hierarchy of noble supporters. In Weberian terms he must routinize his charisma by transforming the very symbols of his rebellion into symbols of economic and governmental stability. In Pauline terms, he must prevent dissent from cropping up among the original dissenters by incorporating his rebels into his political body.

There are several problems with this project, however, the most prominent being that Henry's promises to Hotspur and the others (in *Richard II*) to reward their loyalty to him once he becomes king were acts of a pure charismatic leader, definitely not the acts of an ensconced lineage authority (Hotspur eventually scorns the promises as a "candy deal of courtesy" [*1*.1.3.247]). One of the hallmarks of a pure or personal charismatic movement is the lack of rational economic organization: the charismatic leader awards his followers according to other-than-rational criteria, such as honor, loyalty, and courage. Thus Henry, as early as *Henry IV, Part 1*, runs into the conflict between his attempt to routinize his distribution of wealth in the kingdom and the irrational—that is, not rationalized—promises he made at the height of his charismatic dissent. Shakespeare might easily have deduced from Holinshed the importance of those promises for Henry's institutional legitimacy. Holinshed's chronicle of Henry IV begins with a list of all the new officers he created for his court by handing out earldoms, dukedoms, stewardships, and so forth. This sort of beneficence was no doubt common practice with every new regime, yet Holinshed seems to make a point of underscoring it in Henry IV's case while omitting it from Henry V's (and most others'). Perhaps we should not make too much of this; perhaps there were few rational economic alternatives to recommend themselves. But Shakespeare, by heightening the contrast between the rebels' expectations and Henry's responses, seems to dangle an alternative to Henry's methods, albeit a phantom alternative. It is enough to get us thinking about the conflict between the kind of rationalized economic organization Henry should aspire to in transforming his charismatic movement into an institutional form and the kind of irrational distribution he engages in the immediate wake of his coronation.

As I noted, the word *charisma* comes from Paul's first epistle to the Corinthians. The *koiné* Greek term describing the charisms, or charismata, is *diaireseis charismaton*, rendered by the Geneva Bible translators as "diversities of gifts." But in fact the Geneva Bible version misses the complete sense of *diaireseis charismaton*. The Greek *diairesis* tends to mean a dividing-up; like the Vulgate's *divisiones gratiarum*, the Greek implies a distribution of charismata, akin to a dividing up of money or spoils. This sense is somewhat lost in the English translation, but Bolingbroke's behavior, especially at the end of *Richard II* and at the start of *Henry IV, Part 1* (and in Holinshed as well) helps to restore the original notion of charismatic distribution.

Yet Henry IV's somewhat bungled distribution of rewards underscores the difficulty of mixing types of charisma, or of effecting a swift compromise between charismatic and traditional authority during the lifetime of the original charismatic figure. As Henry IV attempts to routinize his charismatic movement with the intention of transforming it into the two legitimate institutions I mentioned earlier, he alienates those followers whose loyalty depended to a large extent on a *personal* relationship to their leader. In my work on charismatic authority and tragedy I spoke of Bolingbroke as possessing what I termed charismatic capital, by which I meant that he had the means to inspire loyalty and that he manipulated his personal ties to his followers as a pirate leader might manipulate his distribution of plunder. Significantly, the term Shakespeare repeatedly uses for Bolingbroke's charismatic bond is *love,* a term that includes implications of both desire and of capital reward.[20] There is clearly a tie between Bolingbroke and his followers which might be called libidinal, and this tie, which of course never becomes eroticized but is instead sublimated in acts of loyalty, nevertheless emphasizes the inescapably personal nature of the relationship that binds Bolingbroke's charismatic movement. To retreat from this personal charisma, even to the limited extent he does as Henry IV, is to call into question the force of the original charisma itself, and thereby to weaken Henry's claim to power.

Coeval with that problem is the legitimacy of the crown itself. To some extent, this is impossible to separate from genealogical legitimacy, so we can consider them together in terms of charisma. Holinshed himself makes explicit Henry's problem in regard to these linked symbols of legitimacy when he records the useless attempt to provide the new king with a bona fide royal lineage: "At the daie of the coronation, to the end he should not seeme to take vpon him the crowne and scepter roiall by plaine extorted power, and iniurious intrusion: he was aduised to make his title as heire to Edmund (surnamed or vntrulie feined) Crooke-backe, sonne to King Henrie the third . . . But not onelie his fréends, but also his priuie enimies, knew that this was but a forged title" (Holinshed 3.3–4). This remark reflects the ham-fisted effort to routinize Henry's personal charisma and to depersonalize it, as if by a kind of back-formation it could be transformed into a legitimate lineage claim. But a forged title to the crown makes the already difficult job of transforming personal charisma into a depersonalized form all but impossible, as Henry finds out, because it calls attention to the revolutionary, personal attributes of Henry's charismatic claim at just the moment when he wants to distract attention from those attributes. His situation through both his plays exacerbates the conflict between pure charismatic and lineage charismatic claims, and the crown hangs in the balance. This is not to suggest that an impersonal kingship along the lines of the Hobbesian impersonal state is ever a possibility in the tetralogy. Rather, the conflict is between kinds of charismatic authority to begin with, and later, under Henry V, between charismatic and legal-institutional authority. And in the latter case the conflict is resolved by the kind of attenuated charisma that is manifest in a remarkable blending of personal charismatic attributes, a de facto lineage claim, and a sudden unification of the established institutions of church and law.

But of course Henry V's successful compromise among competing forms of authority does not have permanent results. As the Chorus reminds us at the end of *Henry V,* the problems experienced under Henry VI will be problems of management, and this too is provocative for the second tetralogy. The infant king (says the Chorus), "Whose state so many had the managing, / That they lost France and made his England bleed" (5.ep.11–12), loses all that his father had gained through the dispersal of his authority. The contrast with Henry V's charismatic management of authority is inevitable, and any such contrast encourages us to look backward and forward from *Henry V* to the different kinds of failure incumbent on the mismanagement of charismatic claims—a personal charismatic claim for Henry IV and a supposedly routinized lineage claim for Henry VI. Among the three, Henry V provides the ideal model of charismatic administration.

In this connection, one of the most provocative post-Weberian theories of charisma has been offered by Thomas Spence Smith, who speaks of charismatic authority using a metaphor derived from Ilya Prigogine's studies of nonequilibrium systems (which are sometimes inaccurately referred to by the umbrella term "chaos theory").[21] Nonequilibrium, entropy-driven systems provide very interesting possibilities when applied to charismatic group formation, and can be exceedingly fruitful in analyzing drama. For example, Smith notes that it may very well be that charismatic groups are unable to survive without some degree of decay. He suggests that certain types of groups survive best in dissipative structures, in the entropy and mild chaos which allow leaders to emerge. One of the constants of charismatic interaction, according to Smith, is that it seeks to preserve itself. Therefore, if mild chaos were to provide a criterion for control, then a charismatic leader might extend or encourage a dissipative structure rather than gravitate toward stability, inasmuch as entropy guarantees a sharp dependency among followers. There is a paradox here, of course, in that we are proposing a structure that defines itself in dissipation. But one can easily imagine such dissipative structures in Shakespearean representations of court life in the second tetralogy.

One way to think, for instance, about Hal's delinquency throughout *Henry IV, Parts 1* and *2,* is to consider the extent to which his conduct organizes his followers—and not merely the tavern dregs he leads by the nose, but, more significantly, the royal court which overnight he will come to lead. His fostering of the mild chaos of what the Archbishop later calls his wildness puts him in the unique position of creating and managing a dissipative structure which he alone can resolve. Similarly, at the other end of the tetralogy, the soldiers' scene in *Henry V* affords a glimpse at the same sort of methodology. King Henry appears to a group of somewhat disgruntled soldiers anonymously. His anonymity allows him to create and manage a bit of mild chaos, what might be called the threat of a dissipative structure. John Bates, one of the three soldiers, wishes he were anywhere but in France. The king, as just another soldier, answers that the king "would not wish himself anywhere but here" (4.1.120). Bates counters: "Then I would he were here alone; so should he be sure to be ransomed, and a many poor men's lives saved" (4.1.121–23). Henry's response pits the notion of being alone against the ideal of the national, and therefore group, honor. What is most interesting about the soldiers' scene, however, is that, by his anonymity, Henry encourages the rambunctiousness, even mild subversiveness, of his interlocutors' opinions. He in effect sets up the soldiers for a surprise (to be sprung in the long revelation of his identity to Michael Williams). Henry's concealment fosters a mild rebelliousness which his later behavior, not to mention winning the battle, will resolve into a trust in his authority. We can therefore see the soldiers' scene as an emblematic dissipative structure *in statu nascendi.* This kind of maneuvering establishes Henry V as a charismatic figure, a king as dependent on the metanoia of followers as on traditional or legal claims for his authority. His authority is not merely a diluted form of charisma in the Weberian sense, but a lively dynamic charismatic force. Both as Hal and as king, he performs a balancing act, demonstrating a management ability absent from both his father and his own son (from the latter in large part because he comes to the throne too early). The contrast is important in that it helps to explain Henry V's successful merging of charismatic attributes with the institutional hegemony he eventually establishes.

We can apply the model of dissipative structures to the practices of both kings in the tetralogy with interesting results. The notion of interdependence which I mentioned earlier, the systemic mutuality crucial to any functioning charismatic organization, takes on a slightly different coloring when we recognize the extent to which the charismatic leader may manipulate the symbols of his (or her) charisma and the circumstances of his or her mission-driven role in order to maintain authority. Henry IV directly addresses this issue. In castigating his son for his wayward conduct in

Henry IV, Part 1, King Henry describes his own manipulation of his charismatic appeal and of the symbols of superiority that brought him to power. His emphasis is on the rarity value of what he calls his "presence," contrasting himself both to the tavern-crawling Hal and, inappropriately I think, to Richard II as well.[22] But King Henry's point is well taken even if Hal rather than Richard supplies the better example. The objective, according to the king, is to manipulate one's presence, to create oneself as a charismatic symbol. "Had I so lavish of my presence been," he admonishes in a well-known speech,

> So common-hackneyed in the eyes of men,
> So stale and cheap to vulgar company,
> Opinion, that did help me to the crown,
> Had still kept loyal to possession
> And left me in reputeless banishment,
> A fellow of no mark or likelihood.
>   (3.2.39–45)

The "mark" he speaks of is the distinction he claims to have transformed into a symbol of divine auspices. "By being seldom seen," he explains, "I could not stir / But like a comet I was wondered at" (3.2.46–47). He had, by his own account, disturbed expectations, creating the kind of dissipative, *dependent* situation that, for example, Othello creates when he refuses to fight Brabantio.

The comet to which Henry likens himself of course has heavenly origins, streaking down from on high like a divine prophecy. What is most significant, however, is that Henry does not blush before the notion that he himself *created the appearance* of divine auspices, that he invented his charismatic presence and manipulated the symbols of his uniqueness. This is a stunning admission, complicated by Henry's assertion that his created charismatic presence had more force than Richard's inherited royal presence:

> And then I stole all courtesy from heaven,
> And dressed myself in such humility
> That I did pluck allegiance from men's hearts,
> Loud shouts and salutations from their mouths,
> Even in the presence of the crowned King.
> Thus did I keep my person fresh and new,
> My presence, like a robe pontifical,
> Ne'er seen but wondered at.
>   (3.2.50–57)

The word "courtesy" echoes ominously with Hotspur's hollowed-out sense of the word, and several critics have seen this passage as proof of the role-playing or theatricality inherent in Elizabethan royal authority.[23] But the speech might also be seen as a prescription for a personal charismatic movement. Henry, clearly a revolutionary figure in confrontation with the "crowned King," first steals courtesy from heaven. He does not *receive* a gift of grace in the Christian (Pauline) sense but takes it himself, and thereby attracts the allegiance of followers. Henry's agency is at the heart of his charismatic movement and he fully expects his son to recognize the superiority of his claim to that of Richard. By the end of the passage he has raised his presence to divine status, likening himself to a "robe pontifical." The irony of the speech is rich: Henry may claim that he somehow converted his stolen courtesy to divine authorization, but not only is the Church (in the person of Carlisle) firmly against him, but also Richard has the more obvious claim to divine auspices. The dead Richard somehow remains the *vicarius Dei,* as Gaunt and Carlisle call him in *Richard II;* and Richard's own words are unforgettable, haunting the entire tetralogy:

> Not all the water in the rough rude sea
> Can wash the balm off from an anointed king;
> The breath of worldly men cannot depose
> The deputy elected by the Lord.
> (3.2.54–57)

There is a significant problem, moreover, in Henry's assertions regarding stolen courtesy and robes pontifical. As Kastan has noted in regard to Henry's concession that "Opinion" helped him to the crown, "it is hypostatized 'Opinion' that he acknowledges, erasing the agency of the people who must hold it."[24] This is an excellent point, recognizing a mistake Henry makes but his son avoids. I would add that it is not merely that "Opinion" has become hypostatized, however, but that the very symbols of Henry's (or Bolingbroke's) original charismatic movement are now hypostatized. Consequently, the manipulation of those symbols which Henry boasts of to his son is no longer possible. Henry must live with a petrified version of his charismatic movement while what he needs is a dynamic model of charismatic transformation: his rulership lacks the dynamism of a self-induced dissipative structure, a mild chaos which Henry might himself manage and appear to resolve. His followers, alienated from the new King Henry after the loss of their personal relationship to his presence and their dependence on his unexpected behavior, are further separated from him by their adherence to the now-hypostatized symbols by which, or because of which, they followed him in the first place. Whereas Henry Bolingbroke created and managed a revolutionary dissipative structure in the realm, Henry IV divorces himself from the

symbols of the dissipative structure and from the allegiance of his charismatic followers to those symbols. The result is a breakdown of group
interdependence, and, predictably, further rebellion, because the symbols
of the group are revolutionary and the charismatic leader, now detached
from the symbols, seeks to establish himself as the embodiment, not of
charismatic, but of traditional and legal authority.[25] There's an interesting
irony connected with this. Dain Trafton has noted the "progressive diminishment of [Henry's] presence on stage" as the tetralogy moves forward:
about half the time in *Richard II,* about one-quarter of the time in *Henry
IV, Part 1,* and only three scenes in *Henry IV, Part 2.*[26] Ironically, this
increasing rarity of presence indicates not a more powerful authority as it
does at the beginning of Bolingbroke's movement, but, to the contrary, a
weakening and less powerful force. It could be said to represent the necessary diminishment of charismatic authority in the augmentation of post-
charismatic, or institutional authority. Unfortunately for Henry, the
diminishment of the former fails to coincide with its transformation into
the latter.

Henry simply cannot make the transition from charismatic figure to
convincing traditional authority, which makes his castigation of Hal all the
more poignant—or more ridiculous. We already know from Hal's famous
"Yet herein will I imitate the sun" speech in *Henry IV, Part 1,* that he has
the same sort of calculating attitude as his father:

> Yet herein will I imitate the sun,
> Who doth permit the base contagious clouds
> To smother up his beauty from the world,
> That, when he please again to be himself,
> Being wanted he may be more wonder'd at
> By breaking through the foul and ugly mists
> Of vapours that did seem to strangle him.
>   (1.1.2.192–98)

Since Hal in fact views his hidden presence among Falstaff and the others as
a means of making himself "more wondered at" later, we would have to
doubt the utility of his father's scolding. By the first act of *Henry IV, Part 1,*
he seems to have learned the lesson of manipulating one's charismatic symbols: his father likens himself to a comet, Hal likens himself to the sun. Both
shine, both have heavenly auspices, both produce wonder in onlookers. The
difference between the two men, as between the two speeches, is that
whereas Henry's emphasis is exclusively on his rarity value, Hal's is on the
transition from hidden to revealed presence. Translated into the terms we
have been using, Hal's speech anticipates the transformation of his charismatic appeal in a way his father's speech and behavior never do:

So when this loose behavior I throw off,
And pay the debt I never promised,
By how much better than my word I am,
By so much shall I falsify men's hopes;
And like bright metal on a sullen ground,
My reformation, glitt'ring o'er my fault,
Shall show more goodly, and attract more eyes
Than that which hath no foil to set it off.
(1.1.2.203–10)

Hal here promises that process of falsification by which he will transform others' opinions of him, and, as Greenblatt suggests, will begin to institute his regal charismatic authority. Either instinctively or with calculation he recognizes that the *transition* from one charismatic status to the next must be the means of producing wonder, if the transformed status is to have any permanence. Thus he prepares himself, as Shakespeare prepares his audience, for the extraordinary transitions to come while also underscoring Henry IV's most prominent shortcoming.

III

The status of institution-building under Henry V is best seen in contrast to that under his father, who, despite a remarkable personal charisma, never manages to convert his dubious lineage claim into an unimpugnable institutional reality. The clash between charismatic and institutional authority inheres in Henry IV himself. He makes an unconvincing institutional figure, perhaps because he comes to power on the ambiguous terms of charismatic appeal and traditional heritage ("As I was banish'd, I was banish'd Herford; / As I come, I come for Lancaster" [*Richard II* 2.3.112–13]). There is a speech by Westmoreland during the rebellion in *Part 2* (4.1) in which Shakespeare seems to present us with this shaky relationship between charisma and institutional stability. Westmoreland is addressing the young Mowbray:

The Earl of Hereford was reputed then
In England the most valiant gentleman.
Who knows on whom Fortune would then have smiled?
But if your father had been victor there,
He ne'er had borne it out of Coventry;
For all the country, in a general voice,
Cried hate upon him; and all their prayers and love
Were set on Hereford, whom they doted on,
And bless'd, and grac'd, indeed more than a King.

> But this is mere digression from my purpose.
> Here come I from our princely general
> To know your griefs, to tell you from his Grace
> That he will give you audience.
>
> (4.1.131–43)

The irony of this speech is that Westmoreland sees the need to invoke the charismatic figure of Bolingbroke—him of the "supple knee" from *Richard II*—to deliver a message from one of the king's *other* sons (Lancaster) regarding an audience. From the perspective of charismatic authority the situation is very clear: the original charismatic figure is invoked as a kind of petrified symbol of the now routinized movement. Significantly, Mowbray recognizes the distinction between the types of authority: "But he hath forc'd us to compel this offer," he replies, "And it proceeds from policy, not love" (4.1.47–48). We recall that Shakespeare uses the word *love* to index Bolingbroke's bond to his followers, and to adumbrate his distribution of the spoils. Thus we easily recognize in Mowbray's complaint that the difference he sees between policy and love is analogous to the difference between institutional requirement and charismatic benison. That Mowbray notices this difference so late in *Henry IV, Part 2* reminds us, if we need reminding, that the king has been unable to make the transition from personal charismatic leader to institutional leader, that his kingly acts are forced whereas his revolutionary acts were supple, and that his followers have been made to choose between one alternative or another rather than being incorporated into a dynamic transformation of forms of authority.

But how do we know that King Henry V is different? How do we know that he, or Shakespeare, resolves the conflict between charisma and its transformations? We can begin by noting that he resolves a great many unstable situations which he inherits from his father. He manages to resolve these problems, I would argue, in large measure because he recognizes the interdependence—or, again, intersubjectivity—that exists between himself and his followers. In the first scene of act 1 of *Henry V,* the Archbishop of Canterbury describes a charismatic infusion that has transformed the wild Hal into a king of the blood—or if not of the blood precisely, then an heir of divine auspices. And we might note here the *OED* definition of the word "institution" in Roman law as the appointment of an heir. "The breath no sooner left his father's body," says the Archbishop,

> But that his wildness, mortified in him,
> Seem'd to die too; yea, at that very moment,
> Consideration like an angel came,
> And whipp'd th'offending Adam out of him,

Leaving his body as a Paradise,
T'envelop and contain celestial spirits.

One could hardly ask for a better description of a gift of grace, which the editor of the Arden edition, J. H. Walter, recognizes in making the appropriate connection to Saint Paul's ecstasies. A distinctly charismatic authority of divine promise comes to Hal like an angel and, like the charismata in 1 Corinthians 12, is made part of his *soma* at the moment that his mortal body becomes the immortal body politic. But this is not merely an individual experience if the Pauline text lurks in the background. For if Shakespeare is indeed referring to the charisms, then his reference would automatically include an emphasis on the group component of Henry's new gift, and on the gift's reciprocal nature. This distinction cannot be underscored sufficiently: the reciprocal nature of the charisms, the intersubjective participation in the body of Christ, carries over in any reference to charismatic infusion. Thus we must acknowledge the very strong possibility that the descent of the angel into Hal's spirit, the whipping away of the offending Adam, the embodiment of the celestial spirit—all these signs of divine intervention in the status of the English monarchy, in language drawn from the Book of Common Prayer Baptism service—have a concomitant condition or stipulation that requires the reciprocal *bodily* relationship of the new king to his followers. With the charisms as a model, Henry V's newfound power is above all a form of intersubjectivity that not only atomizes notions of autonomous or hegemonic personhood but also makes the new king's political successes dependent on a successful shared charismatic experience. Jonathan Dollimore and Alan Sinfield have suggested that "*Henry V* was a powerful Elizabethan fantasy simply because it represented a single source of power in the state."[27] But this is only true, I suspect, if we understand the fantasy to be a vision of power that includes the group share in it.

A good example of Henry V's—and Shakespeare's—awareness of the group share in power is the soldiers' scene, to which I would like to return briefly here. In the disguise of a nameless soldier, Henry provides for his interlocutors a model of intersubjective group conditions, and a warning regarding the dangers of such conditions:

> For though I speak it to you, I think the king is but a man, as I am: the violet smells to him as it doth to me; the element shows to him as it doth to me; all his senses have but human conditions. . . . his ceremonies laid by, in his nakedness he appears but a man; and though his affections are higher mounted than ours, yet when they stoop, they stoop with the like wing. Therefore when he sees reason of fears, as we do, his fears, out of doubt, be of the same relish as ours are: yet, in reason, no man should possess him with any appearance of fear, lest he, by showing it, should dishearten his army. (4.1.101–13)

Much can be made of this passage from the perspective of charismatic relations. Most significant, perhaps, are the last lines. The anonymous Henry affirms the interdependence of the king's relationship with his soldiers: to show fear is to dishearten one's own membership because king and army are one body, one affective system. In a manner of speaking, the individual element has been leeched out of the kingship, despite Henry's protestations of humanness. The individual has been replaced by the communal charismatic group experience. Compare Richard II's notorious collapse into humanness: "I live with bread like you, feel want / Taste grief, need friends—subjected thus / How can you say to me, I am a king?" (*Richard II* 3.2.175–77). No matter what he himself may intend, Richard's humanness means not a bond with other human beings but a destruction of the bond on which he has been relying. In pointed contrast, Henry V's assertions about his humanness lead him to a recognition of his power as a king. In other words, and remarkably, his assertions regarding his human stature confirm the authority of his rulership, reestablishing as a viable charismatic state the institution of the English crown.

Shakespeare uses Henry's anonymity to emphasize this point: Henry is Everyman as the representative of the intersubjectivity of charismatic leadership and, as the audience and reader know, he is also an institutional authority as the king. The mortal body of the king is joined (or rejoined) to the body politic of the king, and, most importantly of all, the king knows it. For reasons outlined already, Henry IV never arrives at a consciousness of himself as simultaneously man and king, simultaneously charismatic and institutional leader. His son, on the other hand, just before the battle that will solidify his fortunes, demonstrates a full consciousness of his dual existence. We can infer, as we could as early as the "I imitate the sun" speech, that Henry V also understands the transformations of charismatic authority that will enable him to be both man and king, mortal body and body politic, personal bearer of a gift of grace and head of an institution legitimated by (and thereby paradoxically legitimating) that selfsame gift of grace.

It may be that the proof of this legitimation can be found in the erotic element Shakespeare introduces with Katharine and the marriage plans at the end of *Henry V*.[28] I spoke earlier about the libidinal ties that are sublimated in the bond existing in a charismatic group between a leader and his or her followers. The social psychologist Donald McIntosh, following Freud, called these "aim-inhibited ties" and noted that the charismatic relationship has a clear erotic component, an erotic charge, but that the libidinal urges attendant on that erotic charge must remain inhibited in aim for the group to remain intact.[29] This would be true predominantly in the case of a personal charismatic claim: the leader's tie to his or her followers would depend in large measure on the maintenance of aim-inhibited libidinal ties between them. The breakdown of those inhibitions, the satisfaction of those aims, particularly on the leader's part, threatens to undermine the affective structure of personally guaranteed group relations.

Princess Katharine might be seen to represent exactly the sort of breakdown of aim-inhibited libidinal ties I am referring to. Simultaneously—and this is deliberate, I think, on Shakespeare's part—the marriage signals the transformation of Henry's personal charismatic claim into an institutional claim in which aim-inhibited ties would not be necessary. The bond at the institutional level is not as highly personal and therefore not necessarily eroticized; rather, it is the result expressly of the depersonalization of charisma and is routinized in custom, rational economic organization, or legality and bureaucracy. Henry's wooing of Katharine, shot through with the language of alliance and leaguing, openly links the erotic to the political—and, as critics have noted, also distorts a species of rape by misrepresenting it as a traditional lover's quest. But the morality of the situation is irrelevant from the point of view of charismatic development. What is important in those terms is the sudden advent of libidinal ties which are definitely not aim-inhibited. This eroticization of Henry's personal charisma not only signals an end to both his tavern- and battlefield-style bonds, but also—and more significantly for the conclusion of the tetralogy—heralds the transformation of his charismatic presence into the combined institutions of marriage, genealogical legitimation, and the rulership of England and France.

But does the final play then leave us with a critique of Henry V or with an affirmation of his ideology of hegemonic rulership, as so many critics have asked? More to the point, does an analysis of charismatic transformations help us to choose between critique and affirmation, or help to place us among what Harry Berger, Jr., terms either the Harry-lovers or the Harry-haters?[30] Probably not: the best that can be said, I think, once we appreciate the status of charismatic transition, is that we feel a puzzled sort of admiration for the hybrid figure who is part god and part charismatic administrator. Yet there is something bittersweet in our admiration.

NOTES

I am grateful to William Carroll and Coppélia Kahn for the invitation to present a version of this essay to the Harvard Shakespeare Seminar, and to the participants in the seminar for their useful comments. I would also like to thank Lena Cowen Orlin and Christoph Irmscher for their advice.

1. This essay extends the findings of a recent book in which I attempted to show the effect of the dissolution of charismatic authority on tragic circumstances. See my *Charismatic Authority in Early Modern English Tragedy* (Baltimore, MD: Johns Hopkins University

Press, 2000). I have borrowed from *Charismatic Authority* especially in discussing Weberian and post-Weberian theories and the origins of the term *charisma*.

2. S. F. Eisenstadt, ed., *Max Weber: On Charisma and Institution Building* (Chicago and London: University of Chicago Press, 1968).

3. See, e.g., *Shakespeare as Political Thinker*, ed. John E. Alvis and Thomas G. West (Wilmington, DE: ISI Books, 2000); Grace Tiffany, "Shakespeare's Dionysian Prince," *Renaissance Quarterly* 52 (1999): 366–81; Norman Rabkin, "Rabbits, Ducks, and *Henry V*," *Shakespeare Quarterly* 28 (1977): 379–96; David Scott Kastan, "Proud Majesty Made a Subject: Shakespeare and the Spectacle of Rule," *Shakespeare Quarterly* 37 (1986): 459–75, and, idem, " 'The King hath many marching in his Coats,' or, What did you do in the War, Daddy?," in *Shakespeare After Theory* (New York: Routledge, 1999), 129–47. For a modified version of the individual subject, see also Constance Jordan, *Shakespeare's Monarchies: Ruler and Subject in the Romances* (Ithaca, NY: Cornell University Press, 1997), esp. 10–11, where Jordan briefly discusses what she terms the "factor of inwardness" in the history plays.

4. Freedom from choice as well as conformity even to a dissenting position bind members to a charismatic group, while simultaneously binding the charismatic leader to his group. Cf. *Charismatic Authority*, 18.

5. See *Charismatic Authority*, 13–14. The relevant passage in Weber comes from his *Economy and Society*, 2 vols., ed. Guenther Roth and Claus Wittich (Berkeley and Los Angeles: University of California Press, 1978), 2.1111–12: "All *extra*ordinary needs, i.e., those which *transcend* the sphere of everyday economic routines, have always been satisfied in an entirely heterogeneous manner: on a *charismatic* basis. The further we go back in history, the more strongly does this statement hold. It means the following: that the 'natural' leaders in moments of distress . . . were neither appointed officeholders nor 'professionals' in the present-day sense . . . but rather bearers of specific gifts of body and mind that were considered 'supernatural' (in the sense that not everybody could have access to them)."

6. Toward the end of his life Weber increasingly believed that charismatic authority had to be disruptive, especially at the start of a movement. See, e.g., *Economy and Society* 2.1117: "Charisma, in its most potent forms, disrupts rational rule as well as tradition altogether and overturns all notions of sanctity. Instead of reverence for customs that are ancient and hence sacred, it enforces the inner subjection to the unprecedented and absolutely unique and therefore Divine. In this purely empirical and value-free sense charisma is indeed the specifically creative revolutionary force of history."

7. Edward Shils, *The Constitution of Society* (Chicago: University of Chicago Press, 1982), 120.

8. Ibid., 118.

9. Quentin Skinner, "The State," in *Political Innovation and Conceptual Change*, ed. Terence Ball, James Farr, and Russell L. Hanson (Cambridge: Cambridge University Press, 1989), 90. Cf. Claire McEachern, "*Henry V* and the Paradox of the Body Politic," *Shakespeare Quarterly* 45 (1994): 33–56; see p. 37.

10. Skinner, "State," 92.

11. Stephen Greenblatt, *Shakespearean Negotiations: The Circulation of Social Energy in Renaissance England* (Berkeley and Los Angeles: University of California Press, 1988), 63.

12. I am less sure about his assertion that "the unequivocal, unambiguous celebrations of royal power" had somehow lost their force. This seems more tendentious, or wishful, than provable. On one hand, were celebrations of royal power ever "unequivocal" or "unambiguous"? On the other hand, ambiguity notwithstanding, royal progresses, coronations, triumphs, funerals—all seemed to inspire a fair share of admiration and literary praise, and maybe even a little awe, in the sixteenth and seventeenth centuries. Greenblatt may be setting the bar too high in terms of the effects of "theatrical force." Indeed, one could probably

stretch the argument to say that such events as royal coronations and funerals, to the extent that they capture the public imagination, *still* carry "theatrical force." But this is not the place to go into such an argument, and, besides, before beginning one would want to sharpen and more rigorously define such terms as "celebrations of royal power" and "theatrical force."

13. Kastan, *Shakespeare After Theory,* 144.

14. Ibid., 145.

15. Ibid.

16. This is not the place to explore this complicated concept. But see *The Cambridge History of Renaissance Philosophy,* ed. Charles B. Schmitt and Quentin Skinner (Cambridge: Cambridge University Press, 1988), esp. 389–408. In this section, which is written by Skinner, there is a discussion of the course of political theory from John of Salisbury's notion that rulers are images of the divine on earth (390) to Azo's remarkable ideas about the *merum imperium* (391) to Jacques Almain's much later concept that "Rulers are seen, in short, as wielding 'a form of *dominium* which is merely administrative in character'; they are not the owners of their sovereignty, but are merely commissioned to exercise it on behalf of their subjects as a matter of convenience" (404).

17. All references to the plays are to the Arden editions. *Richard II,* ed. Peter Ure (London: Methuen, 1956); *Henry IV, Part I,* ed. A. R. Humphreys (New York: Vintage Books, 1960); *Henry IV, Part II,* ed. A. R. Humphreys (New York: Vintage Books, 1966); *Henry V,* ed. J. H. Walter (London: Routledge, 1954).

18. Worth noting too is Hall's emphasis on Henry V as a leader. See *The Union of the two noble and illustre famelies of Lancastre and Yorke* (1550), chapter 2, 16 recto: "Kyng Henry also lyke a leader & not lyke one led, like a sovereigne and not like a soldior ordred hys men for hys most aduantage lyke an expert captaine and a couragious warrior." (This passage appears on pp. 66–67 of the reprinted edition, London, 1809.)

19. Dain A. Trafton maintains that "[e]ven before the end of *Richard II* it becomes clear that Henry's efforts to make himself a sacred king in the old style cannot succeed." (See "Shakespeare's Henry IV: A New King in a New Principality," in Alvis and West, *Shakespeare as Political Thinker,* 102). It may be, as Trafton says, that Henry cannot succeed in making himself into a sacred king, but that should not divert our attention from his efforts to reestablish the institution of the kingship, nor from his intention of making his successors into sacred kings through de facto genealogical inheritance.

20. See for instance *Richard II* 2.3.48–49, where Bolingbroke says to young Harry Percy (soon to be called Hotspur): "As my fortune ripens with thy love / It shall be still thy true love's recompense."

21. See Thomas Spence Smith, *Strong Interaction* (Chicago: University of Chicago Press, 1992), esp. 14, 110–11, 162–99; and *Charismatic Authority,* 19, 94–95.

22. This latter comparison is remarkable, I think, because the Richard we know from *Richard II* hardly seems "Enfeoffed . . . to popularity" (3.2.69) to use Henry's derogatory words, or "sick and blunted with community" (3.2.78). To the contrary, Richard seems isolated and aloof, relying too heavily on his divinely ordained separateness, his lineage charismatic claim. He certainly does not seem to be spreading himself too thinly among his people—at least not in Shakespeare's rendition (this clash with the sources is worth examining, especially since it points to Shakespeare's awareness of Richard's mismanagement of group relations).

23. See Kastan, *Shakespeare After Theory,* 142, and "Proud Majesty Made a Subject," 466; and Vickie Sullivan, "Princes to Act: Henry V as the Machiavellian Prince of Appearance," in *Shakespeare's Political Pageant: Essays in Literature and Politics,* ed. Joseph Alulis and Vickie Sullivan (Lanham, MD: Rowan and Littlefield, 1996), 131.

24. Kastan, *Shakespeare After Theory,* 138–39.

25. One might contrast Marlowe's *Tamburlaine,* in which the opposite is the case: Tamburlaine remains fixed on the petrified symbols of revolutionary disruption while his followers change, seeking less disruptive forms of authority. But of course Tamburlaine is a tragic figure while Henry IV, in Harold Goddard's estimation, only "approximates tragedy." (Goddard, *The Meaning of Shakespeare,* 2 vols. [Chicago: University of Chicago Press, 1951], 1:162).

26. Trafton, "Shakespeare's Henry IV," 94.

27. Jonathan Dollimore and Alan Sinfield, "History and Ideology: The Instance of Henry V," in *Alternative Shakespeares,* ed. John Drakakis (London: Routledge, 2002), 220.

28. See McEachern 1994, 49, on the subject of Henry and Katharine. She suggests that "the consummation of state interest is attended with all the affections of charismatic fellowship." She seems to be referring to the union of England and France, of which the marriage represents "the most violent purification of the body from the body politic." Presumably this purified body is more attuned to a charismatic relationship, but I am not sure how the "violent purification" affects the stages of charismatic development.

29. Donald McIntosh, "Weber and Freud: On the Nature and Sources of Authority," *American Sociological Review* 35 (1970): 901–11.

30. Harry Berger, Jr., "What Did the King Know and When Did He Know It? Shakespearean Discourses and Psychoanalysis," in *Making Trifles of Terrors: Redistributing Complicities in Shakespeare* (Stanford: Stanford University Press, 1997), 250.

Mona Lisa Takes a Mountain Hike,
Hamlet Goes for an Ocean Dip

Bruce R. Smith

ONE OF T. S. ELIOT'S MOST FAMOUS LINES REMAINS his dismissal of *Hamlet:* "Probably more people have thought Hamlet a work of art because they found it interesting, than have found it interesting because it is a work of art. It is the 'Mona Lisa' of literature."[1] With Mona Lisa, Hamlet shares a sense of mystery. The two figures also share a dead-centeredness. Modern studies of perception have demonstrated that a viewer perceives the center of a quadrilateral field to be just above the actual, geometric center.[2] In the case of Leonardo's panel, that point of perceived centrality is occupied by the sitter's open bosom—specifically by the highlighted area above her left breast. Her bosom, the region of her heart, is framed by sinuous river channels flowing down on each side of her body from a horizon line defined by the mist of distant mountains distilling into a large lake. That vaporous horizon is aligned with the sitter's eyes—specifically her left eye—just above the vanishing point (see figure 20). The sense of mystery that centuries of viewers have found in the painting has a great deal to do with the visual power of two central triangles, one formed by the sitter's bosom and the horizon line, the other by her left eye and folded arms. The downward course from mountain mist to lake to rivers invites the viewer to follow, in two dimensions, a similar course from eye to heart and, in three dimensions, from heart to soul or psyche.

Hamlet's centrality has to do with the sheer number of lines he is scripted to speak. He is the most solidly *there* of all Shakespeare's characters. Of the play's 3,776 lines in the Pelican edition, Hamlet speaks 1,422. That's 37 percent of the whole. Claudius runs a distant second with 540 lines, just 14 percent of the total number of lines. (The only other characters in Shakespeare who can claim more than a thousand lines are Richard III [with 31 percent of the play's total], Henry V [with 32 percent], and Iago [with 34 percent].)[3] For readers of the script Hamlet assumes the same kind of presence that the speaker in a lyric poem enjoys or the first-person narrator in a novel or the omniscient voice-over in a film—a position that Hamlet, speaking in soliloquy, does indeed assume in Laurence Olivier's 1948 film performance. Such circumstances help explain why

Figure 20. Mona Lisa with Monocle and Galenic Pacemaker. Underlying image reproduced by permission of Getty Images/Bridgeman Art Library.

Hamlet was the nineteenth century's favorite Shakespeare play. The lyric poem and the novel were, of course, the very genres that dominated litera- ture in the nineteenth century. For much of the twentieth century, Hamlet took a new lease on life as a model patient for Freudian psychoanalysis.

He performs a similarly exemplary function, I believe, with respect to the philosophical issues that occupy us at the beginning of the twenty-first century. In the simultaneity of thought and speech, Hamlet would seem to offer a perfect instance of logocentricism. Consider Derrida's description of that effect in *Speech and Phenomena:*

> When I speak, it belongs to the phenomenological essence of this operation that *I hear myself at the same time* that I speak. The signifier, animated by my breath and by the meaning-intention . . . , is in absolute proximity to me. The living act, the life-giving act . . . which animates the body of the signifier and transforms it into a meaningful expression, the soul of language, seems not to separate itself from itself, from its own self-presence. It does not risk death in the body of a signifier that is given over to the world and the visibility of space. It can *show* the ideal object or ideal [meaning] connected to it without venturing outside ideality, outside the interiority of self-present life.[4]

That is to say, Hamlet's voice confirms in him a sense of presence in which *thinking* a word and *saying* a word seem to be simultaneous events, confirming the speaker's sense that what he says *is*. Deconstruction is ded- icated to undermining that illusion.

In the theater, Hamlet's speaking would seem to work the same logo- centric effect in listeners: the in-filling of the actor's voice in the ears, bod- ies, and minds of the audience would seem to reproduce the same simultaneity of sound and meaning that Hamlet himself enjoys. And yet Hamlet is no less a product of his background than Mona Lisa is. The background in this case is made up, not of mountains and rivers, but of sounds. Consider this sequence:

Bzzzzzzzz. Bzzzzzzzz. Bzzzzzzzz. Bzzzzzzzz. Bzzzzzzzz. Bzzzzzzzz. **Bzzzzzzzz.**
Taranta*ta*. Taranta*ta*. Taranta*ta*.
Bong. Bong. Bong. Bong. Bong. Bong. Bong. Bong. Bong. Bong. Bong. Bong.
Cuck-*kuh*. Cuck-*kuh*. Cuck-*kuh*.
Let us impart what we have seen tonight
Unto young Hamlet; for upon my life,
This spirit, dumb to us, will speak to him.
Taranta*ta*. Taranta*ta*. Taranta*ta*.
But now, my cousin Hamlet, and my son—
A little more than kin and less than kind.
How is it that the clouds still hang upon you?
Not so, my lord, I am too much i'th'sun.

Tarant*ata*. Tarant*ata*. Tarant*ata*.
O that this too too solid flesh would melt,
Thaw, and resolve itself into a dew.

[Applause.]

What you have just witnessed, with your eyes if not with your ears, is the coming-to-presence of Hamlet. By the time Hamlet speaks his first soliloquy ("O that this too too solid flesh would melt"), he has laid claim to center stage.[5] Alone after the departure of Claudius and his court, Hamlet hears only his own voice as he speaks. His thoughts come in quick succession, and as they come he utters them in such quick succession that syntax is stretched to the breaking point. Modern editors turn to dashes and exclamation marks to transcribe these rapid changes in thought and speech:

> That it should come to this—
> But two months dead—nay, not so much, not two—
> So excellent a king. . . .
>
> (1.2.137–39)

Hence the simultaneity of thought and speech that would seem to make Hamlet such a good example of logocentricism. The sequence of sounds you have just read in the transcript and played out in your mind suggests, however, that Derrida's listening has been selective. He has assumed that a speaker's self-identity is articulated in words alone and that how a speaker hears his own voice is a biological given. Both of those assumptions can stand historical scrutiny. *Is* self-identity only a matter of words? *Do* people in all cultures experience sound inside their bodies in the same way? Particularities about the Globe Theater as a physical structure, about early modern techniques for representing character in stage performance, about how sensation is explained in Galenic physiology all suggest that Derrida's model needs to be qualified by historical contingencies. Let us consider Hamlet's coming-to-presence in the play's original performances through three successive frames: a physical frame, a dramaturgical frame, and a physiological frame. I use the word "frame" here, not as a casual visual metaphor, but as a form of the "bracketing" practiced by phenomenologists, whereby ordinary assumptions about an object "out there" in the world are put aside and the perceiver's consciousness of that object is studied systematically, step by step.[6] My aim in all three cases is to consider the experience of character in Shakespeare's theater by attending to one of the component parts of that experience. To refuse Hamlet's rhetorical ploys, to decenter him among the sounds in which he exists, is the aural equivalent of telling Mona Lisa to go take a hike.

PHYSICAL FRAME

It was in the newly constructed Globe that *Hamlet* probably received its first performance during the 1599–1600 season. In stark contrast to the universal, undifferentiated circumstances in which Derrida assumes that coming-to-presence through speech takes place, the 1599 Globe provided a physical surround with distinctive acoustical properties. For the actor speaking Hamlet's lines and for the audience who heard him speak, these acoustical properties related sound to speech and speech to identity in ways quite different from the way they were aligned in other locations. The situation of *logos* was different in the great hall of a castle, in a bed-room, on a ship, in a cemetery—in any of the places where the fictional Hamlet fictionally found himself fictionally speaking. Each of these spaces would have shaped, directed, and propagated sound in distinctive ways. According to its size and shape, each would have amplified the sound of a speaker's voice or dampened it. Each would have emphasized certain fre-quencies over others. Each would have returned the sound of the speaker's voice back to him with varying degrees of delay, and from dif-ferent directions, according to the reflective surfaces at hand.[7] It was not, of course, in a great hall, bedroom, ship's deck, or cemetery that the actor playing Hamlet spoke but from the stage of the Globe Theater.

I'll describe here only briefly the acoustic reconstruction of the 1599 Globe that I attempted in my book *The Acoustic World of Early Modern England*. The Globe offered a listening space of 231,028 cubic feet shaped roughly like a cylinder—a physical circumstance that would have encour-aged a "broad" sound as opposed to the "round" sound shaped by the Blackfriars' rectilinear space. In a cylinder, the main reflection of sound waves is from side to side, making it possible for auditors to locate the ori-gins of sounds, particularly higher-pitched sounds, quite precisely. The presence of a canopy, however, meant that sounds originating under that canopy were reflected from top to bottom as well as from side to side, producing a more diffuse, harder-to-locate sound. The voices of actors standing near the outer edges of the stage are more locatable to auditors than the voices of actors standing under the center of the canopy.[8] As *Hamlet* in fact begins, a single word is spoken by an actor onstage: it emerges out of the noise of the assembling audience. Trumpet blasts momentarily impose a central focus on this noise, but the script itself begins with dispersed sounds rather than a centralized sound:

Who's there?

Nay, answer me. Stand and unfold yourself.

Long live the king!

Bernardo?

He.

(1.1.–3)

The scene continues with such short exchanges until Marcellus, in line 21, finally takes first-person-singular command of the acoustic space and gives it first-person-plural unity as he describes in a seven-line speech "this dreaded sight twice seen of us." It is Horatio, however, whose voice comes to dominate the scene as he fills the audience in on the story prior to act 1, scene 1, and then, in midstory, encounters the ghost of the elder Hamlet. In the Folio text his speech runs to 42 lines—by my calculation, about three minutes of continuous sound. In the 1604 quarto four brief lines from Bernardo interrupt Horatio's voice in midcareer.

The Ghost refuses Horatio's repeated commands to join his voice with the others: "Speak, speak, speak, I charge thee speak," "Speak to me," "Speak to me," "O, speak!," "Speak of it, stay and speak" (1.1.49, 110, 113, 116, 120). The 1604 quarto prints the third and fourth of these charges as single metrically incomplete lines, as if the Ghost's silences filled up the missing syllables. By refusing Horatio's commands, the Ghost throws the other characters off balance, not only in terms of iambic pentameter rhythm, but in palpably *physical* terms:

'Tis here.

'Tis here.

'Tis gone.
(1.1.122–23)

Later the Ghost's dislocated voice entoning "Swear" from under the stage throws Hamlet off balance in equally physical terms (1.5.151ff).

As a speaker, Hamlet comes to presence, therefore, in a physical surround full of dispersed sounds that only on occasion find a center in a single speaker. Hamlet may assume centrality in his soliloquies, but that effect is only momentary. As a physical body, he shares the stage with at least twelve other bodies. As a voice, he provides but one element in a sound-world that includes other human voices in a variety of pitches and timbres, not to mention trumpet blasts, the clank of the watchmen's swords, the thud of feet on wooden scaffolding, the swish of costumes, the crowing of a cock (this in the 1604 quarto), perhaps even a bell sounding twelve midnight before anyone ever speaks. The Ghost, whose repeated interventions serve to dislocate sound and body, points up a more general dislocation of sound in the play. Hamlet comes to presence amid these dislocations. In both visual space and acoustic space, he remains a marginal figure. What does occupy the center

of the wooden O is not an individual speaker, much less an individual listener, but a physical object: the stage itself, a gigantic wooden sounding
board comprising about a thousand square feet in surface area.

DRAMATURGICAL FRAME

Hamlet first comes to consciousness—the audience's and his own—in third
person, as words in someone else's mouth: "Let us impart what we have
seen tonight / Unto young Hamlet" (1.1.150–51). He then becomes an
entity in second person, a "you": "But now, my cousin Hamlet, and my
son" (1.2.64)—a syntactical position that he immediately refuses by asserting his first-personhood in an aside: "A little more than kin and less than
kind" (1.1.65). Reluctantly, he accepts his second-person status, until at last,
in his first soliloquy, he can command the entire acoustic space, presumably standing in the position of greatest acoustic presence, at center stage,
under the canopy. Hamlet's logocentric sense of presence is thus achieved
not through his own voice alone but through the voices of other people. As
Bert O. States observes with respect specifically to Hamlet, "We speak of
actors as feeding each other lines, but it would be more accurate to say
that they feed each other character."[9] It is not other actors' voices alone,
however, that call Hamlet into being but all the other myriad sounds in the
play, including, most immediately, the "flourish" that the 1604 quarto spec-
ifies for Claudius's exit just before Hamlet's first soliloquy.

To maintain that presence, he also needs the voices of his listeners in
the audience—not so much their words as their claps and shouts. Testimony from a number of sixteenth- and seventeenth-century writers suggests that the listeners gathered in the Globe were anything but passive.
Michael Drayton, for one, alludes to "Showts and Claps at ev'ry little
pawse, / When the proud Round on ev'ry side hath rung."[10] Hamlet
emerges, not out of silence, but out of the noise of the audience before the
play begins. As such, Hamlet recapitulates the process through which all
human speech comes into being. Michel Serres in his *Genesis* traces language back to the source of life, to the endlessly roaring sea: "We are
immersed in sound just as we are immersed in air and light, we are caught
up willy-nilly in its hurly-burly. We breathe background noise, the taut
and tenuous agitation at the bottom of the world. . . . My acouphenes, a
mad murmur, tense and constant in hearing, speak to me of my ashes,
perhaps, the ones whence I came, the ones to which I will return. . . . No
life without heat, no matter, neither; nor warmth without air, no logos
without noise."[11]

In Elsinore, the sea is never far away. Hamlet's "acouphenes," his relations
with sound, turn out to be just as Serres describes his own, an emergence out

of ashes and a return to ashes. Hamlet's *alpha* is [a]: "A little more than kin." His *omega,* at least in the Folio text, is "O, o, o, o" (5.2.311). At the moment of death Hamlet's voice devolves into the noise from which it emerged. What follows is anything but the silence that Hamlet predicted—or at least wished for. What follows are the voices of Horatio and of Fortinbras as they offer their respective versions of Hamlet's story—and then, according to the Folio text, the booms of "a peal of ordnance." The play ends, just as it has begun, in a series of single, unified, nonverbal sounds. A "peal" suggests a sequence of shots that answers the trumpet peal with which the play began. After the sound of ordnance being fired comes a return of noise from the audience in the form of applause and shouts. The German traveler Paul Hentzner, in his 1598 account of London's public playhouses, finds the audience's noisy response more worthy of comment than details about the plays themselves. Performances of tragedies and comedies before "very numerous audiences" are concluded, Hentzner says, "with excellent music, variety of dances, and the excessive applause of those that are present."[12] The effect of applause after the play, like the buzz of voices before it begins, is both collective and individual. An individual entering the theater speaks to his or her nearest companions. As more and more people do the same, more and more voices are added to the cacophony, until the combined voices make up the collective roar that the trumpet blasts attempt to silence. Similarly, at the end of the play, the audience responds with applause and shouts that may start out as a collective expression of approval but inevitably end as actions being done by individuals who are about to give up their corporate identity as Audience and leave the theater to go their separate ways.

Through the entirety of the play, in fact, Hamlet has to struggle against acoustic oblivion in the sounds of other people's voices and in prelinguistic noises like the ringing cannon shots that Claudius favors as accompaniments to his drinking. The full repertory of sounds to be heard in the Globe can be imagined as a cycle of sounds that begins in preverbal cries like "oh!," passes through speech to the postverbal syntax of music, disperses into the more random but still meaningful sounds of the ambient sound world, and returns finally to preverbal cries, which take their place in the ambient sound world and mark the beginnings of speech. Heard in this circular context, Hamlet's soliloquies stand out as isolated moments of logocentricism. And they become rarer as the play progresses. The omission of the fourth soliloquy, "How all occasions do inform against me," from the Folio text, means that Hamlet must increasingly compromise his first-person singularity as he performs the last third of the play only in dialogue, as second person to other speakers' first persons, and as first person only in relationship to their second persons. In terms of sound, the passage from "To be or not to be" in act 3, scene 1, to "O, o, o, o" in act 5, scene 2, charts the gradual but inexorable disintegration of the speaking "I"—the reverse of the integration that was sounded in the entry to this essay.

PHYSIOLOGICAL FRAME

Derrida offers his model of logocentricism as a universal condition, as if how one hears oneself speaking or how one hears other people speaking were the same experience in all times and all places. He assumes that human physiology does not change and therefore that the coincidence of thought and speech will be always be experienced in the same way. The medical writings of Galen and his medieval and early modern successors give us reason to doubt that proposition. The actor playing Hamlet in 1599–1600 and the audiences who heard him brought to the theater an understanding of how sounds are related to semantic meaning that is different from our own, precisely because they entertained different ideas about their physical bodies. In 1600 the human body as delivered up by Galenic medicine was only just being called into question by scientific anatomy.[13] Where metaphysics hears *logos,* early modern physiologists heard *passion.* The sixteenth century inherited a model of hearing that derived ultimately from Aristotle's *De Anima,* expanded and worked out in detail so as to accord with the medical writings of Galen. The process by which sound becomes meaning can be rendered thus:

> Sound waves → ear → *spiritus* → common sense → imagination, where converted into *species* (or internal image) → *spiritus* → dispersal through entire body

Anatomical studies and the philosophical criterion of efficiency led sixteenth- and seventeenth-century thinkers increasingly to question the existence of *species,* but authorities like Helkiah Crooke and even Descartes could not give up the idea of the body as a hydraulic system in which *spiritus* does the work of intercommunication among the body's parts. In his description of the physiology of hearing in *Microcosmographia: A Description of the Body of Man,* Crooke demonstrates that he knows all about the nerves as a network of specialized tissue; what he does not know is the workings of electrical impulses.[14]

The notion of *spiritus* means that every sense experience, and every making of meaning, is a whole-body experience. Sound, like other forms of sensation, activates the listener's passions. As Thomas Wright explains in *The Passions of the Mind in General,* "First, then, to our imagination cometh by sense or memory some object to be known, convenient or disconvenient to Nature; the which being known . . . in the imagination . . . , presently the purer spirits flock from the brain by certain secret channels to the heart, where they pitch at the door, signifying what an object was presented, convenient or disconvenient for it. The heart immediately bendeth either to prosecute it or to eschew it, and the better to effect that affection draweth other humours to help him."[15] The listener experiences this visceral bodily response as *passion*. In Wright's scheme, reason stands in an uneasy relationship to the passions. Reason ought to direct the passions, but the passions have a friendlier working relationship with the senses. Indeed, the passions can prevent reason from knowing the truth about objects that the body, through the senses, sees and hears. Again Wright: "Whatsoever we understand passeth by the gates of our imagination, being prevented, yea, and well nigh shut up with the consideration of that object which feedeth the passion and pleaseth the appetite, the understanding looking into the imagination findeth nothing almost but the mother and nurse of his passion for consideration; where you may well see how the imagination putteth green spectacles before the eyes of our wit to make it see nothing but green, that is, serving for the consideration of the passion."[16]

Wright speaks here about the passion disposing a subject to *see* green; what would it be like to *hear* green? That would involve hearing the *totality* of sound, its extralinguistic as well as its linguistic components.[17] It would involve hearing, not just logos, but pitch, timbre, rhythm, and all the sound effects that we know as alliteration, assonance, rhyme, and so on. These phenomena are not just "decorations" applied to semantic meaning but essential elements in the sound event. "O that this too too solid flesh would melt": to hear green is, in this case, to hear the repetitions of [oː], [ð], [s], and [t], the hardness of [d], the softness of [ʃ]—and to delight in those sensations quite apart from what they signify as instances of logos. As Katherine Park notes, the dispersal of *spiritus* throughout the entire body meant that, once aural sensation had been registered in common sense, the sensation was dispersed through the entire body: intellect might attend to the logos component of sound, but other elements of sound sensation would be experienced, via the heart, as passions.[18] Hence, the concern of rhetorical manuals with the passion-inducing effects of artful language.

To claim that making meaning through sound is altogether a cultural construct is, of course, just as partial as to assume physiological determinism. The sense organs of the human body are indeed "hard-wired" in ways that different cultures exploit in different ways. For example, the anatomy of the human vocal tract is such that the sounds produced in even the simplest speech far exceed the phonemes that listeners need to isolate in order to understand the semantic content of the speech. An actor playing Hamlet says, "O that this too too solid flesh would melt."

What members of the audience hear is not the phonemes [oː] [ð] [a] [t]
and so on but a continuous stream of sounds that the listener brackets off
into phonemes that make sense in English via a process that linguists call
coarticulation.[19] Speech in a language one doesn't understand seems so
rapid precisely because the listener is hearing all the sounds coming out
of the speaker's mouth and not just the discrete phonemes that make
sense in that language. In effect, the listener in such a situation is "hearing
green." In performances of *Hamlet,* sounds in the spaces between the
phonemes of English join the sounds of trumpets, cock-crow, and ordnance to produce an acoustic "world of green" in which individual words
figured as isolated events. That is not to say, however, that the boundary
between *logos* and green can be clearly delineated. Rhyme, assonance,
alliteration, and other sound effects occupy the cusp, so to speak, between
the House of Logos and the House of Green. Post-Cartesian understandings of the body attempt to "filter out" all nonsemantic sounds, not only
those of trumpets, cock-crow, and ordnance but the nonphonetic sounds
of human speech. Hamlet stands at that semiotic cusp. Speaking soliloquies that are insistently logocentrifugal, not logocentric, he challenges the
protocols of Cartesian mind/body dualism.

The Horizon Line

What happens when we superimpose the three frames around Hamlet,
the physical, the dramaturgical, and the physiological? What do we see?
The horizon behind Mona Lisa's eyes. Sir John Davies in his philosophical poem *Nosce Teipsum* (1599) locates the nexus between body and soul,
not in the pineal gland, but in the vanishing point:

> God first made Angels bodilesse, pure, minds;
> > Then other things, which mindlesse bodies bee;
> > Last he made Man, th'*Horizon* twixt both kinds,
> > In whom we do the worlds abridgement see.[20]

What do we hear in the three frames? The ocean. Michel Serres's *Genesis,*
like the version in the Bible, begins with water and with words. In the biblical account the spirit of God moves across the waters; his voice calls
forth light, the firmament, dry land, plants, the planets and the stars, fish,
beasts, man. The emergence of forms in Serres is less certain. It depends,
not on a creator-god speaking the words, but on a subject listening to
sound in all its totality: "I hear without clear frontiers, without divining an
isolated source, hearing is better at integrating than analyzing, the ear
knows how to lose track."[21] What we hear in Hamlet is not, I feel, the

logocentricism that Derrida needs for his project in deconstruction. "Hearing green" is, to some degree, always an effect of hearing speech, regardless of how dispassionately the listener attempts to isolate semantic meaning. The green effect is heightened in theatrical performance, which brackets off dramatic speech from ordinary speech and calls attention to its soundedness. The sensation would have been all the greater in a culture like Shakespeare's, a culture that prized the arts of rhetoric and made training in those arts part of every schoolboy's program of study.[22] The fundamental principle of deconstruction is *différance,* the making of all meanings through the binary marking of difference. In sounded speech, however, binary differences are *not* all there is to hear. The logical mind may be bracketing off certain sounds as phonemes and distinguishing them one from another, but all the while the ears are hearing the range of sounds in between. Garrett Stewart has coined the term "phonotext" to refer to the way voiced phonemes "blur" at the edges: "It is in the nature of phonemes to surrender all real discreteness to the rippling flow of speech. It is also in the nature of phonemes in a given speech act to blur at their borders, creating there the possibility of more paradigmatic choices than can simultaneously be made."[23] The result is what Stewart calls "transegmental drift." Stephen Booth hears that slippage as a distinguishing characteristic of poetry. In a given word Booth hears the possibilities of other words that are *almost* present in the sounds of that word.[24] What Stewart and Booth describe is, in effect, an acoustic ghost or echo that attends each word in a script and undoes the seeming fixity of sounded words. Judged by the standards of Stewart and Booth, the main character in *Hamlet* may not be Hamlet at all but the Ghost, sometimes a body, sometimes a voice in a body, sometimes a voice without a body. Tradition ascribes that role to the actor William Shakespeare.

The psychoacoustics of listening to speech corroborates the suppositions of Galenic physiology. Wright is not the only early modern writer to imagine the passions as roiling water. "Wee may compare the Soule without passions," he says, "to a calme sea, with sweet, pleasant, and crispling streames: but the passionate, to the raging gulfe, swelling with waves, surging by tempests, minacing the stony rockes, and endeauoring to ouerthrow Mountaines."[25] Wright's fluid images come much closer than Saussure's s ≠ S in capturing what Hamlet sounds like when he loses his semantic bearings in such moments as "That it should come to this—. . . ." Sir William Cornwallis, whose first book of *Essayes* was published the same year (1600) that *Hamlet* was first acted at the Globe, distrusts speech: "the eare is more deceiued with soundes," he declares, "then the eye with colours." Cornwallis imagines a time before speech, when men were able to know nature directly and needed no traffic in words. The ocean figures in Cornwallis's maritime conceit exactly as it does in Wright's, as volatile and dangerous: "If we were now, as wee were once, though speech should bee superfluous (for all should haue beene good, and I thinke then, all knowledges should haue seene trueth in a like quantitie) yet it had not beene so daungerous: for our vices are the ocean, our wordes the Barkes transporting, and trafficking sin with sin, and imperfection with imperfection."[26] Cornwallis in his essays may imitate Montaigne's introspection and conversational candor, but unlike Montaigne he always pulls back from the abyss. Hamlet plunges in. And so do auditors less suspicious of words than Cornwallis. The continuous stream of sound broadcast by actors' voices englobes auditors and actors alike in a soundworld that engages, not just the mind, but *spiritus* and sinews, heart and diaphragm. Where deconstruction sees subject / object, I propose that we attempt to hear subject / subject.

My strategy in this essay exemplifies a methodology that I have come to call "historical phenomenology." It attempts to reconstruct bodily experience in the past on historically informed terms. Its insistence on historical difference and cultural relativity distinguishes it from phenomenology as practiced by Merleau-Ponty and his followers in the 1950s. In several respects, historical phenomenology differs from the dominant critical methodologies of the moment: New Historicism and deconstruction. Both of these dominant methodologies are concerned primarily with nouns, with naming things and classifying them—or, in the case of deconstruction, with *de*classifying them. To name something is to turn it into an object, to position the analyst here and *it* over there so that *it* can be seen, known, mastered. Lyotard has argued that such a position can never really be achieved, even when the objects being studied are historically removed from the investigator. According to Lyotard, all objects of historical inquiry are never really objects. The analyst is connected with what she analyzes along a continuum of time: the past is both "now" and "no longer" as the future is both "now" and "not yet."[27]

It is not just time that complicates the relationship between the historian and his supposed object of study but the shared fact of a human body. The syntactical unit that best captures the situation of the knowing subject, Serres claims in *The Troubadour of Knowledge,* is not nouns, not adjectives, not even verbs, but prepositions: "*Before* and *after* construct their viscous fluidity; *with* and *without,* the hesitating divisions; *over* and *under,* the false and true subject; *for* and *against,* the violent passions; *behind* and *before,* the cowardly hypocrisies and courageous loyalties; *in* and *outside of,* the corporeal and theoretical" and so on with *between* and *beyond, from* and *via* and *toward.*[28] What Serres describes here is a *relational* way of knowing. With respect to the past, such a way of knowing recognizes the embodiedness of historical subjects and attends to the materiality of the evidence they have left behind at the same time that it acknowledges the embodiedness of the investigator in the face of that evidence.

Such a methodology attempts to undo Descartes' separation of thinking subject and thought-about object. With respect to sound, Descartes and his successors seek to know the sounded message apart from the body of the speaking knower and the listening knower. We might think of the Cartesian model in terms of prepositions: the knower is positioned "opposite" or "against" the thing known. By contrast, the preposition that best describes Hamlet in the theater is "among." According to Charles Taylor in *Sources of the Self*, it is altogether appropriate that we should adopt such a methodology when talking about artifacts like *Hamlet*. It is in the half century after *Hamlet* that Taylor locates a major shift in the localization of knowledge of the self. In the universe assumed by "the Elizabethan world picture," the knower and what he knows exist as objects within the same all-encompassing order. In the universe set in place by Descartes, the knower exists apart from what he knows, as subject to object.[29] Vision, as Plato argues in several places, may be "the *sharpest* of our bodily senses"[30] because it supposedly gives readiest access to immaterial ideas through the comparatively pure medium of fire/light,[31] but hearing depends on a thoroughly material medium, air, in which speaker and listener are both immersed. Sir Francis Bacon describes the situation exactly in *Silva Silvarum:* "The *Species* of *Visibles* seeme to be *Emissions* of *Beames* from the *Obiect seene;* Almost like Odours; saue that they are more Incorporeall: But the *Species* of *Audibles* seeme to Participate more with *Locall Motion,* like *Percussions* or *Impressions* made vpon the *Aire.* So that whereas all Bodies doe seeme to worke in two manners; Either by the *Communication* of their *Natures;* Or by the *Impressions* and *Signatures* of their *Motions;* The *Diffusion* of *Species Visible* seemeth to participate more of the former *Operation;* and the *Species Audible* of the latter."[32] It is ultimately the materiality of air that calls into question the distinction between subject and object that is essential to Cartesian philosophy, even in its latter-day forms of deconstruction and New Historicism.

If Hamlet occupies a position of logomarginality, then what of Shakespeare's other protagonists? In dramaturgical terms, other protagonists in Shakespeare's scripts are even more dependent on other speakers to feed them character. They have voices only in relation to all the other voices in the play. In physical terms, all of Shakespeare's speakers in scripts written for the outdoor public playhouses occupy the same marginal space that Hamlet does, as sound producers whose voices are amplified and distorted in ways characteristic of open cylinders. Furthermore, each of them contributes to a repertory of nonverbal sound effects that, alongside words, constitute the fictional and experiential world of each script. Finally, in physiological terms, all of Shakespeare's protagonists are imagined to be producing sounds that listeners will hear with their whole bodies, as sensations transported by *spiritus* to the heart, where those sensations can be acted upon viscerally as passions or subjected to the censure of reason. The testimony of Michael Drayton, Paul Hentzner, and other witnesses to plays in performance suggests that passion figured largely in audience responses. On the subject of Hamlet, scholars may write essays, precisely isolating each grapheme at the stroke of a key, but in the heat of performance audiences tend to respond, not with words but with applause and shouts. They return Hamlet to the sea of noise from which he emerged.

NOTES

1. T. S. Eliot, "Hamlet and His Problems," in *The Sacred Wood: Essays on Poetry and Criticism* (London: Methuen, 1922), 5.

2. Rudolf Arnheim, *Art and Visual Perception: A Psychology of the Creative Eye* (Berkeley and Los Angeles: University of California Press, 1974), 30–33.

3. William Shakespeare, *Complete Works,* ed. Alfred Harbarge (London: Penguin, 1969), 31.

4. Jacques Derrida, *Speech Phenomena and Other Essays on Husserl's Theory of Signs,* trans. David B. Allison (Evanston, IL: Northwestern University Press, 1973), 78–79.

5. *Hamlet* 1.2.129ff., in William Shakespeare, *The Complete Works,* ed. Stanley Wells and Gary Taylor (Oxford: Clarendon Press, 1988), 657. Further quotations from *Hamlet* are taken from this edition and are cited in the text by act, scene, and line numbers.

6. Don Ihde, *Listening and Voice: A Phenomenology of Sound* (Athens: University of Ohio Press, 1976), 29.

7. Stephen Handel, *Listening: An Introduction to the Perception of Auditory Events* (Cambridge, MA: MIT Press, 1989), 41.

8. Bruce R. Smith, *The Acoustic World of Early Modern England: Attending to the O Factor* (Chicago: University of Chicago Press, 1999), 206–45.

9. Bert O. States, *Hamlet and the Concept of Character* (Baltimore, MD: Johns Hopkins University Press, 1992), 7. From this and other directions Leeds Barroll investigates the illusion of theatrical character in *Artificial Persons: The Formation of Character in the Tragedies of Shakespeare* (Columbia: University of South Carolina Press, 1974).

10. *Michael Drayton,* ed. J. William Hebel, 5 vols. (Oxford: Clarendon Press, 1934–41), 2: 334.

11. Michel Serres, *Genesis,* trans. Geneviève James and James Nielson (Ann Arbor: University of Michigan Press, 1995), 7.

12. Paul Hentzner, *A Journey into England,* trans. Richard Bentley, ed. Horace Walpole (Reading, UK: T. E. Williams, 1807), 22.

13. Nancy G. Siraisi, *Medieval and Early Renaissance Medicine: An Introduction to Knowledge and Practice* (Chicago: University of Chicago Press, 1990), 97–114.

14. Helkiah Crooke, *Microcosmographia: The Description of the Body of Man* (London: William Jaggard, 1616), 606–10.

15. Thomas Wright, *The Passions of the Mind in General,* ed. W. Webster Newbold (New York: Garland, 1986), 123.

16. Ibid., 128.

17. Bruce R. Smith, "Hearing Green," in *Reading the Early Modern Passions,* ed. Gail Kern Paster, Katherine Rowe, and Mary Floyd-Wilson (Philadelphia: University of Pennsylvania Press, 2004), 147–68.

18. Katherine Park, "The Organic Soul," in *The Cambridge History of Renaissance Philosophy,* ed. Charles B. Schmitt (Cambridge: Cambridge University Press, 1988), 464–84.

19. Handel, *Listening,* 134–62, 185–217.

20. Sir John Davies, *"Nosce Teipsum,"* 881–84, in *The Poems of Sir John Davies,* ed. Robert Krueger (Oxford: Clarendon Press, 1975), 34.

21. Serres, *Genesis,* 7.

22. See T. W. Baldwin, *Shakspere's Small Latine and Lesse Greeke,* 2 vols. (Urbana: University of Illinois Press, 1944), and Marion Trousdale, *Shakespeare and the Rhetoricians* (Chapel Hill: University of North Carolina Press, 1982).

23. Garrett Stewart, *Reading Voices: Literature and the Phonotext* (Berkeley and Los Angeles: University of California Press, 1990), 26.

24. Stephen Booth, "Poetic Richness: A Preliminary Audit," *Pacific Coast Philology* 19, nos. 1–2 (1984): 68–78.

25. Wright, *Passion,* 59.

26. Sir William Cornwallis, *A Second Part of Essayes* (London: Edmund Mattes, 1601), sig. MM5.

27. Jean-François Lyotard, *Phenomenology,* trans. Brian Beakley (Albany: State University of New York Press, 1990), 111–32.

28. Michel Serres, *The Troubadour of Knowledge,* trans. Sheila Faria Glaser with William Paulson (Ann Arbor: University of Michigan Press, 1997), 146.

29. Charles O. Taylor, *Sources of the Self: The Making of Modern Identity* (Cambridge, MA: Harvard University Press, 1989), 199–207.

30. *Phaedrus* 250d, emphasis added, in Plato, *The Complete Works,* ed. John M. Cooper (Indianapolis, IN: Hackett, 1997), 528.

31. *Timaeus* 45, in Plato, *Complete Works,* 1248.

32. Francis Bacon, *Sylva Sylvarum, or A Naturall Historie,* ed. William Rawley (London: William Lee, 1626), sec. 268.

Part IV
Artificial Persons
(Title of Leeds Barroll's First Book, 1974)

Psychoanalysis and Early Modern Culture: Lacan with Augustine and Montaigne

Catherine Belsey

I

IS IT LEGITIMATE TO READ EARLY MODERN TEXTS in the light of psychoanalysis? Can we, that is to say, appropriately bring to bear on work of the sixteenth and seventeenth centuries a vocabulary, and the insights inscribed in it, that cannot be said to have existed before the late nineteenth century? Whether we date psychoanalysis from the *Studies on Hysteria,* initially published by Josef Breuer and Sigmund Freud between 1893 and 1895, or from Anna O.'s identification in 1881 of the "talking cure" recorded there,[1] the invocation of psychoanalytic theory in the interpretation of early modern texts seems to imply that what psychoanalysis uncovered was a universal, transhistorical truth of human nature, and this assumption sits very uneasily indeed with current historicist convictions that values, sympathies, emotions, and behavior change as culture changes. Do we, in other words, contradict ourselves if we use psychoanalytic theory to *historicize* the texts of a more distant epoch?

To some degree, the answer must depend on what we use psychoanalysis *for.* It surely gave itself a bad name in the early days, when it was seen as a way of understanding the artist's unconscious impulses or, worse, the pathology of the fictional character, in Freud's account of Leonardo or Ernest Jones's reading of *Hamlet.* As a thematic content of the psyche, able to be invoked as the explanation of the work of art, the Oedipus complex too easily takes on the role of a key to all mythologies. More recently, the Oedipal narrative, apparently understood as a timeless truth, has been brought to bear on early modern drama in order to account for the misogyny critics have found in the plays. Lacanian psychoanalysis, too, remains a sourcebook for universal themes, though of a different kind, in the work of Slavoj Žižek, who brilliantly but still ahistorically attributes to the death drive the final cause of the antagonism that characterizes human nature. If psychoanalysis represents the inscription of eternal truths, it is radically incompatible with history.

One of the effects of the centrality of New Historicism since about 1980 has therefore been a tendency to marginalize psychoanalytic readings,[2] on the grounds that, explaining everything, and in the same terms, they appear ultimately to explain very little. Besides, the relationship between children and their parents that Freud described was surely itself historically specific, and can be held to tell us more about turn-of-the-century Vienna than about any supposed universal human condition. The classic New Historicist case is eloquently put by Stephen Greenblatt himself in "Psychoanalysis and Renaissance Culture." Greenblatt argues that psychoanalysis cannot be adduced to interpret early modern culture, on the grounds that it represents the completion of the Renaissance project, not its explanation. Freud gives us a universalizing account of the human condition and a totalizing version of the self, on the basis of an understanding of subjectivity inaugurated four hundred years earlier. The early modern account of the subject, Greenblatt maintains, is both developed and supplanted when psychoanalysis redoubles consciousness with an unconscious whose content is concealed. Psychoanalytic theory, itself a cultural construct, thus both completes and supersedes an early modern account of subjectivity: "The problem, I suggest, is that psychoanalysis is at once the fulfilment and effacement of specifically Renaissance insights: psychoanalysis is, in more than one sense, the end of the Renaissance."[3]

It is hard to disagree. How, then, in an era dominated by historicist criticism, could we possibly justify putting psychoanalysis at the center of historical scholarship itself? Oddly enough, however, we owe new insights into the period to some of those who have done exactly that.[4] Such critics commonly turn to Jacques Lacan's reinterpretation of Freud in the light of Saussure, and some defend their position on the grounds that the content of Lacan's symbolic order, the order of language and culture, is itself historically specific, with the consequence that the unconscious is implicated in history.[5] Lacan himself would have had reservations about this "culturalist" view,[6] but the textual specificity of readings by Lacanian critics prompts the paradoxical reflection that the crucial value of psychoanalysis for reading and interpretation might not be psychological at all. Instead, perhaps its use is textual, not thematic, illuminating, that is to say, not content, but a relation to language? What if, to be more precise, the Freudian account of the unconscious, modified and developed by Lacan's recognition of Saussurean linguistics, were to offer us, rather than a version of the human condition, whether eternal or historically relative, an approach to the necessary condition of meaning? Then the advantage of psychoanalysis for historicists would lie not in its account of themes, or what is meant *by* early modern texts, but rather in its perception of the waywardness of textuality itself. Psychoanalysis would illuminate, in other words, not a signified, either constant or historical, but the instability of signifying practice.

Its contribution would be methodological rather than explanatory, a way above all of paying attention to the workings of the texts.

Emphasis on the Oedipal story, the death drive, or neurotic pathologies tends to dwell on what the unconscious hides from thought. But suppose we laid the stress on the prefix as pointing instead to what is simply missing from consciousness. If the *un*conscious, reread in relation to Ferdinand de Saussure's theory of the sign, were seen as what Jacques Derrida calls a "radical alterity," not a presence but instead a subtraction from what the text sets out to communicate, an element "definitively taken away from every process of presentation,"[7] then psychoanalysis would impel us to read more attentively—more *closely*, in fact. This would not, however, be the close reading that outstayed its welcome as New Criticism, but the kind of attentiveness practiced by the analyst, who listens for the slippages, lapses, and incoherences in the speech of the analysand. Psychoanalysis dwells on the moments when the utterance fails to create consistency, evades its own inevitable thetic, or thesis-making, obligations, but instead both withholds and amplifies the information it promises, by *fading* from view. The result of such a mode of interpretation would be more history, not less, and more nuanced history, where it is inevitably so tempting to settle for updating or amplifying in the light of our current social and political concerns—sexual, say, or postcolonial—the old reassuring cognitive totalities of the Elizabethan world picture and the early modern mind.

Is there still, even in the treatment of psychoanalysis as access to the condition of signification, rather than the content of the unconscious, a trace of the universality historicism finds unpalatable? Possibly. It is at least arguable, on the other hand, that the psychoanalysis which emerged in the late nineteenth century, and has developed and refined itself ever since, shares a framework of ideas with an earlier model of human experience that goes back at least as far as Saint Augustine, whose shaping influence on both Catholic and Reformation Christianity can hardly be overestimated. If this case can be made, if such a framework was available in the Renaissance, the most rigorous historicist would surely be willing to concede that certain aspects, at least, of psychoanalysis might illuminate early modern culture. Greenblatt's point is that psychoanalysis completes what was begun earlier, in history and in culture. If we take him at his word, is this not exactly why it can illuminate retrospectively texts that anticipate in practice some of the insights Freud and Lacan would go on to formulate as theory?

II

The argument for a line of descent from Augustine through Freud to Lacan starts with sex, though it does not end there. The lineage passes through the essays of Michel de Montaigne, first published in French in the 1580s, and in John Florio's English translation in 1603, but influential in early modern England even earlier. Montaigne was, as we know, an avid reader, whose library of a thousand volumes evidently included an edition of Augustine's *City of God,* with a commentary by the Spanish humanist, Vives.[8] If Montaigne occasionally took incidental issue with Augustine,[9] he more commonly appears as an orthodox Augustinian, and most notably when it comes to sex. Montaigne, who ignored nothing human, took a considerable interest, as did Augustine, in the behavior—and its implications—of the anarchic male sexual organ.

Montaigne's essay, "Of the Force of Imagination," for instance, records the remarkable capacity of fantasy to bring about physiological effects. Imagination, Montaigne maintains, is so powerful that it can transform us: people can die purely of fear; some attribute the stigmata of Saint Francis to imagination; Augustine himself, Montaigne claims, gave an example of a man who would faint in sympathy whenever others were unhappy. And among its other powers, imagination can radically affect masculine sexual prowess. Anxiety, or intensity of passion, or suspicion of sorcery can all deflate the most ardent lover; conversely, imagined magical remedies can reinstate potency when nothing else has changed. Indeed, Montaigne goes on, the penis commonly takes all too little account of external reality. On the contrary, it seems to lead a life of its own: "Men have reason to checke the indocile libertie of this member, for so importunately insinuating himselfe when we have no need of him, and so importunately, or as I may say so impertinently failing, at what time we have most need of him; and so imperiously contesting by his authority with our will, refusing with such fiercenes and obstinacie our solicitations both mentall and manuall."[10]

This account of the unruly organ is close enough to Augustine's to suggest that Montaigne may well have had the text open in front of him. In John Healey's seventeenth-century English version, Augustine complains that the penis "will be sometimes importunate against the will, and sometimes immovable when it is desired, and being fervent in the mind, yet will be frozen in the body."[11] The word that describes this behavior in Montaigne's French and Augustine's Latin, as in Florio's English translation of Montaigne and Healey's of Augustine, is consistently "importunate."[12] Augustine's theological point is that, just as the Fall represented a refusal to obey the will of God, its consequence, appropriately enough, is that our own sexual organs refuse to obey *us:* "And in one word, what reward, what punishment, is laid upon disobedience but disobedience? What is man's misery other than his own disobedience to himself: that seeing he would not what he might, now he cannot what he would?"[13]

Psychoanalysis too is crucially interested in the behavior of the genitals. According to Freud, of course, the child's sexual response to the mother is subject to punishment by the threat of castration. In consequence, children renounce incest early, and submit to the paternal law which represents civilized morality. From this moment on, culture depends on sublimation, the capacity to find legitimate outlets for sexual impulses. Like Augustinian theology, psychoanalysis allots a central place to the conflict between law and desire. As a historian of the penis puts it, "For the Bishop of Hippo, original sin is passed from one generation to the next by semen, and the punishment for Adam's insult against God is erections we cannot control. For Freud, the killing of the primal father and the sexual appropriation of the mother is passed on as the Oedipus complex, and the punishment is a civilization that controls our erections."[14] Like Augustine, psychoanalysis treats the phallus as lawless, irrepressible, for ever in conflict with propriety.

While Augustine shows no special interest in female sexuality, his general assumption seems to be that women are subject to much the same sexual reflexes as men. In Freud, however, gender difference comes into being with the resolution of the Oedipus complex. As is well known, the phallic phase of infantile sexual pleasure is the same for little girls and little boys. But when the children discover the anatomical difference between them, the psychical consequences determine to a high degree their distinct sexual destinies. According to Freud, the little girl acknowledges that she is already castrated, and either succumbs to penis envy or settles down to wanting a baby as a substitute. The little boy, meanwhile, sees with horror that castration is a real possibility, and promptly submits to the values of civilization, deferring his desire for his mother until such time as he is entitled to find a socially acceptable substitute in a marital partner outside the family.

The sexual stereotyping in Freud's account, and the misogyny of the differentiation he makes, have been variously pilloried as sexist or historicized as no more than can be expected of his cultural moment. In defence of psychoanalysis, however, it is worth pointing out that Freud goes on to treat the civilization that endorses these "opposite" sexes as a place, for both boys and girls, men and women, primarily of discontents. There is in Freud no divine comedy, no happiness as a reward for conformity, but instead a permanent tendency for both sexes to deviate from the appointed, monogamous, heterosexual path, and to face the perpetual likelihood of sexual disappointment. Civilized adults, torn between the impulsions of the drive and the imperatives of culture, Freud proposes, face "the possibility that something in the nature of the sexual instinct itself is unfavourable to the realization of complete satisfaction."[15]

Psychoanalytic castration reenacts the Fall; thereafter, in each case, people are no longer at one with themselves. Both Augustine and Freud, in other words, locate human beings in a world of exile and loss; and both identify sex as the place where that loss is most evident.

III

Male and female genitals also play a part, of course, in Freud's *Interpretation of Dreams,* where they are commonly represented symbolically, and understood to betray unconscious desire. It is no doubt the conjunction of these two sources, the role of the genitals in the Oedipus complex and their representation, oblique or otherwise, in dreams, that leads Lacan in his Saussurean reading of Freud to identify the phallus as the *signifier* of unconscious desire.

How should we interpret the Lacanian phallus? Lacan's prose is characteristically evasive, mimicking the speech of the analysand, who wants to tell—and at the same time wants to conceal—whatever it is that really (unconsciously) matters. In "The Signification of the Phallus," Lacan insists that the phallus is not to be confused with the sexual organ it symbolizes, whether male or female.[16] At the same time, since at one point the lecture reveals that the woman may expect to find it in the body of her lover,[17] the phallus is evidently not entirely remote from the organ that registers, as both Montaigne and Augustine attest, an impulse, or a failure of impulse, that is not amenable to conscious control. It would be a mistake, in my view, to reduce the Lacanian phallus to a biological organ; but it would equally be a mistake to understand it as purely figurative. The general effect of signification in Lacan is to bar access to the world outside representation, the "signifiable,"[18] and to replace it with a signifier, derived from the order of language and culture, which exists outside us, and always betrays, in consequence of that Otherness, the organism on whose behalf it speaks. It follows that the signifier is as close as we get to the real thing, but we can never get back to organic being itself. The Lacanian phallus, as the signifier of unconscious desire, represents the sexual organ *as it plays its part in culture.*

What the phallus as the signifier of desire shares, however, with the unruly member invoked by Freud, as well as by Montaigne and Augustine, is its anarchic character. Desire in Lacan always conflicts with Law, where Law is the discipline imposed by the tyrannical superego as representative of what Freud calls "civilization." Lacan differs from Freud, on the other hand, in his account of the role language plays in the constitution of the human subject. Let us go back to the (Lacanian) beginning. Desire comes into being for Lacan when the little human organism submits to the Otherness of the symbolic order, the discipline of language and culture. This order already exists outside us, and constitutes for the child the condition of being able to make its wishes known. But to the degree that these wishes are necessarily subjected to the preexisting language, the Other, the very process of formulation means that our demands always *alienate* the wishes themselves; the name never quite matches what we want. Desire is the difference between the wish and the demand; it is what cannot be put into words; it is in consequence *un*conscious. Unconscious desire is not amenable, or indeed accessible, to reason; it lives a life of its own; it repudiates what Lacan dismissively calls "the goods" (propriety, virtue, self-sacrifice, good deeds); and its signifier is the phallus.

Human life may be understood, Lacan urges, as a "dialectic of demand and desire."[19] Demand, belonging to the symbolic order, consistently betrays desire, and desire equally consistently asserts itself, *insists* in dreams, jokes, and lapses, or as psychosomatic symptoms, marks on the body. In hysteria the organism reasserts itself, puts on physical display the symptoms of the unsatisfied desire that springs from its subjection to the discipline of the symbolic. Even Aristotle knew that much, Lacan affirms, since he produced "a theory of hysteria based on the fact that the uterus is a small animal which lives inside the woman's body, and which moved about bloody violently when it wasn't given something to tuck into. Obviously he used this example because he didn't want to take a far more obvious one, the male sexual organ, for which you don't need any sort of theoretician to remind you of its surgings." The project of psychoanalysis, the talking cure, is to elicit in dialogue and thus bring to consciousness the specific desires of the analysand. Analysis might be understood as a dialogue with unconscious desire. In a sense, then, the analyst's interlocutor is the phallus, and Lacan exploits this remarkable possibility when he goes on to distinguish the Aristotelian theory of hysteria from psychoanalysis: "Except Aristotle never thought matters would be helped by having conversations with the little animal inside the woman's belly. In other words. . . . it [Aristotle's hungry womb, Lacan's phallus, unconscious desire] is not open to reason. If the experience of speech has an effect under these circumstances, it is because we are somewhere other than Aristotle."[20] "We," that is to say, analysts, are somewhere other than Aristotle thanks to Saussure, who detached meaning from reference, its anchorage in things in the world, or in preexisting ideas in people's heads, and thus made possible a recognition of the lack of fit between desire and demand, what we want and what we can say we want, as well as between the phallus as signifier and the penis or clitoris as organ. As the signifier of unconscious desire, the phallus is not open to reason; but the talking cure makes a difference, all the same, because it consists in a form of dialogue that escapes the constraints of rationality, interpreting what is said when reason fails and the subject fades into inconsequentiality, slips of the tongue, denial, or silence.

According to Lacan's paradoxical thinking, while the phallus is and is not the organ, desire is and is not sexual. He makes very clear that sex is not in any sense desire's origin. Instead, desire finds its source in the split between the real of the organism and the signifying subject constituted in the symbolic order. At the same time, the recurring theme of psycho-analysis is sexual, because sex so readily "occupies" the field of desire created by the split. The sexual concentrates human energies at the level of both the organism and the signifier. This is the place where demand struggles most resolutely (and perhaps most ineffectually) to avoid misrepresenting desire. In naming the phallus as signifier, Lacan is true to Freud's account of the castration complex, and the feminist proposal to substitute some other organ simply misses the point. But he is also true to an older tradition, embodied in Augustine and Montaigne, that dooms all mortal beings to the unhappiness of a desire and an organ that does not obey our conscious wishes, and evades our best efforts at rational or moral control.

IV

If this lawless desire, signified by the phallus, occupies a nodal point in Lacan's psychoanalytic theory, the anarchic member is also nodal for the Augustinian account of Christian theology, in so far as it concerns human life in this world.[21] To Augustine, the unruly sexual organ symbolizes the human condition. In this, as in all things, he argues, we ourselves are not able to help ourselves. Try as we might, we cannot, by an act of will, achieve virtue, since even our own bodies do not obey us. According to Augustine, the original disobedience, the Fall, explains the existence of evil, as well as the need for divine Grace. While our models are those Old Testament figures like Abraham, who obeyed the will of God however hard it seemed, human beings are redeemed not by their own volition, which cannot ensure submission to the good, but by the ultimate obedience of Christ, the second Adam.[22] Without this promise of redemption, Augustine tells God, people are restless, footloose creatures who have no hope of satisfaction, since "our heart cannot be quieted till it may find repose in thee" (inquietum est cor nostrum, donec requiescat in te).[23] Lacan, meanwhile, would have repudiated the metaphysical solution (and the address to the deity), but he would have recognized the anxiety, as well as the restlessness that precedes conversion in the discontented pagan protagonist of Augustine's *Confessions*. He would also have shared Augustine's perception of a double self, rational, deliberate, willing the good on the one hand, and arbitrary, unaccountable, incapable of obedience to the law on the other.[24]

While the Lacanian phallus and the Augustinian penis are nodal, Montaigne's essays, laconic, relaxed, apparently moving easily from topic to topic by a kind of free association, are nowhere consecutive enough to display obvious nodes. But, even so, the anarchic behavior of the unruly member plays a critical part in his reflections too. Augustine concerns himself mainly with men; Lacan includes women, then disqualifies them again, and then backtracks on that too;[25] only Montaigne credits women with the dubious advantage of a sexual appetite, and a corresponding unruliness, at least equal to men's: "The Gods (saith *Plato*) have furnished man with a disobedient, skittish, and tyrannicall member; which like an untamed furious-beast, attempteth by the violence of his appetite to bring all things under his becke. So have they allotted women another as insulting, wilde and fierce; in nature like a greedy, devouring, and rebellious creature, who if when he craveth it, hee bee refused nourishment, as impatient of delay, it enrageth."[26] Like the Aristotelian womb in Lacan's account, Montaigne's sexual organ acts up if it's not given something to tuck into. Law and desire are at odds. In view of the disobedience of this organ in both sexes, Montaigne argues, love is incompatible with marriage, since wedlock is a lasting institution designed to foster posterity, companionship, respect: "A good marriage (if any there be) refuseth the company and conditions of love; it endeavoureth to present those of amity. It is a sweete society of life, full of constancy, of trust, and an infinite number of profitable and solid offices, and mutuall obligations."[27] Marriage is lawful and law-abiding; desire is unpredictable and not amenable to discipline.

Montaigne follows Augustine to the degree that he sees a perpetual conflict between sex and propriety. We do it in private, both insist, because the loss of control it entails is shameful.[28] Moreover, Montaigne concedes that this disobedience of the body is evidence of our fallen nature: "Surely it is an argument not onely of our originall corruption, but a badge of our vanity and deformity."[29] Montaigne's tone is different from Augustine's, however. True, sex absorbs our attention in a way that no other physical activity does, he recognizes, just as Augustine does,[30] distracting the mind from intellectual pursuits, and eclipsing thought, so that "its imperious authority makes brutish and dulleth all *Platoes* philosophy and divinity." But Montaigne adds, as Augustine does not, "and yet he [Plato] complaines not of it."[31] Montaigne, in other words, also sees the other side of the story. His Cupid is comic, as well as dangerous, "a roguish God," whose contest with devotion and justice is "sport."[32] Ancient societies deified the phallus, he notes;[33] and if Nature had indeed invested it with any privilege, she would have done right, after all, in view of its role as "Author of the only immortall worke, of mortal men."[34]

If he looks back to Augustine, then, Montaigne also looks forward in this ambivalence to Lacan, for whom, if desire conflicts with Law, it also constitutes the only genuine good. Lacan concedes that desire is arbitrary and absurd; it is dangerous, too, since in the end its imperatives cannot be disentangled from the death drive; but the alternative is the fierce and exorbitant tyranny of Law itself, the demanding and destructive superego, or conscience. For this reason, we should never struggle to suppress desire. On the contrary, from the point of view of the Last Judgment, if it were humanly possible to look back on our life from such a place, Lacan affirms, "the only thing of which one can be guilty is of having given ground relative to one's desire."[35] We should pursue desire wherever it leads. And in case this should be interpreted as a plea for the most callous hedonism, it is worth bearing in mind first that desire is unconscious, so that its object is not what we mistakenly suppose it to be. What we want is not that man, that woman or, indeed, that child, who is only a stand-in for the unnameable object itself. And second, we should remember that the sexual drive is ultimately inseparable from the death drive. In Lacan's *Seminar 7,* the resolute and heroic pursuit of desire leads not to pleasure but to the living death of Antigone, walled up in her own tomb because she has done what she had to with respect to an unconscious imperative more powerful than Creon's law.

V

Montaigne, in short, can be seen as investing with a wry sympathy the Augustinian account of anarchic desire, symbolized by a sexual organ that ignores the imperatives of law and order. Meanwhile, there is direct evidence of Lacan's familiarity with the works of both Augustine and Montaigne. Indeed, he refers more than once to each of them, and always with respect. Fully familiar with his cultural heritage, Lacan was aware of the parallels between psychoanalysis and Christian theology. Like redemption, culture is won at the price of a loss. The psychoanalytic experience, Lacan acknowledges, leads, "Freud in the van," to original sin.[36] But the child's incestuous desire, he declares, is a "*felix culpa,*" a fortunate transgression, since its sublimation gives rise to civilization.[37] The theological paradox that good comes of evil enjoyed wide currency in Reformation Christianity, and the idea of the *felix culpa* (though not the phrase, which was liturgical) can be traced back to Saint Augustine.[38]

Moreover, Lacan knew the writings of Augustine directly, and mentions him several times. His essay on "Aggressivity," presented as a paper in 1948, explicitly claims that Augustine "foreshadowed psychoanalysis," commenting sardonically that, although his own moment resembled Lacan's in its social upheaval (barbarians had just sacked the Roman Empire), at least Augustine was fortunate enough to have lived at a time when there wasn't any trouble from the behaviorists. The instance of continuity Lacan gives here is the passage from the *Confessions* where Augustine describes a child pale with jealousy as it observes its foster brother at the breast, and in properly Augustinian terms Lacan names the episode evidence of "original" aggressivity.[39] He returns to the implications of infant rivalry throughout his work, but most notably, perhaps, six years later in *Seminar 1,* where he mentions a case of his own, a little girl who was found, at an age when she could scarcely walk, absorbed "in the application of a good-sized stone to the skull of a little playmate from next door." And he adds, invoking Augustine's paradigm instance, "The deed of Cain does not require very great motor sophistication."

This murderous, but perfectly normal, little girl made no attempt to conceal the truth of what she had done. Indeed, she had no sense of guilt, but laid claim to her deed "with assurance and peace of mind."[40] In Lacan's account, guilt will come with the acquisition of Law, when in due course the child submits to the discipline of the symbolic order. Guilt belongs, in other words, to the signifying subject. So, in a manner of speaking, does truth; or at least, it is only the world of language that makes truth into an issue. Truth is what we tell—or deny. There is no question of truth before there is language. Lacan not only acknowledges the Augustinian anticipation of psychoanalysis; he also treats with equal deference Augustine's account of the relation between truth and the signifier. One of the seminars of 1954 is virtually turned over to an exposition (by Father Beirnaert at Lacan's invitation) of Augustine's theory of language. If Augustine foreshadowed Freud, it seems he also anticipated Saussure, whose work Lacan explicitly brought together with Freud's in order to reread the founding texts of psychoanalysis. Augustine's *De Magistro* is, Lacan announces, "one of the most glorious" texts one could read, and linguists "have taken fifteen centuries to rediscover, like a sun which has risen anew, like a dawn that is breaking, ideas which are already set out in Saint Augustine's text."[41] The ideas in question include a nonreferential theory of language, in which signs are not signs *of* things, and if for Augustine truth is ultimately extralinguistic, metaphysical, as the Christian truth must in the end be, Augustine sees, even so, Lacan maintains, that it is the independence of the signifier, its detachment from things, that makes truth into a problem.

Montaigne, too, elicits Lacan's repeated attention and endorsement. "Psychoanalysis is a dialectic," Lacan says; it is "what Montaigne in Book III, chapter VIII, calls *an art of conversation.*"[42] If psychoanalysis goes beyond Montaigne's observations on human nature, it recognizes their accuracy too. The subject is not a unity, Lacan says, "not only not free from contradiction, as we have known since Montaigne, but much more, since the Freudian experience designates it the place of negation."[43] Temperamentally, Lacan and Montaigne have much in common. For both, prohibition intensifies desire; and conscience in Montaigne, like Law in Lacan, is exorbitant, setting the self against the self.[44] But above all, Montaigne anticipates Lacan's interest in the *fading* of the subject. "I would

show you," Lacan asserts, "that Montaigne is truly the one who has cen-
tred himself, not around scepticism but around the living moment of the
aphanisis of the subject. And it is in this that he is fruitful, that he is an
eternal guide," who goes beyond the historical turning point that was his
own time.[45] *Aphanisis* (disappearance) was a term first used by Ernest
Jones, who argued that the subject's ultimate fear was that desire would
disappear. Lacan appropriates the term to discuss the disappearance, or
sometimes the "fading," of the speaking subject itself, as it loses its purchase on meaning. I can disappear from what I am saying, and in the
process make apparent the provisional character of subjectivity.[46] *Aphanisis* resides at the heart of the analytic process, and at the heart, too, of the
Lacanian account of the human condition.

The historical turning point where Montaigne stands as the eternal guide
to *aphanisis* is the inaugural moment, Lacan says, of humanism in early modern culture, and its other representative is Descartes, whose philosophy
excludes the unconscious. The object of desire for Descartes, Lacan points
out, was certainty, but the certainty he longs for, and believes himself to have
found, resides entirely at the level of the *Cogito*. His mistake, according to
Lacan, is to claim possession of this certainty, to believe he has achieved it,
and not to "make of the *I think* a mere point of fading."[47] Concealed in
humanism, with its overconfidence in consciousness, there is always, in consequence, a "skeleton in the cupboard," the threatened return of the disruptive and deadly drive.[48] Montaigne, by contrast, reveals the "living" moment
when the subject fades, surpassing in his practice of writing whatever of
humanism he may also share with his epoch.

Lacan says no more here about Montaigne, leaving his audience to
construe how this proposition is to be understood. My own best guess is
that Lacan finds in Montaigne's apparent inconsequentiality, in the
appearance of free association that characterizes the essays, a contrast with
the rigorously thetic, law-abiding self-discipline of an Enlightenment philosophy confident that nothing in principle exceeds its totalizing grasp.
Montaigne himself draws attention to the lawless quality of his writing,
and laments that such unruliness also characterizes his mind itself, which
he describes as capricious. He is prone, he declares, to pick up verbal
habits from others, and reproduce them out of context. He can be totally
inconsistent, he goes on, affirming seriously one day what he said as a
joke the day before. Moreover, "All arguments are alike fertile to me. I
take them upon any trifle. And I pray God this were not undertaken by
the commandement of a minde as fleeting. Let me begin with that likes
me best, for all matters are linked to one another. But my conceit dis-
pleaseth me, for somuch as it commonly produceth most foolish dotages
from deepest studies; and such as content me on a suddaine, and when I
least looke for them; which as fast fleete away, wanting at that instant

some holde fast." He goes on to describe how his train of thought is easily distracted by the most minor interruption. Ideas that come into his head unpremeditated slip out again as unaccountably, leaving him to "chafe, spight and fret in pursuite of them."[49] It is as if, then, the inconsequentiality of the essays dramatizes in their own mode of address an involuntary disobedience to the discipline of rational composition, an *importunate* practice of writing where an anarchic self refuses accountability to the self that tries in vain to master it. Instead, he complains that his mind, left to its own devices, "begets" in him "extravagant *Chimeraes,* and fantasticall monsters. . . . orderlesse, and without any reason, one hudling upon an other," full of "foolishenesse and monstrous strangenesse."[50]

The essay genre itself, Montaigne's invention, is precisely tentative, provisional, allusive, and anecdotal. Its form runs counter to the totalizing pretensions that would go on to characterize the philosophy of Descartes and his successors. Enlightenment prose sets out to follow a rational sequence and eschews digression. It was not until the early twentieth century, when modernism challenged Enlightenment ideals by introducing the stream of consciousness, that writing began once again to permit the deliberate representation of inconsequentiality. The project of this literary device was to do justice to the unruly way people actually think, and at the same time to enlist the full attention of the reader to the opacity of thought processes themselves. Lacan's own writing and, indeed, the seminars, transcribed from recordings by Jacques-Alain Miller, take advantage, in high modernist manner, of this technique, with a view to mimicking the speech of the analysand in its apparent inconsequence, as well as the claim its opacity makes on the auditor's attention.

Montaigne's skepticism represented a starting point for Descartes: the one thing Descartes claimed he could be sure of was his own doubt. Equally, Cartesian overconfidence in the capabilities of consciousness represented a starting point for Lacan, who early on declared himself opposed to "any philosophy directly issuing from the *Cogito.*"[51] No wonder, then, that Lacan returned to Montaigne as a guide to the moment when the subject "fades." If Lacan is difficult, where Montaigne is relaxed and apparently casual, they share, nonetheless, a repudiation of the Enlightenment mode of address that condemns digression as a deviation from the rigorous linearity of the declarative text.

VI

Montaigne, then, takes Lacan beyond the Augustinian account of unruly desire. Offering an alternative to the law and order that drives Enlightenment rationalism, Montaigne's mode of address also presents an instance of the "fading" that characterizes the Lacanian subject. *Aphanisis* represents more for psychoanalysis, however, than a "fading" manner of writing or speech. Human beings constantly "choose" between the world of meaning they inhabit as speaking subjects and the real of the organism that they also are. To choose meaning, culture, the symbolic order, is to invoke the mismatch between desire and Law, and thus to relegate an element of what we wish to say to the unconscious. Conversely, to opt for the real in an attempt to escape subjection by language as the inscription of culture is to lose all purchase on meaning and subjectivity itself.

Lacan introduces the analogy of the highway robber or the mugger who demands, "Your money or your life!," and the violent parallel is evidently not accidental. If you choose your life, you lose your money, he explains, but if you choose to hold on to your money, you lose both. Similarly, the subject that chooses meaning loses part of it to the unconscious, while to choose being is to lose access to meaning, and thus to everything that defines the signifying subject as fully human.[52] There is in these circumstances no such thing as a subject in the full possession of meaning that the Cartesian *Cogito* presupposes. Certainty is not an option, unless at the price of repressing the unconscious, that element of nonmeaning that necessarily attends the process of signification. Something, not a presence, not a thematic content, and certainly not sex, but a radical alterity, is definitively taken away from every process of presentation. The signifier always betrays us, as it must; language is incapable of transmitting a full thematic content, a complete, coherent world picture, or a cognitive totality of any kind. This is not to say, of course, that *something* isn't said, but it is necessarily both more and less than we consciously had in mind.

Language permits the little human infant to name its wishes and make demands; it enables us to relate to one another in ways that are not simply bodily. But because language also betrays those wishes, the naming never achieves the perspicuity that is the goal of Enlightenment philosophy. As an analyst, Lacan speaks both of the analytic situation and of dialogue in general when he says, "It follows that the place of the 'inter-said' (*inter-dit* [exchanged/censored]), which is 'the intra-said' (*intra-dit*) of a between-two-subjects, is the very place in which the transparency of the classical subject is divided and passes through the effects of 'fading' that specify the Freudian subject."[53] This "fading" is the basis of Lacan's opposition to any philosophy directly issuing from the *Cogito*. The scandal of psychoanalysis has been that it refuses the Enlightenment identification of the subject with consciousness, and the dualism of mind and body on which the Cartesian moment so explicitly depends. Freud and Breuer found that unconscious psychic disturbance manifested itself organically, in the coughs, disrupted vision, and paralyzed body parts of their hysterical patients. But then that same disturbance, in Freud's account, depends in turn on the fact that the instinctual in civilized human beings is never fully surmounted, but survives in the drive as its represented form. According to Lacan's rereading of Freud in the light of Saussure, unconscious desire marks the distance between the organism and the speaking being, as a reminder of that inextricable element of need which is lost in the demand that comes from the symbolic Other. For this reason, the subject is unable to be present to itself as pure thought. Instead, the Otherness of language and culture ensures that "I think where I am not, therefore I am where I do not think." These are, Lacan goes on, "Words that render sensible to an ear properly attuned with what elusive ambiguity the ring of meaning flees from our grasp along the verbal thread."[54] As the fading of the subject into nonmeaning, or into that alternative mode of meaning that characterizes dreams, jokes, and slips of the tongue, and that requires an active reading to make it signify, *aphanisis* demonstrates that the *Cogito* depends on the repression of the organic remainder that makes itself felt in the psyche as unconscious desire.

Descartes' case depended on mind-body dualism, privileging thought as the place of identity: "I think, therefore I am." But like Lacan, like Freud, his immediate predecessor, Montaigne, regards dualism, as he does asceticism, with suspicion. As his essay on "Imagination" demonstrates, mental images have physical consequences. Conversely, mental processes depend on physical health. There is no energy in the products of his intellect, he says, if there is none in his body; they belong together and the one does not work without the other. The mind too easily follows the imperatives of the organism; indeed, "if hir companion have the chollicke, it seemes she also hath it."[55] Temperance, meanwhile, makes him stupid, he insists.[56] Philosophers, Montaigne claims, believe that it is possible to satisfy the body without involving the mind. He finds their position "somewhat rigorous," and adds, "May we not say, that there is nothing in us, during this earthly prison, simply corporall, or purely spirituall? and that injuriously we dismember a living man?"[57]

If the vocabulary here is reminiscent of Plato, and of philosophy's founding antithesis between the sensible and the intelligible,[58] Montaigne's question challenges that opposition. His antidualist view might be seen, on the other hand, as compatible with Augustine's account of the fallen human condition. Contrary to immediate appearances, Augustine is not a mind-body dualist either. Once again, Lacan, Montaigne, and Augustine are aligned against the division between matter and spirit that informs the dominant tradition of Western philosophy. If the Fall has thrown mind and body out of kilter, destroying the God-given harmony between the mortal body and the immortal soul, that is our fault, Augustine affirms, and not part of the divine plan. The opposition that structures his thinking, however, is not between flesh and spirit, but between two cities, the earthly city we inhabit here and now, and the heavenly city to which all Christians ultimately belong. The first lives according to human, secular values, and the second in accordance with the will of God.

Augustine's prime opponents in this context are the Manichaeans, who imagine an eternal division between good and evil, and this is reproduced in the opposition they define between soul and body. By contrast, Augustine insists on valuing the body: procreation, he argues, was a glory, commanded by God, and sexual intercourse would have taken place in Eden, though in perfect obedience to the will and without the perturbation of mind that accompanies the act in the fallen world. At the Last Day we shall rise again as bodies, and not simply as disembodied souls, though our new forms will retain no vestige of corruptibility.

Augustine has to reckon, of course, with Saint Paul, who consistently opposes flesh and spirit. But he interprets this first Christian theologian in the most resolutely antidualist manner. If the earthly city is defined as carnal, we should understand that term to refer to its values. In the earthly city, they live according to the flesh, but this is not to say that they seek bodily pleasures. Instead, they dedicate themselves to human, secular, and worldly commitments. "Two loves therefore have given origin to these two cities, self-love in contempt of God unto the earthly, love of God in contempt of one's self to the heavenly."[59] The flesh, Augustine maintains, is given by God and was good, at least until the Fall made it corruptible. Moreover, it would be a mistake to suppose that the flesh is the cause of sin. On the contrary, it was "the sinning soul" that "made the flesh corruptible." There are sins of the flesh, certainly, but the worst sins are envy, pride, wrath, deceit, all characteristic of the devil, who, after all, has no flesh.[60] It was pride and the wickedness of the will, not the flesh, that caused the Fall.[61] As Andrew Marvell's debating Body would later put it, "What but a Soul could have the wit / To build me up for Sin so fit?"[62] After the Fall, Augustine insists, Adam became carnal in mind and body, with the result that another imperative in both flesh and spirit came to undermine his once-unified longing to obey the law of God.

In consequence of all this, Augustine takes issue with the Platonists, as well as the Manichaeans. The Platonists are not quite so wide of the mark, he allows, as the Manichaeans, since they make God the Creator of the visible world, as well as the origin of the intelligible one. But they err in attributing sin to the desires of the flesh.[63] The penalty for the Fall is made visible in the flesh, as the lawless behavior of the unruly sexual organ, but the meaning of this punishment is the loss of control, the disobedience of the self to the self. In this sense, the penis for Augustine is the *signifier*, we might want in a post-Lacanian world to say, of lost mastery.

Just as Augustine's human being is divided against itself, asserting desire against the dictates of the will, the subject of psychoanalysis is other than it is, divided between conscious intents and unconscious desires. In neither case is the conflict reducible to a distinction between mind and body. Instead, in each instance an irrepressible imperative other than the law intrudes, insists, and overturns the best efforts of consciousness to command behavior. If their values are antithetical, Augustine's metaphysical, identifying the law with the will of God and eternal life, and Lacan's secular, defining the Law as both human and deadly, if one appeals to Grace to save him from desire, and the other insists that desire is the only genuine good, they share, nevertheless, a theoretical framework that the Enlightenment would repudiate, a conception of the self at odds with the self in a conflict where victory cannot be achieved by willpower.

The early modern period represents the meeting point of two incompatible knowledges, whose most representative figures we might now want to see as Descartes and Montaigne respectively. Descartes pointed forwards to the Enlightenment; but Montaigne, who looked back to Augustine in so many ways, also anticipates in some respects our own postmodern, post-Enlightenment sensibilities. Of course, the historical differences are as great as the theoretical similarities. Psychoanalysis was radically new in its own modernist period: there is no conception of the specifically psychoanalytic unconscious in Augustine or Montaigne. But I have a sense that both Augustine and Montaigne might have found Lacan congenial, or at least intelligible, in a way that Descartes would not. And if so, we are not entirely anachronistic in allowing certain aspects of his work to illuminate the texts of the period that is our shared concern.

Those aspects, I have suggested, are not so much thematic as textual. What psychoanalysis offers us, in my view, is a way of reading, an attention to the signifier that acknowledges the dialectic of Law and desire that informs all writing. This is apparent in the importunate irruption of unexpected meanings into the most thetic, the most disciplined of pronouncements, and the tendency of the writing subject to *fade* at the critical moment. Reading for *aphanisis* would withhold the promised mastery of world pictures and the illusory certainty of cognitive totalities, but would give us instead an early modern culture at least as divided, as complex and, indeed, as inventive as our own.

VII

In his brilliant, provocative and sometimes mischievous essay, "What is Postmodernism?," Jean-François Lyotard, surely the most Lacanian of philosophers, claimed Montaigne for postmodernity.[64] Fifteen years later, in 1997, the year before he died, Lyotard wrote the first half of a projected book on Augustine's *Confessions*. The surviving text is elusive, subtle, lyrical, more prose-poem than commentary on Augustine's text, the first-person figure who appears there as the writing subject ostensibly Augustine himself, but perhaps also interchangeable with Lyotard. The primary theorist of the postmodern finds in Augustine's Christian theology a temporality that resembles at once the timelessness of the Freudian unconscious and the future anterior of the analytic experience. Lyotard also singles out for attention the unruliness of sexual desire that conflicts with the most righteous resolutions of the will, as well as the other self that in Augustine's text makes itself felt in dreams, a lecherous figure who wakes when the conscious, virtuous self is asleep. In Lyotard's paraphrase, "Sleep does not belong to I. Another principle, another prince exercises at its own pace on the stage of the dream the languorous and lascivious illusions. When the master's lieutenant, controlling the passions and upright in chastity, is on leave, what can the master do? Has he not given the conjuror the reins?"[65]

Intensely aware, as this quotation shows, of the resemblance between psychoanalysis and Augustinian thought, Lyotard additionally finds in the *Confessions* a story of reading. Trying to compensate for the originary loss, we read, interpreting both books and the Book of Nature, in order to possess the truth. For the postmodern philosopher, as for the Christian theologian, the longed-for object is the *absolute,* unattainable in the world we ourselves inhabit, but infinitely desirable in spite of that, or perhaps for that very reason. Lyotard mimics Augustine's text, with its direct address to God: "Chased out of the paradise of your intimacy, we are left for memory by you the collection of your works, the world, a text of which we form as much a part as its readers. Decipherable decipherers, in the library of shadows."[66] But the truth reaches us obscured: "We mumble our way through the traces left by the absolute that you are; we spell the letters."[67] The angels, Lyotard goes on, still paraphrasing the *Confessions,* read quite differently. They have no need of the intervention of language, the signifier that Augustine regarded with such suspicion. Instead, they encounter the Logos directly, "The very thought of the author," "A presence of which we have no idea, an infinite ocean of light without shadow."[68]

Augustine records his own conversion as a scene of reading. In despair in the garden, he hears a voice repeating, "Take up and read." He at once read Romans 13, the chapter where the book fell open, and all doubt vanished.[69] Thereafter, the daily struggle against sin is no less, but mysteriously, mystically, something is known, if only that the time of perfect knowledge is not yet.[70] Is there envy or identification in Lyotard's account of this recognition? "The absolute, absolutely irrelative, outside space and time, so absolutely far—there [it] is for one moment lodged in the most intimate part of this man. . . . The soul has not penetrated into the angelic spheres, but a little of the absolute—is it thinkable?—has encrypted itself within it."[71]

Augustine (or Lyotard?) is thus more, as well as less, than he is: not only at the mercy of an anarchic desire, but aware of the Other, which is the source of meaning and truth, and yet does not exist as substance, but only as signification. "What I am not yet, I am. . . . What is missing, the absolute, cuts its presence into the shallow furrow of its absence."[72]

As cultural critics and historians of culture, we do not, it seems to me, aspire to the absolute as the object of our reading. On the contrary, our aim is not the truth beyond the signifier, but the contours of signification itself, while the absolute, with its supernatural resonances, can safely be left to philosophy. Instead, our task is to spell the letters that do no more than trace the anxieties as well as the ideals, the hopes, uncertainties and dissonances, that inform the writing of a past culture. In that project, a postmodern and psychoanalytic acknowledgment of the incompleteness of every text, its silences and its potential incoherences, its propensity to "fade," is a necessary ally, the material of a deeper historicism and a sharper awareness of historical difference. On those grounds, and because in its Lacanian form it is not inconsistent with certain critical early modern convictions, psychoanalysis surely deserves to be brought in from the cold.

NOTES

1. Josef Breuer and Sigmund Freud, *Studies on Hysteria,* ed. Angela Richards, Penguin Freud Library, 3 (Harmondsworth, UK: Penguin, 1974), 83.

2. "As the New Historicism attempts to strengthen its hold over reconfiguring the Renaissance (and in particular the Renaissance 'subject'), psychoanalysis, implicitly or explicitly, finds itself marginalized" (Elizabeth Bellamy, *Translations of Power: Narcissism and the Unconscious in Epic History* [Ithaca, NY: Cornell University Press, 1992], 4).

3. Stephen Greenblatt, "Psychoanalysis and Renaissance Culture," *Literary Theory / Renaissance Texts,* ed. Patricia Parker and David Quint (Baltimore, MD: Johns Hopkins University Press, 1986), 210–24 (210 quoted).

4. See for example Joel Fineman, *Shakespeare's Perjured Eye: The Invention of Poetic Subjectivity in the Sonnets* (Berkeley and Los Angeles: University of California Press, 1986); Juliana Schiesari, *The Gendering of Melancholia: Feminism, Psychoanalysis, and the Symbolics of Loss in Renaissance Literature* (Ithaca, NY: Cornell University Press, 1992); Lynn Enterline, *The Tears of Narcissus: Melancholia and Masculinity in Early Modern Writing* (Stanford, CA: Stanford University Press, 1995) and *The Rhetoric of the Body from Ovid to Shakespeare* (Cambridge: Cambridge University Press, 2000); Christopher Pye, *The Vanishing: Shakespeare, the Subject, and Early Modern Culture* (Durham, NC: Duke University Press, 2000); Philip Armstrong, *Shakespeare in Psychoanalysis* (London: Routledge, 2001).

5. Bellamy, *Translations of Power,* 14; Schiesari, *Gendering of Melancholia,* 23–24.

6. Jacques Lacan, *Écrits: A Selection,* trans. Alan Sheridan (London: Tavistock, 1977), 284–85.

7. Jacques Derrida, "Differance," *"Speech and Phenomena" and Other Essays on Husserl's Theory of Signs,* trans. David B. Allison (Evanston, IL: Northwestern University Press, 1973), 129–60, 151–52.

8. *Les Essais de Michel de Montaigne,* ed. Pierre Villey, 2 vols. (Paris: Presses Universitaires de France, 1965), 1:xli–xliii.

9. On the question, for example, of breaking wind, *The Essayes of Michael Lord of Montaigne,* trans. John Florio, 1.20, 3 vols. (London: Dent, 1910), 1:99.

10. Ibid., 1:92–104 (98 quoted).

11. Augustine, *The City of God,* 14.16, trans. John Healey [1610], 2 vols. (London: Dent, 1945), 2:47. The modern edition slightly corrects Healey's orginal.

12. "On a raison de remarquer l'indocile liberté de ce membre, s'ingerant si importunement, lors que nous n'en avons que faire, et defaillant si importunement lors que nous en avons le plus affaire" (Montaigne, *Essais,* 1:102); "Sed aliquando importunus est ille motus poscente nullo, aliquando autem destituit inhiantem, et cum in animo concupiscentia ferveat, friget in corpore" (Saint Augustine, *The City of God Against the Pagans,* 14.16, vol. 4, books 12–15, trans. Philip Levine, Loeb Classical Library [London: Heinemann, 1966], 354).

13. Augustine, *City,* 14.15 (trans. Healey), 2:45–46. I first encountered this argument in 1990 in a copy that Leeds Barroll kindly lent me of Elaine Pagels, *Adam, Eve, and the Serpent* (New York: Random House, 1988).

14. David M. Friedman, *A Mind of Its Own: A Cultural History of the Penis* (New York: Free Press, 2001), 193. I am grateful to Cynthia Dessen for this book.

15. Sigmund Freud, *On Sexuality,* ed. Angela Richards, Penguin Freud Library, 7 (Harmondsworth, UK: Penguin, 1977), 258. See also Sigmund Freud, *Civilization and Its Discontents,* and Jacqueline Rose, "Femininity and Its Discontents," *Sexuality in the Field of Vision* (London: Verso, 1986), 83–103.

16. Lacan, *Écrits: A Selection,* 285.

17. Ibid., 290.

18. Ibid., 284, 288.

19. Ibid., 290.

20. Jacques Lacan, *Seminar 2, The Ego in Freud's Theory and the Technique of Psychoanalysis,* ed. Jacques-Alain Miller, trans. Sylvana Tomaselli (Cambridge: Cambridge University Press, 1988), 225–26.

21. Slavoj Žižek also notes the parallel between the Lacanian phallus and the Augustinian penis (*The Sublime Object of Ideology* [London: Verso, 1989], 222–23).

22. Augustine, *City,* 14.15 (trans. Healey), 2:45.

23. Augustine, *Confessions,* 1.1, trans. William Watts [1631], 2 vols. Loeb Classical Library (London: William Heinemann, 1912), 1:3, 2.

24. Michel Foucault also took an interest in Augustine's account of the unruly member, seeing it as bringing into being a new form of self-subjection. Augustine refocuses attention, Foucault argues, from the relationship between the libido and other people to that between the self and the self. At this moment "sexuality, subjectivity, and truth were strongly linked together" to bring the subject into line, or rather, to induce subjects to bring themselves into line ("Sexuality and Solitude," in *Ethics, Subjectivity and Truth,* ed. Paul Rabinow [Harmondsworth, UK: Penguin, 2000], 175–84, 183 quoted). Foucault repudiates psychoanalysis on much the same grounds: it insists on subjecting us to the "truth" of our sexuality. Psychoanalysis "promises us at the same time our sex, our true sex, and that whole truth about ourselves that secretly keeps vigil in it" (*Herculine Barbin,* trans. Richard McDougall [Brighton: Harvester, 1980], xi).

25. In "The Signification of the Phallus" the phallus symbolizes the penis or clitoris indiscriminately; unlike men, women tolerate frigidity; men, by contrast, commonly seek out more than one woman; and yet "if one looks more closely, the same redoubling is to be found in the woman" (Lacan, *Écrits: A Selection,* 290).

26. Montaigne, *Essayes,* 3.5, 3:84. "In men the nature of the genital organs is disobedient and self-willed, like a creature that is deaf to reason, and it attempts to dominate all because

of its frenzied lusts." The corresponding unruly organ in women is the womb, which longs to bear children, and causes all kinds of maladies if this gratification is deferred or denied (Plato, *Timaeus* 91 B and C. *Timaeus, Critias, etc.,* trans. R. G. Bury, The Loeb Classical Library [London: William Heinemann, 1966], 248–51).

27. Montaigne, *Essayes,* 3.5, 3:74.

28. Ibid., 3:106–7; Augustine, *City,* 14.19 (trans. Healey), 2:50.

29. Ibid., *Essayes,* 3:106.

30. Augustine, *City,* 14.16 (trans. Healey), 2:47.

31. Montaigne, *Essayes,* 3.5, 3:106.

32. Ibid., 3:98.

33. Ibid., 3:82.

34. Ibid., 1:100.

35. Jacques Lacan, *Seminar 7, The Ethics of Psychoanalysis,* ed. Jacques-Alain Miller, trans. Dennis Porter (London: Routledge, 1992), 319.

36. Lacan, *Écrits: A Selection,* 317.

37. Lacan, *Seminar 7,* 6.

38. A. O. Lovejoy, "Milton and the Paradox of the Fortunate Fall," *ELH* 4 (1937), 161–79.

39. Lacan, *Écrits: A Selection,* 20; Augustine, *Confessions,* 1:19–22.

40. Jacques Lacan, *Seminar 1, Freud's Papers on Technique,* ed. Jacques-Alain Miller, trans. John Forrester (Cambridge: Cambridge University Press, 1988), 171–72.

41. Ibid., 247–60 (249 quoted).

42. Ibid., 278.

43. Jacques Lacan, *Écrits* (Paris: Seuil, 1966), 179 (my translation).

44. Montaigne, *Essayes,* 2.5, 2:45–6.

45. Jacques Lacan, *The Four Fundamental Concepts of Psycho-Analysis,* ed. Jacques-Alain Miller, trans. Alan Sheridan (Harmondsworth, UK: Penguin, 1979), 223–24.

46. Lacan, *Écrits: A Selection,* 300.

47. Lacan, *Four Fundamental Concepts,* 224.

48. Lacan, *Four Fundamental Concepts,* 223.

49. Montaigne, *Essayes,* 3.5, 3:104–5.

50. Ibid., 1.8, 1:44.

51. Lacan, *Écrits: A Selection,* 1.

52. Lacan, *Four Fundamental Concepts,* 211–12.

53. Lacan, *Écrits: A Selection,* 299.

54. Ibid., 166.

55. Montaigne, *Essayes,* 3.5, 3:66.

56. Ibid., 3:62.

57. Ibid., 3:123.

58. Derrida, "Differance," 133.

59. Augustine, *City,* 14.28 (trans. Healey), vol. 2, p. 58.

60. Ibid., 14.3 (trans. Healey), 2:29.

61. Ibid., 14.13 (trans. Healey), 2:43–4.

62. "A Dialogue Between the Soul and Body," *The Poems and Letters of Andrew Marvell,* 2 vols., ed. H. M. Margoliouth (Oxford: Clarendon Press, 1971), 1:23.

63. Augustine, *City,* 14.5 (trans. Healey), 2:31.

64. Jean-François Lyotard, "Answering the Question: What is Postmodernism?," *The Postmodern Condition* (Manchester, UK: Manchester University Press, 1984), 81.

65. Jean-François Lyotard, *The Confession of Augustine,* trans. Richard Beardsworth (Stanford, CA: Stanford University Press, 2000), 18–21 (20 quoted).

66. Ibid., p. 41.

67. Ibid., p. 40.

68. Ibid., p. 42.

69. Augustine, *Confessions*, 8.12, 1:464–5.

70. Ibid., 13.15, 2:406–7.

71. Lyotard, *Confession*, 53.

72. Ibid., 57. Compare (and contrast!) Lacan: "Desire is affirmed as the absolute condition. Even less than the nothing that passes into the round of significations that act upon men, desire is the furrow inscribed in the course; it is, as it were, the mark of the iron of the signifier on the shoulder of the speaking subject" (*Écrits: A Selection*, 265).

Abdiel Centers Freedom

Susanne Woods

THE ANGEL ABDIEL IN BOOKS 5 AND 6 OF MILTON'S *Paradise Lost* is a marginal character used to center a principal theme: God's creatures are free to stand or fall. The Abdiel episode is interesting for a number of reasons, three of which I want to highlight in this essay. The story comes at a crucial moment in the history of the idea of freedom in English-speaking culture, it exemplifies Milton's technique of inviting the knowledgeable reader to make choices, and it helps to clarify one of the larger ambiguities of *Paradise Lost*, the question of whether or not the fall of man was fortunate, a *felix culpa*.

In his cultural biography of *Anna of Denmark, Queen of England*, Leeds Barroll rejects the view that "the early modern English state [is] a binary, with the Crown (synonymous with the 'state') in ideological opposition to those whom the Crown rules."[1] Rather, Barroll posits "the early modern English state" as a "polymorphic body politic," where peerage, gentry, and merchants (none of these categories monolithic), along with the Crown, "made up the early modern state by relating to one another within a general formation characterized by the constant mobility of power centering" (3). While Barroll illustrates this formulation through Queen Anna's complex and fluid cultural and political influence as an active and self-conscious Queen Consort, this observation has implications well beyond the Stuart court. In particular, it suggests that a variety of Englishmen had, or could develop, the autonomy and social importance that signify personal and political freedom.

The concept of freedom, in Tudor times associated with order and safety, was to become increasingly destabilized in the period between the beginning of the first and the end of the second Stuart's reign.[2] Between 1603 and 1649, the assertion of a monarch's absolute power, and therefore ultimate control over the freedom of his subjects, moved to the assertion that God's power, revealed to the individual conscience, was not necessarily coordinate with the monarch's, and could override it. In 1609, King James was able to evoke his divine right and challenge the legislative rights of Parliament by claiming that when "kingdoms began to be settled in civility and policy, then did the kings set down their minds by laws, which are properly made by the king only."[3] By 1628, his son Charles I, under financial pressure, was conceding the power of Parliament through the Petition of Right, one of the founding documents of personal freedom in the tradition of the American Bill of Rights (and the source, among other things, of the doctrine of habeas corpus). And in January 1649, Charles would lose his head under a Parliamentary order that accused him of tyranny, a charge of misrule and abrogation of his subjects' freedom.

Theological disputes further complicate the idea of freedom in this period. It is one thing to sort through the competing claims of the "polymorphic body politic," and quite another to consider whether fallen souls have any free will, and therefore any inherent ability to make autonomous choices on their own behalf, a prerequisite to political freedom. The question of free will was of course one of the principal controversies of the Reformation.[4] By the time of the early Stuarts, however, Protestant thinkers who followed Luther and Calvin in denying the ability of a person to choose salvation, nonetheless allowed for free choice in the ordinary motions of daily life. William Perkins, for example, a late Elizabethan former Catholic and a Protestant apologist whom Milton much admired, distinguished between our physical and ethical agency, which we retain after the Fall, and our spiritual agency, which original sin has lost us absolutely: "Human actions are such as are common to all men good and bad, as to speak and use reason, the practice of all mechanical and liberal arts, and the outward performance of Civil and Ecclesiastical duties, as to come to the Church, to speak and preach the word, to reach out the hand to receive the Sacrament, and to lend the ear to listen outwardly to that which is taught. And hither we may refer the outward actions of civil virtues: as namely Justice, temperance, gentleness, and liberality. And in these also we join with Rome and say (as experience teacheth) that men have a natural freedom of the will, to put them or not to put them in execution."[5]

With this confluence of political and religious complexity, it is no surprise that the early to mid-seventeenth century was a time of disagreement and turmoil over ideas of freedom, which would eventually (through John Locke, Thomas Jefferson, and others) become a centerpiece of English-speaking cultural self-definition. Milton is the first important writer in English-speaking culture to put ideas of freedom at the center of almost everything he writes. His self-described devotion to liberty, "religious, domestic or private, and civil," pervades his prose and is at the core of *Paradise Lost*.[6] So much is commonplace. What is less well understood is how Milton invites understanding of what he means by liberty, and not only invites understanding, but urges his reader's enactment of the liberty he describes.[7] The story of Abdiel, a narrative within the narrative, is told by the Archangel Raphael to Adam as part of God's care to inform his human creation fully. Abdiel's brief appearance exemplifies the choice Adam does not make, and the reader is encouraged to judge the angel's circumstances, decision, and its consequences against Adam's. In that judgment, the reader enacts the liberty Milton advocates, and the ambiguities that surround the question of a fortunate fall permit an uncoerced judgment, a legitimate freedom. In this story, Milton invites his reader to step beyond the conflicts of his own day, to visit the fundamental choices that underlie both theological and political freedom.

A caveat: exemplary as Abdiel is to Adam, and both Abdiel and Adam to Milton's reader, the parallels are necessarily inexact. Abdiel's angelic nature is characteristically intuitive while Adam's is characteristically rational, and the choices of prelapsarian angel and man are of a different order—both more free and more consequential—than they are for Milton's postlapsarian reader. Milton and his internal narrator, Raphael, acknowledge the problem but assert the utility of comprehensible illustrations:

> What surmounts the reach
> Of human sense I shall delineate so,
> By lik'ning spiritual to corporal forms,
> As may express them best, though what if Earth
> Be but the shadow of Heav'n, and things therein
> Each t'other like, more than on earth is thought?
> (5.571–76)

"What if," indeed. This deliberate uncertainty demands and therefore liberates individual judgment in the exercise of interpretive choice. Both Raphael and the narrator of *Paradise Lost* suspend the reader a step above simple didactic narration. Rhetorical and structural devices still create the context from which the reader will make interpretive choices. They literally *inform* those choices, creating the opportunity for the knowledgeable choice that, in Milton's view, separates liberty from heedless license.[8]

The formal situating of Abdiel's story is a case in point. Abdiel appears and disappears within three hundred lines of *Paradise Lost*. However, as Joseph Summers observed, Abdiel's resistance to Satan's rebellion comes at the structural center of the first (ten-book) edition of *Paradise Lost* (1667), and remains central in the twelve-book version (1671).[9] The exemplum begins about one hundred lines from the end of Book 5 and continues through another two hundred lines at the beginning of Book 6. At the outset, Abdiel is an obscure angel among Lucifer's group in heaven ("who under me their banners wave," 5.687) and responds naively to Beelzebub's call to gather and prepare for a visit from the newly pronounced Messiah. Abdiel shortly emerges from his obscurity to proclaim, with intuitive clarity, against the fallen Lucifer's dangerous plans. As creatures beyond temporal reasoning, angels' logic should not be sequential or disjunctive, yet that is the rhetoric Abdiel encounters and resists.

The archangel henceforth known as Satan has turned preparation for the Messiah's visit into an insinuating invitation to rebellion. He says he has gathered his forces

> to consult how we may best
> With what may be devis'd of honours new
> Receive him coming to receive from us
> Knee-tribute yet unpaid, prostration vile,
> Too much to one, but double how endur'd,
> To one and to his image now proclaim'd?
> (5.779–84)

From an assumption of tribute due to the Messiah, Satan has moved with breathless speed to a new assumption: that tribute to God is "vile," and doubly so if it must now include the Messiah. He goes on to appeal to the angels' sense of individual dignity, suggesting that angels are equal to the Messiah and even to God. At the same time, he is careful to insist that angels among themselves are

> not equal all, yet free,
> Equally free; for Orders and Degrees
> Jar not with liberty, but well consist.
> (5.791–93)

Nonetheless,

> Who can in reason then or right assume
> Monarchie over such as live by right
> His equals, if in power or splendor less,
> In freedom equal?
> (5.794–97)

From an intuitive truth, that both God and the angels are free, Satan argues that angels are therefore equal to God and His Son, even if they are "in power or splendor less." Satan as putative monarch must maintain his own hierarchic preeminence even as he denies the fundamental preeminence of God and the Son. The conclusions do not follow the premises, but the most basic premise, that all are free, is enticingly true. From this Satan exhorts his followers to exercise their freedom by disobeying God, by seeing themselves as "being ordain'd to govern, not to serve" (5.802).

Of all the gathered angels, "innumerable as the stars of night" (5.745), only one speaks up. "In a flame of zeal severe" (5.807), Abdiel perfectly judges Satan's rhetoric: "O argument blasphemous, false and proud!" (5.809). It is "blasphemous" because it denies the primacy of God, asserting that, since both are "free," the Creator is equal to his creation.[10] It is "false" because it argues that angels will somehow be demeaned and oppressed by being asked to obey an "equal," although what God has actually offered is a closer angelic relation to the deity by uniting them with the godhead through the Son, who, as Abdiel intuits, was God's agent of creation (5.835–44). Satan's argument is "proud" because it advocates placing the disobedient self above God.

Milton resisted bishops and monarch, serving the parliamentary government and then Lord Protector Cromwell during the interregnum. Abdiel's argument in favor of divine monarchy would therefore seem to fly in the face of Milton's own experience, but, as Roger Lejosne points out, Abdiel's arguments, with their tantalizing echoes of Milton's intellectual adversary Salmasius, confirm the unique kingship of the Son of God.[11] Even through Milton's republican partisanship, he saw himself as a singular voice of conscience against the easily swayed mobs, whether royalist or puritan. Abdiel, in his courageous isolation, is therefore Milton's kind of rebel-prophet:

> The flaming Seraph fearless, though alone
> Encompass'd round with foes, thus answerd bold.
> O alienate from God, O spirit accurst,
> Forsak'n of all good; I see thy fall
> Determind, and thy hapless crew involv'd
> In this perfidious fraud, contagion spred
> Both of thy crime and punishment.
>
> (5.875–81)

Abdiel's prophetic rhetoric invites the reader's questions: how does he know Satan will fall and "contagion spred"? Milton seems to suggest (but not demand) that we see Abdiel's vision as a function of his obedience to God. As long as he remains obedient, his angelic nature with its intuitive apprehension of truth remains intact. Satan's fall into self is a fall into the narrower confines of temporal logic; to Abdiel, the false logic itself shows Satan's "fall / Determind."

Book 5 concludes with Abdiel, "among the faithless, faithful only he" (5.897), moving through the crowd's "hostile scorn," to turn his back "on those proud Towers to swift destruction doomed" (5.903, 907). This might have been the end of his story, or it might have concluded, as an afterthought, with the brief mention of Abdiel near the middle of Book 6 where he is given a moment of recognition amid hordes of other unnamed angels fighting faithfully the war in heaven. There we find him overthrowing three of those former colleagues who jeered him on his way from Satan back to God:

> Nor stood unmindful *Abdiel* to annoy
> The Atheist crew, but with redoubl'd blow
> *Ariel* and *Arioc,* and the violence
> Of *Ramiel* scorcht and blasted overthrew.

The narrator, Raphael, continues his story noting that he could name others just like Abdiel but it would be beside the point.

> I might relate of thousands, and thir names
> Eternize here on Earth: but those elect
> Angels contented with thir fame in Heav'n
> Seek not the praise of men.
>
> (6.369–76)

After this brief moment of battle, Abdiel appears no more in Raphael's narrative nor in *Paradise Lost.*

There is more, however, that Raphael (and Milton) want to show Adam (and the reader) about the virtues of obedience. By the time he fades back into the crowd, Abdiel has not only illustrated courage in the face of mob psychology but also the personal consequences of the choice to stand. Book 6 begins with the cheers of the faithful at Abdiel's return, as "on the sacred hill / They led him high applauded" (6.25–26). In this moment of approval, Raphael presents Abdiel's obedience as the object lesson for Adam and Milton's reader. "Servant of God, well done," says the the "voice / From midst a Golden Cloud" (6.30, 28–29). He has gone from the jeers of one crowd to the approbation of another, but more importantly he has earned and confirmed his own name (Abdiel means "servant of God"). He has, ironically, fulfilled what Satan's temptation to rebellion claimed to provide: freedom and individual dignity. By standing, Abdiel has exercised his freedom and affirmed his personal strength. By serving God, he governs himself and achieves his fame.

As Raphael invites Adam, so Milton invites the reader to understand what, exactly, Abdiel has done well, and why it is so important. The message is one of individual courage. As Raphael stresses to Adam that the power to stand or fall resides individually in him, so Abdiel

> single hast maintained
> Against revolted multitudes the Cause
> Of Truth.
>
> (6.30–32)

As if to underscore the difficulty of such a task, the voice of God acknowledges that Abdiel has met the charge of obedience in the most difficult

circumstance. In the face of Satan's enticing rhetoric and the most severe
peer pressure, he has

> for the testimonie of Truth . . . born
> Universal reproach, far worse to bear
> Then violence: for this was all thy care
> To stand approv'd in sight of God, though Worlds
> Judg'd thee perverse.
>
> (6.33–37)

Unfallen Adam cannot imagine that it will be difficult to obey God
(5.512–18). It seems right and natural to him. Abdiel's moment of glory is
an admonition to all who think obedience to God is easy. What may seem
simple is filled with temptation and adversity, and "Worlds" may judge
you "perverse." Perhaps because it is easier for Milton's fallen reader than
for unfallen Adam to understand the temptations that lead away from
God, Milton chooses to underscore the rewards of standing as well as the
dangers of falling.

Abdiel receives as his reward not only God's praise and that of his (obedient) peers, but the particular righteous pleasure of striking the first blow
against his adversary. In the process, the obedient angel counters Satanic
falsehood with God's truth and flings phrases that, since *Paradise Lost* began
properly in medias res, we know will haunt Satan's fall. Satan was the master
of rhetoric in Book 5, but here in Book 6 Abdiel gets the good lines:

> This is servitude,
> To serve the unwise, or him who hath rebell'd
> Against his worthier, as thine now serve thee,
> Thy self not free, but to thy self enthralled.
> . . . .
> Reign thou in Hell thy Kingdom, let mee serve
> In Heav'n God ever blest.
>
> (6.178–81, 183–82)

At last, midway through the epic, we have the response to Satan's glamorous declaration that it is "better to reign in Hell, then serve in Heaven"
(1.263). More poignantly, perhaps, Abdiel has also prophesied the self-
enthralled Satan: "which way I flie is Hell; my self am Hell" (4.75). More
than the blow that Abdiel strikes providing Satan's first setback and his
first pain, these words will resonate through the fallen condition.

Abdiel's story is deeply embedded in the texture of Milton's narrative; it is a tale within a tale within a tale. Milton tells of Raphael's visit
to Adam, Raphael tells Adam of the war in heaven, which in turn contains this small narrative of obedience, surrounded by rebellion and

divine triumph. Raphael's narrative is itself constructed like a Chinese box: it begins and ends with the elevation of the Son, includes within it rebellion first verbal then violent, and includes within that rebellion Abdiel's rebellion against the rebels. Like the allegorizing of sin and death, Raphael's structural artifice draws attention to itself, focusing Adam's attention on the center, Abdiel's story, where the true moral for Adam resides.

But as we move out from the structural center to the wider stories, what are we to make of Raphael's description of the war in heaven and of the Messiah's elevation and ultimate triumph? Milton has accomplished something unexpected with his boxes—he has created not a static balance, but a dynamic energy that both propels the larger narrative and exemplifies it. What is true for Abdiel is always true, even as he recedes from the fame of Raphael's earthly tale to the enigmatic but absolute fame of heaven, with which the "elect Angels" remain "contented" (6.374–75).

This apparently marginal character, embedded in a larger and more complex narrative, is example and foil for both Satan and Adam. His very marginality makes his heroism the more pronounced. Surely if the least of the angels can stand up to one of the greatest, then the originary and therefore greatest of mankind can stand up to a fallen angel and, even more, the fall of his own presumed inferior, Eve. Abdiel's small story and great victory accentuate Adam's grand story and pitiful defeat. Adam does not stand in the face of Eve's fall.

So Adam falls, but might his fall be fortunate? God in *Paradise Lost* is ultimately "Merciful over all his works, with good / Still overcoming evil" (12.565–66). Fallen Adam, to whom the Archangel Michael gives a vision of God's plan for redemption, wonders logically

> Whether I should repent me now of sin
> By me done and occasioned, or rejoice
> Much more, that much more good thereof shall spring.
> (12.474–76)

The story of Abdiel and its surrounding context says no; to fall is to fail. Milton's angelic narrators, Raphael in Books 5 and 8 and Michael in Book 12, seem to offer contradictory visions of the happiest human condition.

Raphael introduces his narration of the war in heaven with an admonition to Adam:

> Attend: that thou art happy, owe to God;
> That thou continu'st such, owe to thyself,

> That is, to thy obedience; therein stand.
> (5.520–22)

Through the story that follows, Raphael stresses two points: all of God's creatures have free will and are free to stand in happiness or fall into misery, and it is far better to stand than to fall. God's favorable judgment of Abdiel confirms it ("this was all thy care / To stand approv'd in sight of God"). Before he leaves Adam, Raphael reiterates the warning even more pointedly:

> Be strong, live happie, and love, but first of all
> Him whom to love is to obey, and keep
> His great command; take heed least Passion sway
> Thy Judgment to do aught, which else free will
> Would not admit; thine and of all thy Sons
> The weal or woe in thee is plac't; beware.
> (8.633–38)

By the time the reader comes to Adam's enraptured recognition of God's mercy at the end of Book 12, it is easy to forget Raphael's insistence and Abdiel's example that it is better to stand. As Raphael concludes his warning in Book 8, the choice truly is Adam's own and, with Raphael's story and explicit warnings, Adam is presented as complete and sufficient to make that choice correctly:

> . . stand fast; to stand or fall
> Free in thine own Arbitrement it lies.
> Perfet within, no outward aid require;
> And all temptation to transgress repel.
> (8.640–43)

Michael, on the other hand, reveals to Adam the biblical plan that culminates in the incarnation, sacrifice, and resurrection of the Son of God. Adam learns what the reader has known since the council in heaven in Book 3, that "Heav'nly love shall outdo Hellish hate," that mankind will be raised with the Son, whose "Humiliation shall exalt / With [him his] Manhood also to this throne" (3.298, 313–14). Further, as Michael tells Adam, the final judgment will transform the earth beyond even its prelapsarian joys. At that moment the Messiah shall again come down from heaven,

> With glory and power to judge both quick and dead,
> To judge th'unfaithful dead, but to reward
> His faithful, and receave them into bliss,
> Whether in Heav'n or Earth, for then the Earth

> Shall be all Paradise, far happier place
> Then this of Eden, and far happier daies.
>
> (12.460–65)

This vision prompts Adam to see that his fall will bring "To God more glory, more good will to Men / From God, and over wrath grace shall abound" (12.477–78).

Even so, Adam claims to have learned that "to obey is best" (12.561). Few things are stressed so thoroughly in *Paradise Lost*, and nothing else is so purposefully centered, as this message: God's creatures have both the free will and sufficient strength to make the right choices. However mercifully God overcomes evil by the good of his redemptive plan, there is presumably nothing fortunate about the Fall itself nor is it inevitable. What is fortunate is not the Fall but rather God's willingness to overcome the evil of man's disobedience, despite the inevitable consequences.

Yet *Paradise Lost* is not oppressively didactic, directing the reader to an authorial conclusion. Instead it invites the exercise of personal freedom, political and religious, that is the work's subject. The choices we make, Milton's narrative argues, derive from our free will but affect a community, present and future. The model of Abdiel—marginal character at the center of the work—informs the reader's own set of choices about the more central examples of Satan, Adam, and Eve. God's transforming mercy at the end of the work may, on the other hand, confirm not just the similarities between Abdiel's situation and Adam's, but its differences. While both angel and man are undeceived, the temptation may be greater for Adam than for Abdiel, as individual passion may be a greater temptation than peer pressure. The point is arguable, however, and that, I would argue, is the point. In *Paradise Lost,* Milton invites the reader not only to see the value of liberty, and its potential loss in choosing away from God, but also to exercise that liberty. Is it better to stand than to fall? Of course. Now that the world is fallen, is it possible to find "a Paradise within [us], happier farr" (12.587)? Of course, given Milton's vision of a merciful God, but what came naturally and easily before the fall comes with great difficulty after. Abdiel is a constant reminder, if we choose to believe it, that it is possible to know good by knowing good, and that we do not have to fall into evil to know good.

As so often in *Paradise Lost*, either/or propositions are a challenge to see either/and. It is both better to stand, and better to seek a Paradise within, happier far. In the supreme paradox of the epic work, we are invited both to choose, and not to choose, to affirm Abdiel's choice, and to affirm the necessary choices of our fallen condition as well. Like Adam and Eve at the end of *Paradise Lost*, the world is all before us, to choose is to be human, but Providence remains our guide. Milton's narrative places each reader, like Abdiel and Adam, at both the margin and the center of his vision of God's plan and in a dialectic of unfolding, individual choices.

By the time Milton published *Paradise Lost*, his hope for an English Republic, and for the fullest opportunity for the exercise of individual freedom, seemed forever deferred. When Charles II restored the English monarchy in 1660, those who executed his father paid with their lives, and Milton, whose *Eikonoklastes* (1649) and other works on behalf of Cromwell's government made him a visible representative of the old regime, was lucky to escape with his. Yet if the basic pieces of political power appeared the same in the 1660s as they had some fifty years earlier, the fluid relations among Crown, peerage, gentry, and merchants were already changing in a direction that would have pleased Milton. His principal gift to the process turned out not to be the two versions of *The Ready and Easy Way to Establish a Free Commonwealth*, desperate arguments published on the very eve of the Restoration in 1660, but the voices and examples of freedom in *Paradise Lost*, Abdiel's centrally among them. Instead of placing cultural power in court masques and in the co-optation of the peerage, Milton's work invites the individual reader and the individual hero to make choices founded on conscience and responsibility. In centering individual freedom, Milton changes the cultural dynamics.

NOTES

1. Leeds Barroll, *Anna of Denmark, Queen of England: A Cultural Biography* (Philadelphia: University of Pennsylvania Press, 2001), 2.

2. See, e.g., Joel Hurstfield, *Freedom and Corruption in Elizabethan England* (London: Jonathan Cape, 1971), 11–76, and, for a somewhat different view that gives more importance to Parliament, G. R. Elton, "The Rule of Law in Sixteenth-Century England," in *Tudor Men and Institutions: Studies in English Law and Government*, ed. Arthur J. Slavin (Baton Rouge: Louisiana State University Press, 1972), 265–94. For a summary of the destabilization process, see Gerald R. Cragg, *Freedom and Authority: A Study of English Thought in the Early Seventeenth Century* (Philadelphia: Westminster Press, 1975), esp. 67–68 and 301–2.

3. James I, "A Speach to the Lords and Commons of the Parliament at Whitehall, on Wednesday the xxi of March, Anno 1609" in *The Political Works of James I*, ed. C. H. McIlwain (Cambridge, MA: Harvard University Press, 1918), 309.

4. See, e.g., Erasmus, *The Free Will*, and Luther, *The Bondage of the Will*, in *Erasmus-Luther: Discourse on Free Will*, trans. and ed. Ernst F. Winter (New York: Continuum, 1999).

5. William Perkins, *A Reformed Catholike* [1597] (1605 *Works*, Lll5r-Sss6v), Mmm2r. I have modernized the spelling.

6. John Milton, from "The Second Defense of the English People," in C. A. Patrides, ed. *John Milton: Selected Prose* (Columbia: University of Missouri Press, 1985), 71. *Paradise Lost* and all poetry quotations are from *The Complete Poems of John Milton*, ed. John Leonard (New York: Penguin, 1998).

7. I have elsewhere suggested some of the rhetorical techniques by which Milton (and his "sage and serious" predecessor, Edmund Spenser) invite readers to make choices, and

therefore enact a vision of freedom as knowledgeable choice. I have also explored how narrative poets who preceded Milton, notably Spenser and Aemilia Lanyer, use marginal figures to center their themes. Here I am interested in how Milton adds the technique of centering a marginal figure to his rhetorical arsenal in service to engaging an active reader. See "Elective Poetics in Milton's Prose," in *Politics, Poetics and Hermeneutics in Milton's Prose,* ed. David Loewenstein and James Turner (Cambridge: Cambridge University Press, 1990), 193–211; *Aemilia Lanyer: A Renaissance Woman Poet* (New York: Oxford University Press, 1999), chap. 2, "Spenser and Lanyer"; "Making Free with Poetry: Spenser and the Rhetoric of Choice," *Spenser Studies* 16 (2001).

   8. E.g., in *Areopagitica*: "As therefore the state of man now is [i.e., fallen], what wisdom can there be to choose, what continence to forbear, without the knowledge of evil?" *Selected Prose,* 213. Cf. also Sonnet 11, "I did but prompt the age to quit their clogs," in anger at the uninformed:

> [They] bawl for freedom in thir senseless mood,
>   And still revolt when Truth would set them free,
>   Licence they mean, when they cry liberty,
>   For who loves that must first be wise and good.
>   (*Complete Poems,* 82)

   9. Joseph Summers, *The Muse's Method* (London: Chatto & Windus, 1962), 112–13. In the twelve-book version, "the significance of [Abdiel's] action remains, but the emphasis has changed; for in the final version the War in Heaven and the Creation of the world are clearly at the center. Milton seems to have discovered that in the poem which he had written the true center was not the angelic exemplum of man's ways at their most heroic, but the divine image of God's ways at their most Providential."

   10. Satan disputes the very notion of creation. "We know no time when we were not as now; / Know none before us, self-begot, self-rais'd / By our own quick'ning power" (5.859–61). John Rogers makes the point that this was not as outrageous a position as it may sound, given Milton's interest in vitalism, or the inherent quickening power of matter (*Matter of Revolution: Science, Poetry and Politics in the Age of Milton* [Ithaca, NY: Cornell University Press, 1996], 124.) Milton appears to assume, however, that the unfallen created nature will intuit its own creation, as even Adam is able to do (8.277–82).

   11. Roger Lejosne, "Milton, Satan, Salmasius and Abdiel," in *Milton and Republicanism,* ed. David Armitage, Armand Himy, and Quentin Skinner (Cambridge: Cambridge University Press, 1995), 106–17. "If the sole truly legitimate king was the 'son of God,' then whatever Salmasius and the other royalists said of earthly kings was true of him, but of him only" (116).

Artificial Intensity:
The Optical Technologies of
Personal Reality Enhancement

Barbara Maria Stafford

FOR A LONG TIME, LEEDS BARROLL HAS DEMONSTRATED that literature was a branch of history and history was a branch of literature. His myriad reflections on Shakespeare and, more broadly, on the political culture of the Renaissance reveal that both kinds of authorial practices were part of the same craft. The combined artisanal/theoretical activities of the dramatist in the early modern period—his immersion in tangible realities as well as the business of mimesis—influenced the choice of my homage to Leeds.

For, I argue, virtuoso products of art increasingly fabricated in the early modern period were pervaded by similar intersecting domains of trade, industry, and magical technology. Images, especially those generated with the aid of optical devices, possessed poetic, religious, prophetic, and visionary qualities. Just as the focus of the literary artist was fixed on an ideal grounded in more than impartial copying, the visual artist was bent on putting the real in question by exploring the hyper-real. That is, from painting to print-making to perspective box constructing, we are offered insight into how the observer is constantly crossing frontiers and extending outwards the limits and possibilities of vision. I propose a subjective history of instrumentation, then, as opposed to the standard view of instruments in the objective construction of knowledge.

Aby Warburg proposed that visual images—that complex knot of imaginative spatial forms ranging from high art to popular media—rouse the eyes into action.[1] But these fleeting shapes and mutable figures also excite our memory, consciousness, and desire by their ability to intensify, and so alter, reality. Not surprisingly, then, such vivid apparitions—spun merely from light, shadow, and color—engage the total person at the sensory, psychological, and social levels (see figure 21).

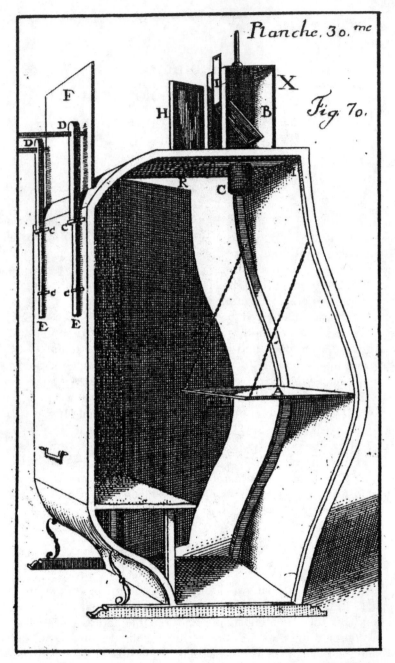

Figure 21. Camera Obscura. From Gravesande, *Essai de perspective,* **plate 30. Courtesy of the Research Library, The Getty Research Institute, Los Angeles.**

Figure 22. Magic Lantern (Lanterne magique à Alexandre). Chalk Lithograph with scraping. Courtesy of the Research Library, The Getty Research Institute, Los Angeles.

When *optical devices*—such as mirrors, lenses, magic lanterns, peepshow boxes, or computer screens—are placed between our eyes and the world, "natural" images become ramped up into high fidelity. Perception-amplifying technology is entangled with quests for otherworldly revelation, escapist entertainment, and worldly pursuits of knowledge. It lures us with the prospect of boundlessness, immediacy, connectedness. Viewers are swiftly displaced from their normal surroundings and effortlessly thrust into a synthetic or better-than-ordinary hyperrealm.

The exhibition *Devices of Wonder: From the World in a Box to Images on a Screen* offers a haunted view of eye-machines, old and new (see figure 22).[2] This installation has less to do with tracing the function of modern scientific equipment in art—from the futurist and constructivist movements and their enthrallment with machines to kinetic sculpture, space imaging, artificial intelligence, and CAVE Automatic Virtual Environment VR systems[3]—than with exposing the enduring fascination for personal-reality enhancers. Part of what it means to be human has increasingly involved the instrumentalization of the biological self. We routinely construct our emotional and cognitive states not just from the inside out but from the

Fig. 13—The Elephant, and

Fig 14—The Bird, and

Fig. 15—The Cat, were perfected by Trewey.

Figure 23. Trewey, *Art of Shadowgraphy*, book plate 5. Courtesy of the Research Library, The Getty Research Institute, Los Angeles.

outside in—with gadgetized additives. Yet since the sixteenth century, mind-bending apparatus has been busy altering solid bodies into more vibrant virtual events. These dazzling artificial entities are made, not begotten.[4]

We also wanted to propose the paradox that, frequently, what persists within the cultural imaginary is the obsolete artifact most remote from the future-obsessed present. Even the most dead-seeming media hint at an undercurrent of unsatisfied desires still alive, but submerged, in the new media world. The potency of sense-extending instruments links today's motorized joysticks, mobile mouses, and haptic touchpads to the "optical contrivances" of a prior, curiosity-ridden age.[5]

Ten years ago, I was very fortunate to be invited by Salvatore Settis to become a Getty Scholar. I had just completed my *Artful Science* book. It investigated a host of interactive special-effects gadgets—first described in late Renaissance books on natural magic and cresting with the experimental "mathematical recreations" of the Enlightenment—that distracted in order to instruct. These illustrated works dramatized, in spectacular demonstrations, the uncanny exchanges between visible and invisible forces harnessed by showmen through refined, if eccentric, equipment. Simultaneously occult and practical, entertaining and educational, these ancestors of today's wireless assistive technologies were smart tools to conjure by and think with (see figure 23).[6]

During my year's residency at the Getty, my greatest good luck was to meet and eventually collaborate with Frances Terpak and Isotta Poggi. Fran, a historian of photography and curator of Special Collections, had recently acquired key pieces from Werner Nekes's important collection for the Getty Research Institute. These constituted a delightful, if daunting, accumulation of seventeenth-, eighteenth-, and nineteenth-century optical toys, animated games, and boxed instruments generally classified as "precinematic." Isotta Poggi—soon to become master of databases—had just gotten a degree in library and information science. She was faced with the Herculean task of helping to strike order in this mountain of unruly material, stored in a forbidding warehouse on Euclid Street in Santa Monica.

We three were to spend many months navigating that sealed metaverse bristling with tantalizing plastic-shrouded machinery *à la Christo*. In retrospect, I believe it was the frequent immersion in that cavernous, computer-game-like space (a bit like *Dungeons and Dragons!*)—teeming with enigmatic and alluring objects—which convinced us that reality has long had a competitor.

Initially, the idea of the exhibition had been simple enough. Using the former Nekes material, plus major items from the Getty Rare Books Department, and the Painting and Decorative Arts sections of the Getty Museum—fleshed out by key loans from around the world—we wanted to blast these complex and ingenious artifacts out of the developmental narrative of film, an exclusive story of progress which tends to see such devices only as imperfect stages on the road to moving pictures and convincing simulations. Optical technology is a vast and diverse region. It contains legions. We hoped to recuperate glimmers of its multiple functions and multiple realities, its polyopticalities, by demonstrating the vicissitudes of instrumentation's supernatural, wonder-inducing, and knowledge-producing evolution that have become obscured over time.

As our labors continued in the *Wunderkammer*-warehouse on Euclid—stocked with secret marvels occluded from sight—we came to realize, however, that even the most arcane mechanism is as much an extension of as a stand-in for reality. Visual technology has been used in collaborative, intimate ways for centuries. Among its irresistible attractions, apparently, is the promise both to extend us prosthetically and to deliver transcendence.

This almost viral draw of instruments down the ages was to become an important concept in the exhibition. The folks at Microsoft, DreamWorks, and Electronic Arts may be at the leading edge of breaking the boundaries of the monitor, but the tendency of fictional experience to bleed into real life and real life to emancipate itself through sublime gadgetry started much earlier. From rococo automata—rouged, powdered, and bewigged—to Steven Spielberg's and Stanley Kubrick's *A. I.*—with its winsome robot child—biology has been steadily leaking into cybernetics.

Both early modern and posthuman engineered organisms resonate with this symbolism of domesticated technology. Whether we consider Vaucanson's refined eating, digesting, and defecating *Duck* (1733–34), Von Oeckelin's virtuoso android *Clarinetist* (1838), or Spielberg's industrial prototype, David—waiting to be persuaded by his programming that he exists in the flesh—they inhabit a familiar, if ambiguous, informatic universe. In the digital hereafter—just as in the rhapsodic rhetoric of virtual reality—the goal is to extend the rule of mind over matter. As David Melville mystically said, "the idea is to have a function without the object."[7]

SCENES FROM THE EXHIBITION

Perhaps only contemporary viewers can fully appreciate that the early-modern cabinet of wonders is no mere period piece. Its global project to order an actual complex world of information, coming from many different fields and standpoints, still beckons and vexes us. This is why the first room of the exhibition contains a fully deployed and retrofitted seventeenth-century *Wunderschrank*. The mysterious gatherings concealed inside are hinted at by the encyclopedic mountain of creation's marvels crowning the top.

The remainder of the gallery space—all six thousand square feet—is a voyage of discovery in pursuit of the afterlife of the singular components in this universal toolbox and the optical collecting devices they provoked. The visual dynamics of this museum-in-miniature[8]—in which apparently unrelated objects are juxtaposed to encourage the search after deeper resemblances—underpin the spatial organization of the exhibition. Merritt Price, Brian Consadine, and Tim McNeil constructed a visible environment where the concept of analogue and digital media crisscrossing in time and space can be experienced as well as imagined. As in phylogenetics, which tries to show how species—both extant and extinct—are related,[9] the potency of these objects derives less from sheer number than from their complex branchings, surprising groupings, and multitudinous interactions with the changing environment.

Both a crafty *container*—secretively housing a microcosm of natural and artificial prodigies—and an absolute *instrument*—drawing into itself no less than everything—the *Wunderschrank* invites the user to explore an uncharted universe by mapping its disjointed fragments into a network of correspondences.[10] This experimental procedure of handling or performing the elusive contents in order to understand them connects the *Wunderschrank* to the domains of scientific investigation, commerce, and theater. As late as the 1770s, Sir Ashton Lever (1729–88), founder of the *Holosphusikon* in Leicester Square, London, was described by a contemporary "as busy in the arrangement of his curiosities as a tradesman in his shop."[11]

Collections of rarities: shells, gems, coins, sculpture, painting, clocks, and automata produced new kinds of aesthetic objects the way "windows," web pages, and avatars proliferate in our digital culture. Transforming the relationship of human beings to matter, these struggles to uncover general categories or cognitive patterns from myriad particulars were signs of the turn toward empirical observation emerging in the sixteenth and seventeenth centuries.[12]

An intersensual medium for personal realization and transformation, such complex assemblages constituted a cultural inventory and artisanal archive exposing the collective heritage of nature's and humanity's greatest handiwork. What hasn't been remarked, however, is that these amazingly wrought substances also pointed elsewhere. They broadened horizons by suggesting the existence of an intangible and undiscovered region lying *beyond* the boundaries of the unaided senses and accessible only through optical devices. A land of wonders and secrets—cloaked by the mists that normally obscure human vision—awaited this clearing of passages through instruments so as to penetrate the concealed core of existing things or open up alternative realities.

Cabinets and instruments share certain *formal* properties. As A. S. Byatt said about the crammed display window of Puck's Girdle—a traveler's curiosity shop specializing in booking uncommon journeys—it was "deep in small things."[13] The practice of confining and isolating diminutive rarities in a compressed space (ranging from Europe to China and Japan) intensifies the aura and strangeness of those objects. (Think of Joseph Cornell's hyperreal constructions—those densely packed shrines that transform discarded scraps into precious relics.)

Like the wooden cabinet with its squirreled-away oddities, optical devices similarly capture and frame transitory phenomena. Just as the *Wunderschrank* compartmentalizes the scattered bounty of the cosmos in niches and drawers to accentuate them, so instruments "box" a universe of disembodied images. The rush of space and time is stopped for an instant in flat and curved mirrors or halted temporarily inside the lenses of microscopes and telescopes letting us observe miniscule objects in great detail. Thus sharpened and concentrated, these alien visions appear doubly real and hallucinatory at the same time.

Excess drove the Baroque machinery of transcendence. Fantasy, religious anguish, and a parade of witty metamorphic devices blurred the lines between the natural and the supernatural. Instead of providing a smooth repetition of outward appearances, cylindrical and pyramidal mirrors exaggerated and tormented shapes. They thinned and thickened, fragmented and overturned regular forms, warping them beyond recognition into irregular or hybrid creatures only to miraculously restitute them again.

Bodily deformations and monstrous transformations shimmered in the glazed catoptrical cabinets of the Jesuits. Among the hundreds of "mathematical" mechanisms[14]—from the hydraulic to the magnetic—devised by the natural magician, Athanasius Kircher, for the Jesuit museum in the Collegio Romano, many were perception-altering crystalline boxes. These glassy metaphysical instruments, manipulated in ocular demonstrations, ingeniously probed the hidden workings of creation. Anamorphic apparatuses exposed secrets: whether—at the organic level—it happened to be the transposability of the human into the nonhuman, i.e., the biological into the geological; or, at the symbolic level, it was the revelation that fallen humanity inhabits an inverted moral universe whose skewed perspective must be righted by spiritual converting machines.

The ascent of glass in secular surroundings is evident in the wealthy residences proliferating throughout pre-Revolutionary Europe. Large mirrors—limpid and ripple-free—multiplied the flesh-and-blood occupants of Parisian salons and London drawing rooms generating bright companions, airy artificial persons that came and went according to the viewer's movements and position. Their cool presence intensified the emotional heat of the moment.[15] Not just a replicating technology but a taut coordinating system, bouncing reflections swiftly transfigured the material, spatial, and social dynamics of a room. The solid world of interior decoration generated an unstable, parallel land of illusion where light plays with everything it touches. Crisscrossing emanations sprang from gleaming woodwork and rebounded from shiny fixtures to optically network the home. During the Enlightenment, living quarters mimicked the practical magic of the laboratory. Projecting and focusing furnishings—concave or convex porcelain cups and saucers, knobby silver knives, and faceted crystal bowls—were the entrancing stuff of experiment.

Shadow arises from the expanding and contracting effects of light swiftly traveling over a surface. Shades are phantasms. These faint and fleeting apparitions suddenly climb the walls of a room or invade the hallucinatory chamber of the mind. They belong to a dark, urgent universe where people are trapped in spatial systems beyond their control. At the dawn of human history, sputtering torches magnified or diminished human and animal shapes inside dim caves. Modern projection technologies are the spectral descendants of this ancient shadow-show that cast mobile silhouettes, first on natural rock faces and later on muslin sheets and translucent screens. This distortion of translucent or volumetric forms into an opaque, mutant, or flat physiognomy continues on and off the computer screen.[16] We see it in the liquid architecture of Greg Lynn's digitized folds and blobs, in the canted floors and walls of Morphosis, and in Kara Walker's mordant caricature cutouts of black and white racial stereotypes.

David Hockney is right to see various sixteenth- and seventeenth-century lenses as having developed, in part, from mirrors.[17] The concave mirror (Archimedes' "burning mirror" used to incinerate a fleet of ships by intensifying the sun's rays), especially, has the wondrous property of projecting images as well as reflecting them. This amazing "painterly" ability to thrust the three-dimensional—and even extradimensional—world onto a two-dimensional surface lurks behind a spate of mechanized projections creating entities separate from our bodies.

Magic lanterns, first referred to by the physicist Christiaan Huyghens, were primarily used to amaze and edify in the seventeenth century. Figures were painted on mica or glass slides and cast from a light-emitting box so as "to make strange things appear on a wall, very pretty." Like the *Wunderschrank,* these popular demonstrations conducted with the help of mechanical intermediaries opened up spaces of excess, flickering displays of worldly and otherworldly powers.

At first, the subjects were scary, rooted in the religious upheavals of the Reformation and Counter-Reformation, and invoked hellish regions: skeletons, devils, demons, phantoms. Later, they displayed exotic flora and fauna for the stay-at-home and views of distant lands for the would-be tourist without ever abandoning the destabilizing repertory of comical and frightening phantasmagoria. Projective technology also became a powerful tool in the Enlightenment critique of irrationalism, superstition, and the "despotic" alliance of wonder to thaumaturgy. It exposed the dangerous proximity of the visionary to the grotesque.

The craze for boxing light—as dematerialized colors, tones, and shifting sights—was fed by a succession of room-size and portable "dark chambers" in whose confines images glowed and sparkled with a preternatural clarity. The camera obscura—the poetic device probably used by Vermeer to paint his odd, yet measured, interiors that appear so easy to walk into[18]—is basically a dim booth equipped with an aperture that may or may not contain a rectifying lens. This cabinet for images meant-to-be-seen-in-the-dark compressed the ceaseless flow of visual representations coming from the outside world into an intense beam that projected them upside down on the back wall. The dreamy effect of such hovering phantoms—a sort of natural automaton—is at once filmy and lucid.

Smaller perspective boxes similarly play with disorienting and orienting illusions. From a predetermined angle—usually dictated by a peephole fitted with a lens—the viewer is rewarded with that rarest of visions: a perfect, spatially coherent artificial universe wrested from an imperfect world. Perspective—a theory of vision as well as a technique of pictorial representation founded on geometry—promises an essential or truthful depiction.

To the unequipped eye, the anamorphically painted interiors of these small boxes look chaotic. But since the composition is rooted in a mathematical system for rendering space, its elements are precisely locked together. So when the beholder shifts to the correct viewpoint, scrambled signals become magically aligned. An ideal invisible grid pulls disorder into order in a snap. These domestic microcosms are also allied with stage sets where actors, props, and scenery do not just copy reality but dramatize it. Like the *Wunderschrank,* the trompe l'oeil still lifes they contain embody a radicalization of naturalism, a better-than-real realism.

In the seventeenth century, perspective boxes remained elite objects elevating curiosity and interiority. By the eighteenth century, myriad pleated paper theaters—to be viewed with or without a box—popularized charming dumb shows on every conceivable topic, secular and profane, from the Lisbon earthquake to the interior of famous churches and notable museums. Mass-produced folding *Engelbrecht Theaters,* and their many variants and descendants, had the uncanny ability to have every shape appear both as its sculptural self in depth and as a flat silhouette. This simple toy was also a sophisticated apparatus that turned a sequence of images into a play. Such freestanding set pieces recall the "number operas" of the period where a chain of separate musical movements are linked together to form a dramatic "fabric."[19] Users were encouraged to imagine the sets from the inside by emotionally participating in a fictional story and animating the silent scenery.

Prints were often technically repurposed from their fine art categories into broader cultural applications. The *Guckkasten*—which wandered into the middle-class parlor from open-air fairs and markets—utilized pricked, hand-colored, varnished, and oiled engravings or etchings pirated from famous *vedusti* like Piranesi. Through a flourishing cottage industry, these opaque scenes were then tortured into transparency the way nineteenth-century photographs, originally documenting travel or destined for souvenir albums, could be altered into postcards.

Magic lanterns by night and *Guckkasten* by day provided thrilling intimacy with rootless visions projected from inside a sealed box. Commodious and episodic, these loosely linked collections of glowing images had no overall plot that rolled them into a single unified picture. Like camcorders, high-resolution television, and video games, these customized—but still circumscribed—do-it-yourself kits prefigured the impending privatization and internalization of mass media. While not yet a fulfillment of Ray Kurzweil's misty assertion that technology's rapid pace of change, so rapid, in fact, "that people may not notice it, because in its wake it will leave a very good facsimile of the real world,"[20] they forecast the ascent of the in-house electronic sanctuary. Ubiquitous computing, with its exaltation of the "aware user," and the emergence of "experience design," similarly promise an almost divine, direct interactivity at the interface. As in certain religious cults, personal experience is the ultimate form of credibility.

By contrast, the engulfing panorama looked ahead to the rise of streamlined industrial design. A new glass-and-iron building technology supported urban high-tech mass entertainments like the "all-view."[21] At the beginning of the nineteenth century, the development of the comprehensive wraparound picture redrew the boundaries between the painter, architect, engineer, inventor, and entrepreneur. Vast murals seamlessly collated and standardized the tinkered topographic *vedute* featured in hand-sized zograscopes and *optiques,* transforming them into hyperbolic collections in the round. An endless flow of metropolitan landmarks like the Crystal Palace, suburban landscapes of leisure from Naples to Hamburg, and grim battlefields like the frozen wastes that decimated the Bourbaki army in Switzerland (exhibited in Lucerne's famous panorama building and glimpsed in Jeff Wall's sweeping lightbox, *Restoration*) surged around viewers perambulating on an elevated platform and gazing down at the fray from above.

These immersive ensembles drowned the spectator in self-contained and pre-programmed ambient media—insulated from the polluted, crowded physical geography of the booming cities and manufacturing centers of the Victorian Age. Analogously, the encompassing electronic environment is often described as a noetic "new space"—woven from an infinity of invisible nets, webs, and threads—that both transcends mortal flesh and connects the far reaches of the globe.

At first blush, the relentless quest after augmenting digital technologies that insulate us from physical realities while vaulting us into the hyperreal must appear remote from the creaking wooden boxes, crude cardboard devices, and overt apparatuses of the premodern era. Yet a number of older and younger techno-artists are tapping into this rich repertory to escape the spate of rapidly morphing computer graphics spinning endless simulations of terrifyingly lifelike creatures and violently vivid mortal combat.

As part of his ongoing Roden Crater Project in the Arizona desert, James Turrell has produced a dreamlike series of three-dimensional "skyscapes" that demand leisurely viewing and tap into our reveries. These hovering video projections—literally boxing a translucent cube of luminous blue air— manage to be as immersive, and as contained, as the monumental color-field paintings of Ellsworth Kelly. Diana Thater's dioramic video of scudding clouds evokes the meteorology of cyberspace: either blank or shifting with the mounding nebulosities of electronic information.

Tiffany Holmes's computer and sensor-based installation, entitled *amaze@getty.org,* relies on liveware—that is, real-world and real-time viewer collaboration—not hardware. Hidden throughout the *Devices of Wonder* exhibition are tiny spy cameras that capture people looking at and interacting with other works in the show (e.g. multiplying spectacles, salon camera obscura, and the *Mondo Nuovo* peepshow). The live video is ported wirelessly into a computer that integrates the imagery into a large montage displayed on a plasma screen. The space around the plasma screen acts as the interface for the piece.

In its resting state, with no viewers in front, the screen displays a panoramic image of Robert Irwin's garden lying just outside the museum's walls. When a viewer approaches the screen the animation changes. Slowly, the video is fractured by small rectangles; as they multiply, the larger image of the gardens is replaced by smaller still images grabbed earlier by the hidden cameras. The longer the viewer stays to watch, the more fractured the panoramic image becomes. Conceptually, the piece draws on the metaphor of armchair travel, moving from material terrain into datasphere. The longer the viewer lingers in the gallery, the more she "travels" virtually, away from the seemingly infinite landscape into a series of highly localized spaces that ultimately incorporate the watching subject into their confines.

This multimedia installation thus links earlier optical technologies (*Wunderschrank,* mirror, camera obscura, Engelbrecht theater, panorama) with contemporary digital tools to create an interactive piece in which a coherent and collective field of vision (the big landscape) yields to a fragmented field of data (spy shots, maps, computer code). In the process, the viewer is made acutely aware how visual technology structures perception and how we structure visual technology. The observer of the projection not only becomes the observed, but also the creator of the rupturing tableaux.

BACK TO THE FUTURE

Recently, William Gibson declared that "the nonmediated world has become a country we cannot find our way back to." He goes on to say: "I don't think it's possible to know what we've lost, but there is a pervasive sense of loss, and a sense of Christmas morning at the same time."[22] The science fiction writer encapsulates our technological ambivalence in a nutshell. We seem to vacillate between elegy and marvel, estrangement and enthusiasm. But is such nostalgia accurate history? Was there ever a past free of optical technology, given that the eye was the first tool extending humans beyond the outer edge of their bodies? I have been arguing that visual devices have shaped our sense of interiority since the beginning.

Devices of Wonder explores the surprising age, depth, and complexity of the *mediated* world. It works to undo our forgetfulness by recognizing that visual technologies are both discrete implements, thriving within specific historical contexts, and interrelated events that become layered and superimposed over time. The pattern of intensifying reality, and the practice of visually or virtually collecting the world in some sort of integrating box, cross-link an array of apparatuses from the late Renaissance to the twenty-first century. By recovering a bit of the imagination and excitement aroused when these old, experience-augmenting gadgets were new, perhaps we can better understand why people now play multiuser global online games or animate and simulate galaxies of synthetic objects.

We live in an era that longs for direct interaction. The desire for faster links ranges from manipulating the interior of our brain through intimate neuroprostheses to accessing an interactive dimension in real time. This futuristic third space—whether diminutive or distributed—has many names: nanospace, cyberspace, hyperspace, data space, information space, netscape, ethernet, connective Web.[23] But this contemporary urgency for immediacy that, paradoxically, can only be achieved through media is not revolutionary. It evolved from a vast reservoir of earlier mechanisms casting the beholder into supernatural, spooky, and wondrous dimensions. There has always been something so beautiful, beguiling, or terrifying about technologically produced images that they make us believe in the existence of another reality. In this sense, the exhibition points to what *does* seem to be novel about current technology. Instead of extreme fictions breaking out of the monitor to merge symbiotically with reality, "legacy" applications possessed modest gifts of compression and intensification that were as limited, impermanent, and mysterious as life. Becoming aware of the huge corpus of devices can help us recognize the traditions that shape us. Then we can begin thinking of sensory technology as arguments that make serious claims on us, rather than just another set of options we might want to choose or not choose.

NOTES

An earlier version of this essay appeared as "Künstliche Intensität"—Bilden Instrumente und die Technologie der Verdichtung," in *Kunstkammer, Laboratorium, Bühne: Schauplätze des Wissens im 17. Jahrhundert,* edited by Helmar Schramm, Ludger Schwarte, Jan Lazardzig (Berlin: Walter de Gruyter, 2003), 339–58.

1. See Georges Didi-Huberman, "La tragedie de la culture: Warburg avec Nietzsche," in *Visio: Les statuts de l'image/The State of the Image* no. 4 (Winter 2000–2001), 5, 13.

2. See my introductory essay, "Revealing Technology/Magical Domains," in Barbara Maria Stafford, Frances Terpak, and Isotta Poggi, *Devices of Wonder: From the World in a Box to Images on a Screen,* an exhibition catalog (Los Angeles: Getty Museum of Art, 2001).

3. This has been done. See NTT's Intercommunication Center, in Tokyo's Shinjuku district. This gallery is dedicated exclusively to high-tech art and includes a timeline representing the history of technology in art. Also see the spate of recent shows devoted to new technology: *Bitstreams* at the Whitney Museum, *ArtCade* at the San Francisco Museum of Modern Art, *Game Show* at the Massachusetts Museum of Contemporary Art in North Adams (all these in the Spring/Summer of 2001).

4. See the illuminating discussion of the poet as maker in J. Leeds Barroll, *Artificial Persons: The Formation of Character in the Tragedies of Shakespeare* (Columbia: University of South Carolina Press, 1974), 4.

5. Barbara M. Benedict, *Curiosity: A Cultural History of Early Modern Inquiry* (Chicago: University of Chicago Press, 2001), 13.

6. See my *Artful Science: Enlightenment Entertainment and the Eclipse of Visual Education* (Cambridge, MA: MIT Press, 1994).

7. Quoted in Fred Moody, *The Visionary Position: The Inside Story of the Digital Dreamers Who Are Making VR A Reality* (New York: Times Books, 1999), 65.

8. As a comprehensive collection of singularities it resembles those "nouns of multitude," "group terms," and "terms of venery" analyzed by James Lipton in *An Exaltation of Larks: The Ultimate Edition* (New York: Viking Penguin, 1991), 5–6.

9. See Henry Gee, *In Search of Deep Time: Beyond the Fossil Record to A New History of Life* (New York: Free Press, 1999) on "cladistics" or phylogenetics which attempts to reconstruct the evolutionary relationship of organisms.

10. Roberto Calasso has spoken of poetry as "absolute literature." See his *Literature and the Gods* (New York: Alfred A. Knopf, 2001), 171. I take the *Wunderschrank* to operate in an analogously inclusive way.

11. Clare Haynes, "A 'Natural' Exhibitioner: Sir Ashton Lever and his *Holosphusikon,*" *British Journal for Eighteenth-Century Studies* 24 (Spring 2001): 3.

12. On the profound shift of early modern European culture toward material things and the impetus for this in a craft tradition, see the excellent essay by Pamela H. Smith, "Science and Taste: Painting, Passions, and the New Philosophy in Seventeenth-Century

Leiden," *Isis* 90 (1999): 421–461. Also see Lisa Jardine, *Ingenious Pursuits: Building the Scientific Revolution* (New York: Nan A. Talese, 1999), 7.

13. A. S. Byatt, *The Biographer's Tale* (New York: Alfred A. Knopf, 2001), 124.

14. Thomas L. Hankins and Robert J. Silverman, *Instruments and the Imagination* (Princeton, N. J.: Princeton University Press, 1995), 34. On the "mixed" domain of Jesuit mathematical tradition, see Amir R. Alexander, "Exploration Mathematics: The Rhetoric of Discovery and Rise of Infinitesimal Methods," *Configurations* 9 (Winter 2001): 3.

15. Lynn Hunt and Margaret Jacob, "The Affective Revolution in 1790s Britain," *Eighteenth-Century Studies* 34 (Summer 2001): 510–11, speak of the importance of a "pattern of affective experimentation," but they don't consider the role of instruments in furthering it.

16. Anthony Vidler, *Warped Space: Art, Architecture, and Anxiety in Modern Culture* (Cambridge, MA: MIT Press, 2000), 245.

17. David Hockney, "When the Mirror Becomes a Lens," essay-fax sent to Frances Terpak, January 5, 2001.

18. See the fine analysis by Philip Steadman, *Vermeer's Camera: Uncovering the Truth Behind the Masterpiece* (Oxford: Oxford University Press, 2001).

19. Peter Kivy, "Music in the Movies," in *Film Theory and Philosophy,* ed. Richard Aden and Murray Smith (Oxford: Clarendon Press, 1997), 310–13.

20. See www.kurzweilai.net.

21. Carla Yanni, *Nature's Museums: Victorian Science and the Architecture of Display* (Baltimore, MD: Johns Hopkins University Press, 2000).

22. See/hear William Gibson in Mark Neale's film, *No Maps for These Territories* (2001), at www.nomaps.com.

23. Andrew Leyshon and Nigel Thrift, *Money/Space: Geographies of Monetary Transformation* (London: Routledge, 1997), 325.

Notes on Contributors

CATHERINE BELSEY is a long-term beneficiary of Leeds Barroll's good will and excellent wit. She is Distinguished Research Professor at the Centre for Critical and Cultural Theory at Cardiff University. Her books include *Critical Practice* (1980 and 2002), *The Subject of Tragedy: Identity and Difference in Renaissance Drama* (1985), *Shakespeare and the Loss of Eden: The Construction of Family Values in Early Modern Culture* (1999), and *Culture and the Real* (2005).

HARRY BERGER, JR., is the author, most recently, of *Fictions of the Pose: Rembrandt Against the Italian Renaissance, The Absence of Grace: Sprezzatura and Suspicion in Two Renaissance Courtesy Books* (both 2000), and *Situated Utterances: Texts, Bodies, and Cultural Representations* (2005). His current projects include book-length studies of seventeenth-century Dutch group portraiture, Books 1–3 of Spenser's *Faerie Queene,* and *Othello.* He is in the eleventh year of his official career as Professor Emeritus at the University of California, Santa Cruz, and in the fortieth year of his unofficial career as an admirer of one of the great academic presences of our generation—a presence whose sonority and perpetual delight now cresting in new forms deepens the resonance of our golden years.

PHILIPPA BERRY is the author of *Shakespeare's Feminine Endings: Disfiguring Death in Tragedies* (1999) and *Of Chastity and Power: Elizabethan Literature and the Unmarried Queen* (1989). She was Fellow and Director of Studies in English at King's College, Cambridge until 2004 and is currently a Visiting Fellow in the Faculty of Arts, University of Bristol. Pippa has been a long-time admirer of Leeds's work, both on Shakespeare and on early Stuart culture, and her chapter in this collection was inspired by his groundbreaking work on Mediterranean politics in the early modern period. She wrote the first version of the essay for a panel on Venice and questions of ethnicity, organized by Leeds for the World Shakespeare Congress at Valencia in 2001.

RAPHAEL FALCO is a Professor of English at the University of Maryland, Baltimore County, where he knew Leeds Barroll as a mentor, a colleague, and a friend. He has published *Conceived Presences: Literary Genealogy in Renaissance England* (1994) and *Charismatic Authority in Early Modern English Tragedy* (2000), and is completing a book on cultural descent tentatively called "Cultural Genealogy."

JEAN E. HOWARD is William E. Ransford Professor of English at Columbia University. An editor of *The Norton Shakespeare* (1997) and general editor of the Bedford contextual editions of Shakespeare, she has also written several books, including *Shakespeare's Art of Orchestration: Stage Technique and Audience Response* (1984), *The Stage and Social Struggle in Early Modern England* (1994), and, with Phyllis Rackin, *Engendering a Nation: A Feminist Account of Shakespeare's English Histories* (1997). Her new book, *Theater of a City,* studies the representation of London in Jacobean and Caroline drama. She is deeply grateful to Leeds Barroll for sustaining friendship over the course of many years and for his numerous and incisive contributions to the world of Shakespeare studies.

LENA COWEN ORLIN is Professor of English at the University of Maryland, Baltimore County and Executive Director of the Shakespeare Association of America. She recognizes a seminar Leeds Barroll led at the Folger Shakespeare Library in 1979 as the defining moment of her career, and she thanks him for this as for the twenty-five subsequent years of his high standards, generous mentorship, and good fellowship. She is the author of *Private Matters and Public Culture in Post-Reformation England* (1994), editor of *Material London, ca. 1600* (2000), and co-editor with Stanley Wells of *Shakespeare: An Oxford Guide* (2003). Her current book projects are "Locating Privacy in Tudor London," "The Textual Life of Things in Early Modern England" and the Palgrave "Sourcebook for English Studies: The Renaissance."

PATRICIA PARKER is Margery Bailey Professor of English and Dramatic Literature and Professor of Comparative Literature at Stanford University. She has edited numerous critical anthologies, including *Shakespeare and the Question of Theory* with Geoffrey Hartman (1985) and *Women, "Race," and Writing in the Early Modern Period* with Margo Hendricks (1994). Author of *Inescapable Romance* (1979), *Literary Fat Ladies: Rhetoric, Language, Culture* (1987), and *Shakespeare from the Margins* (1996), she is currently completing two new books on racial and religious configurations in early modern writing, and editing new Norton and Arden editions of *Twelfth Night, Much Ado About Nothing,* and *A Midsummer Night's Dream.* Her entry for this volume was inspired by the Ottoman conference organized at the Folger Shakespeare Library by Leeds Barroll, whose friendship and support have been without bounds.

A former President of the Shakespeare Association of America, PHYLLIS RACKIN has published numerous articles on Shakespeare and related subjects as well as three books on Shakespeare: *Shakespeare's Tragedies* (1978), *Stages of History: Shakespeare's English Chronicles* (1990), and *Engendering a Nation: A Feminist Account of Shakespeare's English Histories* (1997), which she wrote in collaboration with Jean E. Howard. Her contribution to this volume is taken from her new book, *Shakespeare and Women* (2005). She is delighted to have this opportunity to express her gratitude to Leeds Barroll. Like so many others, she has been enriched by his innovative scholarship, by his work in establishing and sustaining such central institutions of our profession as the Shakespeare Association of America and the Folger Institute, and by his warm and gracious presence in our academic lives.

BRUCE R. SMITH is College Professor of English at the University of Southern California, where he also holds an appointment as Professor in the School of Theater. The convergence of theatrical performance and sound in his contribution to this volume continues interests first explored in *Ancient Scripts and Modern Experience on the English Stage 1500–1700* (1998) and *The Acoustic World of Modern England: Attending to the O-Factor* (1999). Leeds Barroll's book *Artificial Persons: The Formation of Character in the Tragedies of Shakespeare* has suggested the focal point for the convergence of performance and sound specifically in the illusion of character. The original forum for several ideas advanced in this essay was the seminar program at annual meetings of the Shakespeare Association of America. In founding that organization, Leeds Barroll proceeded from principles of equality and inclusiveness among participants that persist to this day.

BARBARA MARIA STAFFORD is William B. Ogden Distinguished Professor of Art History at the University of Chicago. Her work investigates key intersections between the arts, sciences, and myriad visual technologies from the seventeenth century to the contemporary era. Her recent publications include *Devices of Wonder: From the World in a Box to Images on a Screen* (with Francis Terpak, 2002), and *Visual Analogy: Consciousness as the Art of Connecting* (1999).

PETER STALLYBRASS is Annenberg Professor of the Humanities at the University of Pennsylvania. His most recent books are *O Casaco de Marx* ("Marx's Coat"), published in Brazil in 1999, and *Renaissance Clothing and the Materials of Memory,* written with Ann Rosalind Jones (2000). He is at present working on a material history of reading and writing.

SUSANNE WOODS is Provost and Professor of English at Wheaton College in Massachusetts and has also taught at the University of Hawaii, Brown University, and Franklin & Marshall College. Her publications include *Natural Emphasis: English Versification from Chaucer to Dryden* (1985); the Oxford edition of *The Poetry of Aemilia Lanyer* (1993); *Lanyer: A Renaissance Woman Poet* (1999); and *A Handbook of Literary Feminisms,* with Shari Benstock and Suzanne Ferriss (2002). Leeds Barroll's work on the court of Queen Anna was especially valuable to her reseach on Lanyer and her context, and she is grateful for his many kindnesses.

Index